SOUTHEAST ASIA IN INTERNATIONAL POLITICS 1941–1956

Southeast Asia in 1956

SOUTHEAST ASIA IN INTERNATIONAL POLITICS 1941–1956

EVELYN COLBERT

CORNELL UNIVERSITY PRESS

ITHACA AND LONDON

International Standard Book Number 0-8014-0971-3
Library of Congress Catalog Card Number 76-28008
Printed in the United States of America by York Composition Co., Inc.
Librarians: Library of Congress cataloging information appears on the last page of the book.

To Claire Holt
    who opened ten thousand doors
And to Andrew Colbert
    who, in his short life, opened many
In loving memory

ACKNOWLEDGMENTS

For stimulation, insights, and major contributions to such knowledge as I possess, I owe a debt of many years' standing to my colleagues in the Office of Strategic Services, the Department of State, and the Intelligence Community. For the Federal Executive Fellowship that allowed me an extended period of uninterrupted research, I am grateful to the Department of State and the Brookings Institution. For their help in bringing this about, I owe particular thanks to Harry Feinstein and William Gleysteen.

Fred Greene assisted at the birth of this project and provided acute criticism at every step of the way. Others who read all or part of the manuscript, preserving the author from error, providing valuable material, and provoking re-evaluation and reconsideration, included Patricia Barnett, William Bundy, Frederick Bunnell, Paul Kattenburg, Charlton Ogburn, Ruth Russell, Richard Stuart, Allen Whiting, and Eric Willenz. Evi Blake and Josephine Nypaver, secretaries extraordinary, brought the same unfailing intelligence, accuracy, and devotion to this enterprise as to all others.

My husband patiently endured this long process and provided constant encouragement and support.

For my opinions as well as my errors, I take full responsibility.

EVELYN COLBERT

Washington, D.C.

CONTENTS

INTRODUCTION

By the end of the nineteenth century the patterns of colonial domination of Southeast Asia, which had been in the making for some four hundred years, seemed almost immutable. Only Thailand was independent. Elsewhere the control exercised over Asians by the western empires—the British in Burma, Malaya, and Singapore, the Dutch in Indonesia, the French in Indochina, the United States in the Philippines—was untroubled by conflict among them. Nor was it seriously challenged by the aspirations of subject peoples.

World War I did nothing to disturb these patterns, but, in little more than a decade after the end of World War II, colonial domination had all but disappeared; only Malaya and Singapore, whose independence was already in prospect, remained under western control in 1956. War had played an important part in the emergence of the Southeast Asian states into an independent role in the international community. With the war between the old imperialism of the West and the new imperialism of the Greater East Asia Co-Prosperity Sphere having left in its wake militant and confident nationalist movements in much of the area, Japan's surrender was quickly followed by war between emergent nationalism and resistant colonialism in both Indonesia and Indochina. In Indonesia, a bitter struggle brought early independence. In Indochina, however, war was pursued on a heightening scale and became inextricably intertwined with the East-West struggle. Outside Indochina the broader great-power contest was also reflected, or seemingly reflected, in internal wars between local contenders for power, with Communist insurgents in the forefront of those who sought to displace the rulers of the newly independent states.

By the end of the first postwar decade, it seemed possible that some new stabilization would result from the events of Geneva—the Indochina Conference of 1954 and the Summit of 1955. Instead, however, the turning point that seemed possible in the mid-fifties was to be postponed for another two decades.

Western expansion, beginning in the sixteenth century, had been largely confined to the archipelagos and coastal areas until early in the eighteen-hundreds. To an important degree, European interest was whetted by Southeast Asia's traditional role as both bridge and barrier between India and China, countries whose cultures had joined with indigenous ones to shape the institutions of the intervening region. Themselves unable to resist the western advance, the Indians ceased to play any part in the international politics of Southeast Asia in the eighteenth century and the Chinese late in the nineteenth. Not only the weakness of Asia's major powers, but also the international politics of the Southeast Asian subregion, facilitated the progress of the western drive, the occasion for western intervention often being provided by conflicts between local rulers moving out toward what have become the territorial boundaries of the contemporary states.[1]

For many years, the dependencies of Southeast Asia entered into international politics only as appendages of western empires. Of the independent states, Thailand performed its principal international role as a buffer between French and British possessions; Australia and New Zealand, in the area but not of it, looked to the home country to protect and advance their very limited interests in the outside world.

Later adjustments to independent participation in international affairs were nevertheless affected by the external influences exerted on the region during the colonial period. Dependent status itself created problems for the future conduct of foreign policy. Linked to their western capitals, the Southeast Asian colonies had little contact with each other. Colonial borders having been fixed largely as the outcome of im-

1. The interplay of Chinese and Indian influences with the indigenous cultures and politics of mainland Southeast Asia before the intrusion of the West is best covered in G. Coedè's *The Making of South East Asia*. D. G. E. Hall's *A History of South-East Asia* deals with this subject for the entire area and also provides a detailed account of its later subordination to the West. Charles A. Fisher gives particular attention to the geographic factors that facilitated the western advance in his *South-east Asia* and, in more condensed form, in his contribution to *Conflict and Stability in Southeast Asia*, edited by Mark W. Zacher and R. Stephen Milne.

perial competition, growing consciousness of national identity could not wholly displace the particularism and mutual antagonisms of diverse ethnic groups. Ruled from abroad, Southeast Asians participated in varying degrees in the administrative process but, except in the Philippines, they played virtually no part even in domestic policy making. Integrated into the economies of the metropolitan powers, Southeast Asians provided food, raw materials, markets, and investment opportunities while having little or no say in the design or management of their economic role. Moreover, the local entrepreneurial class, such as it was, tended to be heavily Chinese, as overseas Chinese communities grew and prospered in the hospitable climate afforded by western control.

Variations in the colonial experience were equally important for the future. In Burma, for example, the weakly-rooted political elite of the colonial period was displaced by the young nationalists who led the struggle for independence during and after the war. In the Philippines a political and economic elite, nurtured during the period of American rule, provided continuity of leadership during the progression through successive stages of autonomy to independence. In Indochina and Indonesia, the postwar experience was significantly shaped by the interaction between new leadership emerging from the nationalist movement and traditional elites—both aristocratic and bureaucratic—that had been incorporated into French and Dutch governing mechanisms.

Throughout Southeast Asia the impact of the colonial experience went far beyond the interplay between the policies of a particular governing country and the institutions of its colony. Nationalist aspirations were influenced by the political norms and institutions that had matured in the western democratic and nationalist revolutions of the modern era. The Russian revolution reinforced earlier Marxist influences, while Moscow and the Communist parties of the West provided guidance and support for the Communist components of Southeast Asian resistance to continued alien control. Closer to home were the examples provided by nationalist movements in India and China and by Japan's drive for equality with the western powers.

Japan's intrusion into western arrangements seemed at the outset nothing more than a revival of the old struggle for empire. But nationalism was vastly stimulated by the Asian victory over Europeans and by the Japanese occupation. Moreover, while Southeast Asians were now cut off from their rulers in the West, they were not cut off from Allied propaganda, which heightened expectations that a new era would follow the war's end. As the Indonesian nationalist leader, Mohammad Hatta, observed in August 1945, "It was the 'Atlantic Charter' which succeeded in holding all men's minds in thrall," carrying "the solemn assurance of the Big Powers that they recognize the right of all peoples to live under a government of their own choice."[2]

The European powers, however, were quite unaware of the attitudes and expectations developing in territories now occupied by the Japanese. Their policy makers tended to envisage a world in which the economic and political development of subject peoples would continue to be shaped according to the conceptions and interests of their rulers. Even the United States, in principle dedicated to ultimate independence for all, regarded its achievement as the last step in a very gradual process carried out, on the Philippine model, under benevolent western tutelage. Indeed, it appeared to many in the West, even those who regarded themselves as among the most enlightened on the colonial issue, that the enormity of wartime damage and destruction made continued western control even more indispensable.

Unexpectedly confronted with what Hatta described as the "common view"—the assumption by colonial peoples that the end of the war was "the beginning of their national existence as a free people"[3]— the reactions of western governments differed. The United States, whose original acquisition of the Philippines had been unpopular at home on principled and economic grounds, fulfilled its commitment to postwar Filipino independence and protected Thailand from what it regarded as the imperialist pressures of Britain and France. Britain, after some hesitation, bowed to Burmese demands; its prior decision to grant independence to India had provided a precedent while undermining the rationale for retaining Burma. Moreover, with the Labour Party in office, the government was less responsive to British business interests than it might otherwise have been. The Dutch and French in contrast embarked upon an increasingly costly effort to reimpose their sovereignty in Indonesia and Indochina. In the early postwar years, the national consensus in the Netherlands and France supported the effort to retain colonies whose contribution to the economic well-being and

2. Mohammad Hatta, *Portrait of a Patriot,* p. 501.
3. *Ibid.,* p. 502.

political importance of the metropoles was regarded as essential and whose success in detaching themselves from the mother country was seen as likely to encourage unsettling developments elsewhere. In 1949, when the Netherlands government yielded to demands for independence that it had been unable to suppress, it did so largely because of international pressures in which the American ingredient had become increasingly important. By the time the French abandoned the struggle in 1954, domestic pressures, which had made it impossible to persist, outweighed American pressures to continue the fight. Well before this, however, the victory of the Chinese Communists and the outbreak of hostilities in Korea had brought the Cold War into Southeast Asia, fatefully affecting the American view of the area and dominating the international political environment to which the new states were making their difficult adjustments.

Particularly in the wake of the Korean War, the United States and its European Allies—seeking to strengthen the western world against Moscow's threats, whether military or subversive—began to view Southeast Asia as another arena of the same struggle. The contiguity of Moscow's Chinese Ally, the weaknesses of the indigenous states, and the western and Japanese withdrawal from the region seemed only to add to the gravity of the peril. Impelled by this view, the United States—the only western country now capable of deploying substantial wealth and power into the area—began the process of involvement that was to establish it as a major protagonist in the Indochina War and as Southeast Asia's principal source of economic aid and military support.[4]

The view the United States took of an area with which it had been little concerned until the beginning of the Japanese advance was heavily conditioned by its experience in Europe and the lessons learned there during and after World War II. There was first the assumption

4. While noting its importance in encouraging an unprecedented American role in Southeast Asia, it is worth noting also that the Korean War inspired an even more unprecedented American peacetime role in Europe. As Fred Greene points out, "Even the Korean War of 1950–53 seemed to reinforce the preeminence of Europe. It contributed to: the dispatch of four American divisions to Germany, the appointment of Dwight Eisenhower as SHAPE [Supreme Headquarters Allied Powers in Europe] commander, a substantial military assistance program and modernization of armed forces in Europe, the creation of a NATO infrastructure, . . . and finally, the determination to re-arm West Germany and bring it into NATO" (*U.S. Policy and the Security of Asia*, p. 23).

that to yield anywhere—to cut losses or abandon an unprofitable investment—was invariably disastrous, leading to greater weakness on the friendly side and a more aggressive enemy posture.[5] With the Korean War affording persuasive evidence, it was believed that Moscow was as intent in Asia as in Eastern Europe on extending its power outward. American and European experience also supported the view that the local Communist parties were no more than instruments of Moscow functioning in pursuit of some pre-established blueprint; when American observers could find no evidence that Moscow was providing directives to Ho Chi Minh, they concluded that it was because, as a well-trained Communist and former Comintern agent, he was trusted to make day-to-day decisions on his own.[6] In the earliest days of Communist control in Peking, the People's Republic of China (PRC) was seen in similar terms as little more than an adjunct to Moscow—its own orthodox response to Titoism reinforcing the view that it was unlikely to take an independent stance any time soon. Especially after its intervention in the Korean War, concern with China as an actor on its own increased. Its military capabilities and intentions were now viewed with much greater alarm, but it was still seen as indissolubly linked with Moscow.

The economic factor, as it operated to shape American policy in an area where concrete interests were relatively slight, took a rather paradoxical form.[7] Thinking shaped by the experience of total war supported the expectation that a Communist-controlled Southeast Asia might again be totally closed off to America and its Allies. In this context, the region was seen as a prize of great consequence, the raw materials and markets of which could be harnessed by the Communists to delay western and Japanese recovery and to strengthen a war machine directed against the non-Communist world. But, viewed as a target of Communist subversion, its poverty and other economic weaknesses were recognized and, in thinking shaped by the success of the

5. The impact of the Munich and Yalta analogies is discussed in Arthur Schlesinger, Jr., *The Bitter Heritage*, p. 89.

6. *Foreign Relations of the United States (FRUS)*, 1948, VI, 54.

7. In 1946, U.S. direct investment in Asia, Africa, and Oceania together accounted for 8.3 percent of total direct American investment abroad (Zacher and Milne, p. 358).

Marshall Plan in Europe, western aid programs were expected to strengthen resistance to the Communist advance.[8]

The United States did not see Southeast Asia wholly in Cold War terms however. It recognized that under nationalist auspices a genuine revolution was taking place in the region, congenial to the American tradition and reflecting drives too deep-seated to be effectively suppressed. In the case of Indochina, if the United States seemed to put less stress than was warranted upon this aspect of the situation, it was not so much because of a failure of sympathy or perception as because of an order of priority. This, for quite weighty reasons, put American interests in Europe first, and acted always as a limit on American pressures on the French to satisfy nationalist aspirations. Outside Indochina, however, it was easier to reconcile conflict between American global Cold War stakes and sympathetic interest in the nationalist drive toward independence and betterment. Both interests could be served by economic and military assistance to Allied countries; the neutralist countries, although given occasion to take umbrage at American style, were nevertheless assisted on terms they found consistent with their international stance.

Although American interest in Southeast Asia was greatly magnified by Cold War considerations, never during the first decade after World War II did the United States accord Southeast Asia the importance it gave to Europe and Japan. Military influence, with almost complete consistency, worked against too deep an involvement; little is more evident during this period than the resistance of American military leaders —Dwight D. Eisenhower included—to the notion that American forces

8. The many references in National Security Council papers to the economic importance of Southeast Asia have confirmed to such writers as Gabriel Kolko and Richard DuBoff the primacy of economic considerations in determining U.S. policy in Southeast Asia (see their contributions to Volume V of Senator Gravel's edition of *The Pentagon Papers*). They overlook the compulsions on those who draft such papers—more often justifications for existing policies than efforts to chart some new course—to look for practical arguments for proceeding along the predetermined path. Richard Barnet remarks in this connection, "Leaders as well as citizens often try to make the irrational rational by emphasizing dollars-and-cents reasons when the real decisions may be made for such costly uneconomic reasons as glory, honor, fear, or the sheer fun of winning" (*Roots of War*, p. 160).

should be employed on the Southeast Asia mainland.[9] Congressional opinion, although supporting tendencies toward confrontation with Communist China, also operated to contain tendencies toward carrying this confrontation to what might have seemed its logical conclusion. Differences among the Allies also operated to brake American involvement. Quite apart from the unlikelihood that Australia, New Zealand, and the Philippines would willingly have accepted Japan as a partner, brief interest in a regional military alliance was extinguished by Japan's unwillingness to participate. France proved unwilling to persist in Indochina even with greater Allied support. And finally, while Britain, and Australia and New Zealand as well, believed with the United States that the loss of Vietnam to the Communists would place the rest of Southeast Asia in significant jeopardy, the Commonwealth countries saw no practical alternative to a compromise moving the protective border southward and, in addition, were anxious to engage the neutralist forces of the region—with which India and Ceylon were then associated—in closer partnership.

Moscow also played less of a role in the area than Cold War doctrine suggested it might. On Peking's scale of values, Southeast Asia, if only for geographic reasons, ranked higher than it did on Moscow's. Nevertheless, for the Chinese as for the Russians, it was a secondary theater, one in which both operated with great caution and increasingly according to the dictates of national interest and conventional diplomacy rather than of ideology.

In the years immediately following World War II, motivated by optimism over Communist prospects in Western Europe, Moscow was prepared to sacrifice the interests of the Viet Minh to the desire of the French Communist Party to remain within the national consensus; elsewhere the difficulties encountered by the prewar Comintern in dealing with the complexities of nationalist revolution continued to confuse postwar Communist policies. By the late forties the international position had been clarified. The militant "two-camp" thesis rejecting any

9. The military demand—supported in Congress—for continued American control over islands taken from the Japanese during the war in the Pacific reflected views on the importance of bases from which to deploy American forces in some future repetition of such a conflict. Mainland Southeast Asia was seen in quite a different light as an area in which an American investment—however it might be justified for political reasons—could not be supported on military grounds alone.

middle course between the two blocs was now applied to the Southeast Asian states whose leaders became the target of bitter attack and whose Communist parties were urged to follow the Chinese revolutionary path.

Single-minded support for Communist insurgency against nationalist governments, however, was more rhetorical than practical and also proved to be short-lived. By the early fifties, Moscow and Peking had recognized the limited prospects of most of the indigenous Communist parties, the fact that continued turbulence in colonial areas was not preventing the economic recovery of the capitalist world, and the prospect that the followers of the third path they had previously condemned could, under appropriate circumstances, be helpful to Communist purposes. For these and other reasons, in Southeast Asia as elsewhere in the Third World, Moscow and Peking turned their attention to cultivating the existing governments, whatever their complexions. Considerations of national interest also governed policy in Indochina. The Lao Dong Party, alone among the Communist parties of Southeast Asia, had shown itself both as worth investing in and as requiring an investment that was neither unduly large nor excessively risky. But, whatever the view in Hanoi, by 1953 Moscow and Peking had concluded that it was time to take advantage of growing French opposition to the war and seek a settlement which, while taking into account the gains made by the Viet Minh and providing opportunities for further advance, would remove an obstacle to their broader "peaceful coexistence" policies.

Even though stronger interests elsewhere imposed limits on the activities of the two blocs in Southeast Asia, the policies of the regional states could not but be heavily influenced by the Cold War rivalries and concerns of the great powers. Moreover, while the bloc struggle may have seemed remote to Asians before 1950, its advent in Asia was not merely a contest of great powers; local interests were also involved. A strong and united China was inevitably of concern to small countries on its periphery, whatever its complexion. And this was even more the case when its leaders were committed to doctrines calling for revolution abroad as well as at home. Indigenous Communist pressures—particularly insurgent ones—against independent Southeast Asian governments suggested that the new China would be an expansionist one; at the very least, it was assumed that Communist parties and overseas

Chinese communities would act as instruments for spreading Peking's influence.[10] Especially before the Communist return to united-front tactics in the fifties, Southeast Asian governments, still attempting, however imperfectly, to follow the parliamentary path, had little reason to regard the local parties as anything but inimical to their existence. Even after insurgent tactics were largely abandoned, the course of events in China and then in territory controlled by the Democratic Republic of Vietnam (DRV) left no doubt that, whatever their external stance and their professed commitments to the united front, Asian Communist governments were no less ruthless and uncompromising in their totalitarianism than their Eastern European counterparts.

Southeast Asian leaders were thus as convinced as were western ones that Moscow and Peking would take what opportunities they could to subvert existing governments and institutions. Like the western powers, they also believed that Communist subversion fed on economic weakness and looked upon foreign aid as an essential ingredient in the effort to achieve domestic political stability. And, in these years, notwithstanding suspicions of the imperialist motives of the West and frequent charges that western powers were betraying their political heritage, the attraction of western democracy over eastern totalitarianism remained strong.

While equally wary of the Communist threat at home, Southeast Asians tended to differ with the West and with each other in their prescriptions for coping with foreign Communist powers. To the Philippines from the outset and increasingly to Thailand, safety seemed to lie in close association with the United States. The neutralist path—followed by Burma and Indonesia and, after the Geneva settlement, by Laos and Cambodia as well—appeared to its proponents to avoid involvement in remote but potentially explosive issues while reducing the risk of antagonizing Moscow and, more importantly, Peking. Even more, as the ranks of the Third World swelled, it began to seem to its supporters that the neutralist course not only might protect the countries following it, but also might enable them to help soften the conflict between the two great power blocs. The proponents of both views found some confirmation in the events of the mid-fifties. Although the

10. For discussion of the influence of Chinese Communist rhetoric on Southeast Asian attitudes see Allen S. Whiting's foreword in Jay Taylor, *China and Southeast Asia*.

regional members were far from satisfied with the guarantees it provided, advocates of alliance found the Southeast Asia Treaty Organization (SEATO) reassuring; the Manila Pact, while strengthening the American commitment to Southeast Asia, might also reduce such temptations as existed in Peking to act against China's weaker neighbors. For those of neutralist persuasion, the compromise at Geneva, Peking's altered attitude, and success at the Bandung Conference in bringing together the aligned and nonaligned of Africa and Asia seemed to support the argument for pursuit of the third path.

Although the international politics of the region were thus markedly shaped by Cold War considerations in the first postwar decade, the countries of Southeast Asia gained some benefit from being seen by the two sides as prizes in the bloc contest, but, despite rhetoric to the contrary, as prizes of relatively low priority. Located in an area of competition between the two blocs, the Southeast Asian countries could, if they chose, benefit from the interest of each, while counting on greater involvement elsewhere to contain competition in their own area within safe and tolerable grounds. Strong interest led both sides, first the West, but then the countries of the Communist bloc as well, to woo the countries of the area with political, military, and economic support. But limited interest preserved the area from what might otherwise have been a broader struggle spreading outward from Indochina and was important in making possible the settlement of 1954.

To be sure, in the decade after Japan's surrender, the high hopes with which Southeast Asian leaders entered the postwar world were much dimmed. Aspirations clashed with obstinate facts: the theoretical commitment of a westernized elite to democracy came up against political inexperience, contrary traditions, and inhospitable behavior patterns; the desire to advance economically along nationally controlled paths came up against the heritage of one-sided colonial development, the destruction of war, and the inadequacies of infant administrations; the hope of expanding and strengthening national consciousness and unity came up against ethnic and local particularism; the vision of a united Asia against national differences, lack of a common world view, and very limited capacities and opportunities for cooperation on a mutually beneficial basis.

Nevertheless, in the mid-fifties, with Vietnam, Cambodia, and Laos now independent, and independence for Malaya and Singapore in prospect, the new Southeast Asian state system seemed to be assuming permanent and stabilized form. Vietnam to be sure was divided, but this was not without precedent either in its own past history or in the contemporary world. At least to outside observers, the division seemed neither intolerable nor too unsatisfactory: it ended a war of increasing scope and intensity; it gave the Communists tangible recognition of political and military success; and, at the same time, it gave their opponents to the south a firmer base for political competition than they had ever before possessed. Elsewhere in Southeast Asia, divisions between aligned and nonaligned reflected both the wider power struggle and strong differences of view among the countries concerned. But no real polarization had taken place; the sense of Asian community, although more symbolic than otherwise, and the common feeling that small powers must seek to contain the influence exerted upon them by the great, provided something of a bond. While it was difficult for the countries of the region to join together, they were not torn violently apart by their historic animosities, differences, and rivalries. These, though real enough, were rarely explosive. The world into which they had entered as independent states was a singularly dangerous one. But paradoxically it proved to be a world in which it was easier to preserve independence than it had been in the past. It was no longer a world in which to be poor, weak, unstable, and divided invited outright colonial conquest. Now, the powers, in seeking to expand their influence, were more inclined to offer material assistance and protection. Whether they were aligned or nonaligned, the terms of the competition provided the new states with some degree of maneuverability and leverage. In the mid-fifties, it appeared that competition remained strong enough to provide Southeast Asians with opportunities to reap benefits from both sides, but not so strong as to threaten the stability of the area in which they lived. That in the next decade confrontation was revived and intensified reflected, to be sure, the events of the preceding years—whether inevitably so is another question.

PART I

Decolonization and After

CHAPTER 1

THE COLONIAL ISSUE
DURING WORLD WAR II

Two weeks after Pearl Harbor, Franklin Roosevelt and Winston Churchill met in Washington with their military advisors. Eighteen months earlier, Japan and the Vichy government had reached the first of the agreements that were to integrate Indochina into the Japanese military system while yet retaining French sovereignty for most of the war.[1] Even before the beginning of 1942, Japanese forces had taken Guam and Wake and were attacking Malaya and the Philippines. When Roosevelt and Churchill met, the Japanese held Manila. There was no question of abandoning the "Europe first" strategy adopted at the secret U.S.-British staff talks of early 1941, but it was agreed that the enemy should be prevented from capturing Singapore, the Philippines, and the East Indies. But, when Corregidor fell on May 5, 1942, Singapore and the Indies were already in Japanese hands. The Americans, the British, and the Dutch were now completely expelled from their dependencies in Southeast Asia. Thereafter, Japanese control in Southeast Asia was not to be seriously challenged until the last months of the war, and then only in the Philippines and Burma.

Nor were the Allies ever to coordinate their plans or reach agreement concerning the ultimate fate of their dependencies. Indeed, they differed significantly in their basic assumptions. For those who saw themselves as most enlightened—the British and Americans particularly—colonial rule was a "sacred trust," justified to the extent that rulers carried out their civilizing mission and trained dependent peoples to assume their own burdens and responsibilities. Even so, there were important differences between the United States and Britain, especially

1. But not over all of Indochina; in May 1941, France had been forced to cede territory in Cambodia and Laos to Thailand.

as to whether, after the war, the international community should have some authority over the Allied dependencies as well as former enemy ones. The French and the Dutch, although no doubt as convinced of their rectitude as the Anglo-Saxons, were less concerned with progress toward self-government.

Americans wanted to do more than save the old order; war aims must include the creation of a new and better order, with Roosevelt's Four Freedoms applied "everywhere in the world." Moreover, some argued, if no action were taken until the war's end, Japanese propaganda would "emphasize heavily the exploitation by Western powers of Far Eastern peoples." Accordingly, said a member of the State Department's Far Eastern Division a month after Pearl Harbor, the United States should urge the British to give dominion status to India and Burma and permit increased native participation in government in other colonial areas, with the Dutch to do likewise in the Indies.[2] Americans saw the Philippine path—phased steps toward self-government and a fixed date for independence—as an appropriate model for the postwar period. They had no confidence, however, that Old World rulers, lacking the anticolonial traditions of the New, would follow it unless directed and supervised by the postwar international organization. American postwar planning accordingly tended to revolve around the role the anticipated international authority would play in enforcing the rights of colonial peoples and ensuring progress toward self-government and ultimate independence.

The European Allies, however, saw no reason why the terms of peace should reduce their colonial empires or their freedom to manage them. The December 1943 Cairo Declaration pledge to deprive Japan of its post-1895 acquisitions seemed an appropriate way to restore China, punish aggression, and reduce prospects for revived militarism. But the Europeans also assumed that, when Japan had been expelled from territories "taken by violence and greed," the New Order in East Asia would be replaced by the Old and the relationship between metropolitan and dependency would be restored, perhaps somewhat reformed and liberalized, but essentially intact.

During the war—with the European colonies in any case occupied by the Japanese—Allied cooperation, particularly Anglo-American

2. Akira Iriye, *The Cold War in Asia*, pp. 69–70.

cooperation, seemed much more important than pressing for new commitments on colonial questions. Then, as the end of the war approached, the American position was diluted by two strategic decisions. One—the decision to launch the final assault on Japan from the Pacific, not from the Asian mainland—correspondingly reduced American interest in Southeast Asia and removed any prospect that American forces would participate in expelling the Japanese from Indochina or Indonesia. The other—the decision to seek unrestricted American control over the Japanese-mandated islands—brought the American position on international supervision of colonial administration much closer to the European one. Ultimately, the fight for a significant role for the international organization was left largely to the less influential voices of Australia and New Zealand and of countries recently emerged from one or another form of colonial experience.

The Future of the Colonial Empires: The Views of the Powers

Undersecretary of State Sumner Welles, speaking on Memorial Day in 1942, declared, "The age of imperialism is ended. . . . The principles of the Atlantic Charter must be guaranteed to the world as a whole—in all oceans and in all continents."[3]

A few months later, however, Secretary of State Cordell Hull took a more restricted position. The United States would "use the full measure of our influence to support attainment of freedom by all peoples who, by their acts, show themselves worthy of it and ready for it."[4] Hull's formulation reflected more accurately Roosevelt's views and those of most Americans officially concerned with the colonial problem. Independence was not a right to be granted immediately. It was a privilege to be won by colonial peoples as they learned to exercise its responsibilities according to standards set for them by others. Ideally, some impartial international body would set these standards and ensure that dependent peoples were trained to meet them. But the process was to be a gradual one, probably extending over decades.

In discussing the problem with Soviet Foreign Minister Vyacheslav Molotov, Roosevelt himself suggested twenty years. The conversation illustrated Hull's comment that the President tended to apply the prin-

3. Ruth B. Russell, *A History of the United Nations Charter*, p. 83.
4. Harley Notter, *Postwar Foreign Policy Preparation, 1939–1945*, p. 109.

ciple of international trusteeship to areas ranging "from the Baltic to Ascension Island in the South Atlantic and to Hong Kong."[5] It encapsulated also the principal components of the President's thinking on Southeast Asia: ignorance of the area; indifference to the modalities of progress from colonialism to freedom; and a sure political instinct for the nationalist drive to come. Strategic islands, Roosevelt said—including Japanese and Allied mandates—"ought not to belong to any one nation. . . . The easiest and most practical way to handle the problem of these islands over a long period would be to put them under an international committee of three to five members." On other colonial possessions, in which he included Thailand as well as Indochina, the Netherlands East Indies, and the Malay States, he was less precise. He attributed to Chiang Kai-shek the notion "that some form of interim international trusteeship" might administer these territories "until they were ready for self-government." Each would require a different period "but a palpable surge of independence was there just the same, and the white nations thus could not hope to hold these areas as colonies in the long run."[6]

The President, however, did not encourage his foreign-policy planners to develop a strategy for decolonization. Hull, as firm an anti-colonialist as the President, favored leaving colonial rule in existing hands; it should, however, be exercised under internationally established and enforced principles. Meanwhile, in the earliest years of the war, the United States was inclined to assure the Europeans that their empires would be restored, seeking to encourage continued resistance if possible, or to keep hope high even if resistance had come to an end. As Hull observed, wanting to cooperate as closely as possible with the western democracies, the United States "could not alienate them in the Orient and expect to work with them in Europe."[7] In a memo to the President, Hull cited "the more important" American statements which "generally . . . looked toward the restoration of French territories after the war."[8] Between August 1941 and November 1942 there were six addressed to Vichy or Free French authorities; in one, Acting Secretary Welles declared that "the Government of the United

5. Cordell Hull, *Memoirs*, II, 1305.
6. Robert Sherwood, *Roosevelt and Hopkins*, p. 573.
7. Hull, II, 1598.
8. *FRUS*, 1944, III, 770 ff.

States recognizes the sovereign jurisdiction of the people of France . . . over French possessions overseas" and "fervently hopes that it may see the reestablishment of the independence of France and of the integrity of French territory."[9] Roosevelt, writing to explain the Europe-first policy to Queen Wilhelmina in the dark spring days of 1942, said that "the Netherlands Indies must be restored—and something within me tells me that they will be."[10]

Another factor arguing against detailed planning was the unpredictable shape of things to come. This was emphasized by Harley Notter, official historian of the State Department's postwar planning effort which got under way in 1942. As he put it, the many imponderables and uncertainties, the growth of new desires, and the rise of new leaders made it essential and unavoidable to postpone commitments on territorial questions until after the war. Meanwhile, "the vital interests of the United States lay in following a 'diplomacy of principle'—of moral disinterestedness instead of power politics."[11]

The "diplomacy of principles" notwithstanding, practical problems arose affecting colonial questions. When they did, the United States tried to stay aloof, if possible, or, if not, to postpone decision. American civil affairs officers, it was decided, should not be assigned to the Southeast Asia Command set up under Admiral Lord Louis Mountbatten in August 1943, because a civil-affairs presence "would further increase the belief among the peoples of India and presumably throughout the Far East that our policy and that of the British in Asia are the same."[12]

Postponed decisions were particularly evident in the case of Indochina despite the President's well-known view that French control should not be restored.[13] At the Quebec Conference of August 1943, the

9. Department of State Bulletin (DSB), April 18, 1942, p. 33.

10. Herbert Feis, Churchill, Roosevelt, and Stalin, p. 41.

11. Notter, p. 123.

12. FRUS, 1944, V, 1195.

13. All of Roosevelt's statements to this effect, and there are fewer than one might think, have been endlessly reiterated and will not be repeated here. Because of subsequent controversy over American policy in Indochina and the consequent focus on every aspect of the conflict, it is easy to exaggerate the attention that the President and other Americans gave to this subject during World War II. Edward R. Drachman's United States Policy Toward Vietnam, 1940–1945, a very useful, complete, and careful, if somewhat uncritical, compilation, includes everything said on this subject by Americans, ranging from the President to the

first of the Roosevelt-Churchill meetings to focus on the war in the Pacific, the newly established Southeast Asia Command was empowered to carry on clandestine activities against the Japanese in Indochina. Free French pressures for participation in such activities were soon joined by debate over French participation in future military operations and civil administration.[14] By the second Quebec Conference in mid-September 1944, with the liberation of France well under way, the British had requested concurrence in steps looking toward a French role in liberating Indochina. This concurrence, then and later, Roosevelt was not willing to give. On November 4, the State Department was instructed to tell the British that the United States had made no final decisions on Indochina.[15] At the end of December, Hull reported the British Foreign Office view that "it would be difficult to deny French participation in the liberation of Indochina in light of the increasing strength of the French Government in world affairs . . . [and that] unless a policy to be followed toward Indochina is mutually agreed between our two Governments, circumstances may arise at any moment which will place our two Governments in a very awkward situation."[16] But Roosevelt still did "not want to get mixed up in any Indochina decision." It is a matter, he thought, for postwar decision. "From both a military and civil point of view, action at this time is premature."[17]

---

members of that tiny band of Office of Strategic Services and military officers whose presence in postsurrender Hanoi has given rise to so many French myths of U.S. responsibility for Ho's success and American myths of opportunities lost. All of this, plus the necessary background data on events and personalities in Indochina and elsewhere, Drachman covers in 165 pages. It is hard to think of any problem regarded as really important during World War II that could be treated with equal detail in so little space.

14. Philippe Devillers, *Histoire du Viet-nam de 1940 à 1952*, pp. 114–115; *FRUS*, 1943, China, pp. 882–883.

15. *FRUS*, 1944, III, 780.

16. *Ibid.*, p. 783.

17. *FRUS*, 1945, VI, 293. How much of the President's emphasis on Indochina stemmed from his anticolonialism and how much from his dislike of the French and especially of General de Gaulle is hard to say. Roosevelt's treatment of the civil affairs agreement for liberated France is instructive. Early in September 1943 the French Committee of National Liberation (CNL) asked to be made responsible for civil administration in areas regained from the Germans and outside combat zones. By December 1943, the State Department had joined

Committed to the principles of anticolonialism but without plans for applying them, sensitive also to differing British views of China, Americans were quick to suspect the motives of their Allies. To Harry Hopkins and others, Churchill's misgivings over the campaign in northern Burma to reopen the land route to China (a plan on which American military opinion had also been sharply divided) and his preference for an amphibious campaign in the southwest Pacific to regain Singapore and Sumatra were evidence of greater British interest in preserving their Empire than in the war against Japan.[18] Americans also tended to read efforts to get on with preparations for expelling the Japanese as evidence of imperialist conspiracy and as the occasion for reminding all concerned that the United States expected to be consulted on any arrangements as to the future of Southeast Asia.[19] When a small French military mission arrived at Mountbatten's Kandy headquarters in November 1944 there was consternation in the China theater where relations with the Southeast Asia Command, never particularly amicable, were headed toward a major eruption over command arrangements in Indochina. The British, the French, and the Dutch, reported Patrick J. Hurley, U.S. Ambassador to China, had secretly established a "Council of the Three Empires" which proposed to use American lend-lease supplies to re-establish dominion over Southeast Asia and undermine U.S. policy in China. Later, he identified in Kunming a "Southeast Asian Confederacy" established by the British to the same end.[20] "It would appear," the Office of Strategic Services representative in Kandy commented, "that the strategy of the British, Dutch, and French is to win back and control Southeast Asia, making the fullest

the Foreign Office in urging a civil affairs agreement with the CNL similar to those already made with the Belgian, Dutch, and Norwegian governments-in-exile. Roosevelt would not agree, however, nor would Churchill (who also disliked and distrusted de Gaulle), press Roosevelt to change his mind. In consequence, a civil affairs agreement was not signed until July 10, 1944, a month after the Normandy landing. Details are in E. Llewellyn Woodward, *British Foreign Policy in the Second World War*, pp. 261–268.

18. Feis, pp. 248–256.

19. Woodward, p. 427; *FRUS*, 1944, V, 1285; *FRUS*, Conference of Berlin (Potsdam), 1945, I, 916.

20. William D. Leahy, *I Was There*, p. 288; Drachman, pp. 64–65; *FRUS* (Potsdam), 1945, I, 915–917.

use possible of American resources but foreclosing the Americans from any voice in policy matters."[21]

The British tended to dismiss American thinking as the product of ignorance, however benevolent. The official historian of British wartime foreign policy observed that neither Roosevelt nor Hull "knew much about recent developments in colonial government and administration in territories controlled by Great Britain and other European Powers. They also did not realize the practical difficulties in the way of international control. Mr. Hull had been more interested in the furtherance of free international trade than in political control, but he and the President were inclined to regard Mr. Churchill's vehement opposition to any proposals for 'trusteeship' as due solely to his wish to maintain an out-moded British Empire."[22]

Churchill's vehemence on the subject of the British Empire is well known; he was as easily aroused by any mention of international trusteeship—however limited the context—as Roosevelt was by references to Indochina. When the international organization's role in colonial matters was raised at Yalta, he said, "I will not have one scrap of British territory flung into that area. After we have done our best to fight in this war and have done no crime to anyone, I will have no suggestions that the British Empire is to be put into the dock and examined by everybody to see whether it is up to their standard. No one will induce me as long as I am Prime Minister to let any representative of Great Britain go to a conference where he will be placed in the dock and asked to justify our right to live in a world we tried to save."[23]

The British generally opposed international direction or supervision in colonial matters; even the Labour Party, although its 1943 platform accepted "the principle of international supervision and accountability," in the course of the war apparently moved toward the idea of commonwealth partnership.[24] An international administration seemed particularly undesirable; in discussing this point with Roosevelt, An-

21. *FRUS,* 1944, III, 779.
22. Woodward, p. 530.
23. James F. Byrnes, *Speaking Frankly,* frontispiece. There are other versions, but it seems likely that Byrnes—whose shorthand Leahy says was excellent—got Churchill's words down most accurately.
24. Ernest B. Haas, "The Attempt to Terminate Colonialism: Acceptance of the U.N. Trusteeship System," *International Organization,* VII (Feb., 1953), p. 13; Norman Harper and David Sissons, *Australia and the United Nations,* p. 71.

thony Eden pointed to the French-British condominium in the New Hebrides as an example of the difficulties likely to arise when more than one country was involved in the day-to-day government of a dependent area.[25]

Proposals specifically defining independence as the goal of colonial rule also seemed to conflict with British concepts of the Empire and Commonwealth as an association infinitely capable of accommodating different peoples at different stages of political development up to and including full partnership. Churchill, to be sure, confined the principles of the Atlantic Charter to "the states . . . now under the Nazi yoke." But, with the same pride that Americans took in their Philippine performance, he also pointed to "the progressive evolution of self-governing institutions in the regions and peoples that owe allegiance to the British crown." Statements already made concerning the development of constitutional government in India, Burma, and other parts of the Empire, Churchill said, are "complete in themselves, free from ambiguity, and related to the conditions and circumstances of the territories and peoples affected" and "entirely in harmony" with the Atlantic Charter.[26] Elsewhere, however, in America and more fatefully in India, Churchill's remarks were read not as committing him to self-government, but as a blunt reminder that the British Empire was solely the business of the British. Nor did others, particularly in the dependencies, fail to observe that progress toward self-government seemed often to owe more to nationalist agitation than to British high-mindedness.

Specific promises for the future did not fit very easily into British patterns. Indian pressures for commitments to complete postwar autonomy and the right to secede had been irresistible but Burma's were not. In February 1940, its House of Representatives had made Burma's willing participation in the war effort dependent upon immediate recognition "as an independent nation entitled to frame her own constitution." In response, the British government, affirming dominion status the ultimate goal, postponed decisions as to how and when it might be attained until after the war. [27] Almost two years later, on the

25. Woodward, p. 441.
26. Hansard, 5th Series, H.C., Vol. 374, Cols. 68, 69.
27. Nicholas Mansergh, *Survey of British Commonwealth Affairs, 1939–1952,* p. 241.

eve of Japanese invasion, Burmese Prime Minister U Saw went to
London seeking a definite commitment to dominion status after the
war. Instead, the Secretary of State for India expounded simultaneously on the excellence of British intentions and the impracticality of
specific proposals. "It is to that high position of Dominion Status—a
position to which we would not lightly admit outside people without
full consideration of the character of their Government or the responsibility which it might involve—that we wish to help Burma to attain as
fully and completely as may be possible under certain contingencies immediately after the victorious conclusion of the war. . . . With a situation at the end of the war which no one can yet foresee, it is out of
the way to give a categorical assurance of such a nature as might result
in gross misunderstanding and disappointment."[28] Again, in 1943, after
the Japanese had granted their version of independence, Sir Reginald
Dorman-Smith, who had been governor of Burma when the invasion
began, pressed unsuccessfully for a commitment. Meanwhile, London's
plans reflected British business pressures for a strong postwar government, with politics as well as political progress suspended until the
economy had been rehabilitated. After Burma's recapture, it was these
pressures that were reflected in the May 1945 White Paper. Self-government was the "ultimate objective"; for the shorter term the White
Paper proposed a three-year period of rehabilitation during which such
representative institutions as had been established under the constitution of 1937 would be suspended.[29]

Even while refusing to commit itself to independence, the British
government, no less confident of its rectitude than the American, was
equally ready to define the general principles that should govern colonial administration. In December 1942, the cabinet tentatively accepted a draft declaration on colonial policy. In July 1943 the Colonial
Secretary, Oliver Stanley, declared in the House of Commons that
trusteeship had long been the central and proclaimed purpose of
British colonial policy which had "brought to millions of people security for life and property and an even-handed justice which they have
never known before." But, now that many prefer "to combine with the
status of trustee the position of partner," Britain is pledged to guide
the colonies toward self-government within the imperial framework,

28. John F. Cady, *A History of Modern Burma*, p. 429.
29. *Ibid.*, pp. 491, 494; Mansergh, *op. cit.*, p. 243.

Rapid and spectacular advances might win applause, but self-government cannot be awarded to those not yet trained in its use. Colonial policy accordingly must be directed toward the two main pillars "upon which any sound scheme of political responsibility must be based"— economic development and educational advance, including education through political participation. Much could be done by cooperating with neighboring and friendly nations, and the establishment of Regional Commissions to provide effective and permanent collaborative machinery would be particularly welcome. But "the administration of the British colonies must continue to be the sole responsibility of Great Britain."[30]

The British also disagreed with Roosevelt on the future of French Indochina. The President dismissed British uneasiness on this score as arising from fear that the dissolution of the French Empire would spell the doom of the British. Britain undoubtedly did share the opposition of other colonial powers to policies aimed at dissolving their empires. But its major concern was with the likelihood that discrimination against France would reduce its future role in Europe.

Less confident than the Americans that Moscow's postwar policy would be constructive, and uncertain also of what part the United States would play in Western Europe, British policy makers regarded a powerful postwar France as indispensable to containing Germany. Eden pressed these points with Churchill. But the Prime Minister, influenced in part by his own distrust of General Charles de Gaulle, was unwilling to risk his relations with Roosevelt in disputes over such issues as the French Empire.[31] Nevertheless, in April 1945, when the question of the French role had become a more immediate one, Churchill wrote to the President: "It would look very bad in history if we failed to support isolated French forces in their resistance to the Japanese . . . or if we excluded the French from participation in our councils as regards Indochina."[32] With these views, it was natural that the British should repeatedly raise the question of French participation in the Asian military operations that were expected to precede the fall of Japan.

To the extent permitted by practical constraints, American views, and the imprecise dividing line between the responsibilities of the

30. Hansard, 5th Series, H.C. Vol. 391, Cols. 47–70.
31. Woodward, pp. 222–223.
32. *FRUS* (Potsdam), 1945, I, 819.

Southeast Asia and China commands in Indochina, the British were hospitable to a limited French presence in their theater. This presence was important to de Gaulle who believed that military participation in the war in the Pacific might be indispensable to the restoration of French rule in Indochina. Their case, the French believed, was a good one; the Japanese occupation of Indochina, they argued, had not changed the French juridical situation there any more than it had changed the British juridical position in Malaya and Burma, or the Dutch in Netherlands East Indies.[33] But de Gaulle knew that France was not regarded in the same light as Britain and the Netherlands, least of all by Roosevelt. Looking back over his efforts to ensure the use of French forces in the Pacific, de Gaulle wrote: "Measuring the shock inflicted on France's prestige by Vichy's policy, knowing the state of public opinion throughout the Union, foreseeing the outbreak of nationalist passions in Asia and Australia, aware of the hostility of the Allies—particularly the Americans—in regard to our Far Eastern position, I regarded it as essential that the conflict not come to an end without our participation in that theatre as well."[34]

In October 1943 the French Committee of National Liberation made the first of what was to be a series of requests for United States approval and support of plans for military action in Indochina. Despite rebuffs then and subsequently, planning continued: military formations in Algiers were designated for eventual employment in Indochina; more French officers were sent to Mountbatten's theater; a "French Detachment in the Indies" was organized in Calcutta and became the French Section of the British Clandestine Force 136; and contacts were established with French officers in Indochina to whom the Royal Air Force dropped weapons and supplies. By January 1945, the French were prepared to offer two divisions against the Japanese in Indochina in addition to the 50,000 French troops already there.[35]

General de Gaulle's recollections almost certainly accord the exaggeration of hindsight to his foreknowledge of rising nationalist pressures. Nevertheless, the French recognized a need to accompany their military planning with some public elaboration of their postwar intentions, if only for the American audience. The first of these state-

33. *FRUS,* 1945, VI, 295.
34. Charles de Gaulle, *The War Memoirs,* III, 187.
35. *FRUS,* 1943, China, pp. 882–883; Devillers, pp. 114–119, 145–146; Leahy, p. 286.

ments, made in December 1943, promised the Indochinese a new political status within the French community; the only specific concession was the promise that "within the framework of the federal organization . . . the Indochinese will finally have access to all the public positions and functions of the State."[36]

Recommendations for the Empire as a whole were adopted by the Brazzaville Conference of January 1944 where colonial governors met under the chairmanship of René Pleven as Commissioner for Colonies. Independence, and even autonomy, were out of the question: "the aims of the work of civilization which France is accomplishing in her possessions exclude any idea of autonomy and any possibility of development outside the French Empire bloc. The attainment of 'self-government' in the colonies, even in the most distant future, must be excluded." The purpose of the conference, said Charles de Gaulle, is to clarify the conditions that would permit the overseas populations "to become integrated into the French Community." The proposed political reforms were correspondingly limited: the establishment of universally elected colonial assemblies with both European and native representation, and greater native participation in the higher grades of colonial administration.[37]

A year of study by a special commission produced a more detailed plan for Indochina that was embodied in the Declaration of March 24, 1945. The plan offered little advance toward self-government. A federated Indochina composed of five states, Laos, Cambodia, and the three divisions the French had established in Vietnam—Cochin China, Tonkin, and Annam—would become part of the French Union, with France retaining control over foreign affairs and defense and appointing the High Commissioner. He in turn would select ministers responsible to him. The assembly was to be "chosen in accordance with the mode of elections best suited to each of the States of the Federation" with powers limited to approving the budget and discussing matters presented to it.[38]

Like the French, the Dutch in the years before World War II had

36. Royal Institute of International Affairs, Arnold J. Toynbee (ed.), *Survey of International Affairs (SIA)*, 1939–1946, p. 263.

37. Donald Lancaster, *The Emancipation of French Indochina*, pp. 122–123; Guy de Carmoy, *The Foreign Policies of France, 1944–1968*, p. 128.

38. Ellen J. Hammer, *The Struggle for Indochina*, pp. 111–112; Joseph Buttinger, *Vietnam: A Dragon Embattled*, I, 302–303.

not thought themselves responsible for leading their colonies toward self-government, much less independence. The theorist of Dutch colonialism, H. Colign, was almost unique among conservatives in recognizing that nationalism was more than the aberration of a tiny group of intellectuals. His belief that the best response was to make clear that "the authority of the Netherlands is as fixed as Mont Blanc in the Alps,"[39] was reflected in the response of the Dutch government-in-exile to the Wihoho Resolution of February 1940. Passed by the Volksraad—a European-Indonesian assembly of no great authority— the resolution called for self-government within the framework of the Netherlands constitution, cabinet responsibility to an expanded Volks-raad, and reduction of the powers of the Governor General. The government-in-exile in London took six months to respond that political reforms could not be considered until after the war. Until the government returned to The Hague it wished neither to consider the merits of the resolution nor to draw up plans for the constitutional development of the Indies.[40]

By the beginning of 1942, however, with the United States in the war and Japan already embarked on its conquest of the Indies, Alpine fixity no longer seemed appropriate. Starting in January with a commitment to a postwar round table on the future of the Kingdom, the move toward greater flexibility culminated in a radio address by Queen Wilhelmina on December 6. "I am convinced," she said, "that after the war it will be possible to reconstruct the Kingdom on the solid foundation of complete partnership. . . . I visualize, without anticipating the recommendations of the future conference, that they will be directed toward a commonwealth in which the Netherlands, Indonesia, Surinam, and Curacao will participate with complete self-reliance and freedom of conduct for each part regarding its internal affairs, but with the readiness to render mutual assistance." The commitment was vague enough; those most closely concerned with colonial policy believed its principal result would be greater decentralization, giving a Dutch-dominated administration in the Indies greater independence from The Hague.[41]

39. Whitney T. Perkins "Sanctions for Political Change—The Indonesian Case," *International Organization*, XII (Winter 1958), p. 28.

40. George McT. Kahin, *Nationalism and Revolution in Indonesia*, p. 98.

41. H. J. van Mook, *The Stakes of Democracy in Southeast Asia*, pp. 180–181; Paul M. Kattenburg, *The Indonesian Question in World Politics*, p. 45.

Like the French, the Dutch were anxious to participate in the Pacific war. A call for volunteers, after the southern part of the Netherlands was liberated in the fall of 1944, brought a good response. But then, as later, shortage of transport and higher Allied priorities elsewhere blocked Dutch plans even though the Netherlands did not face the problems of status that bedeviled France. Roosevelt, apparently satisfied by his conversations with Queen Wilhelmina and by her December 1943 declaration, had never suggested that the Dutch Empire should be dismantled. The Dutch had resisted the enemy valiantly, first at home and later in Indonesia. Their government-in-exile had been promptly recognized. They were officially represented in General Douglas MacArthur's Southwest Pacific Command, established in Australia in March 1942; in Melbourne, Dutch officials were planning the reoccupation and directing propaganda and intelligence efforts; and in December 1944 a civil affairs agreement was signed.

Although as anxious as their western Allies to expel the Japanese, the Chinese had no particular desire to see colonial rule restored. They had themselves suffered from western dominance and exactions, and, in relatively recent times, they had seen their traditional primacy in Southeast Asia replaced by that of the West. Generally, they were not particularly active in discussions of colonial issues; the proposal made by the president of the Legislative Yuan in March 1942, that postwar independence be guaranteed to Vietnam, Korea, and the Philippines was a rather rare public intervention.[42] Nevertheless in their conversations, Chiang Kai-shek and Roosevelt seemed always to agree on trusteeship and related matters.

For the Chinese, as for Roosevelt, Indochina was a special case— considered the pathway to China's riches by French and British competitors for control of Southeast Asia and, more recently, by the Japanese as a source of supply and sustenance to China that must be cut off. The Chinese government, with considerable American sympathy, anticipated a voice in Indochina's ultimate disposition; mean-

42. King C. Chen, *Vietnam and China, 1938–1954*, p. 57. The Chinese Communists also do not seem to have had much to say on the subject during the war. However, toward the war's end, Mao said to a party congress "In regard to the nations of the southern seas—Burma, Malaya, Indonesia, Vietnam, the Philippines—we would like that, upon the rout of the Japanese invaders, the people of these countries should achieve the right to build their independent democratic states." Quoted in David J. Dallin, *Soviet Foreign Policy after Stalin*, p. 76.

while, it was hoped Chinese aid and hospitality to Vietnamese nationalists might weaken the Japanese hold now and the French later.

China's interest in Indochina added yet another strand to the cat's cradle of conflicting objectives, command rivalries, freewheeling clandestine operations, personal and national jealousies and antagonisms, aborted plans, and frustrated hopes within which the Allies conducted the war on the Asian mainland. The prospect, late in 1943, of shifting responsibility for future operations in Indochina and Thailand from the China to the Southeast Asia Command incensed the Generalissimo, who argued that the change would be a blow to Chinese morale and would support Japanese contentions that the war was being fought to re-establish British control. An understanding ensued that SEAC was to attack from the south when the time came, and the Chinese from the north.[43] This understanding, however, although portentous for the future, did not end wartime bickering.

Even more portentous was Chinese hospitality to Vietnamese nationalist refugees. The connection was an old one, dating from the early years of the century. Vietnam's leading nationalist party, the VNQDD,[44] had modeled itself on the Kuomintang. It was in Canton in 1925 that Ho Chi Minh founded the forerunner of the Indochinese Communist Party, the Revolutionary Youth League. Communists and non-Communists alike sought safety in China from the French police and were welcomed as channels of increased Chinese influence in Indochina. Once the Japanese had established themselves in Indochina, Vietnamese could be usefully employed in espionage against them. Because the Communists brought superior organizational resources to this task, their Chinese hosts increasingly accorded them the major role that they would otherwise have preferred to see played by the nationalists.[45]

The French Committee of National Liberation, represented in Chungking and in Yunnan Province since 1942, was aware of these activities. In 1944, the temporary reduction of the Communist role in the Chinese-sponsored united front organizations was attributed to French pressures. The possibility of Chinese troop movements into Indochina aroused Vichy in 1941 and the Committee of National

43. *FRUS*, Conferences at Cairo and Tehran, 1943, pp. 391–392.

44. Viet Nam Quoc Dan Dong (Viet Nam Nationalist Party).

45. Harold C. Hinton, *China's Relations with Burma and Vietnam*, p. 11; Buttinger, I, 269–271.

Liberation in 1943 and 1945 to vigorous protest. Hearing reports of a Chinese plan for a three-army invasion, the French predicted that any such moves would immediately cause a rising against the Allies, because for the Indochinese "the Chinese . . . represent the hereditary enemy." Commenting on this contention, John Carter Vincent of the State Department's Far East Division called it "grossly misleading, if not actually false." The Chinese government, he added, "should be consulted and its views given full consideration in regard to plans for the future of Indochina."[46]

Although Roosevelt often claimed that Joseph Stalin supported his views on the colonies, the Russians actually said very little. Stalin and his Foreign Minister Molotov, usually responded to the President's remarks with brief expressions of understanding, with implied approval, or, less frequently, with anti-French diatribes. But the Soviet position on the restoration of empire and the postwar regulation of colonial rule remained obscure. Indeed, until San Francisco, the Soviets seemed interested in the trust concept only in connection with Korea and Italian territory in Africa. Moreover, although Stalin made it clear at Teheran in December 1943 that the other half of Sakhalin and all of the Kuriles were the price for war against Japan, it does not appear that trusteeship for these territories was ever proposed or considered.[47]

The Russians also showed little interest in the Far East. The Soviet press, reflecting Kremlin preoccupation with Europe, gave the Asian theater little coverage.[48] Moscow as leader of the world's revolutionary forces showed little more interest than Moscow as national capital. Nikolai Lenin had declared at the Comintern's Second Congress in 1920 that "the breaking up of the colonial empire, together with the proletarian revolution in the home country, will overthrow the capitalist system in Europe."[49] Although, after the Second Congress, Moscow's directives concerning cooperation with nationalist movements against the imperialist powers were to waver and change, opposition to these powers themselves remained a fixed feature of Communist doctrine. In 1935, however, at the Seventh Congress this stance was abandoned in favor of cooperation with the colonial powers against the greater

46. *FRUS*, 1943, China, pp. 855–856; Devillers, pp. 196–197; Chen, pp. 72–73. For 1941 and 1945 protests, see *SIA*, 1939–1946, p. 28; *FRUS*, 1945, VII, 55.

47. Feis, p. 255.

48. Charles B. McLane, *Soviet Strategies in Southeast Asia*, p. 249.

49. *Statuts et Résolutions de l'Internationale Communiste*, pp. 90–93.

dangers of fascism, a position which, except for the period of the Nazi-Soviet pact, the Communists held to for a decade. As usual, inconsistencies with past dogmas were not found troublesome; in 1942, when Britain rejected the Indian Congress Party's demand for immediate independence, a Soviet writer commented that this was not the moment for India's independence since "the war against Fascist aggression requires maximum mobilization of India's forces."[50] With even China's increasingly powerful Communist Party receiving little Soviet or Comintern attention, the small, weak parties of Southeast Asia, now further isolated by the Japanese occupation, appear quite logically to have received no attention at all.

While the Communists seemed to have abandoned their revolutionary interest in colonial peoples, Australia and New Zealand, both under Labour Party governments, took positions more in line with traditional socialist views. Both countries emphasized the obligations of trusteeship and its universal colonial applicability. Said Australian Minister of External Affairs Herbert V. Evatt in September 1942, "We must found future Pacific policy on the doctrine of trusteeship for the benefit of all Pacific peoples." To which a New Zealand policy paper added in 1944: adherence to the principle of trusteeship is not enough when the application of the principle is contested, "the crucial point being supervision."[51]

Given an adequate supervisory system, however, Australia and New Zealand were at one on the desirability of re-establishing the prewar juridical situation. "We have no desire," said Evatt in 1943, "of prejudicing the sovereignty of the Netherlands, France, and Portugal in the Pacific."[52] He made the same point more sharply in 1944, stimulated by Roosevelt's claim to Churchill that the people of Australia and New Zealand backed him in opposing the return of New Caledonia to the French. Australia, he wrote to the Secretary of State, "is under a deep obligation to Fighting France. It is publicly pledged to do its utmost to maintain the sovereignty of France in its present South Pacific possessions."[53]

50. McLane, p. 250.
51. W. J. Hudson, *Australia and the Colonial Question at the United Nations*, p. 15; F. L. Wood, *The New Zealand People at War*, p. 320.
52. Hudson, p. 17.
53. *FRUS*, 1944, III, 187.

In the same note, Evatt referred to a problem of great wartime concern to Australia and New Zealand, the tendency of the big powers to make decisions affecting the two dominions' interests without consulting or even informing them. The Cairo Declaration with its sweeping reference to Japan's possessions was a particular shock. Their response, the ANZAC Agreement of January 1944, in turn seemed to the United States and Britain a shocking gesture of antipodean self-assertion. Proposing regional defense arrangements and supporting the doctrine of trusteeship, the two powers demanded that there be no change in the sovereignty or system of control over any island in the Pacific without their consent and no final disposal of enemy territory until the ultimate Pacific settlement in which they would participate.[54]

Trusteeship and the United Nations

In 1942 when the State Department began to plan for the future international organization, two colonial problems were involved: defining responsibilities to dependent peoples, and devising a procedure for international supervision. Solutions would need to reflect American anticolonial emotions while in some degree reconciling American views with those of others, particularly the British, who could reasonably expect to have a voice in the peace settlement. The really restrictive pressures on the American position, however, were to come not from the British but from military leaders and their congressional supporters concerned with protecting an American claim to unrestricted control of strategic islands in the Pacific.

From the outset, it had seemed somewhat easier to define obligations to dependent peoples than to cope with how and where these obligations should be enforced. On the latter point there was some disagreement between Hull and Undersecretary Welles. Hull worried about the political acceptability of Welles' proposals for according authority to the international organization and to regional councils. Writing to Roosevelt in November 1942, he proposed two alternative courses. One called for immediate international control only for League of Nations mandates and for territories detached from the enemy; colonies were to be placed under the same systems later. The other prescribed trusteeship only for mandates and detached areas; elsewhere colonial

54. Alan Watt, *The Evolution of Australian Foreign Policy, 1938–1965,* p. 75.

powers would merely pledge themselves to certain principles and standards of administration. The latter he thought more feasible and therefore preferable.[55]

There was division also on principles and standards. But on this question a draft, at least, was submitted to the President in March 1943, subsequently circulated to the British, and tabled, but not discussed at the Moscow Conference in October. According to the draft, the prime obligation was to prepare dependencies for independence. Continuous support was to be given to the political, social, economic, and educational advancement of dependent peoples, who must be employed to the fullest extent possible in local administration, increasingly given powers of self-government, and assured of independence by dates fixed at the earliest practicable moment.[56]

At midsummer, with the Big Four soon to convene at Dumbarton Oaks, the draft had been substantially changed. To accommodate the British, the term independence was abandoned, nor was there any mention of fixed dates. Those responsible for dependent people were to foster the development of political institutions suited to their needs and to develop their capacity for self-government. While metropolitan responsibilities were prescribed less rigorously, dependencies were obliged "to make every effort to prepare themselves for the corresponding duties and responsibilities and to demonstrate their capacity to maintain stable government and to safeguard the political and civil rights of the inhabitants." Trusteeship was to be applied to colonies only by the voluntary act of the administering authorities; it was to be applied automatically only to territories held under League mandate or detached from the enemy.[57]

Automatic application of trusteeship to the mandates, however, was precisely what American military leaders did not want. Their views had begun to take shape as the campaign in the Southwest Pacific, initiated in June 1943, prepared the way for the conquest of the Japanese mandates, the Marshalls and the Marianas—some 98 islands with less than 900 square miles of land surface. By December, the Navy, already proceeding with military government plans, was seeking political

55. Russell, p. 85.

56. *FRUS*, Conferences at Washington and Quebec, 1943, pp. 717–719; Hull, II, 1235.

57. Russell, pp. 337–341; Notter, p. 606.

guidance from the State Department. In December also, the Cairo Declaration had announced that the islands the Japanese held in the Pacific would be removed from their control but had not provided for their disposition. And, in January, the ANZAC Agreement aroused suspicion in American naval and Congressional circles that Australia and New Zealand were attempting to exclude the United States from the South Pacific.[58]

The President's views had also alarmed the military leaders. At Teheran in December 1943, Roosevelt told Stalin and Churchill that he thought the international organization should exercise sovereignty over the mandates, while Harry Hopkins said much the same thing to Eden and Molotov. Before the Teheran meeting, the President had explained to the Joint Chiefs that his proposal would not preclude establishing the necessary U.S. military bases. However, the military, persuaded by the bitter island-by-island campaign that the archipelagos must never again fall into hostile hands, wanted not base rights but unrestricted control. Talking with the President, Chief of Staff William D. Leahy "argued vigorously that the United States, for its own future security, should keep and exercise sovereignty over any of the Japanese mandated islands that we captured." In March, Leahy put the same point to Hull: "The conquest of the islands," he said, "is being effected by the forces of the United States and there appears to be no valid reason why their future status should be the subject of discussion with any other nation."[59] In July, the State Department draft and the imminence of the Dumbarton Oaks conversations brought the issue to a head. With U.S. interest in the colonial question well known, the other participants would certainly expect American proposals for the future international organization to include a chapter on trusteeship. Civilians and military remained in deep disagreement, however, and no such chapter was included in the American draft, nor was the subject discussed at Dumbarton Oaks.

Further decisions were to be made at Yalta in preparation for the general international conference. In an interagency committee set up at State Department instance, contention over international discussion

58. *FRUS*, 1944, III, 168–201; V, 1186–1187; Wood, pp. 317–318; Watt, pp. 76–77.

59. Leahy, p. 210; *FRUS*, Cairo and Teheran, 1943, pp. 258, 571; *FRUS*, 1944, V, 1201.

of trusteeship continued unabated. The question of trusteeship was not relevant to the Pacific islands at all, the military argued. The islands should not be regarded as colonies but as defense posts, acquisition of which Secretary of War Henry L. Stimson said, "does not represent an attempt at colonization or exploration . . . it is merely the acquisition by the United States of the necessary bases for the defense of the Pacific for the future world. To serve such a purpose they must belong to the United States with absolute power to rule and fortify them." But, in an international discussion of trusteeship, these islands would be seen in the wrong light, and other countries, particularly minor ones, would want to impose restrictions on the United States. Congress also joined the fray. In January 1945 a bill was introduced in the House of Representatives putting under naval administration all U.S. dependencies in the Pacific, including any coming under U.S. jurisdiction as a result of the war. At the same time, the House Committee on Naval Affairs established a subcommittee to consider the need to retain or acquire Pacific islands in the interest of U.S. defense.[60]

The State Department, for its part, placed a high priority on establishing the trusteeship system at the United Nations Conference and feared that failure to present a plan would diminish American influence over final decisions. Accordingly, the civilians attempted to meet military objectives by defining principles and procedures while leaving territorial dispositions for postwar discussion. Thus, the Yalta protocol, signed by the United States, Britain, and the Soviet Union, restricted the application of the trusteeship system to existing mandates, territory detached from the enemy, and territory voluntarily submitted while excluding discussion of actual territories from the forthcoming San Francisco Conference.[61]

The President had not objected to the omission of the trusteeship section from the draft the United States submitted at Dumbarton Oaks or to the truncated handling of the question at Yalta. But he continued to express his expansive view of trusteeship and the international organization, referring specifically to the desirability of placing the mandates under the United Nations (UN), not only in his private conversations but also publicly as in his press conference on April 5. By this time,

60. *FRUS,* The Conferences at Malta and Yalta, 1945, pp. 58–59; Russell, pp. 510–514; Walter Millis (ed.), *The Forrestal Diaries,* p. 28; Leahy, pp. 286–287.

61. Russell, pp. 510–511; *FRUS,* Malta and Yalta, 1945, p. 977; Notter, p. 387.

moreover, continued interagency divisions had clearly created the necessity for presidential choice. State and Interior had agreed to the concept of strategic trusts as a separate category under terms virtually excluding the possibility of international interference. War and Navy did not think the concept provided adequate protection, and Stimson worried that the American delegation might make "quixotic gestures" at San Francisco. Confronted with conflicting recommendations Roosevelt agreed to meet with the three Secretaries on April 19.[62]

But by April 19 Roosevelt was dead, and the decision was made by a new president with no commitments of his own on trusteeship to weigh against the strategic argument. The United States would indeed present a proposal on the trusteeship system at the San Francisco Conference, but, as agreed at Yalta, there was to be no discussion of specific territories. To limit international supervision within the framework of the Yalta agreements, trust territories were to be divided into strategic and nonstrategic areas; the General Assembly and the Trusteeship Council were to have no role with respect to strategic trusts, which would lie wholly under the jurisdiction of the Security Council; and trusteeship arrangements were to be reached in agreement with the administering authorities.[63]

The United Nations charter as it emerged from the San Francisco Conference implicitly rejected the notion that the sovereignty of Allied countries over areas they had controlled before the war would be called into question when the war ended. There was no requirement that the trusteeship system be applied to any particular dependent areas, even former mandates and territories detached from the enemy. Article 73, defining the obligations assumed by administering powers to all their dependencies, was an unprecedented international affirmation of the sacred-trust doctrine. But, as compared with earlier American statements and drafts, it was a pallid formulation.

The substance of the American position had been drastically altered by strategic considerations and its spirit by Roosevelt's death. But since organizing the United Nations required accommodation among the great powers—by this time defined to include France—the outcome might not have been substantially different, even if the United States had argued for its earlier views. To be sure, at the end of 1944, there

62. *FRUS,* 1945, I, 197; Russell, pp. 582–587; Millis, p. 37.
63. Russell, p. 589; *FRUS,* 1945, I, 350–351.

had been indications that the British might accept a system of international supervision. But when the American shift became clear at Yalta, much of the incentive for a British shift was removed.[64] At San Francisco they were willing to accept principles of trusteeship as binding on all administering powers. But they were prepared to give the international organization supervisory powers only in trust territories. Opposing the strategic-trust concept, the British argued that international supervision would be just as necessary in areas used for strategic purposes, if not more so. As an alternative to strategic trusts, they proposed abandoning the restrictions on militarization imposed by the mandates system and permitting the administering power to mobilize trust-territory resources as a contribution to the maintenance of international peace and security under the provisions of the Charter. This last was a point also pressed by Australia, anxious on the basis of wartime experience to provide more adequately for the defense of New Guinea but with no desire to exempt the territory from international supervision.[65]

The British also continued to object strenuously to the term "independence." In a burst of old colonial oratory, their representative attributed Britain's survival in the early days of the war to the existence of the British African Empire. "And the same I know is true of the French territories which rallied to General de Gaulle and of the Belgian Colonial Empire. These colonial empires in fact were welded into one vast machine for the defense of liberty. Could we really contemplate, as the conscious aim of our deliberations the destruction of this machine or its separation into component parts?"[66]

The French, who objected even to the term "self-government" and would have preferred "the progressive development of political institutions," forthrightly excluded themselves from any system of international supervision which, properly, should be applied only to mandates and former enemy territory. Territories such as Indochina, they said, "unequivocally are excluded from the discussion and will so remain."[67] And the French could speak with some confidence having been assured

64. Wood, p. 323; Russell, pp. 31, 511, 813.

65. Documents of the United Nations Conference on International Organization (UNCIO), III, 609–613; Harper and Sissons, p. 77.

66. Kurt London (ed.), *New Nations in a Divided World*, p. 3.

67. UNCIO, III, 604; Drachman, p. 56.

by James F. Byrnes, soon to become Secretary of State, "that the record is entirely innocent of any official statement questioning, even by implication, French sovereignty over Indochina."[68]

The independence issue caused some division within the American delegation. State Department members of the delegation argued that, if the United States failed to uphold specific reference to the goal of independence, its stance would support British, French, and Belgian colonial rule and "would be very unpopular in the Far East. To take any position short of complete independence would simply not satisfy the colonial peoples."[69] This was not the first warning that the American shift, if carried too far, would make it impossible for the United States to move other colonial powers into new positions and would disillusion dependent peoples. Secretary of the Interior Harold Ickes had said as much in a memorandum to the President during the American debate before San Francisco.[70] When Molotov remarked in a press conference that the international organization should have the power to promote self-government for the dependent peoples, Acting Secretary Joseph C. Grew wrote, "Although this has been our historic role, Russia, I fear, may appear before the world as the champion of all dependent peoples. Molotov's move may confirm in the minds of the people of Asia, their already strong suspicion that the Anglo-American powers are not their real champions and [they] will turn to Russia as their more outspoken friend and spokesman."[71]

Although thus breaking their wartime silence on colonial questions, the Russians—as intent as anyone on asserting big-power control—made no real attempt to seize leadership of the dependent peoples. It was they who proposed including "self-determination of peoples" in the definition of United Nations purposes and principles and, in a subsequent press conference, Molotov made clear that a colonial application was intended. They also proposed three amendments to the American draft on dependent areas: specifying the achievement of full national independence as a goal; including in the Trusteeship Council all permanent members of the Security Council; and somewhat

68. *FRUS,* 1945, VI, 307.
69. *FRUS,* 1945, I, 793.
70. *Ibid.,* pp. 198–199.
71. *Ibid.,* p. 652.

strengthening international inspection powers in nonstrategic trusts. But they went no further than this and, perhaps because they still hoped to be awarded trusteeship of Libya, they accepted the American division between strategic and nonstrategic trusts.[72]

It was left to countries that had themselves passed through the colonial experience, or like China, through something resembling it, to press for a larger international role.[73] Australia and New Zealand led in this endeavor, with the latter's role in debate somewhat circumscribed by Prime Minister Peter Fraser's chairmanship of the relevant committee. Although their proposals were limited by the obvious futility of seeking universal applicability of trust machinery, Australia did propose that the General Assembly nominate territories for trust status. Both emphasized stronger trusteeship machinery and a more comprehensive definition of the obligations owed to dependent peoples.[74]

Practice proved even more limited than principle required; of the ten former mandates all but Southwest Africa were placed under trusteeship, as was the former Italian colony, Somaliland, but no administering power ever offered to place any other territory under the system. The colonial peoples themselves were soon to go far beyond the trusteeship concept. The mood of the future was expressed at San Francisco by the Iraqi delegate. Objecting to such phrases in the British draft as "peoples not yet ready to stand by themselves" and "sacred trust of civilization," he remarked that very few peoples in the modern world could stand by themselves while, among dependent peoples, there were some with a long heritage of civilization.[75] In the two important Southeast Asian colonial conflicts in which the United Nations played a role—the Indonesian and West Irian (Netherlands New Guinea) cases—its authority was invoked under peace-keeping not trusteeship provisions.

72. Russell, p. 811; *UNCIO*, III, 618; Haas, p. 13.

73. This included the Philippines which, like India, attended the San Francisco Conference in anticipation of forthcoming independence.

74. UNCIO, X, 644; Mansergh, p. 320; Wood, p. 340; Huntington Gilchrist, "Colonial Questions at the San Francisco Conference," *American Political Science Review*, XXXIX (Oct., 1945), p. 984.

75. Russell, p. 816.

Potsdam: Further Decline of U.S. Interest

Military decisions at Potsdam were to have a more immediate impact on Southeast Asia than political decisions at San Francisco. The military decisions of July and early August 1945 had been foreshadowed long before, as it became evident that the generally anticipated final assault on the Japanese home islands would not be launched from the mainland but as the culmination of the combined air and amphibious operations that were re-establishing Allied control of the Pacific. At Malta, in February, the war on the Southeast Asian mainland was, in effect, entrusted to the British. After Burma was won, the campaign for recovering Malaysia and Singapore and establishing bridgeheads in Java and Sumatra would be launched. But, in order to concentrate American strength on the higher priority assault on Japan itself, U.S. forces were not to participate, and U.S. interest shifted accordingly.

At Potsdam the shift was formally acknowledged. Indonesia was transferred to the Southeast Asia Command from MacArthur's Southwest Pacific Command, the energies of which were now to be directed northward. In Indochina, formerly indistinct lines of authority were clarified: the area north of the sixteenth parallel was accorded to the China theater; the area to the south to the Southeast Asia Command. The division pleased the Chinese little and the French less. The French, who had been pressing for logistic support so that they could move in their own troops, protested in vain. The Generalissimo asked only that the line be extended to take in northern Thailand as well. Later in August, however, Madame Chiang Kai-shek pressed President Harry Truman on future plans for Indochina, recalling to him Roosevelt's statements about trusteeship. Truman replied that General de Gaulle had given him satisfactory assurances concerning steps toward independence and "that there had been no discussion of a trusteeship for Indochina as far as he was concerned."[76] America no longer had the will to intervene nor plans to establish the military presence that might have given it the power to do so.

76. Devillers, pp. 149–150; *FRUS,* 1945, VII, 149, 550–551.

CHAPTER 2

THE STRUGGLE FOR INDEPENDENCE
AS AN INTERNATIONAL ISSUE:.
INDOCHINA AND INDONESIA[1]

Roosevelt's anticipations of a nationalist upsurge and the concern of the military for strategic positions were considerably closer to postwar realities than were the preoccupations of the planners with the principles and machinery of trusteeship. Cut off from developments in Japanese-occupied Southeast Asia, western planners could not know that the very foundations of the trusteeship principles were collapsing. In the course of the war, the notion that one country was properly the object of the tutelary or civilizing mission of another became increasingly unacceptable, and with it the notion of gradual achievement of self-government. Instead, the nationalists insisted on speedy and unequivocal fulfillment of their right to govern or misgovern themselves. And, under the Japanese, they had gained the military training and the arms to advance their demands by force if they could not win them peacefully.

Initial Japanese success had undermined one of colonialism's major moral arguments—that it afforded defense and protection to the weak and helpless. Thereafter, life under occupation revealed that the machinery of state functioned without the occidental presence much as it had with it. And this was not because all the positions from which occidentals were expelled were filled by Japanese. The Japanese occupied some of these positions, played a large role in administration, and held final authority. But in much of the area they gave new positions and new authority to the indigenous peoples, partly out of war-

1. A shorter version of this chapter appeared in *Foreign Affairs* (April, 1973), copyright 1973 by the Council on Foreign Relations, Inc., from which it is reprinted by permission.

time necessity and partly because the appearance of self-government suited their own political purposes.[2]

Even as the war drew to a close, metropolitan governments and former colonial officials, who exercised considerable influence over political decisions, were slow to appreciate the change. Especially because the Japanese, like the Germans, had been brutal and exacting, ill-founded parallels were drawn between the situation in Europe and that in Southeast Asia. The Europeans expected to be welcomed as liberators. They failed to realize that the Southeast Asians, however much they had detested the Japanese, had welcomed the Japanese expulsion of the colonial rulers. The returning Europeans also failed to realize that Southeast Asians who had exercised authority under the Japanese were not regarded by their countrymen as Quislings or war criminals. It was hard for the colonial powers to accept the new Asian leaders thrown up by the war as other than the self-appointed and irresponsible spokesmen of a noisy and disorderly minority. And many who finally accepted the prospect of independence saw a continued, if temporary, presence as urgently necessary to rebuild and restore war-shattered countries before imposing on them the heavy burdens of self-government.

The United States, having already committed itself to independence for the Philippines, did not encounter the problem of aroused colonial nationalism. The British faced it in Burma and, after some hesitation, accepted it and granted independence, the decision eased perhaps because it was made by a Labour Party government and because of the prior commitment to independence for India. The French and the Dutch proved less flexible. In due course, the independence movements in Indonesia and Indochina, escaping the confines of struggle between metropole and colony, became international problems. By the end of 1949, Indonesia had become fully independent, led by men, many of whom had risen to national importance as Japanese collaborators. The three states of Indochina, by contrast, had been accorded quite limited autonomy within the French Union; in Vietnam the French had been for three years at war with an independence

2. The Philippines was a notable exception. Internal administration had been in the hands of the Filipinos since the inauguration of the Commonwealth in 1935; the role of Philippine officials under the Japanese was thus much more circumscribed than it had been before the war.

movement led by men who had opposed the Japanese and who had given some wartime assistance to the Allies.

The differences in outcome were fatefully affected by external roles. In Indonesia, these tended to strengthen pressures toward settlement on nationalist terms. In Vietnam, the relatively minor importance of external roles, as well as the ways in which they were played, tended to reduce the prospects for settlement. France as a great power could fend off interference in ways not open to the Netherlands. The Communist leadership of the Democratic Republic of Vietnam prejudiced efforts to win non-Communist foreign support, while bringing no real assistance from Communist countries or parties elsewhere. But there were other distinguishing factors. Among the most important was the concern felt by Australia and India over developments in Indonesia. A lesser one was the sympathy felt for the Indonesians by other Asian countries and by the Muslim states of the Near East. And finally, the involvement of the United Nations, weak and hesitant as its initial actions were, worked, over the long run, to Indonesian advantage, and brought in its train pressures on the United States to engage itself more actively, as well as a rather high level of international attention.

The Japanese Occupation: Contrasts in Political Impact

The Japanese occupations of Indonesia and Indochina differed considerably. In Indonesia, after their surrender in March 1942, the Dutch were all interned for the duration. The Japanese did not establish an ostensibly independent government as they did in Burma and the Philippines. Nevertheless, Indonesians in large numbers replaced Dutch officials, particularly in the lower ranks but also, late in the war, in higher ones. With some 23,000 Japanese in the administration in 1945, the Indonesian government servant was now merely the servant of the Japanese instead of the Dutch; however, he was often able to exercise more authority under his new masters because of their ignorance of the country.[3]

In Indochina, the Japanese did not eliminate the French administration until March 1945. Nevertheless, although the French, unlike the Dutch, had not been conquered by Asian arms, they had yielded more and more to superior Asian strength. And the French Governor-

3. F. C. Jones, *Japan's New Order in East Asia*, pp. 372–373.

General Jean Decoux, partly to counter Japan's Greater East Asia appeal, adopted policies that stimulated nationalism, giving much more emphasis to national history and tradition, and increasing the prestige, although not the powers, of the three reigning monarchs— Bao Dai in Annam, Sisavang Vong in Luang Prabang, and Norodom Sihanouk in Cambodia.[4] The national languages were emphasized in elementary education, more schools were established, technical and vocational subjects were introduced, and more Indochinese were admitted to French schools. More Indochinese were admitted also to the administration and permitted to rise higher in its ranks, and, for the first time, Indochinese employees were given the same salaries as their French equivalents. To provide some military training for Indochinese, Decoux organized a youth movement emphasizing physical education and paramilitary training with members numbering in the hundred thousands.[5]

These developments, like similar ones in Indonesia, raised the level of nationalist fervor and vastly expanded the circles in which it was felt. But in Indonesia much more than in the Indochinese states there emerged from the Japanese occupation a new, truly national leadership, able to mobilize mass support and to operate effectively and with relative cohesion in the political arena. Because they were entirely responsible for operating the government, the Japanese found it necessary to utilize the Javanese bureaucratic class, already incorporated into the colonial political structure, in ways that increased its responsibilities and elevated its status. But because they also wanted to mobilize and motivate the masses, the Japanese gave new positions of leadership and political prestige to the secular nationalists and to the Islamic leaders who had been held down by the Dutch. These newly potent elements were exposed to Japanese political mobilization techniques and introduced to a theatrical style of politics, which, unlike

4. Indochina, at this time, consisted of four protectorates—Cambodia, Luang Prabang in Laos, and Annam and Tonkin in Vietnam—and two colonies—Cochin China in Vietnam, and that part of Laos not included in the kingdom of Luang Prabang. In Laos, the effort to heighten national feeling was directed more against the appeal of the ethnically related Thai, who had taken advantage of French defeat and their own entente with the Japanese to detach some of their Lao holdings from the French.

5. Devillers, pp. 81–87; Hammer, p. 31; Buttinger, I, 230–233; Bernard B. Fall, *The Two Viet-Nams*, p. 48.

the Dutch style, was compatible with the Javanese tradition. Provided with the facilities of a far-reaching radio network, and given opportunities to travel in Java and the outer islands, many, like Sukarno and Mohammad Hatta, hitherto known in narrow circles, became national figures. Mass organizations of all kinds were permitted and encouraged; for the first time, the nationalist elite was supported by large-scale organization among the people and an armed and indoctrinated youth. As Benedict Anderson has put it, "By 1945, for the first time in Indonesian history, there were political organizations continuously and fairly efficiently connecting the rural family to the centers of political power and decision-making in the capital."[6]

In Vietnam, in contrast, continued French repression helped to perpetuate the conspiratorial, atomized, and elitist characteristics of prewar political activity. To this the highly autonomous Japanese *Kempeitai* (military police) contributed by their secret activity among local political groups. In Cochin China, the Cao Dai and the Hoa Hao, politically oriented religious sects, tended to use their Japanese connections to enrich and strengthen themselves at the expense of each other and of nonbelievers. The *Kempeitai* also involved themselves in clandestine politics in Tonkin, but, unlike the southern sects, the organizations operating under Japanese patronage in the north had little if any popular following.[7]

In sum, such political activity as existed under ostensible French control neither trained new leadership nor stimulated new, widely supported nationalist organizations. When the Japanese displaced the French in March 1945, titular powers of government in the Indochinese states were transferred to the hereditary rulers. These rulers, although they too aspired to independence, also benefited from the *status quo* and were, therefore, more inclined than the new Indonesian leaders to view the existing state of affairs as something that could be altered only gradually.

Among the Vietnamese nationalist groups, only the Indochinese Communist Party became stronger during the war years. Benefiting

6. Benedict Anderson, *Some Aspects of Indonesian Politics under the Japanese Occupation,* pp. 17–26; Harry J. Benda, *The Crescent and the Rising Sun,* pp. 198–200; Joseph Silverstein (ed.), *Southeast Asia in World War II,* pp. 17–26; Kahin, pp. 108–111.

7. Devillers, pp. 90–94; Buttinger, I, 257–258.

from Chinese hospitality aimed against the Japanese or the French, Vietnamese Communist leaders had taken refuge with other nationalists in Yunnan. Their fellow exiles had followers but no organization. The Communists had both a highly disciplined Leninist party structure and a nationalist front organization, the Viet Minh.[8] The Chinese would have preferred their own protégés to dominate the nationalist movement and tried to help them when they could. But they had to recognize the superior organization and capabilities of the Viet Minh, which became a major element in the Chinese-sponsored Dong Minh Hoi[9]—joined also by the VNQDD and eight other nationalist organizations.

Meanwhile in Vietnam, the Viet Minh husbanded its strength, building up an underground organization but not risking it in action, maintaining contact among local groups and with the leaders abroad, and laying the groundwork for the return of its headquarters to Tonkin in October 1944. Guerrilla activities already under way in the northern provinces were facilitated by the removal of French authority in March; by June 1945, the Viet Minh held six provinces between the Chinese border and Hanoi.[10] However, while of all the nationalist groups the Viet Minh was now the strongest threat to the French, its Communist control gave the French a weapon against the nationalist movement that became increasingly potent with time.

For the Indonesian Communists the fortunes of war were almost entirely bad. The Dutch having evacuated political prisoners as they themselves retreated, many of the Indonesian Communists spent the war in Australia in Allied propaganda work; others were in the Netherlands; those who remained in Indonesia were too few to mount the anti-Japanese resistance demanded by current Communist doctrine. When the war ended, three separate parties emerged, and some of the factions tended to take positions in opposition to Sukarno and Hatta. By the time the Communists had pulled themselves together, the nationalist parties were in control of the Indonesian revolution.[11] There-

8. Viet Nam Doc Lap Dong Minh Hoi (Vietnam Independence League).
9. Viet Nam Cach Ming Dong Minh Hoi (Vietnam Revolutionary League).
10. Buttinger, I, 267–296.
11. Arnold Brackman, *Indonesian Communism: A History*, p. 34; McLane, pp. 279–282; Ruth T. McVey, *The Development of the Indonesian Communist Party and Its Relations with the Soviet Union and the Chinese People's Republic*, p. 26.

after, in the ranks of the Republic the Communist Party (Partai Kommunis Indonesia—PKI) became a strong force on the left, and remained so as long as it kept its policies within the nationalist mainstream. Its role was never strong enough to provide the Dutch with useful ammunition against the nationalists generally, while its attempted coup against the Republic in 1948 completely undermined Dutch contentions that the nationalist movement was Communist-oriented.

Taking the Surrender: Contrasting Roles and Consequences

When the Japanese surrendered in mid-August 1945—well in advance of the date assumed for military planning purposes—Britain, France, and the Netherlands were unprepared to return to their colonies immediately and in strength. In a brief but significant hiatus, the exhilaration caused by Japan's surrender reinforced the trends set in motion by earlier victory and by the policies of the last months before defeat. In mid-September, the returning Allies found themselves confronted not by peoples awaiting liberation, but by peoples who, having in their own view liberated themselves, were now seeking a new relationship with their former rulers. In Vietnam, the Potsdam division of responsibility between British and Chinese at the sixteenth parallel facilitated rapid restoration of French rule in the south and strengthened the Viet Minh in the north, increasing the tensions between the French and their opponents but reinforcing the confidence of each in ultimate victory. British responsibility for taking the surrender in Indonesia worked against the Dutch cause, largely because the Netherlands, unlike France, was not able to relieve British forces rapidly.

The liberation of France, little damaged by the war, got underway in mid-1944. Meanwhile, outside of Southeast Asia, the French colonial empire had remained largely intact, providing, among other assets, a base for preparing troops to reoccupy Indochina. The Dutch government, in contrast, did not return to a devastated Netherlands until May 1945. The British in Indonesia, faced by the prospect of prolonged responsibility for preserving order until the Dutch could return, initiated the first of the external pressures on the Netherlands government that were to become a decisive factor in the success of the Indonesian nationalists.

When General Douglas D. Gracey led his troops into Saigon on

September 12, Bao Dai had abdicated after uniting Tonkin and Annam under the old name of Vietnam. In the south, the government set up by the Japanese when the French were displaced, had also resigned, declaring Cochin China part of Vietnam. The Democratic Republic of Vietnam (DRV), proclaimed in Hanoi on September 2 with Ho Chi Minh as president, was Viet Minh dominated, although it included other elements. In Cochin China, where the Viet Minh was weak, the British were confronted by the DRV's local representative, the Committee of the South, an unstable coalition badly divided over whether to resist (the course favored by the Trotskyites, Hoa Hao, and Cao Dai) or to negotiate (as the Viet Minh proposed).[12]

Although the Committee claimed governmental authority, it was unable to control mounting disorder and violence. On September 21, Gracey, who had originally been expected only to accept Japanese surrender and liberate prisoners of war, announced that he would enforce order throughout the occupation zone. Vietnamese were disarmed, Vietnamese newspapers were suspended and, on September 23, French forces—some of whom were newly arrived, some of whom were liberated prisoners—were permitted to wrest control of Saigon's major installations and public buildings from the Committee of the South. To be sure, at meetings with French commanders in Singapore on September 28 and in Rangoon on October 9, the British urged negotiations with the nationalists. But British pressures on the French were neither strong nor particularly influential in contrast with their impact in Indonesia where they had heavier weapons and more urgent compulsions. With the arrival of French troops in increasing numbers the pacification of Cochin China began in earnest. On October 30, Admiral Georges Thierry d'Argenlieu assumed responsibility as High Commissioner and, by the end of the year, with close to 30,000 troops in Indochina, the French became fully responsible for maintaining law and order south of the sixteenth parallel.[13]

Even though resistance continued in the countryside, the French were now able to give more attention to the north. There they faced quite a different situation. The British had been quite simply motivated

12. Buttinger, I, 311–320.
13. *Ibid.*, pp. 319–337; *Documents Relating to British Involvement in the Indo-China Conflict* (CMD 2834), pp. 7, 50–51; F. S. V. Donnison, *British Military Administration in the Far East*, p. 410; Lancaster, pp. 133–134.

—they believed that the position of the juridical sovereign should be protected, and they wanted to carry out their responsibilities as quickly as possible and depart. The Chinese had no desire to assist in restoring French rule, but their motives were mixed, complicated further by differences between the central government in Chungking and the generals who ruled the southern provinces. General Lu Han, who commanded the occupying forces, had the characteristically strong southern interest in political and economic opportunities in Tonkin. He favored a long occupation, which would give the Chinese opportunities to strengthen their own position by supporting the Vietnamese drive toward independence. Chungking, on the other hand, believed that the Chinese should remain only as long as necessary to extract French concessions in exchange for their departure.[14]

The latter view won out but, meanwhile, the Chinese played local politics and supported the Vietnamese against the French. Chiang Kai-shek had disclaimed territorial ambitions and, while expressing support for Vietnamese independence, had promised that the Chinese would remain neutral. This was precisely what they were not; as the British had disarmed the Vietnamese and facilitated the restoration of French administration, so the Chinese provided arms to the Vietnamese and blocked restoration of the French administration. Originally the Chinese had hoped to promote their own protégés, the VNQDD and the Dong Minh Hoi, and, as they moved south, they replaced local Viet Minh committees with their friends. Later they got a commitment from Ho that he would give 50 seats in the national assembly to the VNQDD and 20 to the Dong Minh Hoi whatever the outcome of the January 1946 general elections. But the strength demonstrated by the Viet Minh in these elections, and otherwise, convinced the Chinese all over again that they would profit most from bringing this group under their influence.[15]

It was at this point, however, that there began the negotiations with France from which the Chinese emerged with considerable profit. An agreement signed in Chungking on February 28 restored to China the French concessions in Shanghai, Tientsin, Hankow, and Canton and permitted China to purchase the French-owned Yunnan railway. In Vietnam, China was given a free port in Haiphong, customs-free

14. Chen, pp. 119–126.
15. Hammer, pp. 132–136; Buttinger, I, pp. 351–359; Devillers, pp. 191–204.

transit of goods to the port, and guaranteed protection for its resident nationals. In return, Chinese forces were to be withdrawn by March 31, 1946. Greeting the treaty, Chiang no longer spoke of independence. Instead, he expressed China's sympathy with Indochinese nationalist aspirations and his country's hopes for "an equitable settlement."[16]

Negotiations between the Viet Minh and the French, proceeding intermittently since late August, were indeed speeded by the agreement with the Chinese. Ho wanted to come to an arrangement with the French before the Chinese withdrew in order to gain maximum advantage from their presence. Bolstering his claims to authority, he could show six months of functioning government north of the sixteenth parallel and some success in his campaigns to increase agricultural production and reduce illiteracy, despite the locustlike depredations of the Chinese occupiers. The French, for their part, were anxious to come to terms before the Chinese left so that their own troops would not encounter resistance when they replaced the Chinese.

The upshot was the agreement of March 6, 1946, in which France recognized Vietnam as a free state with its own government, parliament, army, and finances. Vietnam agreed to become part of the Indochinese Federation and the French Union; a referendum would determine whether Cochin China would become part of Vietnam or remain separate. The French troops, of whom up to 25,000 were to be stationed in Vietnam, were to be withdrawn in five annual increments. Much remained unspecified, however, in what was largely a statement of general principles never subsequently translated into concrete arrangements.[17]

In Indonesia, the impact of Allied occupation was quite different. To be sure, when the British landed in Indonesia on September 29, their problems seemed very much like those in Indochina. A self-proclaimed independent Republic of Indonesia had asserted its jurisdiction over the archipelago and made clear its adamant opposition to Dutch return on prewar terms. Moreover, in its six weeks of existence, it had maintained a functioning administration in Java, Sumatra, and much of Madura.

British forces were extremely small, even to disarm the Japanese and liberate prisoners of war and internees; to keep order on any large scale

16. Alfred Grosser, La IVe République et sa politique extérieure, p. 255.
17. Hammer, pp. 152–153; Buttinger, I, 364–368.

would be quite beyond them. But the British could not expect significant Dutch reinforcement for some time to come; indeed, they were destined to remain in Indonesia for more than a year. Because the intelligence gathered by the Southwest Pacific Command had not been turned over to them, the British sent in an advance intelligence team and consulted with the Japanese. From both, they got the same reports of intense nationalist and anti-Dutch emotions. The Japanese advised them to leave the Indonesian administration in place—the Indonesians, they thought, would be happy to cooperate if this would help them toward independence, but slights to their national flag or anthem or war-criminal treatment of President Sukarno or Vice President Mohammad Hatta could have disastrous results.[18]

The British thus had some hope of compensating for their limited numbers by utilizing the Republic's machinery. At a press conference when he arrived, the British commander, Lieutenant General Sir Philip Christison, announced that "things will have to go on as they are" until Dutch civil administrators arrived; this was taken as *de facto* recognition of the Republican administration. The British, however, were also bringing Dutch military and civil personnel in with them— too few to be of much help should the situation get out of hand, but enough to arouse suspicion and heighten emotion. Mounting disorder culminated in November in ten days of intense fighting between British and Indonesian troops in Surabaya. The British now recognized that either they would have to expand their forces in Indonesia very considerably and accept the prospect of major hostilities, or they would have to induce the Dutch to negotiate.[19]

The first course was unacceptable for a host of reasons. The Southeast Asia Command's military resources were already very badly stretched, and its ground forces were predominantly Indian.[20] Use of these forces against Asian nationalists—particularly against Indonesians —was intensely irritating to an Indian government with which

18. Anderson, p. 120.

19. Alastair M. Taylor, *Indonesian Independence and the United Nations*, pp. 7–8; Kahin, pp. 144–145.

20. Indian Army forces made up 80 percent of the Commonwealth total in Malaya, China, Indochina, and Indonesia after the war; of the thirty British battalions that landed in Indonesia in September, 1945, twenty-six were Indian (Donnison, p. 426; Ton That Thien, *India and Southeast Asia, 1947–1960,* p. 71).

Britain was already negotiating the terms of independence. Britain also was deeply involved in efforts to alleviate Asia's postwar food shortage, an effort to which, it was thought, Indonesia's sugar, tea, fats, and oils could make an important contribution. And, finally, having attacked Churchill for his military support of the conservatives in the Greek civil war, the Labour Party, now in office, had no desire to be accused of playing the same role in Indonesia.

Pressure for negotiations was the obvious course, not because the British had any desire to dismember the Netherlands Empire, but because this seemed the best way of saving it at least cost. Some efforts had already been made. Early in October in Singapore, Mountbatten had urged the Dutch to meet with Indonesian leaders, including Sukarno. Thereafter both sides had taken some steps toward each other. On November 6, a statement promised full partnership in a future commonwealth. Sukarno—with whom the Dutch refused to deal—had named Soetan Sjahrir, untainted by collaboration with the Japanese, as Prime Minister, and Sjahrir had brought into his cabinet a number of other noncollaborators. In mid-November, Lieutenant-Governor Hubertus van Mook met several times with Sjahrir under Christison's auspices. And on December 6, at another meeting in Singapore, Christison had been instructed to try to re-establish law and order in as wide an area as possible, while the Dutch had been informed that it was not part of British policy to engage in widespread offensive action against the Indonesians. On December 19, British efforts were reinforced by a U.S. statement urging negotiations.[21]

Pressures were now to be applied at higher levels. On December 27 Prime Minister Clement Atlee held a conference at Chequers with Netherlands Prime Minister Willem Schermerhorn and members of his cabinet. The British agreed to replace Christison, who was regarded by the Dutch as overly sympathetic to the Republic, and the Dutch, in turn, withdrew two "old-guard militarists" who had been leading their forces in Indonesia. The British agreed to make greater efforts to maintain law and order, the Dutch to try more actively to reach an understanding with the Indonesians. On January 19, as an outgrowth of the Chequers conference, Sir Archibald Clark-Kerr (soon to be named

21. Alastair Taylor, pp. 10–13; R. Kennedy and P. M. Kattenburg, "*Indonesia in Crisis,*" *Foreign Policy Reports,* XXIV (1948), p. 176.

Lord Inverchapel) was designated Special Ambassador to assist both sides in reaching a settlement.[22]

The Special Ambassador's instructions made clear Britain's hopes for preserving the Dutch role in some substantial form. The British government, he was told, although vitally concerned with the consequences of continued failure to reach a political settlement, did not wish to become concerned with constitutional issues, which were matters for direct agreement between the Dutch and the Indonesians. But Inverchapel was to seek every opportunity to encourage and facilitate an agreement. The proposals already made by the Dutch, including those of December 6, 1942, and November 6, 1945, offered "a fair and reasonable basis of settlement"; Indonesian leaders should be urged to give them earnest and favorable consideration and to keep in mind British recognition of Netherlands sovereignty.[23]

Inverchapel did not reach Indonesia until February 8. Meanwhile, another development attracted international attention to the British role. On January 21, the Ukrainian representative had lodged a Soviet-inspired complaint in the Security Council accusing the British and Japanese of suppressing the Indonesian national liberation movement and calling for a fact-finding commission. The Ukrainian resolution was prompted much less by interest in Indonesia than by desire to retaliate for an earlier complaint over the presence of Soviet forces in Iran. Easily voted down, it was nevertheless a precedent for future UN action.

On February 10, talks began under Inverchapel's auspices, accompanied thereafter by an enlarging Dutch presence and sporadic violence and ruptures, and influenced by political developments in the Netherlands and Indonesia. Although the talks were for the most part between the Indonesians and the Dutch, at crucial moments the British joined them. Three issues were paramount: the Republic's sovereignty and territorial jurisdiction; its role in the projected United States of Indonesia; and the nature of the union to be formed between Indonesia and the Netherlands.

Finally, on November 15, 1946, the Linggadjati Agreement was initialed. The Dutch recognized the Republic's *de facto* authority over

22. Charles Wolf, *The Indonesian Story*, p. 35; *SIA*, 1939–1946, p. 248.
23. *FRUS*, 1946, VIII, 802–803.

Java, Sumatra, and Madura; the Republic agreed to cooperate in forming a federal Indonesia and a Netherlands-Indonesian Union under the Queen. Both were to be formed no later than January 1, 1949, and the Union was to have its own organs to deal with subjects of common interest such as defense and foreign affairs. Dutch troops were to be withdrawn from the Republic, and disputes not settled by negotiation would be submitted to arbitration.[24]

On November 30, 1946, the British withdrew. As in Indochina, their military forces—reinforced by the Japanese—had helped to restore the islands to the European sovereign. When they departed there were 92,000 Dutch troops in place, 10,000 of them trained by the British who left behind them arms for 62,000.[25] It was also under British auspices, however, that the Dutch had taken the first steps toward accommodation with the Indonesians.

The Metropolitan Governments: Differing Capabilities, Similar Intentions

Given some international status by the Linggadjati Agreement, Indonesia continued to benefit from external pressures on the Dutch, pressures which were thereafter never absent for long. In Indochina, with the British and Chinese departing, France had a free hand made stronger by its ability as an important power to stifle even hints of third-party good offices. The developing Cold War was a major factor influencing the attitudes of the western Allies toward the French and Dutch colonial wars. Both countries, abandoning previous policies— French efforts to act as a bridge between the Soviets and the West, and Dutch reliance on the United Nations and opposition to blocs— had begun to join with the United States in 1947 in strengthening the defenses of Western Europe. But there could be no question about which country was the more important member of the partnership with Europe, and which one therefore had to be treated with more gingerly respect. Instructions to the American embassies in Paris and at The Hague in May 1947 made the difference quite clear. Both embassies were instructed to convey American concern and hopes that conflict would be replaced by voluntary cooperation stemming from

24. Alastair Taylor, pp. 14–17; William Henderson, *Pacific Settlement of Disputes: The Indonesian Question, 1946–1949*, pp. 9–13.
25. Wolf, pp. 24–27.

satisfaction of legitimate colonial aspirations. But, in prescribing how their message was to be delivered, careful distinctions were made. The embassy in The Hague was to present U.S. views at the Foreign Office and leave an aide memoire behind. The embassy in Paris was merely invited to present these views at appropriate times in appropriate conversations with French officials. Moreover, undoubtedly anticipating the embassy's own views, the message conceded that "it might not be desirable [to] make such approach to newly constituted government in first days its reorganization."[26]

The drain on resources imposed by colonial wars was of particular concern to the United States which had undertaken large Marshall Plan expenditures to help reduce the internal threat to Western Europe through economic recovery and to support rearmament as insurance against the external threat. By the end of 1948, the drain on the Netherlands was affecting its contribution to western defense, and there were now a number of other important factors—including American public opinion and the need to uphold authority—impelling the United States toward intervention.

France also was investing heavily in the effort to pacify Vietnam. But in Indochina the United States was not yet confronted with any real need to choose, and the French view that Indochina fell exclusively within its domestic jurisdiction was not yet to be challenged. Regarded as a key to the recovery of Western Europe, and with the alternatives to unstable coalition governments either Gaullist or Communist, France and the French had sensitivities to be treated with circumspection and respect. Moreover, the voice of the European bureau of the State Department was quite crucial in determining policy toward Southeast Asia; the Francophilia of many of its officers—which had no parallel in attitudes toward the Netherlands—played a significant if not precisely definable role.[27]

For their part, France and the Netherlands were equally determined to regain their prewar positions. For France, considerations of economic interest and political prestige were reinforced by fear that, if its posi-

26. *FRUS,* 1947, VI, 495, 924.

27. Grosser, pp. 222–227; Amry Vandenbosch, *Dutch Foreign Policy since 1815,* pp. 301–302; J. Foster Collins, "The United Nations and Indonesia," *International Conciliation,* 459 (1950), p. 181; Arnold Wolfers (ed.), *Alliance Policy in the Cold War,* pp. 242–243.

tion in Indochina weakened, its position in Africa would become more vulnerable.

Pursuing similar objectives, France and the Netherlands followed similar policies. Both were prepared to accept general principles that could be interpreted as fulfilling all but the most extreme demands. But when the time came for implementation, liberal principles seemed to evaporate. Thus, when Ho went to France as a recognized Chief of State for talks on carrying out the March 6 (1946) Agreement, he was kept waiting for a month. Then, when negotiations began at Fontainebleau, he was confronted with technicians not authorized to deal with political questions. He returned to Vietnam with nothing more than the *modus vivendi* of September 14, which dealt largely with cultural and economic matters and left all the political issues unresolved. Similarly, the Netherlands, having agreed in principle to the juridical standing accorded to the Republic by the Linggadjati Agreement, sought, in practice, to reduce the status of the densely populated Republic by putting it on an equal plane with small Dutch-created states through the device of a federal state, the United States of Indonesia. The French, although less favored by geography and indigenous traditions, also looked to forms of federalism to weaken their principal opponent. Ignoring the requirement for a plebiscite in the March 6 Agreement, they recognized a separate Cochin Chinese government on June 1, 1946, just as the Vietnamese delegation was leaving for Fontainebleau.

When stalemates developed, both metropoles acted on the belief that negotiations would be more fruitful if preceded by military action. In their first Police Action of July 1946, the Dutch succeeded in reducing the territory under the Republic's control; however, they also precipitated UN intervention. International reactions to the second Police Action in December 1948 made Indonesian independence inevitable. Similar French action in November 1946, the shelling of Haiphong, aroused no similar international interest, although the casualties, especially among fleeing civilians, were very heavy.

The Role of the United Nations

The Democratic Republic of Vietnam seems to have made at least five appeals for UN action. In February 1946, in letters to the governments of the United States, China, the Soviet Union and Britain, Ho asked that they bring the Indochina issue before the UN. On August 16, intervention was again requested. Early in 1947, the American Embassy in Bangkok was asked to forward a joint appeal by local representatives of the DRV and of the Lao and Cambodian independence movements. And on September 12, 1947, when hostilities were under way in earnest, the Secretary General was asked to request the UN Security Council to put an end to the war and to initiate peace negotiations on the basis of Vietnamese independence and territorial integrity, respect for French cultural and economic interests, and the withdrawal of French armed forces. A similar appeal was made by Ho to India's Jawaharlal Nehru in October 1947.[28] None of these requests seems to have elicited any response or comment, although, by the time of the last two, a precedent had already been set by Security Council action on the Indonesian question. In any case, with the French free to veto, it seems unlikely that much would have come out of Security Council consideration.

Even though the signing of the Linggadjati Agreement had prompted eight countries, including the United States and Britain, to accord the Republic *de facto* recognition, it was not without considerable debate over the issue of sovereignty that the Security Council agreed to take up the Indonesian question and called for a cease-fire.[29] Both sides having accepted the cease-fire on August 4, the Security Council during the remainder of the month took two steps of more lasting significance. Machinery was created to keep the Council informed and to assist the parties in reaching agreement: the reporting function was assigned to the career consular corps in Djakarta; the conciliatory function was assigned to a Good Offices Committee with three members (Belgium selected by the Dutch, Australia selected by the Indonesians, and the United States selected by the two other members). The other significant move advanced the juridical status of the Republic by inviting it to join in the Security Council discussions as a party to the dispute. The proposal that the Dutch-created states of West Borneo and East Indonesia be invited also was voted down.

28. *FRUS,* 1946, VIII, 27, 55–56; *FRUS,* 1947, VI, 56–57; Hammer, p. 213; Thien, p. 124.

29. The most detailed and useful accounts of the United Nations role are in Alastair Taylor, *Indonesian Independence,* and Henderson, *Pacific Settlement,* from which this brief summary is drawn.

As negotiations proceeded under the auspices of the Good Offices Committee bitterness rose on both sides over cease-fire violations, and the Indonesians were increasingly pressed by Dutch military and economic measures. In mid-January 1948, negotiations on board a U.S. naval vessel produced principles for further negotiations. Known as the Renville Agreements, these consisted essentially of a truce arrangement, the Twelve Political Principles—drafted by the Dutch and heavily weighted in their favor—and the Six Additional Principles, proposed by the Good Offices Committee to offset somewhat the severity of the Dutch terms. Even with these amendments the Agreements were quite unfavorable to the Republic on all crucial points—the location of the cease-fire line, the issue of Netherlands sovereignty, and the nature of the proposed federation. Within several months, deadlocks had developed on central issues, and truce violations became increasingly frequent. Finally, on December 19, the Dutch embarked on a full-scale military offensive, the second Police Action.

Planned in every detail, the Police Action achieved complete surprise. Most of the Republic's territory was over-run, and most of the members of the government—including Sukarno, Hatta, and Foreign Minister Hadji Agoes Salim—were captured. But politically it was a disaster for the Dutch. They were bitterly criticized for defying the United Nations. A Security Council resolution, passed on January 28, 1949, called upon them to restore the government of the Republic to its capital, Djogjakarta; the resolution also strengthened the authority of the Good Offices Committee (now the Indonesian Commission) and—in a new step—established a timetable for the transfer of sovereignty, to take place not later than July 1, 1950. Confronted with these requirements, and also with defections among the Indonesian Federalists, the prospect of continued guerrilla warfare, and mounting opposition at home, the Netherlands proposed a conference at the Hague to settle all outstanding issues. The Security Council, finding the Dutch proposal somewhat unresponsive, in providing neither for a cease-fire nor for restoring the Republic's government, called attention to these requirements in March in the so-called Canadian Directive. Meanwhile, the General Assembly had voted to take up the Indonesian question. The continuing pressure, reinforced privately by the United States, brought results. On May 7, before the date scheduled for the Assembly debate, in the Roem-van Royen Agreement, the Dutch agreed to restore the Republican government, release political prisoners, and refrain from fostering new federal states on territory conquered from the Republic. Seven months later the work of the Round Table Conference was completed with agreement reached on all points (except the deferred issue of New Guinea), and sovereignty was transferred on December 27, 1949.

Until the second Police Action, the role of the United Nations tended to favor the Dutch, partly because influential Security Council members, including the United States, were highly sensitive to the issue of Dutch sovereignty and partly because, to get anywhere at all, even the most pro-Indonesian members had to accept substantial elements of the *status quo,* which most favored the Dutch. Nevertheless, often UN involvement acted in many ways as a restraint upon both parties, particularly the stronger one. For example, the November 1, 1947, resolution favored the Dutch in permitting them to remain in control of territory they had conquered between the initiation of the Police Action and the August 4 cease-fire. But it also acted as a deterrent to the Dutch who made no further important inroads on Republican territory until December 1948. Similarly the Renville Agreement would have been even more unfavorable to the Indonesians without the Six Principles proposed by the Good Offices Committee. And the decisive reaction to the second Police Action derived a good deal of its intensity from the Dutch defiance of an agreement reached under UN auspices. In the American Congress, where concern over the situation had been rising, the move to cut off Marshall Plan aid was supported by warnings that the United Nations might go the way of the League of Nations if its members permitted its authority to be flouted. Senator Frank Graham, earlier the American representative on the Good Offices Committee, told his colleagues: "The ghosts of Ethiopia and Manchuria . . . haunt today the chambers of the United Nations."[30] The desire to vindicate UN authority thus reinforced the impetus to action supplied by the desire to settle the Indonesian question. As van Mook later summed up, it became "an aim in itself to maintain the authority of the Security Council in the single instance of a political conflict about which its decisions had not been partially or completely disregarded. This unique success could not be jeopardized whatever the Dutch might contend. And they were not strong enough to resist

30. *Congressional Record,* Vol. 95, Part 3, p. 3847.

the Council, as others might have done under more favorable conditions.[31]

The United Nations also provided the Indonesians with a stage and sounding board that reinforced the favorable impression Sjahrir and his group of westernized intellectuals in particular had made on Americans and others. In addition, supporters of Indonesia—small countries like Burma and the Philippines—had a place in which to express their views. The attention of the world was intermittently focused on the problem by Security Council debates. And the reporting of members of the United Nations staff in the field probably cast a clearer light on events than would otherwise have been available.[32]

The Activists: India and Australia

In the diplomatic activities so crucial to Indonesian decolonization, India and Australia were the Republic's major supporters. Joining Australia in initiating Security Council action in July 1947,[33] India was carrying on a policy that it had adopted as early as October 1945, when Nehru offered help and issued the first of a series of protests against the use of Indian troops. India did what it could to bolster the Republic's international standing: agreeing to an exchange of goods in April 1946; according it *de facto* recognition after the Linggadjati Agreement was signed in March 1947; providing a plane to fly Sjahrir to a hero's welcome at the Indian-sponsored Asian Relations Conference that same spring; proposing the Republic's admission to the Economic Council for Asia and the Far East (ECAFE) in June 1948; and appointing a consul-general in Djakarta in November 1948. After the first Police Action, the Indians prohibited Dutch planes from landing in or overflying their territory; after the second, Nehru invited the Republic to form a government-in-exile in India, and postponed indefinitely the departure of India's first ambassador to The Hague.

31. Van Mook, p. 260.

32. Wayne Wilcox et al, *Asia and the International System*, p. 124. Devillers points out (in W. L. Holland, ed., *Asian Nationalism and the West*, p. 200) that the world had only the official French version of the circumstances surrounding the outbreak of civil war in Vietnam. According to his account, no French or foreign newspaper had a correspondent on the scene.

33. India participated in the Security Council debates throughout, having participated in bringing the case before it, but was not a member of the Council in any of the years when it was actively considering the Indonesian question.

Most importantly, however, Nehru convened the conference on Indonesia in New Delhi in January 1949 at which fifteen Far and Middle Eastern countries called upon the Netherlands to restore the Republic and proceed expeditiously to the transfer of sovereignty.[34]

India believed with moral fervor that the time had come to end imperial rule; the Indians, having won their own freedom, could not, said Nehru, "conceive it possible that other countries should remain under the yoke of colonialism."[35] The Indian representative in the United Nations bitterly dismissed the arguments advanced in support of suppression or delay. The Dutch, he claimed, were using all the stock arguments of the colonial apologist: "The people of the colonies concerned are unfit or unable to govern themselves, are unfit or unable to enforce law and order in their country, and . . . their interests are better looked after by outsiders than by themselves. Another favorite line of attack is to charge the indigenous population with being undemocratic and sometimes even to charge them with having imperialistic and expansionist tendencies. . . . Then there is the attempt to win over the sympathy of the entire group of colonial exploiters, by pointing out that the indigenous population concerned is hostile not only to those who oppress it, but to all foreigners."[36] Added to these strong feelings was outrage over the use of Indian troops to suppress nationalists. The Indians, Nehru said, were watching these troops doing "Britain's dirty work against our friends" who are fighting the same fight as we . . . with growing anger, shame, and helplessness."[37]

Indian statements condemning the use of their troops or asserting the universal right to freedom usually referred to Indochina as well as Indonesia. The shelling of Haiphong was widely condemned: the president of the Indian Congress Party called it Hitlerism; student and trade-union organizations passed resolutions; and there were unofficial efforts to recruit volunteers, and to collect money, food, and clothing. But official assistance to the DRV was conspicuous by its

34. Thien, pp. 88–99; Alastair Taylor, pp. 9–14, 27, 48–49.
35. Thien, pp. 59–60.
36. Security Council Official Record (*SCOR*), Aug. 22, 1947, p. 2154.
37. Allan B. Cole, *Conflict in Indo-China and International Repercussions*, p. 50. There does not seem to be any evidence that the troops themselves were outraged. Harold Isaacs (in *No Peace for Asia*, p. 161) describes those he encountered in Indochina as fierce and ruthless professional soldiers who showed no sympathy for the nationalist cause.

absence. When government action was suggested, Nehru replied, "So long as the Government of India is not at war with another country, it cannot take action against it." In February 1947, the Indian government did take some action: in response to Ho's request for termination of the operations of the French purchasing mission and the repair and refueling of French planes and ships in Indian territory it merely cut off French military overflights.[38]

A few months later, while the Indonesian delegates to the Asian Relations Conference were being enthusiastically welcomed, the Viet Minh representatives met a cool reception. Moreover, invitations to the conference had been extended not only to the DRV but also to a delegation speaking for the French-supported governments in Cochin China, Cambodia, and Laos. The DRV representatives joined with the Indonesians in calling for support: "We have used enough words about Asian unity. Now let us act." Concrete help was needed, they said; arms and ammunition manufactured in countries represented at the conference were being used in Indochina; the Indian delegates should ask their government to recognize the DRV, bring the problem before the United Nations, and join in efforts to prevent the French from bringing in additional troops. Nehru was sympathetic but noncommittal. As summarized in the official account, "he did not see how the Indian Government could be expected—or for that matter, other Asian countries—to declare war on France. That was not the way to proceed and by such precipitate action they were likely to lose in the long run. Any wise government would try to limit the area of conflict. It would, however, bring sufficient pressure to bear but that could not obviously be done by governments in public meetings."[39]

Clearly the Indian government treated Indochina quite differently from Indonesia; the reasons why this should have been so are less clear. The troop issue, of course, remained alive longer in Indonesia than in Indochina, perhaps helping to keep up greater interest. Communist control of the Viet Minh probably contributed to Nehru's cool attitude but, until later when the Cold War had settled into Southeast

38. D. R. Sar Desai, *Indian Foreign Policy in Cambodia, Laos, and Vietnam, 1947–1964*, pp. 11–18.

39. *Asian Relations, being the report of the proceedings and documentation of the First Asian Relations Conference* (*Asian Relations Conference*), pp. 63, 77–78.

Asia, it would not have been a decisive factor. The Indians, however, did have very practical interests in remaining on good terms with the French. In those early postwar years, they expected negotiations over the return of French enclaves to move fairly swiftly (in fact they moved very slowly) and did not wish to do anything to disturb their progress. And as long as the Kashmir dispute (which had been submitted to the United Nations in December 1947) remained under consideration, it was important not to antagonize a veto-wielding power.[40]

Probably of greatest significance were the intangible ties binding India to Indonesia but not to Indochina. One was culturally Indian-ized, the other Sinicized. In Indonesia, Indian religions and culture had been of crucial influence in many traditional spheres. In the modern era, the Vietnamese nationalists had looked to Sun Yat Sen and China, while the Indonesian nationalists, whose contacts with Indian leaders went back to the 1920's, acknowledged an intellectual debt to Gandhi and to India. Strategic and political considerations reinforced these ties for India. Commanding the passage between the Indian Ocean and the Pacific, Indonesia must have seemed far more important to India in the forties than a small country on the south-eastern fringe of the Asian land mass. And by supporting Moslem Indonesia, India could perhaps demonstrate to the Arab world that its difficulties with Pakistan need not affect its relations with other Islamic countries.[41]

Increasing Australian support for Indonesia against the Dutch re-flected the growing weight of preoccupation with the nearby area and growing pessimism over the prospect that the evolutionary doctrines of the war years could be put into effect. During World War II, the Labour Party government had both urged international supervision of colonial administration and supported restoring the Southeast Asian colonies to their former juridical status. Evatt had said in July 1944, "Our relations with the Netherlands East Indies are of the most im-mediate character. We have received great aid from them . . . There is in Australia today the nucleus of the government of the

40. House Committee on Armed Services, *United States-Vietnam Relations 1945–1967 (Pentagon Papers)*, VIII, 116; Sar Desai, p. 19; Vidya Prakash Dutt and Vishal Singh, *Indian Policies and Attitudes Towards Indo-China and S.E.A.T.O.*, p. 8.

41. Thien, pp. 86–87, 117; Werner Levi, *Free India in Asia*, p. 21.

Netherlands East Indies, which will resume occupation of its territory after the war."[42] After the war, performing functions originally assigned to it as a component of the Southwest Pacific Command, Australia assisted in taking the Japanese surrender in some of the Outer Islands, also selling to the Dutch large quantities of arms and equipment in Borneo. And in voting against the Ukrainian resolution, Australia had emphasized that Council action could be justified only by a threat to international peace.[43]

Nevertheless, even before the first Police Action, the Australian government had been sympathetic to the Republic. In the wake of the Linggadjati Agreement, it accompanied its *de facto* recognition of the Republic by referring to it, much to Dutch annoyance, as "a future essential element in the Interim Federal State." In part, this benevolent interest stemmed from general Labour Party support for the rights of colonial peoples. In part, it reflected Prime Minister Joseph Chifley's conclusion that it was impossible to reimpose western rule on unwilling Southeast Asians. In part, it stemmed from Evatt's determination to assert a leading role for Australia in Southeast Asia as the European powers departed. Geographically, Evatt said, "Australia is closely linked with Southeast Asia. Those who are devoted to Australia's welfare will desire to live in the closest harmony with these new neighbor nations."[44] Indonesia's proximity gave these general considerations a weight they did not have for Indochina. Said the Australian representative in the Security Council, "Not only is Indonesia adjacent to our territory, but we are bound by the closest economic and commercial ties with this important area . . . we feel that the interests of Australia are especially affected by the dispute."[45]

The first Police Action aroused public opinion as well. The Communist-dominated Waterside Workers Federation, hitherto alone in its boycott of Dutch shipping, was joined by other important and less radical unions. In calling for Security Council action, Australia in effect

42. Amry and Mary Belle Vandenbosch, *Australia Faces Southeast Asia,* p. 34.
43. Werner Levi, *Australia's Outlook on Asia,* p. 181.
44. Council on Foreign Relations, John C. Campbell (ed.), *The United States in World Affairs, 1948–1949* (*USWA*), pp. 319–320.
45. *SCOR,* July 31, 1947, p. 1622. Australia held a nonpermanent seat on the Security Council in 1947; when its term expired on Feb. 17, 1948, it continued to participate in the debate as a member of the Good Offices Committee.

abandoned its previous emphasis on Netherlands sovereignty. Thereafter Australia was to be in the vanguard of those who preferred arbitration to conciliation and who wanted cease-fires to be accompanied by Dutch withdrawal to previous positions, while, in the Good Offices Committee, the Australian representatives worked hard to protect the Republic and advance its cause.

When Australia invoked UN jurisdiction the government moved with popular support. Later, however, public opinion polls indicated some shift toward the Dutch. Pro-Dutch sentiments were particularly strong among the Liberals, whose leader, Robert G. Menzies, still saw merit in doctrines of trusteeship and responsibility. Self-government, he warned, should not be confused with the "abject abandonment of legitimate material interests and administrative responsibilities of which many millions of colonial peoples still warmly approve." The Liberals also found it difficult to accept Evatt's view that the realities of power politics were tending to bring Australia closer to the Asians and reduce its ties with Europe. They saw the Dutch as potentially much more useful Allies than the Indonesians. "We have been assisting to put the Dutch out of the East Indies," said Menzies. "If we continue to do that the same process will no doubt in due course, eject the British from Malaya and the Australians from Papua and New Guinea." This, he said, was "the very ecstacy of suicide."[46]

Fellow Asians and Others

In their fight for independence the Indonesians won the support of their fellow Asians and of other countries belonging to what is now called the Third World. The Vietnamese did not. The forum provided by UN consideration of the Indonesian question was an important factor, as was the reaction to the DRV's Communist leadership. Asian leaders tended to lack enthusiasm for what they regarded as crusades against Communist countries and—with the outcome in China still in doubt—found Cold War issues rather remote. But virtually all of them had had bruising experiences in cooperation or conflict with the Communists of their own countries. The DRV, well aware of the resulting suspicions, worked hard to dissipate them. It attempted to keep Communist control of the Viet Minh and the government as inconspicuous

46. Harper and Sissons, pp. 160, 312–313; Paul M. Kattenburg, p. 204; Levi, *Australia's Outlook*, p. 182.

as possible, took neutral positions on Cold War issues, and avoided vituperative attacks on countries that came to figure prominently on Moscow's enemy list, even praising some of them like Burma and India.[47] But these efforts seemed to bear little fruit with other Asians, whose distrust only increased when Communist violence erupted in India, Burma, the Phillippines, Indonesia, and Malaya in mid-1948, threatening the ability of newly independent states to survive and of those not yet independent to achieve their freedom.

During three years of Security Council concern with Indonesia, the Philippines, Burma, and Pakistan, at their request, were invited to participate in the debate. Carlos Romulo, the Philippine representative, was a frequent and eloquent speaker. Rejecting Dutch allegations concerning Indonesian atrocities he said, "It is a queer trick of language that the desperate acts of ill-armed people fighting for freedom on their own soil are called atrocities, but not the deliberate acts of a people armed with cannon and tanks and bombing planes against another people armed with little more than bamboo spears. The latter, we are told, is civilized warfare."[48]

The Indonesians themselves successfully courted their fellow Muslims, to whom they were already well-known from their well-financed prewar pilgrimages, encouraged ironically enough by the Dutch. Hadji Salim—a prominent Muslim leader with old ties to Arab and other Muslim nationalists—led a delegation to the Middle East, setting up a headquarters in Cairo and establishing contact with the Arab League's New York headquarters. By mid-June 1947, the Republic had received *de facto* recognition from Iran, Egypt, and Syria (which held a seat in the Security Council at that time) and promises of assistance from Transjordan, Saudi Arabia, and Yemen. Pakistan also associated itself with the Indonesian cause, joining India and Ceylon in closing its harbors and airfields to Dutch craft en route to Indonesia.[49]

Third World support for the Republic reached a climax at the January 1949 Conference on Indonesia held in New Delhi and attended by representatives from Afghanistan, Australia, Burma, Ceylon, Egypt, Ethiopia, India, Iran, Iraq, Lebanon, Pakistan, the Philippines,

47. Frank N. Trager (ed.), *Marxism in Southeast Asia*, p. 163; Ruth McVey, *The Calcutta Conference and the Southeast Asian Uprisings*, p. 15.

48. *SCOR*, Oct. 9, 1947, p. 2536.

49. Wolf, p. 135; Kattenburg, pp. 218–219.

Saudi Arabia, Syria, and Yemen, with observers from China, Nepal, New Zealand, and Thailand. The resolutions called for the restoration of the Republic, the establishment of an interim federal government, general elections for a constituent assembly, transfer of sovereignty, and the withdrawal of Dutch troops, all within a specified and quite limited time period.[50]

Only the Republic of China seemed to take an interest in Indochina as well as Indonesia. Its interest in Indochina, however, diminished markedly with the withdrawal of its troops and mounting troubles at home, although in conversations with U.S. representatives, Chinese diplomats made no secret of their belief that the French would fail unless they came to terms with Ho, and of their distaste for Bao Dai as a French tool. Twice in 1946—first shortly after the withdrawal treaty was signed and again at the end of the year—Nanking showed some interest in proffering good offices. The DRV, for its part, continued to cultivate Chinese Nationalist good will, limiting Communist activities among the Chinese community in Hanoi and Haiphong, at the Asian Relations Conference expressing gratitude to the Generalissimo for Chinese kindness during the occupation, and making an abortive effort later that year to send a good-will mission to Nanking.[51]

Because of its seat in the Security Council, China's interest in Indonesia, although in fact less immediate than its interest in Indochina, could be given more effective expression. In part, this interest reflected the size of Indonesia's Chinese community. In June 1946, for example, the Foreign Minister, concerned over Dutch use of force, thought China, Australia, the United Kingdom, and the United States might do well to urge a negotiated settlement on the Netherlands. He conceded that it was the Indonesians not the Dutch who had massacred Chinese. Nevertheless, he argued, it was the Dutch, in the long run, who must make the concessions necessary for peace, and it was with the long run that the Chinese in Indonesia had to live.[52]

In the Security Council, the Chinese did not align themselves with countries consistently favoring maximum intervention, instead frequently joining the United States in middle positions. In debate they

50. Lawrence K. Rosinger and Associates, *The State of Asia*, p. 427.
51. *FRUS*, 1946, VIII, 29, 75–83; *FRUS*, 1947, VI, 66, 91, 114–115; *Pentagon Papers*, VIII, 121–122; Chen, pp. 176–179; *Asian Relations Conference*, p. 78.
52. *FRUS*, 1946, VIII, 828–829.

often came to Indonesia's defense; early in 1948 the Indonesian representative expressed particular gratitude to them and to the Indians, saying that, "having experienced the struggle for freedom, they showed in their statements a natural understanding and sympathy for our struggle which is an indication that Asia knows how to form a united front when it comes to matters of vital importance."[53]

Only in Thailand, and for obvious geographic and political reasons, was interest in Indochina greater than in Indonesia. For a brief period the Thai permitted Viet Minh propaganda and purchasing agents to operate in their territory, and provided aid and asylum to Lao rebels, some of whom were associated with the Viet Minh. These activities reflected continued Thai-French differences over the return of Lao territory, traditional Thai interest in Laos, and the views and attitudes of the then-dominant Thai political figure, Pridi Phanomyong. They ceased shortly after Pridi's downfall in November 1947.

The Soviet Union and the Communists: National Interests versus Revolutionary Solidarity

When the Indonesians achieved their independence, they had little reason to thank the Soviet Union. Moscow, for its part, now fully committed to vilifying noncommunist nationalists, had already identified Sukarno and Hatta as imperialist running dogs; it vetoed the resolution welcoming the Round Table Agreement on the grounds that Indonesia's new status was merely a variant of colonialism. Paradoxically, however, caught in compulsions to act created by the Security Council involvement, Moscow, before this, had been a good deal more helpful to Sukarno's Indonesia than to Ho Chi Minh's DRV. Confusion and contradiction stemmed primarily from Moscow's predominant interest in Europe which, in turn, contributed to the slow development of postwar Communist doctrine on the colonial issue.

Moscow's attitude toward Indonesia and its leaders, as expressed by Soviet publicists and experts writing in *Pravda* and elsewhere, was inconsistent and seemed intermittently to be influenced by the activities and status of the PKI. Its policy in the UN, however, remained very much the same until the very last days of the debate.

In October 1945, *Pravda* noted fighting between Indonesians and Dutch. Somewhat increased coverage thereafter was devoted largely to

53. *SCOR*, Feb. 21, 1948, p. 239.

military operations, to attacks on the Dutch and the British, and to criticism of the Americans for failure to act. The Republic was treated as Indonesia's rightful government, and statements concerning Sukarno, Hatta, and Sjahrir were usually noncommittal, sometimes favorable, but, in Sukarno's case at least, sometimes hostile. Analyses of the anticolonial struggle were not always consistent, nor did they seem particularly well informed; through 1947, there was only one analysis of the PKI.[54]

Moscow was critical of the Linggadjati Agreement and did not grant *de facto* recognition to the Republic. However, in June 1948, it ratified a consular convention, initialed just before the fall of the Amir Sjarifudden government by an Indonesian representative, himself a Communist, and the Soviet Ambassador in Prague. Sjarifudden had headed a strongly leftist cabinet, including a member of the PKI as Minister of State, and he himself later claimed that he had been a secret Communist for many years. During his tenure (July 3, 1947– January 28, 1948), Indonesia was treated with greater warmth in international Communist circles; at the first meeting of the Cominform it was the only non-Communist country other than Finland listed among states associated with the antiimperialist camp. By the time the Soviets ratified the consular agreement—apparently to complete Indonesian surprise—Sjarifudden had been out of office for some months, his replacement by Hatta having been attributed in a Soviet foreign affairs journal to the machinations of Wall Street. Criticism of Hatta was not pursued, however, nor was any attention paid to the fact that the PKI-centered opposition was the strongest and most vigorous yet organized in the Republic. *Pravda* hailed the consular agreement as a blow to U.S. and Dutch efforts to deny Indonesia the right to maintain independent foreign relations; the PKI-led opposition welcomed it as recognition of the Republic and a pledge of Soviet aid—which was not, however, forthcoming.[55]

Later in 1948, apparent confusion over Indonesia reached a peak. At the Communist-sponsored youth conference in Calcutta in Febru-

54. Ruth T. McVey, *The Soviet View of the Indonesian Revolution*, pp. 3–4, 13–14; McLane, pp. 285–288; Max Beloff, *Soviet Policy in the Far East*, pp. 215–216.

55. McLane, pp. 401–404; McVey, *Soviet View*, pp. 35–39, 48–49; Kahin, pp. 268–269.

ary, which brought Andrei Zhdanov's two-camp thesis to Asia, Indonesia was described as having attained "the highest form of armed struggle." In August, a veteran Communist leader, Musso, long exiled in Moscow, suddenly arrived in Indonesia. In mid-September, the Communists attempted a coup centered in Madiun—the third largest city in Republican territory—that took three months to crush. Although the sequence of events fed suspicions that Moscow was behind the Communist coup attempt, the Soviet press paid no attention to Musso's return or to subsequent PKI developments, covered the result itself in a few short, confused, and extremely cautious reports, and continued to describe the Republic as courageously defending its independence. Meanwhile, the revolt itself, despite the further burdens it imposed, proved essentially helpful to the Republic's cause. The Republic's military campaign against the Communists provided its friends with the opportunity to underline the importance of pressing the Dutch to compromise; within days of each other, Australian and Indian representatives called on a receptive State Department to convey this message.[56]

Not until the beginning of 1949 did Soviet media elaborate on Madiun. In January, *New Times* accused Hatta of having provoked the revolt with U.S. support in order to behead the progressive movement and crush democracy. This analysis, leaving open the question of whether indeed the Indonesian Communists had decided to resort to the armed struggle recommended at Calcutta, was repeated in February by the Secretary-General of the Dutch Communist Party. Describing Sukarno and Hatta as having been first Japanese and then Dutch and American tools, he accused them also of having capitulated to the second Police Action according to a plan to "behead the revolution" first by striking at the Communists and then at the Republic. The shift to systematic vilification of Hatta and other Indonesian leaders, however, apparently stemmed more from the international doctrinal developments that had accorded the same fate to the leaders of India and Burma than from any particular developments in Indonesia.[57]

Meanwhile, at the United Nations, until late in 1949 the Soviet

56. *FRUS*, 1948, VI, 345–346, 360.
57. *Cominform Journal*, Feb. 15, 1949, p. 4; Kahin, pp. 256–303; McVey, *Soviet View*, pp. 71–73; McLane, pp. 409–415; Beloff, pp. 218–219.

Union consistently supported the Republic and its leaders and attacked the "imperialist" powers. Throughout the debates, it was a strong supporter of arbitration rather than good offices; it pressed for enforcement machinery representative of Security Council membership; and it favored coupling requirements for Dutch troop withdrawals with cease-fire arrangements. Unlike Australia, with which it frequently voted on resolutions embodying these principles, the Soviet Union generally abstained on compromise resolutions.

When the Round Table Conference reached its successful conclusion and the independence of Indonesia was in sight, Moscow apparently decided to bring its UN policies into conformity with its now year-old opposition to the Republic's leaders. Charging that the transfer of sovereignty was "a gross deception," the Soviet representative declared that Indonesian freedom was being sacrificed to the interests of the colonial powers. The Indonesians, he said, were once again "wearing the chains of colonial enslavement with the complicity of the representatives of the Hatta clique, which has betrayed the interests of its people."[58] The Burmese delegate commented bitterly that the Soviet speech "only shows that one needs to be saved from one's so-called friends as much as from one's sworn enemies. There are many countries like Burma, India, Pakistan, and the Philippines which, having won their political independence recently at heavy cost, have not, as the representative of the USSR so flippantly and so insultingly imagines, followed the dictates of the colonial Powers in this last phase of the battle against colonialism in the Far East."[59]

External Communist assistance to the DRV was blocked by Soviet interests in Europe and by the interests of the French Communist Party. Soviet focus on Europe was a primary factor affecting its interest in and even understanding of the revolution Ho was leading. More specifically, Moscow's expectation of Communist parliamentary victories in western Europe, especially in France, made it anxious to avoid any action likely to cast a shadow on French Communist Party prospects. Accordingly, while Moscow expressed appropriate sympathy for the Viet Minh and hailed the Indochinese struggle on the correct Communist occasions, no practical assistance was provided through either diplomatic or international Communist channels. Typical of its

58. *SCOR*, Dec. 13, 1949, pp. 5–11.
59. *Ibid.*, p. 24.

treatment of events during this period was the comment on the *modus vivendi* of September 1946 published in December, after the shelling of Haiphong: "The further development of Vietnam depends to a significant degree on its ties with democratic France, whose progressive forces have always spoken forth in support of colonial liberation."[60]

As far as the French Communist Party was concerned, ambivalence about colonial liberation developed well before World War II in parallel to increased party strength.[61] Thus, the 1937 French Communist Party Congress supported self-determination and the right to independence but, quoting Lenin's saying, "the right to separation does not signify the obligation to separate," found the interests of French colonies to lie in a "free, trusting, and paternal" union with democratic France. Reflecting even stronger postwar motives for not alienating voters, an article in *Cahiers du Communisme* in October 1946 declared: "At the present time, faced with imperialists' designs, the common interest of all Overseas people and the French people is to remain united and to put everything to work so that the brotherhood of diverse races be really assured. In a world where, the war barely ended, and apart from the fifth of the globe where socialism is being built, the great world powers are looking for new pretexts, every attempt to leave the French Union can only lead to an illusory and momentary pseudo-independence and the strengthening of imperialism."[62]

The French Communist position did not go unopposed within the party; internal disquiet was apparently partly responsible for the fact that, while Communist cabinet members voted for the Indochina war appropriations in March 1947, Communist deputies were permitted to abstain.[63] Even more evident was the disquiet of the Viet Minh. Commenting on the post-Haiphong telegrams from Indochina, which had been bombarding French Communist leaders, and the appeals to trade

60. McLane, p. 271.

61. Ho had occasion to complain publicly of the inadequacy of French Communist support as early as 1925. At the Fifth Comintern Congress he said, "I as a native of the colonies and member of the French Party ought to say regretfully that our French Party has done very, very little for the colonies" (Adam B. Ulam, *Expansion and Coexistence,* p. 160).

62. Trager, pp. 142, 326–327.

63. Bernard Fall, "Tribulations of a Party Line," *Foreign Affairs,* XXXIII (April, 1955), p. 501.

unions for a dock strike to bar the transport of troops and supplies, the American Embassy observed: "This pressure has been of considerable embarrassment to the French Communist Party coming, as it does, at a time when party is trying to persuade French public that Communist government would be safe custodian of France's international interests, and more particularly, to persuade Radical Socialists to enter left-wing coalition government."[64]

Although the Communists left the government in May 1947 on another issue, they still hoped to win power through the ballot and only slowly shifted their Indochina stance. It was not until December that they began to express their support of the DRV as a member of the anti-imperialist and democratic camp. More slowly still, Moscow's line shifted also, as disappointment with Communist prospects in the west was reflected in the "two camps" doctrine of the Cominform. In neither case, however, was the shift quickly reflected in concrete assistance; only in 1950 did the French Communists embark on a campaign of strikes and demonstrations to obstruct troop and supply movements to Indochina.[65]

The United States: A Reluctant Role

In American priorities at the end of the war, Europe came ahead of Asia, and—within Asia—Japan, China, and Korea overshadowed the rest. John Carter Vincent, speaking in October 1945, listed the Southeast Asian colonies last among Far Eastern problems, giving precedence to "a defeated and so far unregenerate Japan; . . . Korea, which is to start on the road to independence after two generations of subjection to Japan; . . . China, our Ally and long-time friend, whose principal problems, now that the menace of Japan has been removed, are political unity and economic reconstruction; . . . Siam, an independent nation which has for the past five years been under the domination of Japan." It was evident that the United States hoped to remain aloof from problems between colonies—in whose advancement toward self-government it continued to have a strong but somewhat abstract interest—and European colonial powers—in whose friendship, stabilization, and reconstruction it had an immediate interest and large investment.

64. *FRUS*, 1946, VIII, 65–66.
65. Fall, "Tribulations," p. 503; McLane, pp. 432–435; Rosinger and Associates, pp. 254–256.

The United States government, said Vincent, does not question French sovereignty in Indochina or Dutch sovereignty in the East Indies, but hopes for early agreement "between representatives of the governments concerned and the Annamese and Indonesians. It is not our intention to assist or participate in forceful measures for the imposition of control by territorial sovereigns, but we would be prepared to lend our assistance, if requested to do so, in efforts to reach peaceful agreements in their disturbed areas." This, however, said Vincent, does not mean the United States has abandoned the view that the prime duty toward dependent peoples is to help them "prepare themselves for the duties and responsibilities of self-government and to attain liberty."[66]

At the same time, the United States did its best to disassociate itself from the colonial policies of its Allies. A few days after Vincent's speech, Secretary Byrnes announced that the British and Dutch had been requested to remove U.S. insignia from military equipment they were using in Indonesia. At the beginning of 1946, the War Department was informed that it was not in accord with U.S. policy to employ American flag vessels or aircraft to transport troops, arms, ammunition, or military equipment to Indonesia or Indochina. Official statements continued to reiterate the availability of American good offices, American respect for existing sovereignty, and American conviction that a peaceful and equitable solution would emerge if both sides proceeded responsibly and in good faith.

There were, of course, voices urging that Asians would read this seeming even-handedness as evidence that Americans were denying their heritage and joining forces with the European colonialists. Thus the U.S. political adviser at Mountbatten's headquarters warned at the end of 1945 that the reservoir of good will—filled by belief in America as the champion of democracy and liberation—was already beginning to dry up.[67] Moreover, as time went on, the elements of the

66. *DSB,* Oct. 21, 1945, pp. 645–646.

67. *FRUS,* 1945, VI, 1388–1389. This often-used argument overlooks Asian ambivalence toward the United States. Especially among those of the first postwar generation who were heavily exposed to Marxist argument, it was just as easy to think of the United States as the country of the robber barons, gunboat diplomacy, and Sacco and Vanzetti as it was to think of America in terms of the Declaration of Independence, the Emancipation Proclamation, and the Atlantic Charter. In the mid-twenties, when Sukarno, who was much given to quoting from American scripture, saw U.S. action as likely to facilitate Indonesian inde-

dilemma confronting them became increasingly clear to American policy makers. An early 1947 State Department cable spelled them out in some detail: setbacks to the Western European powers anywhere were setbacks to the United States; but South and Southeast Asia were also areas of great importance where newly emerging nations run grave danger of internal discord or domination by Communism or pan-Asianism, both antithetical to the West; close association between newly autonomous peoples and their former rulers would be the best safeguard against these and other dangers; but this must be voluntary —attempts to perpetuate the relationship on any other grounds would redound against the West as a whole; the United States, while inescapably concerned and anxious to be helpful, had no solution to offer and did not propose to intervene.[68]

Aspiring to maintain the best of relations with colonial powers while promoting the progress of colonial peoples, the United States found it difficult to resolve the conflicts between its European and Asian interests. In Indochina, these conflicts continued to plague American policy until 1954; meanwhile nonintervention was helpful to the French, and intervention, when it finally came in 1950, was on the French side and was of sufficient scale to compensate for the irritation of constant American reformist pressures. In Indonesia, on the other hand, when the first Police Action precipitated the problem into the Security Council, nonintervention became an impossible posture, while the second Police Action forced a choice between Asian and European interests in favor of the former.

Thus, although it was extremely reluctant to see the United Nations intervene, the United States came to play a major part in the decolonization of Indonesia largely through its relationship with the UN and with the UN machinery developed in connection with this issue. In

pendence, he was anticipating opportunities arising from the "inevitable" clash between U.S. and Japanese imperialism. Ho's willingness to temporize with the French—which caused him serious difficulties with the VNQDD, the Trotskyites, and other proponents of more radical action—probably resulted more from his hope that the French revolutionary tradition would reassert itself than from expectations derived from the American tradition. He was not above trying to capitalize on the latter when he thought he could, but it was his confidence in the early victory of the French left that kept alive his hopes for peaceful victory in Indochina.

68. *FRUS,* 1947, VI, 95–96.

stimulating U.S. interest in, and ultimately support for, Indonesia, other factors were also important. In contrast to Indochina, which had been effectively sealed off from non-French economic activity, there was an American economic interest; in the Far East, Indonesia had come third, after China and the Philippines in U.S. direct investments before the war. In oil alone these were estimated at $70,000,000 and in rubber at $40,000,000.[69] Although the amounts were comparatively small, and economic factors as such do not seem to have been very important in shaping policy, the mere existence of an American investment contributed to American interest.[70]

The differing roles of the Communists in Vietnam and in Indonesia also affected the American stance. With respect to Vietnam, the United States argued, as it was to do for many years thereafter, that unless France made the concessions to a non-Communist government that would enable it to rally nationalist support, Ho's hand would be strengthened, and his prospects for establishing a state "dominated by Communists and almost certainly oriented toward Moscow" would be much enhanced.[71] But, with no alternative leadership to propose, the American belief, that French policy in Indochina was more likely to strengthen the Communists than weaken them and thus work against American objectives in Asia, could not take precedence over immediate and vital interests "in maintaining in power a friendly French government to assist in the furtherance of our aims in Europe."[72]

In Indonesia, in contrast, the United States could urge a positive course upon the Dutch not that they find some alternative to the Communists, but that they make concessions to prevent an already established non-Communist leadership from being displaced by a Communist one. Not only in the State Department but also in Congress doubts were resolved and the argument reinforced by the suppression of the Communist revolt. The Indonesians, Senator Wayne Morse ob-

69. Helmut G. Callis, *Foreign Capital in Southeast Asia*, pp. 31–32.

70. Policy papers of the period argued with respect to both Indochina and Indonesia that resolution of colonial conflicts would be more favorable to American business interests than a forced restoration of colonial control or continued armed struggle. Malcolm Caldwell in Mark Selden (ed.), *Remaking of Asia*, p. 37, argues that this expectation was the determining factor in U.S. policy toward Indonesia.

71. *FRUS*, 1948, VI, 28–30, 40.

72. *Ibid.*, pp. 48–49.

served, "are the only people in that part of the world, who, up to this hour, have made a successful fight against Russian Communism within their borders."[73]

But the Security Council role was crucial. Once the UN became seized of the problem, it provided a rallying point both for friends of the Republic and for proponents of a strong international organization who were already dismayed by the impact of the Cold War on UN effectiveness. Involvement in UN operations made U.S. interest self-reinforcing. Americans of some standing, Frank Graham, President of the University of North Carolina, and Coert duBois and Merle Cochran, senior foreign service officers, served in succession as the U.S. representatives on the Good Offices Committee; their own prestige and that of the United States became tied up in its success, and the work of their staffs kept Washington reasonably well-informed. In Hanoi, during the same period, the United States was normally represented by a vice-consul; in Saigon the consulate was not much more heavily staffed and was operated as a satellite of the American Embassy in Paris.

Their UN role seemed to make it easier for American representatives to take the initiative. Thus, when it became apparent to Coert duBois that his warnings of Dutch preparations for further military action were not eliciting new instructions from Washington, he joined with his Australian colleague, T. K. Critchley, in an informal proposal for an elected constituent assembly that would form an Indonesian government and help frame a statute for the Netherlands Indonesian Union. Nothing came of the plan, but Dutch rejection in the face of Indonesian acceptance was another black mark against the Netherlands, intensifying the anger aroused by the second Police Action.[74]

American representatives in Indochina fared less well. In January 1947, Abbot Low Moffat, then in charge of Southeast Asian affairs in the Department of State and en route to Canberra after visits to Saigon and Hanoi, pleaded for a U.S. effort to bring about an end to hostilities in Indochina. He warned that Asians regarded Washington's hands-off policy as supporting French military reconquest. A permanent solution, he argued, could be based only on an independent Vietnam.

73. *Congressional Record*, Vol. 95, Part 3, p. 3668.
74. Letter to the author from Charlton Ogburn, Jr.; *FRUS*, 1948, VI, 237–246; Alastair Taylor, pp. 125–131; Kahin, pp. 247–250.

The French effort at best would bring only a seeming success; the bitterness left behind would ultimately defeat French objectives and threaten all western interests in the area. When Washington rejected his requests to return to report more fully, no further action was open to him.[75]

In response to the first Police Action, the United States and Britain immediately proffered good offices. Both had hoped that the Linggadjati Agreement signalized Dutch willingness to accept self-government within the framework of continued Netherlands sovereignty. Both had granted *de facto* recognition to the Republic and, as negotiations moved toward breakdown, the United States had pressed the Indonesians to accept Dutch proposals for an interim government, promising economic assistance as soon as political problems were resolved.[76] Hopes that the Netherlands would accept good offices and thus stave off UN intervention reflected doubts over the efficacy of Security Council action and, presumably, with the Ukrainian resolution in the recent past, fear that the Soviet Union would exploit propaganda opportunities to good effect against the West. Also of great concern to the United States as well as Britain, however, were the implications of accepting the jurisdiction of the Security Council on what seemed to both essentially a domestic affair.

Once the matter came before the Security Council, the United States sought to keep the UN role in being while fending off proposals for greater UN authority and more extensive requirements than the Netherlands (and its Belgian,[77] French, and British supporters) could be expected to tolerate. It preferred good offices to arbitration, was unwilling to insist that troop withdrawals accompany cease-fires, and opposed allocating responsibility for breakdowns to one side or the other. In contrast, American members of the Good Offices Committee in the field tended to attribute lack of progress more often to the Netherlands than to Indonesia and to be as activist as possible in carrying out their responsibilities.[78]

75. *FRUS,* 1947, VI, 54–55.

76. Collins, p. 124.

77. Belgium's term as a nonpermanent member expired on Jan. 7, 1949; it was replaced by Norway but continued to participate in debate as a member of the Good Offices Committee.

78. Alastair Taylor, pp. 390–400.

After the second Police Action the American posture in the Security Council changed. For the first time, the United States explicitly condemned the Netherlands. "My Government," the American representative said, "still can find no adequate justification for the military action taken by the Netherlands in Indonesia. In many important respects the reasons justifying their action put forth by the Netherlands representative . . . are not supported by the reports of the Committee of Good Offices. . . . The continuance of military action of the Netherlands authorities after the adoption of the Security Council resolution of 24 December was clearly an act of defiance on the part of the Netherlands authorities. . . . In the opinion of the Government of the United States, the representative of the Netherlands has failed to relieve his Government from the serious charge that it has violated the Charter of the United Nations."[79] U.S. pressures were mounted from all sides. American statements and proposed Security Council resolutions became much stronger. On December 22, the transfer to the Netherlands of still unspent aid funds for Indonesia was "suspended pending further developments." Increasingly vociferous congressional critics of Dutch behavior put forward an amendment to the aid bill which eliminated funds for any government failing to comply with a Security Council request; they mustered substantial support, particularly from the Republicans. This was stronger action than the U.S. administration favored at a time of heightened diplomatic effort, and the compromise legislation included instead the article of the Charter prohibiting assistance to any state "against which the UN is taking preventive or enforcement action." In March, Secretary of State Dean Acheson put the need for compliance to the Netherlands Foreign Minister in most urgent terms.[80] For the Dutch government, the new American stance was probably the crucial factor, underlining the futility of continuing to face guerrilla resistance in the Indies, political opposition at home, assaults in the United Nations, Third World opprobrium, and the pressures of its Allies. Beginning with the resumption of Dutch-Indonesian negotiations in mid-April, the road to independence was relatively smooth.

79. Henderson, p. 48.
80. Alastair Taylor, pp. 211–212; Rosinger and Associates, pp. 425–429.

CHAPTER 3

NEW ACTORS AND NEW ROLES
ON THE INTERNATIONAL STAGE

While Indonesia's struggle for independence drew international attention, and less widely noted events in Indochina were in fact the first campaigns of a thirty-year war, developments elsewhere were also affecting the postwar shape of the Southeast Asian region. Before World War II, only one of the Southeast Asian states, Thailand,[1] had succeeded in preserving its independence; now Thailand was joined by Burma and the Philippines as well as Indonesia. Meanwhile, Australia and New Zealand, continuing their move away from dependence on Britain and toward closer relations with the United States, began to take a much more lively interest in their Southeast Asian environment.

The Burmese, who had not had to fight very hard for their independence, and the Filipinos, who had not had to fight at all, entered the world of nations with quite different attitudes toward their former colonial rulers. Burma, led by a new elite owing its prominence to participation in the independence movement, severed its ties with Britain quite completely and, even before its neutralism was fully elaborated, indicated some unwillingness to take sides in the quarrels of the wider world. The Philippines, under an elite nurtured by prewar American administration and still not feeling itself wholly part of Asia, welcomed an association with the United States in which it was clearly a dependent partner. In Thailand also, American influence began to displace British, as the United States, motivated largely by anti-colonialist sentiment, protected the Thai from the full consequences of the ire their wartime behavior had aroused in Britain and France.

1. The name Siam, abandoned in 1939 in favor of Thailand, was resumed between 1945 and 1949. In this text, Thailand is used throughout.

Security preoccupations in the case of Australia, the quest for a regional role in the case of the Philippines, and a general increase in "Asia consciousness" stimulated interest in regionalism and in regional action. Only in the support given to Indonesia, however, was such action of any practical effect. In this case as in others, to the extent that any single Asian leader played a pre-eminent role, it was India's Nehru. His, however, was a prominent voice among those who argued that any formal organization would be premature, since there was still much that divided Asians, and little each country could do to help others with those problems they all shared. Of these, by the end of 1948, one of the most prominent was Communist insurgency which, developing largely in the wake of a Moscow-sponsored conference in Calcutta, was widely seen as Soviet-inspired and -directed.

Thailand Restored

When Japan surrendered, Thailand was not a liberated Ally, not quite an ex-enemy state, and certainly not a neutral. Britain, which had been the most influential of the western powers in prewar Bangkok, was hostile, as was France; the United States was friendly; the Republic of China, neither one nor the other, found Bangkok's uncertain status useful for pushing interests of its own.

National interest in survival had dictated accommodation to Japan. But Thailand's desire to regain territories ceded to France and Britain in earlier years led it beyond submission to active cooperation. The alacrity with which Thailand seized its opportunities to profit from Japanese success owed something to the political dominance of the military element within the ruling group—the so-called "coup group" —which had overthrown the absolute monarchy in 1932. The leader of this element, Prime Minister Phibun Songgram, admired the discipline and military organization of the Japanese, who, for their own purposes, cultivated Thai nationalism and pan-Thai ambitions.[2]

On June 12, 1940, Thailand signed nonaggression pacts with Britain, Japan, and France. Ratification of the pact with France, however, was to await adjustment of the border between Thailand and French Indochina, an adjustment France interpreted as related to

2. Donald Nuechterlein, *Thailand and the Struggle for Southeast Asia*, pp. 67–69.

minor questions concerning the channel of the Mekong and certain small islands, but which was much more broadly interpreted by the Thai. In September, the Vichy regime, having made its peace with Japan in Indochina, proposed immediate ratification of the treaty. The Thai then demanded the retrocession of territory ceded in 1904 and 1907 consisting of the west bank of the Mekong in north and south Laos, and the Cambodian provinces of Battambang, Siem Reap, and Sisaphon. When France refused, the Thai invaded, but it took Japanese and German pressure to get French agreement to a cease-fire in January 1941 and to Thai demands in May. In due course, the Committee of National Liberation repudiated the agreement, and, on December 8, 1941, de Gaulle declared "a state of hostilities" between Thailand and France.

Japan's intervention on their behalf against collaborationist Vichy did not in itself convince the Thai that they had lost the option to remain neutral in any larger struggle. Announcing this as their policy in August 1941, they asked for help from Britain and the United States, but neither was able to comply. Accordingly, when the Japanese invaded in December 1941, the Thai quickly yielded and in that same month signed a treaty of alliance. The treaty permitted the Japanese to move through Thailand against Burma and Malaya; in turn Japan would help Thailand regain the Shan states of Kengtung and Mongpan and the Malay states of Kedah, Perlis, Kelantan, and Trengganu to which it had earlier relinquished suzerain claims. On January 25, 1942, Thailand declared war on Britain and the United States; in May 1943 the Japanese turned over the Shan states (in whose conquest Thai forces had participated) and the Malay states as promised.[3]

With no direct political, economic, or territorial interests that could be adversely affected by Thailand's actions, the United States ignored its declaration of war. It was persuaded by the assurances of the Thai minister in Washington, Seni Pramot, that Phibun's actions were contrary to the will of the Thai people, accepted Seni as leader of the Free Thai movement in the United States, and cooperated with the resistance movement led by the Regent, Pridi Phanomyong, a major civilian member of the 1932 coup group.

3. *Ibid.*, pp. 70–74; Natalie Gurney, *History of the Territorial Dispute between Siam and French Indochina*, pp. 42, 45, 46; *FRUS*, 1945, VI, 1277; Russell H. Fifield, *The Diplomacy of Southeast Asia, 1945–1958*, pp. 235–236.

On August 16, 1945, Pridi, unanimously supported by the national assembly, nullified the 1942 declarations of war; during the war, in 1944, he had succeeded in ousting Phibun as prime minister and replacing him with a fellow civilian, Khuang Aphaiwong. Now, to gain the best possible position for negotiating with Britain and the United States, he asked Seni Pramot to return to Bangkok as prime minister. In addition, he promised to return the territories taken from Burma and Malaya and to provide compensation for damages.[4]

American and British responses differed. Secretary of State James Byrnes on August 20, recalling the Free Thai contributions to the Allied cause, said that the United States "regarded Thailand not as an enemy but as a country to be liberated from the enemy." London's view of Thailand, however, was affected by British wartime experience. From this, concluding that Indochina was the key to defending Burma and Malaysia, they reasoned that future Allied defense of Indochina could be facilitated by using Thai facilities and communications. Accordingly British planners decided in April 1945 that once peace was restored, the Thai government "must be prepared to act on British advice as regards all her defense measures, including the training and equipping of her armed forces and the organization of her air defenses."[5] Moreover, the British believed the Thai should pay some price beyond restoring the territories they had won by submitting to Japan, especially since they had done so not under a puppet government but under one in power since 1938 and since they had suffered far less war damage than their injured neighbors. Britain's attitude toward Thailand, Foreign Secretary Ernest Bevin said, would depend on future Thai action, especially concerning British peace treaty demands. The Thai were to participate in whatever arrangements were made for Southeast Asia's future security and were not to build a canal across the Kra Isthmus without British approval. They were not only to restore extensive British economic interests and assure British rights to participate in the economy, but also they were to agree to sell rubber, tin, rice, and tea at fixed prices, and, most onerous of all, to provide gratis one and one-half million tons of rice for distribution in neighboring countries that were suffering acute rice shortages.[6]

4. Hull, II, 1588; Nuechterlein, pp. 78–85.
5. Iriye, p. 128.
6. Alec Peterson, "Britain and Siam: The Latest Phase," *Pacific Affairs* (Dec., 1946), pp. 364, 370; Nuechterlein, p. 86.

The United States regarded these and other requirements as unduly punitive and intended to ensure the restoration of prewar British economic predominance. It pressed successfully for some softening, but, even so, in the treaty of January 1, 1946, Thailand had to acquiesce in the free delivery of rice. By submitting, Thailand won resumption of diplomatic relations and support for its UN membership, not only from the British but also from the United States, which had delayed in deference to the British. In due course, moreover, British purposes were defeated by the realities of the rice trade which was controlled by Chinese merchants skilled in smuggling goods to the most advantageous markets. Two revisions of the treaty arrangements ensued, the first in May 1946 providing for payment at well below market prices, the second, in December, at market levels.[7]

The postwar settlement with France took longer. The Thai, who were strongly antagonistic to the French, thought they had good prospects for successful resistance. The French war record was itself somewhat anomalous. Britain, Thailand's past protector against France, might join the United States in looking with some sympathy on Thai claims. And Thailand's juridical ground was firmer, since the Lao and Cambodian territories, which were of much greater political and economic interest to Thailand than the Shan and Malay states, had been ceded by treaty.[8]

The British opposed any attempt to differentiate between their claims and those of the French. Washington agreed with the French that the 1942 transfer, made under duress, had been invalid and that the question of restoration was not open to arbitration. But, in American eyes, this did not exclude peaceful readjustment. The Thai, the United States observed, believed their claims to have legal and historic merit. "It is feared that unless assurance can be given them that they will have early opportunity to present these claims by peaceful processes there may be popular Thai resistance to the return of these territories to Indochina and that the potential sources of conflict inherent in the pre-war border may be aggravated."

Encouraged by their awareness of American sympathy, the Thai, while refusing to hand the territories over to the French, sought to demonstrate that they were willing to achieve a peaceful settlement.

7. *FRUS,* 1945, VI, 1283–1286, 1297–1298, 1377–1379; Fifield, pp. 240–241; *SIA,* 1939–1946, pp. 230–231.

8. Gurney, pp. 46–47.

Shortly after Japan surrendered, they proposed joint administration of the territories by Britain, China, the United States, and the USSR, pending a plebiscite. Later they suggested submitting the dispute to the United Nations, with the territories, meanwhile, to be administered by an Allied commission. The British then proposed restoration of all of the disputed territory, to be followed by negotiations with a view to returning to Thailand all that territory in north Laos west of the Mekong. The Thai, however, did not think France would agree, nor were they themselves prepared to settle on unfavorable terms; the domestic impact, they argued, would be highly destabilizing.[9]

By spring, the problem was being further complicated by repercussions in Thailand of Indochinese resistance to the French. In April, Vientiane was occupied by the military forces that were re-establishing French authority in Laos. The Lao Issara (Free Lao) government fled to Thailand, mounting from there a number of cross-border raids which culminated in an attempt to retake Vientiane. French forces, driving the Lao back, pursued them into Thailand, contending that local Thai authorities had failed to control the activities of Lao and Vietnamese rebels and were even protecting them. With three Thai villagers killed, Bangkok appealed to the United Nations. The French, confronted by American and British concern that political instability in Thailand could jeopardize rice deliveries, agreed to take the territorial question to the International Court. Again, in August, Indochinese resistance to the French, this time in Cambodia, complicated the picture. Accusing the Thai of complicity with the rebels, the French withdrew their offer, resumed their uncompromising stance, and reiterated their intention of opposing Thai membership in the United Nations until the return of the territories. With no further hope of success, the Thai submitted. An agreement of November 17, 1946, nullified the 1941 treaty with Vichy, restored the disputed territories to France, and established a conciliation commission to examine border issues (which, in June 1947, found no basis for the Thai territorial claims). France, in return, agreed to support Thailand's application for United Nations membership, which was successfully presented in December 1946.[10]

9. *FRUS,* 1945, VI, 1273–1274, 1346, 1357; *FRUS,* 1946, VIII, 979, 983, 988.
   10. *FRUS,* 1946, VIII, 992–993, 1032–1036, 1082–1092, 1942–1945; Arthur J. Dommen, *Conflict in Laos,* p. 26; Gurney, pp. 50, 136–137; Fifield, pp. 243–245; Nuechterlein, pp. 89–90.

Thailand's admission to the UN had also been blocked by problems with the Soviet Union and China. Moscow's requirements—the establishment of diplomatic relations and the repeal of Thailand's 1933 anti-Communist law—were easily satisfied. Nanking's demands, which included improved treatment of Thailand's very large ethnic Chinese community, were more difficult to satisfy. In January 1946, Thailand agreed to establish diplomatic relations with China, a course it had long resisted, and gave the Chinese in Thailand the same right as nationals of other countries to register their Thai-born children as Chinese nationals. Phibun's 1939 measures limiting Chinese business activities and closing Chinese schools were rescinded, and discrimination against Chinese immigration was removed.

In 1947 and 1948 internal developments, culminating in Phibun's restoration to power, put an end to what had been in British and American eyes heartening progress toward democracy. Postwar civilian unity was short-lived. Pridi, the dominant political figure until November 1947, had been particularly tarnished by rising economic difficulties, corruption, and disunity, and by rumors of his implication in the mysterious death of the young king, Ananda, in June 1947. In November 1947, the military overthrew the cabinet but, remaining in the background, installed Khuang Aphaiwong, now the leader of the opposition Democrat Party, as prime minister in an all-civilian conservative-royalist government. In January, elections were held. Participation was very light—only 22 per cent of the electorate went to the polls, but because the government won by an overwhelming vote in unusually corruption-free elections, the United States and Britain abandoned their reservations about recognition. Three months later, another military move, forcing Khuang's resignation and installing Phibun in his place, reawakened disquiet. However, when the Democrat-dominated National Assembly voted its confidence in Phibun in May, misgivings were again put aside, and the United States and Britain recognized the Phibun government.[11]

Phibun's cautious moves to regain and hold power in a period of marked political instability were paralleled by his careful conduct of foreign relations in a far-from-stable external environment. Partly to

11. *SIA*, 1939–1946, p. 231; Nuechterlein, pp. 47–56, 99–100; Rosinger and Associates, pp. 277–278; Frank Darling, *Thailand and the United States*, pp. 61–67.

discredit his civilian rival but partly also to reassure the Thai, and foreign governments as well, that Thailand could protect itself from the kind of Communist insurrectionary activity already afflicting many of its neighbors, Phibun revived charges against Pridi for Communist connections. But there was no immediate swing to uncompromising anti-Communism on all foreign fronts. Lao and Khmer Issara leaders and Viet Minh purchasing and propaganda agents remained in Bangkok; no effort was made to halt arms smuggling; and, in a July interview, Phibun said he considered the Viet Minh to be a nationalist not a Communist movement. Moreover, Phibun's renewed and highly restrictive policies against the Chinese community were imposed equally on Kuomintang followers and the increasingly numerous supporters of the Chinese Communists.

In June 1948, Malaya's Communist insurrection, known as the Emergency, posed potential problems on Thailand's southern border, but also provided an opportunity for closer cooperation with Britain, still Thailand's most important trading partner. Border officials were instructed to prevent the Communists from using Thai territory as a base and safe haven; and ground forces of both countries were permitted to cross the border as far as ten miles on each side; intelligence was exchanged; and there were occasional joint operations. In April 1949, Britain announced the sale to Thailand of sufficient arms for five infantry battalions to be stationed in the border areas and, in September, arrangements were made to purchase aircraft as well.[12] Meanwhile, relations with the French were also shifting. In September 1948, a Thai military mission went to Saigon and, in November, Bangkok announced that it would deny the use of Thai territory for mobilizing forces and supplies against the French. The Thai, however, did not actively cooperate with the French, continuing to draw a distinction between Malaya and Indochina. Phibun also seemed anxious to disassociate himself from any seeming effort to divide Asians from Europeans. Thus, Bangkok at first rejected the invitation to the New Delhi Conference on Indonesia, arguing that Nehru's initiative might be seen as a step toward an Asian bloc. But, when it became evident

12. Royal Institute of International Affairs, Peter Calvocoressi (ed.), *Survey of International Affairs* (*SIA*), 1947–1948, p. 366; Nuechterlein, pp. 101, 105, 106; Rosinger and Associates, p. 278; A. S. B. Olver, *Outline of British Policy in East and Southeastern Asia, 1945–1950*, p. 40.

that this concern was not shared by others, Thailand decided to send observers.[13]

New States: The Philippines

The Republic of the Philippines became an independent state on July 4, 1946, the first of the former colonies of Southeast Asia to do so. The formal American commitment to Filipino independence dated from the Tydings-McDuffie Act of 1934. Americans as well as Filipinos had pressed for the pledge; American liberals sought fulfillment of the rather vague promises made in the Jones Act of 1916, and agricultural interests wanted to end the free entrance of Philippine agricultural products into the United States. The requirement for a Filipino-drafted constitution was fulfilled in 1935, and by 1941 internal autonomy was virtually complete. During the war the Philippine Commonwealth's government-in-exile, under President Manuel Quezon, participated in the Pacific War Council, the United Nations Relief and Rehabilitation Administration, and the Bretton Woods Agreement as well as in the founding conferences of the Food and Agriculture Organization and the United Nations. When the Japanese occupation ended in October 1944, progress toward independence was resumed. In February 1945, responsibility for civil administration was turned over to the Philippine government under Sergio Osmena who had succeeded to the presidency after Quezon's death.

The new republic faced formidable problems. The Philippines had been devastated by the war; invasion and liberation alike had brought bitter fighting, and there had been much neglect and sabotage in between. Because of the war, negotiations with the United States concerned not only new economic and defense arrangements, which would have accompanied independence in any case, but also compensation for wartime losses, rehabilitation, and veterans benefits.

The U.S. Congress began to consider Filipino rehabilitation problems early in 1942 and, in 1943, President Roosevelt promised to assist the Philippines in "full repair" of war damages. The Rehabilitation Act of April 1946 provided $400 million to cover private claims, $120 million to restore public services, and $5 million to restore U.S. government property. In support of reconstruction activities, property worth $100 million was to be given to the Philippines. However, no payment

13. *SIA*, 1947–1948, pp. 366–367; *SIA*, 1949–1950, pp. 385, 431.

on private claims in excess of $500 was to be made until the Philippine Trade Act of April 1946 entered into effect.

From the American point of view, the trade act was a compromise between agricultural producers, who opposed preferences for the Philippines, and traders and investors, who wanted close ties and free trade. Even after the bill was altered to bring it closer to their views, Filipinos found a number of its provisions objectionable or unsatisfactory. This was especially true of the so-called "parity clause," which required an amendment to the Philippine constitution and gave Americans the same rights as Filipinos to exploit natural resources and own and operate public utilities. Other provisions tied the peso to the dollar, requiring the American president to approve changes in the peso's value, and prohibiting restrictions on convertibility with the dollar or on transferring funds to the United States. Filipino hopes for complete free trade in exchange were disappointed. Free trade was to continue for only eight years, with tariffs gradually increasing on both sides for 25 years thereafter. In addition, as in the Tydings-McDuffie Act, quantitative quotas were imposed for 28 years on such Philippine exports to the United States as sugar, cordage, cigars, certain types of tobacco, coconut oil, and pearl buttons. Early in July 1946, the Philippine Congress, after considerable debate, authorized the conclusion of the necessary executive agreement; it was not until March 1947, however, that the constitutional amendment was approved by plebiscite.[14]

The same month saw the completion of a number of military cooperation arrangements. During the war, both sides had agreed on the inadequacy of the Tydings-McDuffie provisions limiting the post-independence U.S. military presence to naval reservations and fueling stations. The Military Bases Agreement of March 14, 1947, authorized the United States to maintain 23 bases in the Philippines for 99 years. The treaty, other agreements, and American legislation provided also for military assistance and training, and benefits for Philippine veterans; it also established an American military advisory group, defined jurisdiction over crimes committed by U.S. forces, and required

14. Milton W. Meyer, *A Diplomatic History of the Philippine Republic,* pp. 10–14, 24, 377–379; Shirley Jenkins, *American Economic Policy toward the Philippines,* p. 64; George E. Taylor, *The Philippines and the United States,* pp. 125–127; Rosinger and Associates, pp. 383–384.

American permission for purchasing military equipment outside the United States.

It was evident that the Philippines retained some of the characteristics of a dependency and the United States some of the privileges of a metropole. Predictably, Moscow alleged that independence was merely a new form of Asian bondage, preserving the colonial economy, transforming the Philippines into a permanent military base, and suppressing the "national liberation" movement. Nehru was also critical, while the British took some pleasure in pointing out that, unlike the United States, they kept no privileges for themselves in independent India and Burma.[15]

Filipinos were critical too. As Salvador Lopez was later to say: "American policy makers . . . seemed to be more interested in securing parity rights for Americans and ensuring American control of the greatest possible number of military bases in exchange for minimal payments of war damage and Filipino war veterans' claims than in assisting a war-ravaged nation to rebuild its educational and cultural institutions and to rehabilitate its economy. Although the situations in conquered Japan and the liberated Philippines were hardly identical, it is noteworthy that the reform of Japanese political and economic institutions was undertaken with comparatively more sympathetic and vigorous assistance during the brief military occupation of that former enemy country."[16]

George Taylor similarly compared American policy toward the Philippines unfavorably with that toward Japan, saying, "instead of a bold and imaginative program . . . such as was devised for a defeated Japan, the United States Congress served up a sterile compromise based on the restoration of pre-war economic dependence . . . the Congress came up with a series of legislative acts which, in effect, protected American agricultural interests through quotas, protected American manufactured goods through tariff agreements, and protected American investments through currency controls and parity. . . . The key problem, however, was that of the long-term economic development of the Philippines, and to this no branch of the government gave effective consideration."[17]

15. Meyer, pp. 45–48; George Taylor, pp. 128, 132.
16. Frank Golay (ed.), *The United States and the Philippines,* p. 29.
17. George Taylor, pp. 114–115.

The imposition of economic reforms, as well as economic concessions, might have been consistent enough. But the Philippine leaders, who bargained vigorously for fewer American privileges and more American assistance, might have had even more problems with reforms affecting the economic and social position of their own elite class. In any case, they placed a higher priority on securing American defense commitments, and desperately needed economic help, than on freeing themselves from obligation to the United States. Their feelings about the United States were quite different from Burmese views of Britain; they valued the American connection for intangible as well as tangible reasons. At his inauguration in July 1946, President Manuel Roxas spoke of close ideological as well as economic and military ties. Later that year, defending parity and the expanded base presence, he declared, "It is unfortunate that we live in a world in which force and violence are still unchained. . . . But while we do, we must hold fast to strong and tested moorings, and avoid being cast adrift on the angry sea which is apparent to the west of us. . . . I prefer the security of our present plight."[18]

Manila was slow to enter into diplomatic relations with other Asian countries. Until April 1949 the Republic of China was the only Asian state with which the Philippines had established diplomatic relations, and it had done so because of the special interest of both sides in defining the status of the economically important ethnic Chinese minority.[19] The sense of security provided by the American tie may have been partly responsible for this slow pace. Beyond this, the Asian identity of the Philippines was still very weakly rooted. Without any national center or institutions before the Spanish conquest, and largely isolated from the Indian and Chinese influences that had contributed so heavily to the neighboring cultures, the Filipinos had been much more deeply influenced by their western rulers than had other Southeast Asians. With independence, the need Filipino leaders felt to establish the Republic's role in Asia was largely reflected in periodic proposals for regional organization and in Philippine support for anticolonial positions in the UN.

18. Meyer, pp. 31–32.
19. *Ibid.*, pp. 60–61, 114–116.

New States: Burma

The Union of Burma, which became independent on January 4, 1948, had also been devastated by wartime military operations. Again, like the Philippines, it had some experience in self-government (although not as much), serious economic and political problems, and little capacity for self-defense. Yet, far from seeking a similar relationship with Britain, Burma was unprepared even to accept Commonwealth membership. Possibly the Burmese decision was influenced by an unwarranted expectation that India also would cut its ties completely. Then too, the role Asian countries were to play in what had been a white man's club remained untested and unknown. But more basic factors, stemming from the British-Burmese relationship, were at work to ensure that, although remaining closer to Britain than to other western powers, Burma would not accept any formal special relationship.

Aung San, leader of Burma's independence movement, and some of his colleagues apparently saw some advantage in remaining in the Commonwealth but believed that popular sentiment would be opposed. Confirming this view, in May 1947 the national convention of Burma's ruling coalition, the Antifascist People's Freedom League (AFPFL), called for complete independence; the following month the Constituent Assembly unanimously approved a resolution cutting all ties with Britain. Even two years later, the suggestion that Prime Minister U Nu might attend a Commonwealth Prime Ministers' Conference produced a political furor of some intensity.

Although there may have been some sentiment for remaining in the Commonwealth, there was no really strong Burmese support. Unlike the Indians, and perhaps partly because Burma had been governed as an appendage of India for most of the colonial period, the Burmese elite had never become particularly attached to British traditions and culture. The new nationalist leadership had not worked side by side with Britons in the prewar governing structure; those who had been part of this structure were now displaced '(so completely that the former prime minister, U Saw, apparently regarding desperate measures as the only road back to power, instigated the assassination of Aung San and seven of his cabinet colleagues). And, although

Britain moved swiftly once it recognized that the alternative to independence was colonial war, before accepting the inevitable it aroused strong Burmese suspicions that it was seeking pretexts for reimposing the old order.[20]

With these Burmese attitudes, with British strategic interest in Burma vastly reduced by India's independence, and with the limits postwar stringencies imposed on what Britain could provide to others, the grant of independence was not accompanied by elaborate arrangements for the future. Certain Burmese budgetary obligations were canceled, others were assumed by the new government, Britain contributed some £30 million to cover budget deficits and rehabilitation expenditures, and the Burmese promised advance consultation and compensation if nationalization decisions should affect British interests. The Freeman-Bo Letya Agreement enabled Burma to purchase war material, transferred a few small naval vessels, provided financial and technical assistance for the maintenance of three airports, and made training assistance available in Britain and Burma.[21]

Burma in 1948 entered into modest diplomatic activity establishing relations with Britain, France, the Netherlands, the Republic of China, and the United States, and with India, Pakistan, and Thailand, which sponsored its application for admission to the United Nations. In 1947, expressing their solidarity with other Asians seeking independence, the Burmese invited the Viet Minh and the Republic of Indonesia to send representatives to Rangoon; in the following year Burma accorded *de facto* recognition to the Republic of Indonesia and closed its airport to the Dutch.[22]

For two years following independence, the Union's very existence was threatened by Communist and other insurgencies. Even before this perilous situation prompted a search for outside assistance, Burma's leaders had occasionally suggested that national weakness might make alliances desirable. In April 1947, Aung San was reported to have said that such alliances would be indispensable once freedom was attained, and that it would be logical to look to Britain and America for help.

20. Cady, pp. 555–556, 598–599; Mansergh, p. 245; Callis, p. 286; *FRUS*, 1947, VI, 35–36; J. S. Furnivall, "*Twilight in Burma*," *Pacific Affairs*, XXII (March 1949), p. 19.

21. Fifield, pp. 188–190; Cady, pp. 567–569.

22. Hugh Tinker, *The Union of Burma*, pp. 341–343.

U Nu, Aung San's successor as Prime Minister, repeatedly defended the Freeman-Bo Letya Agreement against attacks from the left on the grounds that self-interest and security required good and powerful Allies. In 1948, however, Burma's urgent requests for help from the United States and Britain were greeted coolly. To be sure, the United States had already provided some assistance, even before independence, selling military and other supplies remaining in the country for $2.5 million less than their value. Payments, over a twenty-year period at low interest rates, were to be devoted to jointly agreed educational projects, except for 20 per cent which was to be used for U.S. representational costs. Nevertheless, the United States was not yet prepared for an active role on the Southeast Asia mainland and, in any case, regarded Burma as more appropriately a British responsibility.[23]

The British, in turn, had a number of reservations about the government in Rangoon. U Nu's Fifteen Point Program for Leftist Unity—an attempt to placate the insurgents—had aroused concern over where his government might be heading. The insurgency, mounted by the Karens—who, unlike Burma's other ethnic groups, had responded in large numbers to Christian missionizing efforts—was looked upon with some sympathy in Britain, as well as among American Baptists. Finally, nationalization plans being considered in Rangoon seemed unlikely to provide fair compensation to the British economic interests involved. Nevertheless, it was recognized that prospects for compensation would disappear entirely if the government went under, and Burma's plight had aroused sympathy among fellow Asians in the Commonwealth. In April, India and Pakistan agreed to support Burma's request for arms and assistance at the forthcoming Commonwealth Prime Ministers' meeting. Some assistance was quickly forthcoming; in June 1949, for example, the British provided 10,000 rifles. Agreement over financial assistance from Britain, Ceylon, India, Pakistan, and Australia resulted in a Commonwealth loan of £6 million in June 1950.[24]

In accepting support from the United States and Britain against internal threats, Burma was careful to disavow any implication that it

23. *FRUS*, 1947, VI, 22; Frank Trager, *Burma—From Kingdom to Republic*, pp. 215–218.

24. Cady, pp. 586–588, 597–598; Trager, *Burma*, p. 220; William C. Johnstone, *Burma's Foreign Policy*, pp. 50–51, 59–61.

had joined the side of the West in the Cold War, a contest that it regarded as remote from its own interests. "We are not in the least interested," U Nu said in September 1949, "in anti-Left or anti-Right pacts. An anti-Left pact smacks of aggression on Leftists and in the same way an anti-Right pact smacks of aggression on Rightists . . . we are not interested in any anti-this or anti-that pact except an anti-aggression pact."[25]

New Roles: Australia and New Zealand

The war in the Pacific changed the international outlook of Australia and New Zealand significantly. It brought them into international politics outside the Commonwealth framework. It loosened their ties with Britain, imposed greater dependence on the United States, and caused them to focus more closely on the problems and potentials of the rapidly changing area around them.

Even before Pearl Harbor, the fall of France having put additional demands on British naval forces in the West, Britain had confidentially informed the Pacific dominions that they would have to rely on the American rather than the British fleet if Japan came into the war. Meanwhile, the United States, although its policies seemed increasingly likely to involve Britain as well as itself in war with Japan, was moving only slowly to bolster Pacific security. Then Pearl Harbor and its immediate military aftermath had a shattering effect. Confidence in the invulnerability of Singapore was shown to have been ill-founded, and Australians, particularly, now had reason to believe that greater attention should have been given to their long-standing preoccupation with the Japanese threat and their pessimistic views of the security situation in the Pacific. There could now be no question that the Pacific dominions would have to rely on the United States not on Britain for protection. In his New Year's message at the end of 1941, Australian Prime Minister John Curtin made this point, some thought with unnecessary emphasis: "We . . . shall exert all our energies toward the shaping of a plan, with the United States as its keystone, which will give to our country some confidence of being able to hold out until the tide of battle swings against the enemy."[26]

As the war progressed, Australian and New Zealand leaders became

25. Johnstone, p. 55.
26. C. H. Grattan, *The United States and the Southwest Pacific*, p. 180; Wood, pp. 188–189, 311; Mansergh, pp. 131–132.

concerned that their views seemed to be ignored, even though their countries provided bases of vital importance to the success of the war in the Pacific. In a message to Churchill early in 1942, New Zealand Prime Minister Fraser said: "where the matters under discussion are of immediate and direct concern to us there must be some method devised by which we can intelligently form, and explicitly express our views before action is taken." But, especially in the Cairo Declaration, it became clear that the big powers were not inclined to consult Australia and New Zealand, even on matters that closely concerned them. The ANZAC Agreement of January 1944, while it registered their chagrin, also expressed preoccupations remaining long after the Japanese surrender. The initiative and the decision to publish a formal agreement had been largely Foreign Minister Evatt's. But the view of status and security (as well as of trusteeship) was common to both dominions. Two principles were involved: the importance of the Pacific and arrangements for its future defense; and the central role of Australia and New Zealand in these arrangements.

For the Southwest and South Pacific areas, the two countries proposed a regional zone of defense within the framework of a general system of world security. Based on Australia and New Zealand, which agreed to act together in matters of common concern, the zone was to stretch through the arc of islands north and northeast of Australia to Western Samoa and the Cook Islands. Pending the establishment of this security system, Australia and New Zealand would "properly" be responsible "for policing or sharing in policing" such areas in the region as might be agreed upon. Only a general Pacific settlement could dispose of enemy territory, and Australia and New Zealand were to be represented at the highest level of bodies involved in armistice and peace-making decisions.[27]

Although the ANZAC Agreement had little practical outcome,[28] the attitudes it expressed remained important in Australian and New Zealand postwar foreign policy. The search for some kind of regional security organization continued, with formal proposals made in 1946

27. Wood, pp. 217, 310–314; Grattan, pp. 182–184; F. W. Eggleston, *Reflections on Australia's Foreign Policy*, p. 9; Trevor R. Reese, *Australia, New Zealand, and the United States*, pp. 32–34; Vandenbosch and Vandenbosch, pp. 21–24; Watt, pp. 74–76.

28. Its most lasting result was the establishment of the South Pacific Commission in 1947.

and 1949. The Japanese threat remained of great concern, particularly for Australia. In recognition of Australia's special interest in Japan, an Australian general commanded the small Commonwealth occupation force, an Australian judge presided over the War Crimes Tribunal, and an Australian represented the Commonwealth on the Allied Council.

Australian views that the policies of the Occupation were too arbitrarily determined by General MacArthur as Supreme Commander for the Allied Powers (SCAP), and were insufficiently severe and punitive, caused friction with the United States. Friction arose also over American interest in base rights in the extensive naval facilities that the United States had established on Australian-mandated Manus Island after recapturing the island from the Japanese. The Australians sought to translate this interest into more general security arrangements for the Western Pacific. Said Evatt, "The Commonwealth Government does not recognize the claim that the acquisition of territory by force of arms confers a right to the retention of that territory. . . . Australia is at least as vitally concerned as any other nation in ensuring that provision shall be made for the future security of the Pacific. . . . The Government will enter into no commitment which will lessen the control of the Australian people over their own territories. Any consideration of plans for the joint use of any bases in Australia's dependent territories should be preceded by an overall defense arrangement for the region of the Western Pacific."[29]

In the end, budgetary factors resolved what had become a rather heated dispute between Australia and the United States and a similar, although less acrimonious one, between New Zealand and the United States over base arrangements in Western Samoa. In June 1946, President Truman directed a $650 million cut in naval expenditures; in June 1947, the Australians were informed that the strong American position north of the equator made Manus of slight strategic interest to the United States.

Other wartime preoccupations continued into postwar policy. Concepts rooted in Labour Party doctrines—social and political justice for colonial peoples, the rights of small powers, and the rule of law in international affairs—were expressed at San Francisco, and in United Nations deliberations thereafter. Growing consciousness of neighbors

29. R. N. Rosecrance, *Australian Diplomacy and Japan*, pp. 60–61.

in Asia led to close relations with India, support for Indonesia, and increased receptivity to a role for Southeast Asian states in Pacific security arrangements.[30]

Hints of Southeast Asian Community

Asian regional cooperation was a popular theme of postwar oratory, giving strong play to assertions concerning common traditions, goals, spiritual qualities, and moral force, none susceptible of proof and many rather remote from historic as well as current realities. The latter were more unfavorable than otherwise to the development of the kind of regional institutions then getting underway in Latin America and Europe. History, tradition, and religion divided the countries of the region more than they brought them together. Once independence was gained, and in Southeast Asia this proceeded at an uneven pace, the new countries, differing in their world views and still not secure in their own identities or goals, rarely found common ones they could achieve more readily together than apart. There was little one country could do to help another and there was no desire to assume binding commitments or to sacrifice any element of recently won sovereignty to some joint effort. When combined action was taken to meet pressing postwar economic problems, it was under external guidance and stimulus. Regional political gatherings produced no permanent machinery, while proposals for a regional security organization were stillborn.

The Special Commission in Southeast Asia set up by the British under Lord Killearn, originally as a purely Commonwealth venture, was the earliest form of externally supported economic cooperation. By 1947, fifteen governments were participating, and the staff numbered more than 500. Its organization was stimulated by the Asian rice crisis —in 1946 the Southeast Asian rice available for export was one-sixth the prewar average—and by the need to provide a mechanism for continuing the distribution responsibilities carried out in wartime by the Southeast Asia Command under the jurisdiction of the Combined Food Board. Briefly, the Special Commission performed a political function as the instrumentality of British good offices in the Dutch-Indonesian conflict, but this ended with the Linggadjati Agreement.

30. *Ibid.*, pp. 64–65; *USWA*, 1947–1948, pp. 239–240; Reese, pp. 53–55; Wood, pp. 343–344; Grattan, p. 189; Norman W. Harper, "Security in the South West Pacific," *Pacific Affairs*, XXIV (June 1951), pp. 178–179.

Thereafter, it confined itself to devising and encouraging the adoption of production and distribution programs that would help relieve the South and Southeast Asia food crisis. Periodically, in Singapore, representatives of most of the countries in the area reviewed the food situation, made allocations, and arranged shipments. As the shortage eased, Special Commission activities contracted; in March 1948 the office of the Special Commissioner was merged with that of Governor General of Malaya.[31]

The first postwar Asian political conference, the Asian Relations Conference, was held in New Delhi from March 23 to April 2, 1947. Participation was broad; Asia stretched from Turkey to the Soviet Central Asian republics, taking in, along the way, Arabs and Jews from Palestine and, much to the annoyance of the Chinese, a delegation from Tibet. Japan was invited, but the invitation was rejected by General MacArthur. Australian and New Zealand observers were singled out by Nehru for special mention, the only observers so treated. Coming events cast no shadow before; the Chinese delegation, led by a member of the Kuomintang Central Committee, included no Communist representatives.

From the very outset it was agreed that the conference, convened by the Indian Council on World Affairs, would be unofficial and cultural, with defense and security questions excluded as too controversial. The guiding hand, however, was obviously Nehru's, and the delegations, although representing cultural associations and institutions, also contained a strong official element. In his opening address, Nehru announced the arrival of Asia on the world scene; he called for Asian unity and regional cooperation, and warned against conveying the impression that some form of pan-Asian antiwestern movement was under way. The emotional tone was set by the Indian poet, Sarojini Naidu, "Fellow Asians," she proclaimed, "my comrades, my kinsmen arise; remember the night of darkness is over. Together, men and women, let us march forward to the Dawn."[32]

31. A. S. B. Olver, "The Special Commission in South East Asia," *Pacific Affairs,* XXI (Sept. 1948), pp. 285–287; Olver, *British Policy,* pp. 4, 5; *SIA, 1939–1946,* pp. 224–225; *USWA, 1947–1948,* p. 237.

32. Mansergh, *Survey, 1939–1942,* p. 239; *Asian Relations Conference,* pp. 2–6, 22; Sisir Gupta, *India and Regional Integration in Asia,* p. 34; N. Mansergh, *The Commonwealth and the Nations,* pp. 104–105.

As the discussions proceeded, strong divisions became evident. The Arabs, represented more out of politeness than fellow feeling, were disturbed over the refusal of India's Muslim League to participate. The small countries were concerned that, as western power diminished in Asia, China and India would attempt to take over. The Chinese were worried about measures against their compatriots in Southeast Asia and over immigration restrictions. Rivalry between India and China was pronounced, with the Chinese attempting to block any moves that might encourage India to regard itself as the political center of Asia. Their efforts prevented New Delhi from being selected as the site of the planned second session in 1949; other delegates also suspected India's motives, and the argument that plans could easily be disrupted by civil war between Hindus and Muslims was used with good effect. Accordingly, it was agreed that the 1949 Asian Relations Conference— which never took place—should be held in China.[33]

Of more practical impact was the Conference on Indonesia, held in New Delhi in January 1949 after the second Dutch Police Action. Its objective was not only specific, that is, to demonstrate Asian support for Indonesia and to encourage the Security Council to act vigorously against the Dutch, it was also one readily achieved by the passage of resolutions. Fears in London and Washington that some sort of anti-western, pan-Asian movement was in the offing were set at rest by Nehru's statement that "there is no idea behind this conference of forming an Asian bloc as against European countries or America." It was felt, however, that something more than resolutions should ensue. Nehru, in his opening address, defined another function, to "devise machinery and procedures by which the Governments represented here today can keep in touch with one another for purposes of mutual consultation and concerted action for the achievement of the purposes for which this Conference has met." Carlos Romulo, representing the Philippines, made more concrete proposals. "The Conference might consider further certain measures for the establishing of continuing machinery for the implementation of proposals that may be adopted, including a small permanent Secretariat . . . to serve as a clearing house of information essential to concerted action by our various

33. *Asian Relations Conference,* pp. 71–74; Mansergh, *Commonwealth,* pp. 110–112; *USWA,* 1947–1948, pp. 233–235; Werner Levi, *Free India in Asia,* p. 38.

Governments, and a method of consultation on matters of common interest." On January 22, a conference resolution expressed "the opinion that participating Governments should consult among themselves in order to explore ways and means of establishing suitable machinery, having regard to the areas concerned, for promoting consultation and cooperation within the framework of the United Nations."[34]

The operative word was consultation; as Romulo made clear, plans "to pool material or military resources" were not under consideration. Nehru made the limitations even more apparent when he responded to parliamentary inquiries about the fate of the resolution some months later. We have been thinking about it, he said, and we may have something in a few months' time, perhaps even another conference. But "cooperation can only be the cooperation of independent nations without the least commitment of one to the other . . . there will be no binding covenant in it, and this will be largely an organization for the consultation and cooperation that naturally flow from common interests."[35]

With the boundaries of mutual action so rigidly defined, prospects for a regional defense association were obviously remote, made the more so by the absence of indigenous military strength and the unwillingness of outside powers to lend their support. Britain (although occasionally it gave grudging sanction to Australian initiatives) was determined in this field to do nothing displeasing to India, and therefore to do nothing. The American position was also linked to India's. After the conclusion of the North Atlantic Treaty had once again raised the question of parallel action in the Pacific, Secretary of State Dean Acheson said: "While it is true that there are serious dangers to world peace existing in the situation in Asia, it is also true, as Prime Minister Nehru of India stated in the press the other day, that a Pacific defense pact could not take shape until present internal conflicts in Asia were resolved. He was quoted as saying that the time was not ripe for a pact corresponding to the North Atlantic Treaty, owing to these conflicts. Nehru's view appears to be an objective appraisal of the actual practical possibilities at the present time."[36]

34. India, Ministry of Information and Broadcasting, *The Conference on Indonesia*, pp. 20, 26–27, 37; Lawrence K. Rosinger, *India and the United States*, pp. 91–95.
35. Gupta, p. 42.
36. Reese, p. 114; Olver, *British Policy*, p. 6.

Nevertheless, Australia and the Philippines intermittently advanced proposals for a Pacific defense pact. Australia's notions on the subject were well-defined and dated from the period before World War II when alarm over the adequacy of Pacific defense was aroused by Japan's Manchurian campaign, by Japan's departure from the League of Nations and America's absence therefrom, and by Great Britain's preoccupation with Europe. Then, as in the early postwar years, Australia envisaged partnership with the United States and with the European countries that had colonies in the area. In 1949, however, Australian proposals, stimulated by the anticipated early departure of American troops from Japan, included Asian countries also.[37]

Philippine preoccupation with regional organization during the administration of President Elpidio Quirino, who succeeded to office in April 1948, reflected the same uneasiness over Pacific security that impelled Australian moves. The variety of Quirino's proposals, the vagueness of his concepts, the ease with which he shifted from one to another, reflected an effort to cope with the differing conceptions of the countries to which he was appealing. Even more, however, they reflected the Philippine search for a role in Asia and its ambition for leadership and prestige.

Steps toward the Baguio Conference of May 1950 began while preparations were underway for signing the North Atlantic Treaty; in March 1949 Quirino advocated a similar Pacific Pact to fight Communism in the Far East. When American disinclination to sponsor such a venture became evident, Quirino then proposed a general nonaggression pact with provisions also for economic collaboration. Thereafter, Foreign Secretary Romulo was instructed to emphasize the proposal's nonmilitary rather than military aspects and third-force rather than anti-Communist aspects. In July, however, when Chiang Kai-shek visited the Philippines, the two presidents reiterated the necessity of a Pacific Pact. While Chiang enlisted Syngman Rhee's support, Quirino announced that the proposed organization would mobilize the region's resources against Communism. Meeting with a cool response, however, he reverted in August to the idea of a nonmilitary group to promote economic, cultural, and political cooperation and to be discussed at a meeting at Baguio. At the resulting conference, attended by Indonesia, Thailand, the Philippines, India, Pakistan, Ceylon, and

37. Reese, pp. 53–55, 108–113; Harper and Sissons, p. 30; Levi, *Australia's Outlook*, pp. 81–89.

Australia, the only resolution that was adopted urged joint con-
sultations to ensure that Asian views were taken into account at the
United Nations, and pressed also for common measures to promote
economic and cultural progress; it established no continuing machinery.
Nationalist China and South Korea were not invited; Burma and
New Zealand, although invited, did not attend.[38]

Moscow and the Communists: From Confusion to Calcutta

For some years beyond 1945, Moscow remained indifferent to Southeast Asia, despite the opportunities it might have been expected to see
in the new revolutionary situation. In doctrinal terms, however, the
situation raised a question which Moscow had found intractable:
whether and to what degree colonial Communist parties should cooperate with nationalist movements. Lenin's theses, adopted at the
Comintern's Second Congress in 1920 and elaborated thereafter,
demanded extraordinary talents: the Communists were to be simultaneously rigidly dogmatic and flexibly opportunistic; they were to
support nationalist movements actively, but fight against their bourgeois
tendencies; they were to establish temporary relations or even alliances
with the bourgeois nationalists, but retain the independence of the
proletarian movement; they were to be prepared under shifting circumstances to distinguish between the truly nationalist bourgeois and
those really in the imperialist camp. More often than not, whether
the local Communists followed Moscow's instructions as in China or
defied them as in Indonesia, the results were disastrous.

By the Sixth Congress in 1928, radical changes had occurred:
debacle in China had cast a pall over alliance with the national
bourgeoisie and contributed to the bitter division among Soviet leadership from which Stalin was soon to emerge victorious. The Comintern,
its member parties rigidly encased in the Stalinist mold, was quickly
to become no more than an arm of the Soviet foreign policy struggle
against the West. The complicated question of cooperation with the
nationalist revolution was now quite simply resolved: cooperation was
to be rejected in favor of revolutionary action; henceforth nationalist
movements in the East were to be fought as bitterly as socialist parties
in the West. Significantly, as the new line developed, three of the
Comintern's principal agents in South and Southeast Asia—the In-

38. Meyer, pp. 143–153.

dian, M. N. Roy, the Indonesian, Tan Malaka, and the Hollander, Hendrik Sneevliet (Maring)—broke away; of agents closely familiar with the area, only Ho Chi Minh remained. Thereafter the Comintern and Moscow paid even less attention to Southeast Asia and seemed even less well-informed than in the past. Guided by the parties in the metropolitan countries—assigned this responsibility by the Sixth Congress—the Southeast Asian Communist movement withered and, in some places, barely existed.[39]

In 1935, at the Comintern's Seventh Congress, the line again shifted in response to the exigencies of Soviet foreign policy. With the main enemy defined as "Fascism"—whether European or Japanese—the united front became the order of the day. Unity was difficult to achieve in Asia, however, since the Dutch, French, and British rulers, although no longer the main enemy in the Communist view, had not been so transformed in nationalist eyes. Thus, the Communists in Southeast Asia did not fully share in the growth the Pacific war brought to the nationalist movements. As demonstrated by Ho's successes in Vietnam and by the burgeoning of the embryonic Philippine party, resistance to the Japanese called upon the very conspiratorial and organizational skills that the Communists had tried to develop. But even in Malaya, where resistance to the Japanese vastly strengthened the Communists, the success was a hollow one, since the exclusively Chinese party reached the peak of its strength at the very time when long-dormant Malay nationalism had been aroused—in large part against the Chinese—and was developing rapidly. And, elsewhere, the requirement to resist the Japanese and cooperate with the western colonial powers further isolated the Communists from the mainstream of the nationalist movement, especially in Indonesia, but also in Burma in the first years of the Japanese occupation. In most of the area, the Communists, despite some growth in their numbers, remained a minority within the nationalist movement. Except for Ho Chi Minh, none of the Communist leaders could compare in popular appeal with such figures as Sukarno and Hatta in Indonesia or Aung San and U Nu in Burma.[40]

Almost everywhere when the Pacific war ended, the parties were

39. J. H. Brimmell, *Communism in Southeast Asia*, pp. 39–67; London, pp. 28–30.

40. Virginia Thompson and Richard Adloff, *The Left Wing in Southeast Asia*, passim; Brimmell, pp. 125–246.

badly divided over how to proceed in relation to the nationalists, the policies of the colonial powers, and the choice between political and armed struggle. Even if Moscow had been seriously attentive to events in Southeast Asia, the obscurity and the diversity of the nationalist drive and of the metropolitan response would have complicated the task of finding some iron law of history to guide the Southeast Asian Communists. At least, however, if Moscow had been interested in defining the policy suitable for the new situation, there might have been some resolution of the doctrinal debates that were dividing and weakening the parties. But no such guidance was forthcoming, since, in 1945, Moscow was primarily concerned with Europe. Russian armies occupied all of eastern Europe, eastern Germany, and part of Austria; in western Europe, Communist parties were flourishing and had good prospects of winning power in France and Italy through the ballot; everywhere, economies were shattered, while American interest seemed to be declining rapidly. Soviet national concerns in Asia comparable with those in Europe lay in the north. There the Soviets had acquired southern Sakhalin and the Kuriles, and with them a dominant position in the seas north of Japan, had occupied northern Korea and Manchuria, and remained the pre-eminent influence in Mongolia. Southeast Asia, by contrast, must have seemed extremely unpromising; not yet having become convinced even of a Chinese Communist victory, it is highly unlikely that Stalin had any clue to the potential strength of his putative allies in Vietnam.[41]

Thus, from the end of the Pacific war until some time after the organization of the Cominform in September 1947, Moscow showed little awareness or understanding of developments in Southeast Asia. Initially, Soviet comments even showed some confidence in the prospects for evolutionary change in the colonial relationship and for UN trusteeship. Thereafter, as the drive toward independence gained momentum, Soviet media supported nationalist efforts largely as a point of departure for attacks on the western powers. Moscow was forced into a more active position on Indonesia, at least rhetorically, by Security Council involvement; Indochina remained completely overshadowed by Soviet interest in Europe and the future of the French party.

41. Donald S. Zagoria, *The Sino-Soviet Conflict*, pp. 36–37; *USWA,* 1945–1949, pp. 261–264; McLane, pp. 349–350.

Such commentaries as appeared in the Soviet press were usually written by Asian specialists who were little known outside their field; political or party figures seldom found occasion to express themselves; and the ideological aspects of the Asian revolution were not discussed. Even Asian specialists frequently seemed singularly ill-informed. One such specialist, E. M. Zhukov for example, found sinister ambitions in India's aspirations and its sponsorship of the Asian Relations Conference in 1947. "The fact is that the conference in Delhi was financed, among other things, by certain Indian capitalists. . . . Certain circles had set, as one of the secret rules of the conference, to try on a new basis to revive the idea of 'pan-Asiatism,' and further to make precisely India as the center of the pan-Asiatic movement. As is well known, the imperialist Japan had formerly declared herself as the centre of 'pan-Asiatism.' She explained it in order to 'justify' the Japanese expansion. Now, someone is dreaming of exploiting this Japanese heritage in his own interest."[42]

By 1947, high Soviet hopes for western Europe were being dissipated. Early in the year the Communist parties in France and Italy were excluded from the governing coalitions, third-force tendencies were developing on the left, and the United States was becoming increasingly active, first with the Truman Doctrine and then with the Marshall Plan. Soviet frustrations were expressed in an increasingly hard line epitomized in Andrei Zhdanov's "two camp" speech at the Cominform's inaugural meeting in September 1947. Reflecting the new organization's European orientation[43] Zhdanov, while referring briefly to the crisis of the colonial system and armed resistance in Indonesia and Indochina, made no other reference to Southeast Asia or even to China. Nevertheless, the doctrine preached by Zhdanov had implications for the colonial problem, especially for the problem of relations with the nationalist bourgeoisie. The invective Moscow was already employing against such nationalists as Nehru and U Nu, Zhdanov's rigid division between imperialist forces (led by the United

42. K. P. Karunakaran, *India in World Affairs, 1947–1950,* pp. 90–91; McLane, 253–258, 346–349; Thompson and Adloff, pp. 115–121; McVey, *Soviet View,* pp. 7–8; Philip E. Mosely "Soviet Policy in the Two-World Conflict," *Journal of International Affairs* VIII (1954), p. 95.

43. Its official founders were the Soviet, Yugoslav, Bulgarian, Hungarian, Romanian, Polish, French, Italian, and Czech parties.

States, in alliance with reactionary elements everywhere) and democratic forces (led by the Soviet Union and including fighters for national liberation in the colonies); Zhdanov's complete exclusion of any middle way, and his sharp denunciation of socialists, all suggested that, if applied to Southeast Asia, the two-camp doctrine would prescribe armed struggle against the national bourgeoisie. But, it was not yet so applied and, until early in 1948, Moscow's position—although sharply condemnatory of such nationalists as Nehru and U Nu—continued to be unclear, sometimes seeming to condemn the national bourgeoisie and sometimes to support cooperation with it.

Meanwhile, without guidance, the Southeast Asian parties were pursuing inconsistent policies, and some were badly divided. In Indonesia, the Communists were an important component of a left-wing coalition cabinet pursuing policies little different from its predecessors. In Burma, one Communist faction was already in armed resistance, and the other—increasingly militant and obstructive—had been expelled from the nationalist coalition. In the Philippines, after a period of acute party confusion, armed struggle was already in progress. In Malaya, a united-front policy had been adopted in 1946 but was strongly contested within the party.[44]

By mid-1948, however, these differences had largely evaporated, and Communists were engaged in armed struggle against newly independent governments in Burma, the Philippines, and India, against the nationalist government in Indonesia, as well as against the British in Malaya and the French in Indochina. At the time, it was widely believed that this course had been specifically imposed on the parties at a Communist-sponsored Southeast Asian youth conference held in Calcutta in February.[45] The conference, initiated almost a year before, was sponsored by the World Federation of Democratic Youth and the International Union of Students, two of the many postwar Communist-dominated international front organizations. Except for Thailand, youth groups from all of the Southeast Asian and South Asian countries—independent and otherwise—were represented. The two-camp doctrine was vigorously expressed and widely applied. Asian

44. John H. Kautsky, *Moscow and the Communist Party of India,* pp. 28–30; McVey, *Soviet View,* p. 31; McLane, pp. 354–356; Brimmell, pp. 176–254.

45. Formally, the Conference of the Youth and Students of Southeast Asia Fighting for Freedom and Independence, Feb. 19–25, 1948.

national leaders were judged by the vigor of their resistance to imperialism, with Burmese and Indian leaders criticized for negotiating, and Indochinese and Indonesians hailed for resisting. Indiscriminate condemnation of the national bourgeoisie was the order of the day, and the necessity for Communist leadership of the antiimperialist movement was stressed.

Vigorous as were the calls to action, however, they did not seem to have any specific relevance to the subsequent revolutionary upsurge, which only in Malaya was directed against an imperial power. Moreover, other problems cast doubt on the theory that actual orders were issued at the Southeast Asia Youth Conference in Calcutta. The meeting was of the type normally used by the Communists to propagandize and to mobilize sympathizers, not to issue orders to the faithful. Established Communist positions were not strictly observed—a message from U Nu was read aloud, and tribute was paid to Gandhi when the conference opened. Many of the delegates were not Communists, and some of the members of the Burmese, Indian, and Philippine delegations turned out to be rather energetically anti-Communist. Finally, the trend toward violence implicit in the two-camp doctrine was already underway in a number of the countries before the Calcutta meeting; where it was not, Communist relations with other elements of the nationalist coalition were developing in a direction that made violence at least a possible outcome. In all probability, in the literal sense, no orders or directives were issued at Calcutta. There can be no question that at that time the local parties looked to Moscow for guidance and, if they received no specific directions, sought in its general pronouncements for hints of Moscow's views on the correct path. The role of the Calcutta conference was to make clear that the Zhdanov line meant resistance to the national bourgeoisie, confirming those already moving in this direction that their stance was correct and resolving doubts in the minds of others. If, in following this course to its logical conclusion, the local parties got no material help or even specific guidance, they could nevertheless conclude from propaganda support that they were behaving with complete orthodoxy and according to Moscow's wishes.[46]

Nevertheless, victims of the 1948 wave of Communist violence believed that instructions had been issued in some quite literal sense. The

46. McLane, pp. 357–360; McVey, Calcutta, pp. 13–15, 19–22; Kautsky, pp. 33–41; Beloff, pp. 209–210.

Indian Home Ministry claimed to have conclusive evidence to this effect; even years later, in 1957, U Nu asked, "Can we ever forget that it was the so-called Southeast Asia Youth Conference . . . which was the signal for the start of the Communist rebellion?"[47] In Indonesia, Alimin Prawirodirdjo, leader of the faction that subsequently won control of the PKI, encouraged the notion that the attempted coup in Madiun had not reflected the views of the party but had been the work solely of Musso and his followers.[48] It was easy enough for others to see in this a Communist confession that the uprising had been Moscow's work, not that of the local leaders. Subsequent Russian statements also tended to strengthen belief in the instruction thesis. At the time, for example, nothing in Moscow's response to the Madiun affair suggested that it had anticipated the revolt, much less directed it. But, a year later, a Soviet conference of Orientalists hailed it, together with armed uprisings in Burma and Malaya, as vivid testimony to a new higher stage of development of the national liberation movement. These uprisings and others, moreover, were "not fortuitous, spontaneous outbursts but an organized class conscious struggle of the masses . . . led by the Communist Party . . . against the imperialists and internal reaction."[49]

47. Trager, *Burma*, pp. 224–225; Sar Desai, p. 17.
48. Justus M. Van der Kroef, *The Communist Party of Indonesia*, pp. 44–45.
49. McLane, p. 362.

PART II

The Cold War Comes
to Southeast Asia

CHAPTER 4

THE CHINESE ROLE REVIVED

The Cold War, coming to Southeast Asia only belatedly, was brought there initially by the Communist victory in China. Until the end of 1949, the West had concerned itself with Southeast Asia largely in the context of decolonization, a process in which Cold War issues had not yet become very deeply involved. To be sure, western attitudes were affected by the Communist role in nationalist movements, and liberal policies were urged as a way to counter pro-Communist trends; western concerns with the Communist threat were accentuated by Southeast Asian insurgencies; and, there, as elsewhere, increasing fear of atomic cataclysm imparted a special drama to passing events. From the end of World War II, American policy making was bedeviled by conflicting desires to strengthen western Allies and promote self-government in their Southeast Asian colonies. Contradictions were evident also in Soviet efforts simultaneously to advance national objectives in Europe, remain in the international revolutionary vanguard, and cast discredit on western behavior even when it advanced Asian causes.

The low priority the United States and the USSR had given to Southeast Asia was matched by the relative indifference of Southeast Asians to Cold War issues. To them, the clash of American and Soviet policies, even in Korea and Japan, seemed remote, and European concerns were important only as they impinged on Asian nationalist drives. There were no binding ideological ties to either side. Western cultural traditions were strong among elites, and democratic political institutions were highly regarded. But the West was tainted with the imperialism of the past and with resistance to the continuing nationalist struggles. Socialist economic doctrines were much in vogue, but the Soviet Union's denigration of national leaders, its denial of the possibility of a third path between imperialism and capitalism, and its vociferous approval of Communist insurgencies naturally evoked suspicion and resentment. At first Moscow had failed even to offer help to Southeast Asian countries; when it did, its treatment of the small countries of Eastern Europe was recalled with some concern. Thus, in 1952, the Indonesian Foreign Minister, noting the Czechoslovak experience and others as well, observed "I do not think it would be wise to accept technical assistance now from the Soviet Union."[1]

While European events were of remote concern and the Soviet Union was a far distant power, China could not be overlooked. The prospect of an interminable Chinese civil war was not unwelcome to China's southern neighbors. But, in 1949, as Nationalist defenses crumbled against an inexorable Chinese Communist advance, policy had to be formulated on new assumptions. China now seemed likely to achieve unity under strong and dedicated leaders commanding a disciplined political machine and a huge battle-tested revolutionary army; however enfeebled it might be by war and revolution, their northern neighbor nevertheless loomed large to the new and weak Southeast Asian states, especially with the Soviets helping Peking to move forward.

Nevertheless, if only because of their own weakness, states on China's periphery favored making the necessary re-examination slowly and cautiously. Of the then independent Southeast Asian states only Thailand responded by moving closer to the West. Burma and Indonesia quickly recognized the People's Republic of China (PRC) and, by early in 1950, the Philippines seemed ready to do likewise. In Australia and New Zealand, however, inclinations to join the British in recognizing the new regime fell before the exigencies of an election year in which local Communist activities were an important political issue.

Western perceptions, especially American ones, were sharply affected by the Communist advance in China. Victory there, coupled with the Soviet explosion of an atomic bomb, seemed to more than balance economic recovery and growing political cohesion in Western Europe. Of more immediate concern, Sino-Soviet encouragement to Southeast Asian Communist insurgencies and the extreme militancy of the then-

---

1. Raymond E. Stannard, Jr., *The Role of American Aid in Indonesian-American Relations*, p. 58.

current Communist doctrine suggested, especially to American policy makers, that the pattern of Soviet postwar expansion in Eastern Europe was now to be repeated in Asia, with Peking, as rigidly controlled as the European satellites, serving as Moscow's junior partner and Asian base.

In not the least consequential of its many effects on American behavior and policies, the Chinese Communist victory put in train the movement toward deep U.S. involvement in Southeast Asia. As early as August 1949, it had been determined that the Communist advance in Asia must be checked. Not long thereafter the domino theory was prefigured in a newly formulated strategic concept. The security of Japan, Australia, and India, it was argued, required that Southeast Asia be denied to the Communists. But there was no suggestion that it was an area into which American military power should extend. Instead aid, mostly economic aid, having already demonstrated its efficacy in restoring political stability to Europe, was to be provided to support the same objective in Southeast Asia.

Southeast Asians, whether or not they shared the American view of Peking's hostile intentions, were as persuaded as Americans or Britons of the vulnerabilities that stemmed from their economic difficulties. Recovery from the destruction of war and progress toward national betterment and modernization were taking place slowly if at all. Institutional weaknesses of all kinds, and threats to public order —not the least of which were Communist-inspired—were obstacles to progress and to the consolidation of newly won political power. Even if it had taken the Communist victory in China to bring greater American help, the help was welcome, especially as the United States seemed anxious to direct it primarily along economic lines and apparently expected neither military alliance nor political concessions in exchange.

The Assertion of Revolutionary Leadership

Of the ambassadors accredited to the National Government only the Soviet ambassador accompanied it in its flight from Nanking to Canton in April 1949. The next month, however, he was withdrawn. On October 2, the day after the People's Republic of China was proclaimed, Moscow extended formal recognition. Well before this, the Soviets had hailed the victory of the Chinese revolution and accepted it as the model for Asia, in the process, in deference to Mao Tse-tung's position, abandoning Zhdanov's strictures against cooperation with the nationalist bourgeoisie. This was an important change for Moscow and for the rest of the international movement. Especially after the split between Moscow and Tito's Yugoslavia, nationalism had been anathematized as a phenomenon with which "Marxism-Leninism cannot reconcile itself."[2] Condemnation of nationalism had been specifically applied to the colonial question by the British Communist, R. Palme Dutt. Since World War II, Dutt argued, imperialism had had to seek new Allies among the nationalists; the grant of formal independence, he said, "is the most characteristic technique of im-perialism in the modern period." In countries like India and Burma, the dominant element of the colonial bourgeoisie has "moved from a previously vacillating partial opposition role, to a full counter-revolu-tionary role and a bloc with imperialism." Colonial liberation, he con-cluded, citing principles advanced by Stalin in 1925, can only be achieved by revolution. The compromising section of the nationalist bourgeoisie must be isolated and the petty bourgeoisie freed from its influence.[3]

Meanwhile, however, the Chinese Communists, although they too attacked Tito, had themselves continued to stress the importance of cooperation with the nationalist bourgeoisie—which Mao had defined as a component of the Communist-led united front, together with the workers, peasants, and petty bourgeoisie. Thus, late in 1948, Liu Shao-ch'i's article, "Internationalism and Nationalism," while applauding Yugoslavia's expulsion from the Cominform, called upon the Com-munists in such "colonial and semi-colonial" countries as Burma, Thailand, the Philippines, Indonesia, and Indochina "to enter into an anti-imperialist alliance with that section of the national bourgeoisie which is still opposing imperialism and which does not oppose the anti-imperialist struggle of the masses of the people." Should they fail to do so, he warned, "should they, to the contrary, oppose or reject such an alliance," it would be as grave a mistake as failure to "adopt a firm and irreconcilable policy against national betrayal of the re-actionary section of the big bourgeoisie."[4]

2. McVey, *Soviet View*, pp. 53–54.
3. *Cominform Journal*, Oct. 15, 1948, p. 5; Nov. 1, 1948, pp. 6–7.
4. Kautsky, pp. 87–88.

Moscow did not harmonize its line with Peking's merely in order to strengthen its alliance with the Chinese Communists or enhance their position in Asia. A more flexible attitude was also dictated by the Soviet-sponsored peace movement inaugurated at the World Congress of Intellectuals for Peace in Poland in August 1948. Thus in May 1949 the *Cominform Journal,* commenting on the establishment of NATO, included "elements of the democratically minded national bourgeoisie in the colonial and capitalist countries" among those joining the struggle for peace. Not long after, with Soviet reservations about its prescriptions presumably abandoned, *Pravda* published Liu Shao-ch'i's hitherto ignored article. In June, at a Soviet Orientalist's conference, Zhukov, in his opening speech on the national-colonial struggle, said the struggle for people's democracy in the colonies and semicolonies unites "not only the workers, the peasantry, the urban petty bourgeoisie, the intelligentsia, but even certain sections of the middle bourgeoisie which is interested in saving itself from cut-throat foreign competition and from imperialist oppression."[5] Even after Moscow brought its view of the national bourgeoisie into harmony with Peking's, however, both continued to condemn the governments of Burma and Indonesia as puppets of the imperialists and to call for armed struggle against them.

Accompanying the doctrinal change was a marked shift in the Chinese place in the Communist firmament. In the USSR, the Asian section of the keynote message commemorating the October Revolution was devoted entirely to the accomplishments of the Chinese party; the 1948 message had not even mentioned China. Georgi Malenkov, in his anniversary speech, predicted that from victory in China would flow a "new considerably higher stage" of the "national struggle of liberation of the peoples of Asia, the Pacific Ocean basin, and of the whole colonial world," while developments in China and Mao's writings were increasingly featured in Soviet and Cominform publications.[6]

The Chinese role was celebrated even more conspicuously in November and December when the Asian and Australian Conference of Trade Unions met in Peking under the auspices of the Moscow-dominated World Federation of Trade Unions (WFTU). Liu's open-

5. *Ibid.,* p. 88; Marshall D. Shulman, *Stalin's Foreign Policy Reappraised,* p. 95.

6. McVey, *Soviet View,* p. 32; Shulman, pp. 111–112; Kautsky, pp. 91–92.

ing speech was unequivocal in its claims: "The path taken by the Chinese people in defeating imperialism and its lackeys and in building the People's Republic of China is the path that should be taken by the peoples of the various colonial and semi-colonial countries in their fight for national people's democracy."[7] He was echoed by the Vietnamese delegation's leader, who said that "the path of the 475 millions of Chinese people is the path to be taken to win a decisive victory over the imperialists. The essential principles . . . defined by Comrade Liu Shao-ch'i in his opening speech . . . must serve as the compass for all the workers of Southeast Asia."[8]

Liu's prescribed path was uncompromisingly revolutionary; cooperation with the national bourgeoisie did not mean surrender to their leadership: "They will inevitably compromise half way at the critical moment in the course of the movement and lead it onto the road of defeat and suffering." The resolute fight against imperialism and its lackeys did not exclude the use of legal means of struggle, nor was armed struggle the universal panacea. But, he said, "armed struggle is the main form of struggle for the national liberation struggles of many colonies and semi-colonies. Wherever possible, there must be a Communist-led national army to carry on the armed struggle in the countryside in coordination with legal and illegal action in the enemy-controlled cities."[9]

The departure from normal Soviet behavior in according such great respect to Mao and the Chinese party was striking. Equally so was the Chinese Communists' abandonment of their long-standing circumspection concerning their relations with the USSR. Three months before the establishment of the People's Republic, Mao in his essay "On the People's Democratic Dictatorship" wrote that China belonged internationally "to the side of the anti-imperialist front, headed by the Soviet Union." The choice must be made between the side of imperialism and the side of socialism; there can be no third road and "neutrality is a camouflage."[10] The Sino-Soviet Treaty of Friendship, Alliance, and Mutual Assistance of February 1950 established the

7. New China News Agency (NCNA), Nov. 23, 1949.
8. Chen, p. 218.
9. NCNA, Nov. 23, 1949.
10. Brimmell, pp. 266–267.

specifics of cooperation, but Mao's statement almost eight months earlier had left no room for doubt about the existence of the new alliance.

Not merely for China, but for all countries, a third path between alliance with the Soviet-led Socialist camp or the American-led imperialist camp was excluded. Even in 1948, Liu had echoed Zhdanov's rejection of neutralism: "If one is not in the imperialist camp, assisting American imperialism and its agents to enslave the world or one's own people, then one must be in the anti-imperialist camp. . . . To refrain from lining up on one side or the other and to keep neutral is impossible. . . . So-called neutralism . . . is nothing but deception."[11] Nationalists unwilling to subordinate themselves to Communist Party leadership were excluded from the national bourgeoisie and consigned to the "reactionary section of the big bourgeoisie," the "lackeys of the imperialists." Independent, nonaligned governments in India, Burma, and Indonesia were therefore to be fought by armed struggle equally with the French in Indochina, or the British in Malaya.

With this perspective, the new regime in Peking, although anxious to be accorded recognition, did not seem any more interested than Moscow in carrying on an active diplomatic policy in Southeast Asia. Burma, for example, recognized the PRC in December 1949, the first non-Communist government to do so, but the representative it quickly sent to Peking was unable to present his credentials until August 1950. On the other hand, the advent of Communist power in Peking, even though it encouraged Communists in neighboring countries, appears to have been of material assistance only to the Communists in Vietnam. Moreover, the Liaison Bureau organized at the Peking WFTU meeting failed to fulfill expectations that it would direct and coordinate the Asian revolution, proving, instead, to be merely another propaganda transmitter. Otherwise, Chinese assistance seems to have been limited to strong and frequent endorsement of Communist insurgent activities and whatever private advice may have been offered to such Southeast Asian Communist leaders as Bo Thien Shwe of Burma and D. N. Aidit of Indonesia when they visited Peking.[12]

11. Allen S. Whiting, *China Crosses the Yalu*, p. 7.
12. Johnstone, p. 57; Beloff, p. 211; Brimmell, pp. 208, 311; Kautsky, pp. 99–100; McVey, *Development of the Indonesian Communist Party*, pp. 69–70.

The Southeast Asian Response: Wait and See

Chiang Kai-shek's fall, in itself, aroused no great concern in Southeast Asia. His government had been accepted while it remained in power; such support as it had offered to Asian causes had been welcomed; and, because China had been treated as a great power and a protégé by the United States, it was able to insist on treaty arrangements that such countries as Thailand and the Philippines might otherwise have preferred to avoid. But the Kuomintang was generally regarded as having brought its fate down on its own head and as having survived as long as it did only because of U.S. support which now, it appeared, had been withdrawn.

Control over all of mainland China by a single government was in itself portentous for countries that had come under Chinese suzerainty or pressure in the past. Peking's affiliations with Moscow, its bitter attacks on the leaders of neighboring states, and its endorsement of armed struggle against them were all ominous signs, made the more so by the presence of large Overseas Chinese communities. But it remained to be seen how active a still badly shattered China would be in the international arena and how it would behave there. Meanwhile, Southeast Asian governments—preoccupied with domestic problems, conscious of their weakness and inexperience, and moving only tentatively in international affairs—felt under no immediate pressure to alter existing policies or embark upon new ones.

Vietnam aside, Burma had the strongest reasons for concern and caution. A Communist insurgency, as well as other armed revolts, threatened the government. Its border with China was long, remote, and imperfectly controlled, and substantial sections along its course were in dispute. The British departure had already revived Chinese interest. Even though Burma's relations with Chiang's China (which had been one of the sponsors of Burma's admission to the United Nations) had been cordial, the National Government had made emphatic claim in November 1947 to 77,000 square miles of Burmese territory north of Myitkyina and, in 1948, had refused to accept the annual rent on the Namwan Assigned Tract, which China had leased to Britain in perpetuity in 1897. When the Chinese Communists came to power, their republication of old maps supporting traditional Chinese claims suggested they would take a similar position. In addition, the southward flight of Chiang's Nationalist troops could provide a pretext for action; Chou En-lai's warning in November that "any government which offers refuge to the Kuomintang reactionary armed forces shall bear the responsibility for handling this matter and all its ensuing consequences" had specifically named only France, but had referred to "other bordering countries" as well. Meanwhile, all the considerations that had impelled Burma toward a neutral position were now strengthened by the proximity of the Cold War, and by the expectation that alignment with one side or the other would be positively dangerous. Said U Nu in December: "Our circumstances demand that we follow an independent course and not ally ourselves with any power bloc. Any other course can only lead the Union to ruin."[13]

Indonesia, although also adopting a neutral posture, had a somewhat different perspective on the Chinese issue. Nationalist China had been moderately helpful to the Republic in the UN, and it had not made much of an issue over the brutal treatment of Overseas Chinese during the revolution. But this brutality testified, nonetheless, that, whereas for Burmans, Indians were the scapegoats and the Chinese close, if sometimes difficult, relatives, Indonesian antagonism toward the Chinese was strong, especially in areas where the now politically important Muslim entrepreneurial class had suffered from Chinese competition.

More inclined to distrust Peking and, in their insular position, feeling its pressure less, Indonesians were in no great hurry to recognize the PRC—doing so nevertheless within several weeks after receiving a special request in March 1950. A Chinese Ambassador arrived in Djakarta in August 1950, but Indonesia sent no representative of equal rank to Peking, in this respect repeating a pattern of avoidance it had already established in its relations with the USSR. Moreover, the violently anti-American and pro-Communist speeches of the Chinese Ambassador (the Indonesian-born Wang Jen-shu who had been expelled by the Dutch for Communist activities) quickly became a source of irritation and concern.[14]

Even the Philippines seemed initially inclined to recognize the new

13. Chen, p. 203; Tinker, pp. 341, 343; Harold C. Hinton, *Communist China in World Politics*, p. 310.

14. McVey, *Development of the Indonesian Communist Party*, pp. 66–67; Hinton, *Communist China*, p. 428.

regime, especially as long as U.S. recognition appeared possible. In mid-July 1949, President Quirino of the Philippines had joined with Chiang Kai-shek in calling for an anti-Communist Pacific Pact. But, in October, although Manila did not respond to Chou's invitation to establish diplomatic relations, it did not issue the customary message congratulating the National Government on the Double Ten anniversary, nor did Quirino attend the celebration at the Chinese Embassy. Elected president in his own right in November, Quirino said in his inaugural address: "In our relations with the Chinese people with whom we have had such close contacts over many centuries, we shall maintain an open mind giving due heed to the requirements of our national security and the security of Asia as a whole." Within a week, while visiting the United States, he told the press that Filipino recognition of the PRC was inevitable, although the question of timing was still under consideration. The Philippines, he said, was not worried about the Chinese Communists "as long as they don't bother us." Returning to this theme in February, he declared, "Let China go Communist. Let Japan go Communist. We don't care. We will respect whatever form of government any of our Far Eastern neighbors choose to have."[15]

Of all of China's southern neighbors, Thailand showed the most concern over the possible impact of the Communist victory on its security. In July 1949, answering critics who attacked him for policies too obviously aimed at winning the support of the West, Phibun said his government would never be so strongly anti-Communist as to involve Thailand in open conflict. In September, however, he said he would welcome British and U.S. troops to help Thailand resist foreign aggression. The impact of the Communist victory on local Chinese caused particular concern, and Phibun warned them not to take sides. Peking in turn took up the cudgels on behalf of Thailand's Chinese, mounting a large-scale propaganda campaign in January 1950 demanding revocation of the restrictive measures Phibun had imposed two years earlier. His fears confirmed, Phibun's own inclinations toward close partnership with the United States were thereby strengthened.[16]

15. Meyer, pp. 125–127.
16. Rosinger and Associates, pp. 289–290; Nuechterlein, p. 102.

Australia, although apprehensive over the Communist advance in China, was unconcerned over the fate of the National Government with which its experience had been most unfavorable. Australia's interest in China had been awakened only during World War II; thereafter the Chinese received by far the largest share of the Australian contribution to the United Nations Relief and Rehabilitation Administration (UNRRA), while Australians serving with UNRRA in China were exceeded in numbers only by Americans and Britons. Although Australians, like Americans, had been embittered by Nationalist corruption and mismanagement, Australian bitterness was unmixed with any sense of responsibility for Chiang's fate. Instead, it was intensified by the belief that the National Government, in addition to mismanaging the assistance to which Australia had contributed so heavily, was positively ungrateful and ill-intentioned. Chinese behavior with respect to Manus Island was a case in point. As part of the American withdrawal from Manus, China was to purchase all movable property remaining on the base (using a special UNRRA grant for the purpose), and Australia was to purchase all nonmovables and, in addition, acquire all movables the Chinese did not take by a fixed date. The Chinese, however, were accused of deliberately wrecking equipment and supplies they did not remove and, in addition, of mistreating the island's people. Then, with anger over the Manus incident still simmering, China in the Trusteeship Council bitterly attacked the white Australia policy and gave even greater offense to Australians, proud of a progressive colonial policy, by alleging they were mistreating the New Guineans.[17]

Although antagonism toward the National Government might have smoothed the path toward recognizing Peking, domestic factors worked the other way. In Australia, and in New Zealand also, it was an election year. In both countries, the opposition was charging that the Labour governments had been soft toward the local Communist parties. The issue was particularly lively in Australia, where a prolonged Communist-inspired coal strike had brought general hardship and unemployment to some 600,000 industrial workers. Moreover, anti-Communism among the large Catholic element in the labor move-

17. Henry S. Albinski, *Australian Policies and Attitudes toward China*, pp. 5–12.

ment (which was ultimately to split the Labour Party) was becoming increasingly intense.[18]

The exigencies of an election campaign, where China was not an issue but could easily develop into one, thus became a major factor deterring the Labour Party from maintaining the policy implicit in Evatt's statement of June 1949 that the Chinese Communists should not be given any grounds for believing that cooperation with the West was impossible. Instead, in November, when Australian diplomats, after meeting with a representative of the British Foreign Office, reportedly agreed unanimously that Australia should recognize the PRC, Evatt rejected their recommendation.

Internal factors continued to play an important part in the post-election period. In their first months in office, the victorious conservatives—the National Party in New Zealand and the Liberal-Country coalition in Australia—having made Communism a central campaign issue, were bound to be affected by this in their behavior toward Peking. In Australia, moreover, the Communist issue was kept alive by the government's effort to secure legislation outlawing the party and by a concerted Catholic campaign—stimulated in part by mistreatment of missionaries in China—against recognition. Internationally, both governments were caught between conflicting pressures. Favoring recognition was the desire to remain in harmony with Britain and the Asian members of the Commonwealth who had already recognized the PRC; opposing was the desire to remain in harmony with the United States.[19]

Meanwhile, the Chinese victory served to maintain the interest of the Australian government in an active role in Asia, even though its new Prime Minister, Robert Menzies, was far from predisposed in that direction. Thus, in January, shortly after Menzies took office, his Minister of External Affairs, Percy Spender, citing a "definite" threat of Communism in Southeast Asia, declared that Australia's destiny was "irrevocably conditioned by what takes place in Asia" and that its future increasingly depended upon "the political stability of our Asian neighbours, upon the economic well-being of Asian peoples, and upon

18. Watt, p. 223; A. M. Halpern (ed.), *Policies Toward China*, pp. 173–175.
19. Henry S. Albinski, *Australia's Search for Regional Security in Southeast Asia*, p. 185; Halpern, pp. 173–174, 512; Reese, pp. 153–154.

the development of understanding and friendly relations between Australia and Asia."[20]

The American Response: First Steps toward Involvement

For four years the United States had been relatively inactive in Southeast Asia. It had continued to feel a sense of obligation to the Philippines, and it recognized strong ties of sentiment, language, and tradition with Australia and New Zealand. But it was quite unwilling to embody these sentiments in a formal alliance. It felt impelled by its own traditions to look benevolently upon new nationalism and new states and to express this benevolence, American style, with at least some practical assistance. But its actual policies had been dictated by its interests in Europe. It had come only slowly and reluctantly to support the Indonesians against the Dutch and had been highly circumspect in urging greater concessions to Indochinese nationalism upon the French. To the policy maker, conscious of unprecedented American interests and commitments elsewhere—of which military alliance and conscription in time of peace were only the most conspicuous manifestations—Southeast Asia did not seem to be an area in which the United States should undertake significant responsibilities. When this view began to change in the wake of the Communist victory in China, the shift reflected a mix of domestic pressures and expectations aroused by the postwar experience in Europe as well as by observed Chinese behavior.

For some time, however, the administration resisted pressures for deeper involvement. As early as 1947, and for some time thereafter, Congressional demands for more assistance to Asia were countered by administration arguments pointing to the magnitude of world problems, the consequent need to concentrate resources where they could do the greatest good in the shortest time, and the inapplicability of policies successfully applied in Europe to fundamentally different conditions elsewhere. In Asia, it was argued, a base for using economic measures to build stronger political communities did not exist.

By late 1949, as their very successes seemed to reduce the need for the massively expensive programs the United States had undertaken in Europe and as frictions developed among the western Allies, isola-

20. Albinski, *Australia's Search for Security*, p. 309.

tionist sentiments directed against Europe were reinforcing other pressures for a more active Asian policy. Notwithstanding the circumspect attitude of the executive branch toward a Pacific Pact and despite its objections, Congress, in the Foreign Military Assistance Act of 1949, expressed itself "as favoring the creation by the free countries and the free peoples of the Far East of a joint organization . . . to establish a program of self-help and mutual cooperation designed to develop their economic and social well-being, to safeguard basic rights and liberties, and to protect their security and independence."[21]

Initially, Congressional attention was focused on China rather than on Southeast Asia, but, after the Chinese Communist victory, Southeast Asia began to receive a greater share. As the increasingly popular argument that the United States had lost China became more and more intertwined with accusations of Communist conspiracy in the executive branch, it was also increasingly argued that, without a more active American role, the rest of Asia would be lost as well.

The Truman administration continued to resist the argument that the situation called for further efforts on Chiang's behalf. But apparently the same circumstances impelling the United States toward disengagement in China—the seeming inevitability of Nationalist collapse—were compelling it toward greater engagement elsewhere. In August 1949, the month in which the United States terminated all assistance to the National Government, Secretary of State Dean Acheson announced a committee chaired by Philip C. Jessup to study American policy in Asia and make recommendations for the future. In his instructions to Jessup, the Secretary said: "You will please take as your assumption that it is a fundamental decision of American policy that the United States does not intend to permit further extension of Communist domination on the continent of Asia or in the Southeast Asia area."[22] Soon thereafter policy statements, public and classified, began to define the new approach. In December 1949 the National Security Council (NSC) approved a basic paper on Asian policy that had been in the making since June.[23] In January and

21. *Pentagon Papers*, I, 47; Charles Wolf, *Foreign Aid: Theory and Practice in Southern Asia*, pp. 24–25, 35–36, 53.

22. *DSB*, Oct. 15, 1951, p. 603.

23. Text in *Pentagon Papers*, VIII, 266 ff.

March, in speeches at the National Press Club and the Commonwealth Club,[24] Acheson provided the public rationale. In February, *The New York Times* published an article by Raymond B. Fosdick, a member of the Jessup committee, which was generally regarded as reflecting the committee's views.[25] And in April, Ambassador Jessup himself reported to the nation on the conclusions his committee had reached.[26]

In all of these statements, the administration continued to take a measured view of Asia's importance in American global policy. The NSC did not see the primary strategic interests of the United States as lying there; in war time, Europe would be the theater of strategic offense, Asia a theater of strategic defense carried on with a minimum expenditure of manpower and material.[27] To remain within these limits of commitment while seeking freedom of access to the Asian continent, the United States must retain at least its existing position in the offshore island chain, that is, in Japan, the Ryukyus, and the Philippines. These were to be the locus of its perimeter defense; elsewhere, it should bring to bear such resources as it could in areas where the results were likely to be greatest but stop short of committing military forces.

The NSC defined the U.S. interest in Asia in largely negative terms: it was important to deny an enemy the major advantages presumed to lie in controlling Asia's peoples, resources, and lines of communication. In April, the Joint Chiefs of Staff were more positive, describing Southeast Asia as of critical strategic importance to the United States because of its role as a major source of certain strategic materials required for American stockpiles, a crossroads of communications, and a vital segment in the line of containment of Communism: "The security of the three major non-Communist base areas in this quarter of the world—Japan, India, and Australia—depends in a large measure on the denial of Southeast Asia to the Communists. If Southeast

24. Texts in *DSB*, Jan. 23, 1950, and March 27, 1950.

25. Raymond B. Fosdick, "Asia's Challenge," *New York Times Magazine*, Feb. 2, 1950.

26. Text in *DSB*, April 24, 1950.

27. The NSC defined Asia as including the territory south of the USSR and east of Iran, together with the major offshore islands—Japan, Taiwan, the Philippines, Indonesia, and Ceylon.

Asia is lost, these three base areas will tend to be isolated from one another."[28]

Public statements also stressed resources and communications. But, in addition, they attributed great significance to the non-Communist Asian revolution because it embodied American ideals of independence and human betterment. Asia is important, said Jessup, "because tremendous and hopeful things are happening there, because a great continent and great peoples are anxious to build not only a free but also an abundant society. And that awakening has a profound meaning for us, since we live by these same ideas."

But the United States had not convinced Asians of its interest. The United States, Fosdick suggested, had been seen by Asians as aligned "with the maintenance of the *status quo* rather than with the forces making for a new Asia," as regarding "the people of Asia as pawns in a chess game with Russia." Acheson, granting the American interest in stemming the spread of Communism in Asia, argued that this interest did not derive solely from the conflict with the USSR, but even more from opposition to Communist objectives of capturing the national revolutions, depriving the countries of Asia of their independence and making them "mere tributary states" forced, like China, into the Soviet orbit. The NSC delineated the Soviet role even more sharply. China, Japan, India, or an Asian bloc may some day become a threat, but, now and for the foreseeable future, "it is the USSR which threatens to dominate Asia, through the complementary instruments of Communist conspiracy and diplomatic pressure supported by military strength." The unprecedented degree of equality Moscow had already accorded Peking did not appear to have impressed the NSC. The possibility of later divisions between the two was not excluded but, for the immediate future, Soviet influence in China was expected to become stronger.

As to Southeast Asia, "it is now clear" said the NSC that it is "the target of a coordinated offensive directed by the Kremlin . . . motivated in part by a desire to acquire Southeast Asia's resources and communications lines and to deny them to us," and in part by political objectives. "The extension of Communist authority in China represents a grievous political defeat for us; if Southeast Asia is also swept

28. *Pentagon Papers*, VIII, 308.

by communism we shall have suffered a major political rout the repercussions of which will be felt throughout the rest of the world, especially in the Middle East and in a then critically exposed Australia."

The Southeast Asian states were thought to be particularly vulnerable to Communist subversive techniques because of their political immaturity, their economic problems, their internal divisions, and their difficulties in maintaining law and order. Help to governments seeking to cope with the Communist threat was seen as best provided in ways also forwarding other national objectives. Raymond Fosdick addressed himself to this question with specific reference to President Truman's commitment in his inaugural address in January to provide technical assistance and foster capital investment in underdeveloped countries. "No program in Asia today has meaning or promise which does not integrate itself with the struggle of the common people for a better life. . . . We must prove to the East our traditional concern for the deprived people of the world, and the sincerity of our desire to be of help. . . . That is why Point IV . . . is of such vital significance. . . . It gives us our most effective weapon in halting the spread of communism. For communism grows on tissues made gangrenous by disease, poverty and exploitation and the cause of the malady does not readily respond to a therapy of guns and tanks."

The NSC made the same point, but enjoined the United States to "carefully avoid assuming responsibility for the economic welfare and development" of Asia, while providing measured assistance to supplement self-help and such collective measures as might be taken within the region. The United States "should scrutinize closely the development of threats from Communist aggression, direct or indirect, and be prepared to help within our means to meet such threats by providing political, economic, and military assistance and advice where clearly needed to supplement the resistance of other governments in and out of the area which are more directly concerned."

Regional organization was a desirable means of achieving common ends, but the American approach, the NSC concluded, would have to be cautious. It would be counterproductive for the United States to appear to be taking the lead, and the negative views of countries such as India had to be taken into account. However, the United States should regard Asian initiatives in this direction sympathetically and "be prepared, if invited, to assist such associations to fulfill their purposes under conditions which would be to our interest."

Particularly in order to maintain the western orientation of the new Asian states, the European countries should be encouraged to provide assistance also and to resolve any remaining colonial-nationalist conflict. The United States should continue to influence resolution of the colonial-nationalist conflict so as to satisfy the fundamental nationalist demands while minimizing the strain on the colonial powers, America's western Allies. The Indochina dilemma did not escape notice. "Particular attention should be given to the problem of French Indochina and action should be taken to bring home to the French the urgency of removing the barriers to the obtaining by Bao Dai or other non-Communist nationalist leaders of the support of a substantial proportion of the Vietnamese."

Thus, by early in 1950, there was a new and more active American approach to the problems of Southeast Asia. The Communists' effort to capture national revolutions elsewhere in Asia, as they had captured the national revolution in China, was seen as the area's principal problem. It was anticipated that Communist control of China would strengthen this effort, but that its direction would continue to come from Moscow which would utilize and support Asian Communist movements in pursuit of its own expansionist goals. It was important for the United States to preserve access to Southeast Asia's resources and lines of communication and prevent them from falling under the control of the Communist enemy. It was important, in addition, to support the emerging states in their pursuit of objectives that were also part of the American tradition. There was concern too that further Communist victories would have unfavorable effects elsewhere, psychological ones, especially in other underdeveloped areas of the world, and material ones as well, since Communist control of Asian resources and markets would increase the economic dependence of its European Allies on the United States and adversely affect prospects for speeding Japan's economic recovery through trade with Southeast Asia. At least for the time being, the principal Communist threat was likely to be subversive not military. But, since the new states were weak in so many ways, a subversive threat from externally supported Communists could be a potent one. The new states must, therefore, receive outside assistance, but self-help, including joint efforts to strengthen economic, political, and social institutions, must be the main reliance, since outside assistance could only be limited and would be most useful to the extent that it helped the recipients to help themselves. Moreover, military strength should not be emphasized nor expectations of military alliance encouraged.

Judging by John Foster Dulles' *War or Peace*, published in the same period, the Republican mainstream saw the problem in much the same way. Dulles, who was appointed advisor to the Secretary of State in April 1950, had discovered in Stalin's massive tome of 1924, *The Problems of Leninism*, a sentence, "The road to victory of the revolution in the West lies through the revolutionary alliance with the liberation movement of the colonies and dependent countries," which he believed to be the unshatterable keystone of Soviet policy in Asia, one that explained otherwise mysterious events. Belief in this principle, he said, has led "Soviet Communism" to "vast expenditure in terms of money and of top political thinking. When Mr. Molotov retired as Minister of Foreign Affairs on March 4, 1949, he apparently did so because the Politburo felt that he should devote his entire time to working out the Soviet Communist program for revolution in Asia, a task so important that it deserved the concentrated attention of the best international brains that the Soviet government could command." The new nations, he argued, their governments inexperienced in operating free political institutions and not yet able to ensure economic well-being, were particularly vulnerable to indirect aggression with those in Asia historically open to Chinese influence. The West in response cannot seek to perpetuate the *status quo*. "Any policies regarding Asia and the Pacific must be a logical development of the policy of peaceful evolution to national independence. . . . We should give help where we can and where it is wanted, but we must not seek to impose it under unwelcome conditions."[29]

The British View

Its interest and engagement much less than America's, Britain reacted with much less intensity to events in China. While the United States saw itself as having fought against Japan to preserve the independence of China, Britain saw itself as having fought primarily to defend India and recover Burma and Malaya. After the war, as the United States became even more heavily engaged in China and in

29. John Foster Dulles, *War or Peace*, pp. 76, 228.

Japan also, Britain, except for its position in Hong Kong and its commercial interests, became less so. Britain, to be sure, was concerned over the prospects of further trouble—steps were taken to strengthen Hong Kong's military defenses—and the possibility of intensified Communist activity elsewhere in Asia was not overlooked. But, while conceding the possibility, the British, unlike the Americans, did not accept the certainty.

London's interest in South and Southeast Asia did not disappear because India, Pakistan, Ceylon, and Burma had achieved independence and Malaya would do so when internal order had been restored. Old habits of responsibility persisted; the area's waters were still largely dominated by the British navy; and, most important of all, Britain, having given up much of its Empire, now had a tremendous political and psychological stake in the Commonwealth's success. In the councils of a multiracial Commonwealth, Asia had an important voice, and no Asian voice was more important than India's.

As far as China itself was concerned, it was Britain's inclination, strongly reinforced by India's views, to accept the Communist victory as a fact of life and recognize the new regime, hoping that if the PRC were accorded a normal place in the international community—including admission to the United Nations—this might both moderate its policies and encourage trends toward Titoism. That American attitudes should be so different, the British found regrettable but not decisive. Meanwhile, even though differences over China, and Britain's desire to coordinate its Asian policies with India's, made for Anglo-American frictions, the British welcomed the greater American interest in Southeast Asia and shared the view that technical and economic assistance would contribute to stability and reduce Communism's appeal.[30]

Aid: Winning Hearts and Minds

Experience in Europe had already suggested that economic recovery, political stabilization, and rejection of communism were closely linked. It seemed reasonable enough to assume that the same would

30. Herbert Nicholas, *Britain and the U.S.A.*, p. 96; G. F. Hudson, "Will Britain and America Split in Asia?" *Foreign Affairs*, XXXI (July, 1953), pp. 541–546; H. L. Roberts and P. A. Wilson, *Britain and the United States*, pp. 209–210; Halpern, pp. 13–18; Chatham House Study Group, *Collective Defence in Southeast Asia*, pp. 16–17.

hold true in Southeast Asia. Moreover, it was not only westerners who saw a connection between economic difficulties and susceptibility to communism. In April 1949, the Indian Ambassador to the doomed Chinese Republic, reflecting on the Communist advance "thought the time had come to formulate a policy which would strengthen the economic, social, and political structure of the area. . . . Without immediate and adequate help in the economic field, the political structure of South-East Asia would provide no more than a frail barrier to the expansion of Communism."[31]

There could be no doubt that Southeast Asia was in grave economic difficulties. Production and exports were much below prewar levels with consequent reductions in foreign-exchange earnings. Governments, deprived of revenues normally earned from taxes on international trade and forced by insurgent threats to spend abnormal sums on peace and order, were unable to support public services at former levels, much less invest in development. Nor was public or private investment—greatly curtailed since World War II—sufficient even to maintain existing plantations, mines, irrigation works, and transportation and communication facilities. Throughout the area, inflationary pressures were strong, while attempts to curb them through price and currency controls, import licensing, and rationing encouraged corruption, smuggling, and black markets. Going beyond the immediately disruptive impact of war and revolution were basic structural problems fostered by European control, including an acute shortage of indigenous entrepreneurs, technicians, and administrators.[32]

The United States, with its vast resources, and Britain with its long experience and interest in the area, now had political as well as other reasons for offering assistance. The potential recipients, whether or not they shared western political assumptions, were equally aware of their need for help. In addition, their leaders were anxious for assistance to speed the national modernization that was equated with strength and prestige, to improve the lot of peasants and workers, to provide outlets for elite energies, and simply to help the leaders themselves to maintain their own positions and power.

The first move toward international action was the Colombo Plan,

31. K. M. Panikkar, *In Two Chinas*, p. 55.
32. Samuel P. Hayes, *The Beginning of American Aid to Southeast Asia*, pp. 25–32.

formulated in January 1950. The Plan represented the confluence of three streams of interest: British interest in the economic stabilization and development of the new members of the Commonwealth and the region in which they were located; Australia's similar interest, reinforced by proximity and by the desire to forge closer ties with its neighbors; and the interest of Asians in receiving badly needed assistance as partners rather than as clients. Experience with the Special Commission in Southeast Asia helped shape voluntary and cooperative patterns; the need to accommodate different points of view within the Commonwealth ensured that economic not political objectives would be stressed.

The Plan took its name from the Commonwealth Prime Ministers' Conference in Colombo. The first such meeting to be held in an Asian capital, it had as its major agenda item "the possibility of promoting economic development, raising living standards and ensuring political stability." Its position unaffected by the shift to a conservative government, Australia once again proposed a regional security arrangement, with Britain and the Asian members of the Commonwealth forming the nucleus. But the unenthusiastic response of the Asians, particularly the Indians, was quickly evident, and Australia thereupon substituted a plan for economic and technical cooperation. Ceylon too had come prepared with such a proposal, and it was decided to establish a Commonwealth Consultative Committee to receive proposals from donor and beneficiary governments, to negotiate with other possible participants, draw up a plan of development, and examine ways to coordinate with other international aid programs.[33]

At the committee meeting in Sydney in May and at a subsequent conference in London in September, the mechanisms were developed by which the Colombo Plan was thenceforth to operate.[34] The Plan itself, as published in a White Paper in November, was based on six-year programs submitted by each potential recipient and emphasized

33. Olver, *British Policy*, p. 7; L. P. Singh, *The Politics of Economic Cooperation in Asia*, pp. 175–178; Gordon Greenwood, "Australian Attitudes toward Pacific Problems," *Pacific Affairs*, XXIII (June, 1950), pp. 161, 171; Charles S. Blackton, "The Colombo Plan," *Far Eastern Survey*, XX (Feb. 7, 1951), p. 28.

34. Officially entitled The Colombo Plan for Cooperative Economic Development in South and South-East Asia.

development and improvement of agriculture, transportation, communications, housing, health, and education. It envisaged total costs of approximately $5 billion for the period July 1951 to July 1957, with a little less than half coming from domestic sources. Contributors such as Britain and Australia pledged specific sums to the Plan, but no central fund or allocation machinery was established; within the framework of the plan, assistance was to be provided under bilateral arrangements between donor and recipient. No elaborate structure was required: the Consultative Committee became a ministerial forum meeting annually to review progress and exchange views about common problems of growth and cooperation; representatives of member governments assigned to their national diplomatic establishments in Colombo met periodically as the Council for Technical Cooperation to make recommendations, assisted by the small staff of the Bureau for Technical Cooperation.

It was also decided at these early meetings to extend membership beyond the Commonwealth. In 1951, the original members—Australia, Canada, Ceylon, India, New Zealand, Pakistan, and the United Kingdom—were joined by the United States, which had announced its support for the Plan when it was first devised, and by Cambodia, Laos, and Vietnam. Burma and Nepal adhered in 1952, Indonesia in 1953, and Japan in 1954. Thailand and the Philippines also joined in 1954, largely in response to U.S. persuasion. Both countries, as important U.S. aid recipients, had seen little to gain from participation in the Plan, and Thailand, at least, was initially concerned that membership might result in some diminution of U.S. aid.[35]

The assistance provided through the Plan was small by comparison with aid provided under U.S. programs (the United States also provided by far the largest share of financial assistance made available through the Plan) and much of it was absorbed in South Asia. The Plan had other benefits, however. Because technical assistance played an important part, countries normally on the receiving end—Burma, Indonesia, Malaya, the Philippines, and Thailand—were able to be donors as well. Because of its membership and procedures, the Plan fostered a sense of equality, a feeling that Asians were in control of their own affairs. This confidence, in turn, lowered nationalist tempera-

35. Singh, pp. 183–184, 191–203; Blackton, pp. 28, 29; John D. Montgomery, *The Politics of Foreign Aid*, pp. 188–190.

tures. As one specialist has observed: "Criticisms and suggestions that were exchanged during the annual conferences usually offered greater challenges to national programs and operations than any government would have been willing to accept in bilateral discussions."[36] And because of its loose organization and loosely defined goals, the Plan's purposes could be interpreted to suit individual requirements. Neutralist countries could emphasize economic betterment as an end in itself. To the Australian taxpayer, Spender could justify expenditures under the Plan as the best defense against the "penetration of Communist imperialism" or, in the words of his successor, R. G. Casey, as a potent weapon in that "contest for the minds and hearts of the peoples of Asia that lies at the heart of the power conflict in Asia."[37]

While the Commonwealth countries had been occupied in devising the Colombo Plan, the United States was beginning to carry out the aid commitment made in Point IV of President Truman's inaugural address. American assistance in Southeast Asia was not wholly new, although only in the Philippines had such assistance been of any magnitude. But in the immediate postwar period, aid had been directed toward relieving suffering and repairing damage; now it was to be an active instrument of foreign policy, as it had earlier become in Europe.

Early in the year, Ambassador Jessup traveled throughout the area; in February in Bangkok he chaired a meeting at which American ambassadors in the Far East considered the impact of the Chinese Communist victory on U.S. policy. Not long thereafter the Department of State announced a mission to Southeast Asian capitals to study the technical assistance needs of the area and the ways in which the United States could be of help. The mission was headed by R. Allen Griffin, a California Republican, and a close friend of Senator William F. Knowland, one of the strongest congressional critics of administration policy and performance in Asia. Its activities were accorded an air of some urgency. The mission remained only briefly in each country and, at the conclusion of each visit, cabled its recommendations to Washington. It was felt to be important to demonstrate as quickly as possible that U.S. help was on the way; in addition, there was money immediately available in the form of over $75 million added by Congress

36. Montgomery, p. 190; Charles A. Fisher, p. 755.
37. Harper and Sissons, p. 138.

to the 1949 military-assistance legislation for use "in the general area of China."[38]

The mission's guidelines emphasized that prospective recipients should clearly understand that theirs was the principal responsibility, and that the United States did not contemplate a massive program on the scale of the Marshall Plan. Project, not commodity assistance, was to be emphasized. Proposals were to be judged not only by their economic value, but also by their contribution—as in the case of telecommunications, road, and transport projects—to defense and internal security. Quick-impact projects to demonstrate the strength of U.S. interest were also favored; if this strengthened the government in power, so much the better for enhanced political stability and defense capabilities. Following these guidelines, the mission recommended projects totaling $64,000,000, with more than a third by value in agriculture, roughly a quarter in industry, power, transportation, and communications, and another quarter in health and sanitation. Aid consisted primarily of equipment, technical advisers, and training in the United States. Approximately $23 million was recommended for economic aid to Indochina; something over $11 million each to Indonesia, Thailand, and Burma; and $5 million to Malaya. Of the reported $30 million recommended for military assistance, half was to go to Indochina, $10 million to Thailand, and $5 million to Indonesia.[39]

The United States recognized that the workings of local political and social systems could reduce the impact of its assistance. But in most of Southeast Asia, it was not prepared to go beyond establishing minimum accountability standards, nor would an effort on its part to do so have been acceptable to the recipients. In the Philippines, however, the United States felt justified in accompanying its aid with demands for reform. Because it had been an American colony, the failures of an independent Philippines were bound to reflect unfavorably upon past American policies. And, the persistence of habits derived from the colonial relationship made it seem more natural to Americans to accompany assistance with more than minimum requirements con-

38. Hayes, pp. 5, 25–26, 43; Wolf, *Foreign Aid,* pp. 27, 53; Edwin F. Stanton, *Brief Authority,* pp. 234–235.

39. Hayes, pp. 35–36; Lawrence S. Finkelstein, "U.S. at Impasse in Southeast Asia," *Far Eastern Survey,* XIX (Sept. 27, 1950), p. 170.

cerning its use, and more natural to Filipinos to accept them, even if
somewhat resentfully. The size of aid allocations to the Philippines also
made the United States more demanding; in his National Press Club
speech in January 1950, Secretary Acheson totaled U.S. aid and
benefits to the Philippines since the end of the war at $2 billion, and
felt free to say that "much of it has not been used as wisely as we
wish."[40] Moreover, continued Filipino inability to cope with acute economic difficulties, by stimulating social disorder and increasing the
appeal of the Huk insurgency, could threaten U.S. air and naval bases
and hence affect American security more directly than similar developments in other Southeast Asian countries.

By the time the Griffin Mission was established, it had already been
decided to send a separate mission to the Philippines. Quirino, in discussions in mid-February with Truman, had anticipated a bilateral
group and had even named Philippine representatives but, in due
course, he accepted an entirely American mission chaired by former
Under Secretary of the Treasury David Bell.

The Bell Mission arrived in Manila in July. Its report, released in
October, when the American sense of urgency had been much intensified by the Korean War, analyzed Philippine problems and proposed
remedial action. Since independence, the Mission pointed out, production had been to a considerable degree restored, but population growth
had kept it below prewar per capita levels. Moreover, little had been
done to increase efficiency and diversify industrial production or to
open new lands, improve methods of cultivation, or provide better
conditions for farm workers or tenants. The latter indeed were caught
between two grindstones: low land productivity and landlords who
exacted an unfair share of the crop. Income inequalities, always great,
were found to have become greater: profits earned by businessmen
and large landowners had been exceptionally high, real income had
been transferred from the poor to the rich because of high prices, and
living standards for most people had not yet regained even prewar
levels. The mounting public deficit resulted from lack of forceful
government policy; tax rates and tax collection were wholly inadequate.

The Mission proposed a five-year development program to be sup-

40. *DSB,* Jan. 23, 1950, p. 117.

ported by $250 million in U.S. loans and grants over which the United
States would retain control. The Philippines was to close loopholes in a
tax system that collected only about 25 percent of the revenues due
and tax all imports except basic foods; ensure honesty and efficiency
in government operations; improve education, housing, and health
services; establish minimum wages in agriculture and industry; and
permit the formation of free trade unions.

The report was received with mixed feelings. The commitment to
substantial U.S. assistance was welcome, the accuracy of its analysis
was widely recognized, the reforms it proposed were applauded in
many quarters, and U.S. supervision was widely felt to be advisable
and helpful. On the other hand, charges of corruption met with the
resentful rejoinder that Filipinos had merely learned to follow in
American footsteps, and Americans were reminded that the problems
the Bell Mission had enumerated were in many respects the consequence of a not yet completely abandoned colonial system. The
general reaction, however, was far more affirmative than otherwise. In
November a memorandum of understanding was signed between the
two governments and, by the spring of 1951, most of the necessary
administrative machinery and legislation was in existence.[41]

41. Meyer, pp. 91–95; George Taylor, pp. 138–141; Shirley Jenkins, "Philippine White Paper," *Far Eastern Survey*, XX (Jan. 10, 1951), pp. 2–4; Jenkins,
American Economic Policy, pp. 158–159.

CHAPTER 5

THE KOREAN WAR

The proximity of the Korean War and the various and intertwined questions it raised—the Cold War, the status of Communist China, the United Nations and collective security, the rights of small states—made policy decisions difficult for Southeast Asian states, especially after the PRC entered the war in force. Members of the United Nations, however, were inescapably confronted by the need to make decisions. Burma and Indonesia had to reconcile their support for UN defense of South Korea with their neutrality and their desire to avoid an anti-Communist stance: they found their closest partners in the Arab-Asian bloc led by India. The Philippines, like Thailand, normally voted with the United States. Wanting as well to identify itself with the Arab-Asian bloc, it could not do so consistently, since the views of this bloc and those of the United States were sometimes in sharp conflict. Issues involving Communist China also caused some problems for Australia and New Zealand.

The United States was led by the war to look upon Southeast Asia with an even greater sense of urgency, further heightened by Communist China's entry into the hostilities in October. Two decisions made simultaneously with the decision to assist South Korea related directly to Southeast Asia. Because it seemed possible that the North Korean attack would be followed by Communist thrusts elsewhere, U.S. bases in the Philippines were reinforced. It was also decided to provide more assistance to the French in Indochina. Aid in Indochina —reaching almost $7 billion by 1954—would help contain Southeast Asia's most serious Communist threat, while at the same time releasing French resources for Europe, a defense which was also being strengthened in the wake of the war in Korea.

Other American decisions in the war's train also affected Southeast

Asia, although less directly. Heightened concern over the Asian power vacuum sped moves to restore Japan's sovereignty, ensure its economic recovery, and encourage it to assume responsibility for its own defense. This in turn necessitated formal security arrangements with the Philippines, Australia, and New Zealand, all still fearful that a strong Japan would revert to militarism and expansionism. Finally, the decision to support and protect the Republic of China in its refuge on Taiwan gave Asian neutralism a local point of conflict with U.S. policy and introduced new differences over Asian policy between the United States and some of its Allies.

The expanded role in Indochina notwithstanding, the Truman administration continued to believe that American action in mainland Southeast Asia, Malaya, and Indonesia should be limited and supportive. Action in time of peace was intended to help correct the weaknesses that made the area vulnerable to internal and external threats. Since U.S. forces could not be committed there, Southeast Asia's loss in time of war would have to be anticipated, but this loss, bringing with it an increased threat to vital American offshore defenses, could at least be delayed by improving local military capabilities. Aid for economic development continued, but more stress was placed on economic development as a way to strengthen resistance to Communism, and military assistance became a much larger component of the total aid package. Indochina increasingly became an exception to a policy dictated by still-limited interest; the American posture remained supportive in principle rather than interventionist, but support was increasingly substantial.

The early years of the Eisenhower administration produced heightened rhetoric but little real change in the pattern of involvement and interest. Secretary of State John Foster Dulles set the rhetorical tone in his report on the First Ninety Days: "A new order of priority and urgency has been given to the Far East. Further, it has been made clear that we consider that our Eastern friends, from Japan, Korea, and Formosa to Indochina and Malaya, face a single hostile front, to be met with a common purpose and growing cooperation as between the component parts of freedom."[1] Nevertheless, until 1955, the United States made no defense commitments to mainland Southeast Asia, and

1. *DSB,* April 27, 1953, p. 605.

those to its offshore Allies—Australia, New Zealand, and the Philippines—were no more than had been required by the Truman administration effort in 1951 to gain acceptance of American plans for Japan.

Local Roles and Reactions

All of the Southeast Asian countries, except Indonesia, supported the two initial Security Council resolutions, that of June 25, declaring a breach of the peace and demanding a cease-fire and North Korean withdrawal behind the thirty-eighth parallel, and that of June 27, calling upon UN members to assist the Republic of Korea in repelling the attack and restoring international peace. To the smaller Asian countries, the invasion of South Korea was a reminder of vulnerability, the UN response a reassuring demonstration of the efficacy of collective security. Speaking in the Philippine Senate, Carlos Romulo, President of the 1950–1951 General Assembly, declared: "What has happened in Korea can happen here. What we do to help the United Nations effort in Korea is the first premium we pay on the insurance we now must take against the risk of aggression and the threat of force by an implacable enemy."[2] U Nu declared that events in Korea had dispelled his doubts over whether the UN would avoid the League of Nations' fate and would succeed in performing its most important function, for "as soon as aggression started in South Korea, the United Nations went to its assistance. This has set up a noble precedent."[3]

Somewhat different doubts were resolved in Thailand. Before the war, considerable opposition to accepting military aid from the West had been based on fear that Communist nations would retaliate and that the West would not provide protection. The Korean experience, confirming both the existence of a threat and international support for resistance, ended significant opposition to western military assistance.[4]

The Australian government agreed with the American in seeing North Korea's action as quite possibly presaging similar Communist action elsewhere, especially in Southeast Asia. Every Australian, said Menzies, should regard Korea as his own business, not as some remote frontier incident. The invasion, the government argued, was not intended only to conquer South Korea for Communism, but also to weaken and demoralize Southeast Asia; to forestall aggression there, it

2. Meyer, p. 130.
3. Tinker, p. 344.
4. Nuechterlein, p. 108.

must be countered in Korea. With quickly available forces in Japan, Australia was the first to supply assistance to South Korea, but other countries of the area soon followed. Australia's contribution included an air-force squadron, naval vessels, and ground forces; New Zealand and Thailand contributed naval vessels and ground troops; the Philippines—although initially President Quirino and others opposed military participation—provided tanks and ground troops. All of these countries also contributed foodstuffs (as did Burma) and medicine.[5]

Indonesia, not having become a member of the United Nations until September 1950, had not formally accepted the Republic of Korea as a lawful government, a step Burma took when it voted for the UN resolution to this effect in December 1948. Indonesia, moreover, having viewed UN action against the Dutch with great dissatisfaction, was somewhat cynical about the UN as protector of the weak against the strong. Initially it seemed to place Korea wholly in the Cold War context. "North Korea," its official statement declared, "is under Russian protection and the South Korean Republic is sponsored by the United States. Thus, the so-called civil war in Korea is first and foremost [a] matter concerning the two big powers in the 'cold war' viz, the Russians on one side and American and Britain on the other." Calling it premature to take a position on an issue likely to become "a second Spain," Indonesia pointed to its preoccupation with grave internal problems.[6]

When UN membership put the issues inescapably before it, Indonesia, like Burma, tended to support efforts to maintain or strengthen UN machinery against Soviet bloc assaults, while also favoring North Korean and Chinese Communist participation in discussions and conferences under UN auspices. Thus, both countries voted against the Soviet proposal to disband the United Nations Commission for Korea and in favor of the resolution creating the United Nations Commission for the Unification and Rehabilitation of Korea (of which Australia, the Philippines, and Thailand were members), which also reaffirmed the status of the Republic of Korea as a legal government.[7]

5. Albinski, *Australia's Search for Security,* p. 255; *UN Yearbook,* 1950, p. 226; Meyer, pp. 129, 130.

6. Justus M. Van der Kroef, "Indonesia and the West," *Far Eastern Survey,* XX (Feb. 22, 1951), p. 40; Holland, pp. 175–176.

7. Justus M. Van der Kroef, *Indonesia in the Modern World,* II, 360; Isabelle Crocker, *Burma's Foreign Policy and the Korean War,* pp. 6, 56.

In November Communist China's entry into the war in force introduced new issues. Even before then, the Chinese problem had arisen in connection with the American decision on June 27 to interpose the Seventh Fleet between the Chinese mainland and Taiwan. This appeared to many UN members an unwise, possibly dangerous intervention and, since it was justified in terms of a situation already under UN jurisdiction, a move that should not have been made without wider consultation. MacArthur's northward advance in Korea and the PRC's entry into the hostilities brought the Chinese issue inescapably to the fore. By the last months of 1950 and the first months of 1951 the military threat was so grave that General MacArthur urged blockading and bombing China and using Nationalist forces against the mainland. Meanwhile, the UN was deeply occupied in an effort to cope politically with the consequences of Chinese intervention. The United States was determined that the UN should find Peking guilty of aggression. Opposing forces, of which India was the spokesman, urged the path of conciliation, no matter how long, tortuous, and frustrating it might seem.

In essence, India and the Arab-Asian bloc[8] believed that the Chinese Communist intervention, unlike the North Korean invasion, could not be dealt with as a simple act of aggression. Instead, it had to be considered in the light of General MacArthur's drive northward to the Yalu, a course regarded by this group as one that rashly ignored Peking's warnings and went considerably beyond what the General Assembly had in mind on October 7 in endorsing "all appropriate steps necessary to ensure conditions of stability throughout Korea." India and the Arab-Asian bloc were anxious to avoid steps likely to freeze the Chinese in an uncompromising position, and believed that the Korean problem might be easier to resolve in the context of a general Far Eastern settlement, one dealing also with the status of Taiwan and with Chinese United Nations representation. They tended always to read hopeful signs in Chinese responses, while the United States and its supporters saw in these same responses only that Peking, stiffened by military success, remained obdurate in rejecting UN

8. The Arab/Asian bloc at this time consisted of Afghanistan, Burma, Egypt, India, Indonesia, Iraq, Lebanon, Pakistan, Saudi Arabia, Syria, and Yemen. It was a bloc in the sense that the countries consulted together and jointly sponsored resolutions, not in the voting sense.

authority and required that Communist demands be satisfied before negotiations could even begin.

The Burmese representative, James Barrington, touched upon all of these issues during the debate on the U.S. January 1951 proposal to condemn Chinese Communist aggression. Barrington criticized the resolution for oversimplifying the issues which, he said, went far beyond determining whether or not Communist China had committed an act of aggression. Earlier resolutions seeking an honorable settlement of all issues in the Far East, he argued, had won the support of at least fifty delegations who had favored negotiations encompassing the Taiwan and Chinese representation issues without requiring any pre-liminary condemnation of Communist China. Peking, he contended, had recently indicated its willingness to enter into discussions; why, then, was it necessary to brand it as an aggressor? The U.S. resolution, according to its sponsors, left the door open to negotiations, but a condemned government was hardly likely to cooperate with those condemning it. Moreover, the resolution would not serve the principle of collective security which would require that condemnation be followed by sanctions. It was clear, he said, both from the text of the resolution and the debate that there was no real thought of sanctions: "The tendency to pass a moral judgment offered little comfort, par-ticularly to small nations which had put their faith and their hopes in the system of collective security."[9]

Indonesia's representative, L. N. Palar, likewise sensed some soften-ing of the Chinese Communist position. Any move to condemn Peking "in the present delicate position," he feared, "would only add to the difficulties confronting the Committee in its labourious efforts to maintain peace and might even jeopardize these efforts altogether." On Korea, and on other Far Eastern problems as well, Palar argued, the major powers are on opposite sides of an extremely dangerous dividing line; the objective of the UN must therefore be to bring about negotiations directed toward eliminating that dividing line.[10]

Australia and New Zealand were also uneasy over the possible con-sequences of condemning Peking. Australia's representative, K. C. O. Shann, seeing new problems raised by Chinese intervention, urged

9. *General Assembly Official Record* (GAOR), First Committee, Jan. 29, 1951, p. 578.

10. *Ibid.*, Jan. 20, 1951, p. 521; Jan. 27, 1951, p. 523.

that these be carefully weighed to ensure that any new UN decision be as widely supported as the decision to repel North Korean aggression. Even the slightest possibility of obtaining a cease-fire and an honorable settlement should not be overlooked. Later, after the U.S. resolution had been introduced, Shann agreed that negotiations were not possible as long as Peking rejected a cease-fire before negotiations and insisted that its own views be accepted before negotiations could even begin. Nevertheless, he argued for delaying the vote rather than assuming that Peking's reply ruled out all possibility of honorable negotiations in future.[11]

However, unlike Burma, which voted with India against the U.S. resolution, and Indonesia, which abstained, Australia voted affirmatively. It had its doubts, but it was much more sympathetic with the American position than were the Asian neutralists, while Australian public opinion was as exercised over the Communist issue as American. Moreover, with both houses of the U.S. Congress having recently passed resolutions demanding China's condemnation, and with John Foster Dulles' imminent arrival in Australia to negotiate the long-sought treaty of alliance, the moment was not propitious for public differences with the United States on so sensitive a subject. But Australia's vote for the U.S. resolution was not cast without some doubts. While the UN had to face up to the situation in Korea and must not permit aggressors to profit, Australia still wanted to explore all possibilities for peaceful settlement and believed that the UN should proceed with the greatest caution with respect to sanctions.[12]

Sir Carl Berendsen of New Zealand, while describing Communist China as guilty of an aggression far greater than North Korea's, was as cautious as the Australian representative on sanctions. The United Nations, he said, should not embark upon action likely to have unforeseen results; it should not impose obligations some members would not accept, or adopt courses attractive on paper but ineffective in action. Most especially, any implication that, at this point, the United Nations was committed to any form of action was to be avoided, and more cautious instructions should be given to the Additional Measures

11. *Ibid.*, Jan. 11, 1951, p. 484; Jan. 18, 1951, p. 504.

12. *Ibid.*, Jan. 24, 1951, pp. 539–541; Albinski, *Australia's Policies and Attitudes toward China*, pp. 93–95; Reese, p. 159; Gordon Greenwood and Norman Harper, *Australia in World Affairs, 1950–1955*, p. 210.

Committee, set up to consider what actions should be taken pursuant to the resolution condemning Communist China.[13]

The decision to co-opt the members of the Collective Measures Committee (set up by the General Assembly under the Uniting for Peace Resolution of November 1950) for the Additional Measures Committee caused problems for Burma. Although, unlike Indonesia, it supported maintenance of the Collective Measures Committee in the face of strong Soviet opposition, Burma was unwilling to allow its membership to involve it in an anti-Chinese stance. Thus (like Yugoslavia) it announced that it would be unable to serve on the Additional Measures Committee, citing its preoccupation with domestic difficulties.[14]

If Manila and Bangkok felt any doubts over UN action against China, their reluctance was not expressed in the debates. In Thailand, to be sure, Chinese Communist military successes had been one of the factors contributing to the dissatisfaction with Phibun's policies which ultimately erupted in the navy coup attempt of June 1951. But, in the UN, Prince Wan Waithayakon of Thailand was a firm supporter of the U.S. resolution, as was the more vocal Romulo who particularly stressed the importance of avoiding any form of appeasement. Although, in the first instance, prepared to join members of the Arab-Asian group in seeking a peaceful solution, the Philippines did not share the view of other members of this group that Chinese responses offered any hope of a favorable outcome.[15]

The May 1951 resolution, requiring UN members to embargo the sale of strategic goods to China, caused far less debate. Burma abstained, regarding the embargo as merely making an already difficult situation even more so. In reporting its compliance with the resolution, it pointed out that in 1950 Burma had sold to Communist China an insignificant fraction of its total exports, and, of this, nothing had been on the prohibited list. The Indonesian representative, who also abstained, warned of possibly unfavorable effects on his country's economic welfare, which he said, could not be sacrificed to the policies

13. *GAOR,* Jan. 25, 1951, pp. 548, 599.

14. Frank Trager, Patricia Wolgemuth, and Lu-yu Kiang, *Burma's Role in the U.N.,* pp. 3, 7; Crocker, pp. 30, 34.

15. *GAOR,* Jan. 18, 1951, pp. 506–507; Jan. 22, 1951, pp. 530–531; Nuechterlein, p. 109.

of the western world. His statement reflected the downward shift in prices that began in mid-1951 after a period of great demand had produced a very favorable market for rubber and other primary products. Nevertheless, officially Indonesia observed the embargo, although there was almost certainly some illegal trade.[16]

Australia, while voting for the embargo, again warned against more rigorous sanctions. Speaking in parliament in July, R. G. Casey declared, "It is not our objective to threaten Communist China or legitimate Chinese interests, nor is it our objective to extend the conflict beyond Korea. . . . Proposals for the blockade of the Chinese mainland or for the bombing of Manchuria . . . must be judged in the light of the possibility of so extending the war. If war is to be extended beyond Korea, the responsibility for doing so should not rest with us."[17]

American Interest Confirmed

The importance of Southeast Asia, and the prospect that it might again come under enemy control, were reconsidered in a policy paper approved by President Truman on May 17, 1951.[18] "The demonstrated military capacity of the North Korean and Chinese armies," it was said, "requires a reevaluation of the threat to the free world which the masses of Asia would constitute if they fell under Soviet Communist domination." As in 1949, the importance of the Asian mainland as a source of critical resources and a communications crossroad was stressed. The impact elsewhere of its loss was seen in heightened terms: it would have "disastrous moral and psychological effects in border areas such as the Middle East and a critical effect in Western Europe"; the USSR would be able to concentrate its offensive power in Europe; and the United States would be denied the most direct air and sea routes to India and between Australia and the Middle East.

The Soviet threat continued to be regarded as the central one in the Far East, now itself the area "of most immediate overt threats to U.S. security." Moscow was believed to be seeking to bring the Asian main-

16. Trager, Wolgemuth, and Lu, p. 7; Stannard, pp. 28–35; Van der Kroef, *Indonesia in the Modern World*, II, 359.

17. Albinski, *Australian Policies and Attitudes toward China*, p. 81.

18. NSC 58/5; text in *Pentagon Papers*, VIII, 425 ff.

land and eventually Japan and the other principal offshore territories under its control, primarily through exploiting Chinese Communist resources. Accordingly it should be a principal objective of U.S. policy to detach China from its Soviet alliance. Meanwhile, with Chinese Communist military capabilities taken much more seriously than they had been before November 1950, the possibility of Chinese Communist conquest of Indochina, Thailand, and Burma was not excluded, and it was believed that this would seriously threaten critical United States security interests.

Nevertheless, although the United States had been impelled into military action on the Asian continent in order to deny Korea to the Communists, a similar change in stance was not envisaged for mainland Southeast Asia. Instead, it was believed that the United States should continue its efforts to strengthen indigenous willingness and ability to resist. Within the limits set by local ability to absorb and use aid effectively, support programs should be aimed at enabling the recipients to use their resources effectively and to free-world advantage, to develop sound economies and adequate military establishments, and to resist subversion or aggression.

A year later, an NSC paper, approved on June 25, 1952, reflected considerable perplexity over courses of action in the event of overt Chinese Communist aggression in Southeast Asia.[19] Effective defense would require coordinated political and military measures, but this was not regarded as likely among countries divided among themselves and having little in common. Outside countries could not be expected to participate in the defense of the area except for "some support and token participation at least from the United Kingdom and other Commonwealth countries." Inaction would "permit the communists to obtain, at little or no cost, a victory of major world consequence." But to use American forces against the Chinese would risk Soviet intervention and general hostilities in the Far East, involve the United States in another peripheral action detracting from its global war capabilities, and arouse public opposition to "another Korea." Accordingly, in the event of overt Chinese aggression, the United States should act on the sea and in the air only, and its action should be directed toward interdicting Chinese Communist lines of communication. Thereafter, if

19. NSC 125/2; text in *Pentagon Papers*, VIII, 520 ff.

necessary, action should be taken against all suitable Chinese Communist targets not too close to the USSR. But all of these actions, and others recommended for consideration including a blockade, were to be taken only if the British and French participated at least on a token basis; failing this the United States should *consider* unilateral action.

The NSC was well aware that Britain and France were unsympathetic to action along these lines. In earlier joint discussions, the British and French Chiefs of Staff had opposed any action against the Chinese Communists, except in the area of or along the approaches to land battles. They had been unmoved by American arguments that such wholly defensive action would be indecisive at best and would merely prolong hostilities without improving prospects for ultimate success.[20] In October, joint staff talks in Washington brought greater agreement, but were more diagnostic than remedial. It was agreed that military action in the area of aggression only would probably not cause the Chinese to desist, nor would a complete sea blockade be effective; a combination of coercive measures, including air attacks on lines of communication and all suitable targets would be the best course. But the British contended that air and naval action would be ineffective and beyond Allied capabilities; the French were interested only in Tonkin; and neither agreed even that a blockade should be included among the minimum courses of action.[21]

Although the war stimulated increased emphasis on military assistance, the United States did not abandon its conviction that aid for economic development would contribute significantly to political stability and hence strengthen resistance to Communism. This thesis was reiterated in two influential advisory reports to the President, the Gray Report of 1950 and the Rockefeller Report of 1952. The Gray Report, while giving primacy to rearmament in Western Europe, emphasized that in underdeveloped areas the contrast between the aspirations of the people and their unrelieved poverty "makes them susceptible to domestic unrest and provides fertile ground for the growth of Communist movements."[22] Similarly, Dean Acheson, testifying before the Senate in 1951, declared, "Poverty, disease, illiteracy,

20. *Pentagon Papers,* VIII, 488–489.
21. *Ibid.,* IX, 115–116.
22. Wolf, *Foreign Aid,* p. 112.

and resentments against former colonial exploitations are our enemies.
. . . They represent turbulent forces which the Communist exploits at
every opportunity . . . we must assure that the forces of nationalism
and of the drive for economic improvement are associated with the
rest of the free world instead of with Communism."[23]

Even so, military assistance, already provided in limited amounts to
some Southeast Asian countries, was increased, and the security aspects of
economic assistance were stressed—weak economies were to be relieved
of some of the burdens of the national defense effort, and the morale of
governments resisting Communism was to be strengthened. Ten days
after the North Korean invasion, a State-Defense Economic Cooperation Administration (ECA) mission, chaired by John Melby of the State
Department, departed for Southeast Asia to determine how military
preparedness could be strengthened, to recommend priorities for arms
shipments, and to discuss the composition of American military advisory groups. The Melby Mission spent three months in Indochina,
the Philippines, Thailand, Indonesia, and Malaya, and, like the
Griffin Mission before it, made its recommendations in an atmosphere
of some urgency.[24] Its findings played an important role in the expansion of military assistance in Southeast Asia, nowhere more graphically
illustrated than in the contrast between the appropriations for military
assistance in the original and in the supplementary legislation of 1950.
The original legislation, for which recommendations were prepared
before the outbreak of the war, appropriated $16 million for Korea
and the Philippines; the supplementary request, submitted in August
1950 and passed in full, appropriated $303 million for "the Republic
of the Philippines and other nations in southern and eastern Asia."
Moreover, in subsequent years, as Congress began to look with less
favor on aid appropriations, cuts in administration-proposed military
assistance budgets were proportionately lower than cuts in economic
assistance. In Southeast Asia, overall programs for military-assistance
recipients—Indochina, Thailand, and the Philippines—were reduced
less than programs for Burma and Indonesia. When Eisenhower took

23. *Ibid.,* p. 118.
24. John Kerry King, *Southeast Asia in Perspective,* p. 134. Plans to visit
Burma were cancelled at Rangoon's request; in Indonesia, in deference to the
wishes of the government, the visit was described as unofficial.

office, his potentially conflicting commitments to smaller budget deficits and to a more active Asian policy were reconciled by emphasizing that increased military assistance reduced more expensive requirements for U.S. troops abroad, while aid was cut proportionately less in Asia than elsewhere. In 1954, the Asian share of U.S. aid under the Mutual Security Act rose impressively, from 12.6 percent of the total in 1953 to 54.5 percent. These funds, however, were overwhelmingly concentrated in Korea and Taiwan, and in Indochina. In 1954, for example, $164.6 million was provided for economic and technical assistance for South and Southeast Asia (with India by far the largest recipient); in the same year, U.S. aid to Indochina amounted to $687.6 million.[25]

Legislative language emphasized the defense responsibilities of aid recipients. The objectives of the Mutual Security Act of 1951 and the Act for International Development were defined as: "to maintain the security and to promote the foreign policy of the United States by authorizing military, economic, and technical assistance to friendly countries and to strengthen the military security and individual and collective defenses of the free world, to develop their resources in the interest of the United States, and to facilitate the effective participation of these countries in the United Nations system for collective security." Under the Mutual Security Act, a state receiving military as well as economic and technical assistance was required by article 511a to undertake, among other commitments, to "make a full contribution, consistent with its political and economic capacity, its population, national resources, facilities, and general economic situation, to the development and maintenance of its own defenses and to the defensive strength of the free world." A recipient of technical and economic assistance only was required by article 511b to commit itself "to cooperate in the furthering of international understanding and good will and the promotion of world security, and to take steps as agreed upon for the abolition of international tensions."[26]

Article 511b, applicable to Burma as a recipient of technical and economic assistance, was most carefully scrutinized in Rangoon for consistency with the government's neutral posture. Problems were resolved, however, when it was agreed by both countries that Burma

25. Wolf, *Foreign Aid,* pp. 99, 100, 145, 160; Darling, pp. 97–98.
26. King, p. 156; Herbert Feith, *The Decline of Constitutional Democracy in Indonesia,* p. 199.

would agree to cooperate "within the framework of the United Nations Charter."[27]

The 1951 legislation caused graver difficulties in Indonesia, becoming one of the many factors involved in the fall of the Sukiman cabinet in February 1952. In 1951, in an agreement little publicized by either side, the United States had provided equipment and training sufficient for two mobile police brigades. Accordingly, the question arose whether Indonesia was receiving military assistance and would therefore be required to commit itself under article 511a; regarding this as the case, Ambassador Merle Cochran and Foreign Minister Subardjo early in January exchanged letters in which Indonesia accepted a somewhat modified version of article 511a. When these letters were made public in February, it became known that Subardjo had not discussed the matter with his cabinet colleagues before or even after signing. In consequence, accusations of secret diplomacy were joined with charges that the agreement violated Indonesia's independent foreign policy. After several weeks of debate and proposals to the United States for further changes, the cabinet passed a motion disapproving of Subardjo's handling of the matter. His resignation was followed almost immediately by that of the cabinet which, in addition to its difficulties with the requirements of the Mutual Security Act, had been beset by differences among its constituent parties over a number of important issues, by the dissatisfaction of army leaders with their role in government, and by heightened internal security problems. In resigning, however, the cabinet declared that its action should not be construed as meaning that Indonesia would shirk obligations arising from an agreement with another country. In May 1952, the Wilopo government, which had assumed office in April, decided that it would accept aid from the United States on the basis of article 511b and under conditions similar to those in Burma.[28]

Peace with Japan and New Security Arrangements

Well before the Korean War, the United States had altered its policies in Japan, hoping to reduce its own burdens by speeding Japanese economic recovery. The removal of Japanese assets to provide

27. Hayes, p. 213.
28. Feith, pp. 200–212; Stannard, pp. 47–50.

reparations payments was halted; restrictions on economic concentra-
tration were relaxed; and less favor was shown to trade unions.
Strategic considerations had also come into play: the United States'
position in Japan was regarded as forming part of its perimeter defense; the establishment of predominant Soviet influence there was
regarded as one of Moscow's major goals. Concern over the impact
that Communist control of the Korean peninsula might have upon
Japan's security and orientation was a major factor in the American
decision to support South Korea in force. And it began to seem increasingly urgent to ensure for the long term, not only Japan's economic
viability and friendship for the West, but also its ability to defend itself
and even make some contribution to the defense of the area.[29]

In its new policy toward Japan, the United States had to reckon
with the reluctance of friendly states in Southeast Asia to abandon
punitive concepts. Australia saw two dangers in the concept of strengthening Japan economically. Restoring Japan's economy would restore
its war-making potential; meanwhile, the more rapidly its economic
recovery proceeded, the sooner the nations of the Commonwealth would
have to fear Japan's competition in their foreign and domestic markets.
In addition, Australia's Labour Party regarded lenient treatment of the
zaibatsu and restrictions on trade unions as favoritism toward the Japanese right. This view became less influential when the conservatives
succeeded Labour in office, but the Menzies government was equally
skeptical over the extent to which reform had taken hold, and equally
concerned over the possibility of a resurgent, aggressive Japan. The
Korean War brought with it greater recognition of the desirability of
economic recovery and the development of a self-defense capability, but
it was still felt that Japan should be hedged about with safeguards and
restrictions.

Although conservative thinking was more receptive to the argument
that Japan must be kept out of the Soviet orbit, the Australian perspective differed from the American. Distance made the Soviet threat
appear more remote and, in any case, against this threat, Australians
had no doubt that the United States would protect them. Meanwhile,
it seemed not impossible that a revived Japan, blocked by Communist
power from expanding in north Asia, would find its natural outlet in

29. Frederick S. Dunn, *Peace-making and the Settlement with Japan*, pp.
125–128.

the South Pacific. To the argument that controls over its rearmament would drive Japan into the Soviet camp, they responded that Japan might well rearm in association with the West and then swing over into the Soviet camp. Or, as Spender argued, in the event of a world conflict, to rearm Japan might be a gamble for which Australia would have to pay, a gamble as to "whether Japan would believe that with her renewed military strength she could leave it to the Communist and non-Communist worlds to fight it out between themselves, so that she might reassert herself in the Pacific and in Asia in the exhaustion which such a world conflict would produce."[30]

Filipinos were equally skeptical about Japan's conversion to democracy and pacifism, and equally fearful of a strong, unfettered Japan. In addition, the reparations issue was a burning one in the Philippines, as in Burma and Indonesia. To them their very large claims to indemnification for wartime damages had obvious priority over Japanese economic recovery; to think otherwise was, in effect, once again to subordinate their interests to Japan's.[31]

When the United States decided to press forward on a peace treaty for Japan, it faced what Dean Acheson described as "two central puzzles . . . How could we care for the vital security needs of ourselves, our allies, and the Japanese, and by what method could we accomplish a treaty of conciliation? Any kind of consultative or deliberative peace-conference procedure would end in stalement or disaster. Russian intransigence in the Council of Foreign Ministers would tie up a Japanese treaty as hopelessly as it had the effort for a German treaty. In any larger body the same might still occur, with the added disadvantage that the United States might find itself outvoted by victims of Japan seeking reparations and, at the same time, punitive restrictions on Japanese industry and trade."[32]

To resolve the peace-conference problem, it was decided that John Foster Dulles would first negotiate a U.S. draft with other friendly countries; at the international conference the ground rules would prevent any substantial alteration of the terms. This would leave the

30. Percy Spender, *Exercises in Diplomacy*, pp. 80, 81; Grattan, p. 218; Dunn, p. 125.

31. Robert Strausz-Hupe, Alvin J. Cottrell, and James E. Dougherty, *American Asian Tensions*, pp. 124–125; Dunn, p. 123.

32. Dean Acheson, *Present at the Creation*, p. 429.

Soviet Union only the alternative of not signing, a prospect the United States contemplated with equanimity. To evade the reparations issue, provision would be made for bilateral negotiations after the peace conference. And to resolve the security issue, it would be turned around: instead of restrictions on Japan to deter renewed aggression, the United States would move in a direction hitherto avoided, the establishment of a Pacific system of collective defense which, in the wake of the Korean experience, now looked more desirable in any case. American involvement in war in the Far East was now a fact; a Pacific treaty, therefore, would no longer so clearly involve new obligations and—in the event of new aggression—it would avoid the improvisation that had been necessary to meet the North Korean attack.[33]

This decision made a peace treaty with Japan more acceptable to Australia and New Zealand, fitting in with their own belief in the need for formal security arrangements in the Pacific—whether regional or with the United States alone. The conservatives saw these alternatives rather differently from their predecessors. They were more receptive to a pact with the United States alone, since they were less confident of the United Nations, less optimistic about the efficacy of conciliatory gestures toward the Soviet Union, and less concerned with Asian opinion. Moreover, if a Pacific Pact were to remain elusive, it would be all the more important to secure a formal defense commitment from the United States. On the basis of Pacific War experience, the Australians believed that the American military worked best to prepared plans, which they felt were more likely to be drawn up in good time if alliance machinery existed. They feared that increased American commitments elsewhere might lead to neglect of the South Pacific in the absence of formal undertakings. And, recognizing that NATO decisions, especially those relating to manpower and raw material allocations, could have some impact upon them, they wanted a more regularized form of consultation than normal diplomatic channels alone provided. Australia, said Spender, wanted "to have a suitable voice in the determination of policy and the shaping of events which deeply affect Australia wherever they may take place."[34]

33. *Ibid.*, pp. 433, 539, 540; Princeton Lyman, *Alliances and the Defense of Southeast Asia*, pp. 85–88; Rosecrance, p. 185.

34. Rosecrance, p. 159; Mansergh, *Survey,* pp. 223–224; Lyman, pp. 82–83; Reese, pp. 115–117.

In March 1950, outlining the foreign-policy objectives of the Menzies government, Spender again called for immediate consideration of a regional pact while giving more emphasis than in the past to the United States, "whose participation would give such a pact a substance that it would otherwise lack. Indeed, it would be rather meaningless without her."[35] In June, noting the continued opposition of other Commowealth countries to a Pacific Pact, he said, "Australia alone, if we have a response from the United States of America, will be quite prepared to enter into . . . a pact with that country."[36] Later in the year, Spender pressed his bargaining advantage in Washington. Confronted by Dulles with an outline of American peace-treaty plans, he responded, "Australia could not under any circumstances subscribe to a treaty with Japan unless there were adequate assurances, acceptable to Australia, affording her protection against future Japanese aggression."[37]

As 1951 opened, Australia seemed closer to its goal. When Dulles embarked on his first formal consultations with Japan and other interested parties early in the year, he was authorized to propose a collective defense system linking the United States, Japan, the Philippines, Australia, New Zealand, and possibly Indonesia. With American military opinion remaining strongly opposed to any involvement of U.S. ground forces on the Southeast Asian mainland, the inclusion of Malaya was not to be considered.

Meanwhile, Australia and New Zealand were coming increasingly to prefer a treaty with the United States to a broader arrangement. Britain, at least in Spender's view, did not seem very interested; the British, he concluded, regarded security problems in the Pacific and Indian Oceans as so closely linked that if a security pact could not cover them both—an obvious impossibility in view of American and Indian attitudes—there could be no security pact. But even if Britain were persuaded to join, and especially if France were included also, a multilateral organization might be identified with colonialist resistance to change. Nor would all Asians be welcome. The inclusion of Japan was wholly unacceptable; the inclusion of Indonesia undesirable; inclusion of the Philippines a reluctant concession to the United States.

35. Grattan, p. 213.
36. Rosecrance, pp. 181–182.
37. Spender, p. 45.

Moreover, Australia had little more stomach than the United States for involvement on the Asian mainland. To include Thailand would be unwise, Spender argued, increasing the obligations of the parties without bringing additional strength to the arrangement.[38]

Australia presumably would have been prepared to accept protection for Malaya as the price of British participation. Even so, Australia's opposition to commitment on the Asian mainland had made it very unwilling up to this time to become involved in Malaya. When, in 1949, Australia, New Zealand, and Britain had arranged to coordinate defense planning in what was known as the ANZAM area which included also Malaya, Singapore, Borneo, and the adjacent seas, no commitments were involved. The planning—which took place at staff level—was limited to defending sea and air communications, and Australia and New Zealand undertook no responsibilities in connection with Malaya's Communist insurrection. To be sure, the Australian Labour government met British requests for arms and ammunition for use in Malaya and prevented the waterside workers from imposing a boycott on supplies, but it did not volunteer troops or other support. After the conservatives took over, Menzies said that Australia must be prepared to share in the defense of Malaya and, in June, responded affirmatively to requests for an air-transport squadron and for air-service facilities. However, despite some talk of a volunteer unit, Australian and New Zealand troops were not to be stationed in Malaya until 1955.[39]

By February 1951, when Dulles arrived in Canberra to consult with Australia and New Zealand, the collective arrangements his instructions envisaged were clearly unattainable. In Japan, Prime Minister Yoshida had opposed rearmament to the extent required for Japanese participation in a collective arrangement—for which, in any case, he had no enthusiasm whatsoever.[40] Britain opposed including the Philippines and not Malaya, and any arrangement that imposed obligations for defending the Philippines on Australia and New Zealand while excluding Britain. Finally, Indonesian lack of interest in participating was so quickly apparent that the subject was never formally broached. Ac-

38. *Ibid.*, pp. 57–59, 91–98, 126–127.

39. Chatham House Study Group, p. 20; Albinski, *Australia's Search for Security*, pp. 234–247.

40. Martin Weinstein, *Japan's Postwar Defense Policy*, pp. 59–61.

cordingly, it was decided to proceed with three separate defense treaties, one with Japan, one with the Philippines, and one with Australia
and New Zealand. The previous argument that the American commitment to the latter three was so well understood as to require no
formal arrangements was now discarded. In the official announcement,
which did not come until April 30, Acheson recalled this argument,
saying, "the United States would not tolerate any aggression against
the Philippines from any quarter. . . . In the case of Australia and
New Zealand . . . without formal agreements, it has been clear that
our fates have been joined." But, he added, "discussion of a Japanese
peace settlement has raised the desirability of saying more formally
what had become an underlying fact."[41]

The ANZUS Pact,[42] signed in September 1951, entered into force on
April 29, 1952. Its key article read: "Each party recognizes that an
armed attack in the Pacific area on any of the parties would be
dangerous to its own peace and safety and declares that it would act
to meet the common danger in accordance with its constitutional processes." The Pacific Council, composed of foreign ministers or their
deputies, was to consider questions of implementation and maintain a
consultative relationship with other states and organizations in a position to contribute to the security of the area. Australia set great store
by the Pacific Council as giving it "access to the thinking and planning
of the American Administration at the highest political and military
level."[43] It fell considerably short of achieving this objective, however;
a less exalted American view of its role was indicated by the fact that
in 1953 the United States agreed to a Pacific Council meeting only
after considerable delay, although in 1952 it had been decided that
meetings would be held every year.[44]

The exclusion of Britain caused some public concern, even more in
New Zealand than in Australia, although neither was prepared to
forego the relationship with the United States on this account. Spender
later implied that London had not really been interested in participating, but the evidence is by no means conclusive. Whatever British in-

41. *DSB*, April 30, 1951, p. 685.
42. Formally: Security Treaty between Australia, New Zealand, and the
United States of America.
43. R. G. Casey quoted in Greenwood and Harper, p. 208.
44. Reese, pp. 141–145.

tentions may have been, American unwillingness to protect Malaya and Singapore constituted a formidable problem. Nevertheless, it appeared that although Britain was reconciled to its initial exclusion, it still anticipated membership at some later date. Indeed, in 1951, there was some general expectation—aroused in part by the treaty provision creating the Pacific Council—that new members would soon be admitted, and it was widely believed, incorrectly so, that the matter would be considered at the Council's first meeting in Honolulu in August 1952. Britain's request for observer status at the first meeting of the ANZUS military representatives in September 1952 was rejected, and in 1953 the Council decided that membership should not be increased despite Churchill's pointed remark in Commons: "I did not like the ANZUS Pact at all. . . . I am greatly in hopes that perhaps longer, wider arrangements may be made which will be more satisfactory."[45]

ANZUS was also criticized because the obligation the parties undertook to each other was considerably short of the obligation assumed under NATO,[46] even though the difficulties the NATO phraseology had caused in the U.S. Senate made it apparent that it would have been unwise to use it again. The United States, the critics argued, had agreed only to do what it would have done anyway; said one disgruntled member of the opposition, "This Pact has teeth, but they are irregular and are not a complete set."[47] It was less likely, some argued, that ANZUS would require America to come to the defense of Australia and New Zealand than that they would be involved in a war caused by some American action or commitment. Concern over the ANZUS obligation in the event of a clash between American and Chinese forces in the Taiwan strait heightened in February 1953 when President Eisenhower announced that the Seventh Fleet would no

45. Dean McHenry and Richard Rosecrance, "The 'Exclusion' of the U.K. from the ANZUS Pact," *International Organization,* XII (Summer, 1958), pp. 323–325; Reese, pp. 125, 129; Nicholas, pp. 85–86; E. D. L. Killen, "The ANZUS Pact and Pacific Security," *Far Eastern Survey,* XXI (Oct. 8, 1952), p. 139.

46. In the corresponding NATO article, the signatories had agreed that an armed attack against one or more of them in Europe or North America would be considered an attack against them all, with each taking such action as it deemed necessary, including the use of armed force.

47. Watt, p. 129.

longer restrain the Chinese Nationalists from assaults on the mainland. Responding to this concern with extreme circumspection, the Australian government pointed out that the U.S. action governed only the Seventh Fleet, while adding that, in any extension of the Korean hostilities, Australia would naturally have "material interests." Prime Minister Sidney Holland was similarly cautious. New Zealand, he said, did not question the American right to take action or suspect the President of aggressive intent. But, he hoped that fears that the U.S. move "will directly or indirectly add to international complications, or to the spread of the present Korean conflict, or increase the dangers of another world war, will prove to be unfounded."[48]

The ANZUS treaty was also criticized as having led Australia into too rigid a posture in Asia and into neglect of its relations with Asian countries. However, in Southeast Asia, at least, Australia was more active diplomatically after 1951 than it had been before. In September 1951 in parliament, R. G. Casey, who had visited Southeast Asia after succeeding Spender as Minister of External Affairs, stressed the area's importance to Australia and argued that it be given greater attention. Thereafter, Australian representation in Southeast Asian capitals was augmented, and in 1953 an officer of ambassadorial rank was assigned to Singapore in something of a coordinating role. By 1954, of Australia's 31 diplomatic posts, nearly half were in Asia.[49]

The Treaty of Mutual Defense between the United States and the Philippines was signed in August 1951 and entered into force in August 1952. The language defining the obligation of the parties to come to each other's defense was identical with the corresponding provision in the ANZUS pact and was similarly criticized as providing less adequate protection than NATO. Even as compared with ANZUS, the treaty seemed deficient to the Filipinos. No machinery such as the Pacific Council was established, and, whereas mutual consent was required to terminate ANZUS, either party to the Philippine-U.S. treaty could terminate on a year's notice.

48. *Keesing's Contemporary Archives*, X, 12284; Watt, pp. 129–130; Reese, pp. 138–139; Albinski, *Australian Policies and Attitudes toward China*, p. 87; W. F. Monk, "New Zealand Faces North," *Pacific Affairs*, XXVI (Sept., 1953), p. 226.

49. Reese, p. 146; Watt, p. 144; Albinski, *Australia's Search for Security*, p. 313.

Unlike the Australians, the Filipinos continued to urge a Pacific Pact. When the opposition party complained that the Philippines had not been represented at the Pacific Council's first meeting, Quirino denied government disappointment. Nevertheless, while defending bilateral agreements on the grounds that the countries of the area were not yet able to unite in a single treaty, he hailed the Council meeting as a first step toward a system of collective defense. In a speech in July to the Indonesian parliament he renewed his own campaign, but Indonesia, Burma, and India all quickly rejected the idea of a defensive alliance. Later in August, when the Republic of Korea asked the United States to take the lead in forming a Pacific Pact, Washington pointed to the three existing treaties and said it could not undertake additional commitments in Southeast Asia. Quirino then put forward a proposal for a meeting at Baguio in May 1953 along the lines of the 1950 meeting, but, with no evident interest elsewhere in this proposal, it was soon dropped.[50]

The Reparations Issue

When the peace conference met in San Francisco in September 1951, the security preoccupations of Australia, New Zealand, and the Philippines had been much reduced by the treaties with the United States, but reparations remained a major problem for the Philippines, as well as for Burma and Indonesia. The article in the treaty dealing with this subject reflected Southeast Asian pressures and called upon Japan to enter promptly into negotiations with powers "whose present territories were occupied by Japanese forces and damaged by Japan, with a view to assisting to compensate those countries for the cost of repairing the damage done, by making available the services of the Japanese people in production, salvaging and other work." But any reparations agreement must not impose liabilities on other Allied powers, and the recipients would have to supply any necessary raw materials to avoid foreign exchange burdens on Japan. Because of these restrictions and because the Southeast Asian countries wanted capital goods not technical assistance, the treaty was bitterly criticized; in fact, it was to be many years before all reparations issues were settled.[51]

50. *SIA*, 1952, pp. 407–408; Meyer, pp. 155–156.
51. Laurence Olson, *Japan in Postwar Asia*, p. 16.

In the Philippines, the treaty was so unpopular that Dulles was burned in effigy in Manila. Before the conference an all-party committee established by the President declared the draft unacceptable and asserted that it was calculated to restore Japan to a dominant position in Asia. Romulo, the committee's spokesman, said that the draft had "filled the Filipino people with profound disillusionment and dismay."[52] After the conference, explaining why he had signed so unsatisfactory a document, he said, "We signed the treaty with the greatest possible reluctance. The measure of our attitude is the statement which I made on behalf of the Philippine Government during the San Francisco conference—a statement which has been described as the most bitter that was made there by any country outside of the Soviet bloc. Therefore, there can be no question of our defending the peace treaty as such, but only of explaining the circumstances which constituted a virtual compulsion for us to sign it. . . . That we had to sign it despite the patent inadequacies of the treaty is no more than a frank recognition of the painfully limited area of choice within which we had to act."[53] But the Senate did not agree that the Philippines was without alternatives and did not consent to ratification until 1956.

The reparations arrangements were also a source of bitterness. At the conference, Romulo had said to Japanese Premier Yoshida, "We shall want some clear sign from you of spiritual contrition and renewal,"[54] and his representations and those of Indonesian Foreign Minister Subardjo had evoked public Japanese promises that reparations agreements would be concluded and informal private agreement on some of the items to be covered. Negotiations between Japan and the Philippines beginning in 1952 were quickly deadlocked, however, when the Philippines demanded $8 billion in total reparations over a ten- to fifteen-year period, with an advance cash payment of $800 million. Under an interim agreement of March 1953, Japan was to salvage about 200,000 tons of sunken vessels in Philippine harbors, but implementation was delayed until August 1955, while the two countries haggled over the price of the salvaged scrap. In 1954, after Philippine abandonment of the $8 billion claim made further negotiations possible, the resulting Ono-Garcia agreement giving the Philippines

52. *Keesing's Contemporary Archives*, VIII, 11685.
53. Karunakaren, 1950–1953, p. 93.
54. Jenkins, *American Economic Policy*, p. 16.

an eventual return of $1 billion, created such a political furor that it was not pursued. [55]

In Indonesia, the peace treaty had caused heated political controversy. Even attendance at the San Francisco conference was widely opposed, especially after India and Burma announced they would not go. Critics, including most of the press, argued that Indonesia was associating itself with the American bloc against the Communist bloc. Supporters claimed it would be perfectly in accord with its independent foreign policy for Indonesia to attend the conference and sign the treaty. Moreover, since the treaty would go through in any case, becoming a party would give Indonesia a firmer base for a subsequent reparations agreement. In August, the cabinet decided to send Foreign Minister Subardjo to San Francisco, and in September it voted in favor of signing the treaty. However, the margin was so small and the parties, even of the ministers who supported signature, so divided that a political crisis was avoided only by shelving the matter. Subsequent reparations negotiations were as inconclusive as the Philippine effort. Great differences over amounts, form, and timing persisted, although, as in the Philippines, an agreement was reached late in 1953 on salvage operations.[56]

Ironically, Burma was the first of the Southeast Asian countries to reach a reparations agreement. In November 1954, after a year of negotiations, the two countries signed a peace treaty giving Burma $200 million in goods and services and a $50 million loan over a ten-year period. In addition, Burma's claims (originally for $400 million) were to be re-examined whenever final agreement was reached on the claims of other Southeast Asian countries.[57]

55. Olson, pp. 17–20.

56. *Ibid.*, pp. 16–17; *Feith*, pp. 195–197; Van der Kroef, *Indonesia in the Modern World*, II, 368–369.

57. Tinker, pp. 364–365.

CHAPTER 6

BETWEEN TWO CAMPS

With Communist control in China bringing Cold War issues to the borders of Southeast Asia, the Burmese and Indonesian commitment to nonalignment became even stronger, more reinforced than otherwise by Peking's hostility toward non-Communist Asian leaders and its advocacy of armed struggle. Nevertheless, in each case the bilateral relationship with western countries remained closer than with Communist ones. Shared belief in democratic institutions played some part; the need for foreign assistance was even more significant. Only the West at this time was prepared to provide such assistance while, in Indonesia especially, foreign investment remained central to the operation of the economy. But domestic political pressures as well as international ones made neutralist governments anxious to avoid any implication that hospitality to close economic ties with the West was causing them to respond to western pressures—real or imagined—to lean to one side.

Burma's U Nu became second only to Nehru in articulating neutralist principles. He saw his country as peculiarly vulnerable. Any desire Peking might have to support insurgent Communists or to subvert the ethnic Chinese community would be facilitated by an easily traversed frontier, sections of which, to make matters worse, remained in dispute. In addition Nationalist troops, retreating from China and establishing themselves in the Burmese border area, could cause difficulties with the new regime. In the event, the border problem remained in abeyance. However, the issue created by the presence on Burmese soil of Chinese Nationalist troops embroiled Burma not with the PRC, whose forbearance Rangoon gratefully noted, but with the Republic of China, Thailand, and the United States.

Indonesia was less vulnerable to Chinese pressures. Its neutralist principles impelled it toward early relations with the PRC, but hostility toward ethnic Chinese residents helped to keep relations distant as did the political activities of Peking's embassy in Djakarta. Although the role of foreign capital was hotly debated in the internal political arena, development-minded cabinets continued to seek foreign invest-ment. However, the frustration of Indonesian hopes for early acquisi-tion of sovereignty over West Irian affected both the republic's exter-nal relations and its domestic politics.

The involvement of the international community in the Korean War placed new strains on the neutralists. But it also gave them an opportunity to move from rather passive nonpartisanship to active efforts to mediate and conciliate. This in turn apparently played some part in altering the Communist view of neutralism. At first gradually and imperceptibly and then, by the mid-fifties with great emphasis, Moscow and Peking abandoned their hostility to the leaders of the Third World, seeking instead to gain their sympathy and support. The changed view of neutralist government leaders necessitated also new prescriptions for the proper strategy of the local Communist parties. Thus, armed struggle tactics were replaced by united-front principles and by efforts to enlist broad support for the peace movement that had become a central campaign for Communists everywhere.

The Theory and Practice of Neutralism: Burma

Although Burma's leaders initially contemplated alliances to bolster the defenses of their newly independent country, they were not, even then, thinking of alignment in Cold War terms. On this question, early in the Union's history, U Nu had given voice to the basic concepts that formed the rationale for Burmese neutralism.[1]

In U Nu's eyes, neutralism for Burma was dictated by its location and size and by ethical principles as well. Burma, he said, was "a ten-der gourd among the cactus"; if it were to side with one bloc, the other surely would not look on with folded arms. A tiny nation, unable to fight, it must be friendly with all. If Burma were to take sides, it would have to give blind support to the side it had chosen "in any and every-thing right or wrong." But no country can be right or wrong all the

1. Unless otherwise noted, speeches made by U Nu between 1949 and 1951 and published in *From Peace to Stability* (Rangoon, 1951) are the source for this summary of his views.

time. "Let us be destroyed in the effort but let it be said of us by posterity that we were a people who did right. In order to be able to do right we cannot allow ourselves to be absorbed into any power bloc."

Almost automatically, Burma's leaders regarded democracy as the internal counterpart of national independence. But they did not conclude from this that Burma should link itself internationally to other nations which, however democratic, did not seem to them to be serving the cause of democracy abroad. Thus, U Nu declared in 1953: "In North Africa the United States is supporting the colonial Imperial systems which are most loathsome to the Africans. In Spain also the Americans support the Fascist-Franco regime. In Indo-China they are helping and encouraging the French colonial rulers who are not acceptable any more to all the Indo-Chinese. If you look at China also, you will find that the extreme reactionary Chiang Kai-shek group, which had been ousted from China because the Chinese masses could not stomach them any more, have to be picked on by the Americans to give them support and assistance."[2]

U Nu was equally critical of the gap between Soviet pretensions and practice. In obvious reference to the great purges of 1948–1950, he asked, "What is the nature of Soviet Russia's relations with her immediate neighbors—Poland, Czechoslovakia, Rumania, Hungary, etc.? Why did Marshal Tito, an ardent Communist, become the bitter enemy of Soviet Russia? Why did Soviet Russia have to shut out the world from her and her satellites with an iron curtain?" Proximity made Burma even more wary of Communist China. In an interview in 1951, U Kyaw Nyein, one of the principal members of the government and a leading Socialist theoretician expressed this mistrust: "Small nations always mistrust bigger ones, especially those close by. For years past, every Burman has mistrusted China, whether under Mao or Chiang. . . . We don't consider China a menace, but we accept the possibility of China one day invading us."[3]

In stressing Burma's acute need for foreign aid, U Nu cited, to left-wing critics, Lenin's many statements in the early years of the Soviet Union justifying the search for aid from capitalist countries. War and insurrection, said U Nu, have made Burma "one vast plain

2. Tinker, p. 367.

3. Frank N. Trager, "Burma's Foreign Policy," *Journal of Asian Studies*, XVI (Nov., 1956), p. 93.

of devastation." There must be foreign assistance to permit recovery and the development of resources for the benefit of the Burmese people. Aid should be accepted from anybody, and the criteria must be not the motives of the giver but whether the aid fits Burmese requirements and does not impinge directly or indirectly on Burmese sovereignty. In the late forties and the early fifties, the Soviet Union and the other Communist countries were not offering aid. Accordingly, despite its desire to keep both blocs at an equal distance, Burma's aid requirements dictated much closer relations with the United States than with the Soviet Union. Nonalignment, U Nu argued, "does not exclude us from cooperating closely with the Democracies in matters relating to economic development."

Even within the confines of nonalignment, Burma was notably inactive in foreign affairs. In 1949, for example, Britain, according to U Nu, was the closest to Burma of the three great powers. But, by the end of 1953, Burma's special ties with Britain—its links with a currency board in London and with the British Ministry of Food and the Ottawa Tariffs Agreement—had all been cut, and the British Military Mission, established under the Freeman-Bo Letya Agreement, had been terminated. Feelings of identification with India were fostered by common neutralist views, India's initiatives in obtaining Commonwealth support for Burma, and U Nu's great admiration for Gandhi and Nehru. But even here, there was a good deal of reserve. India, although admired, was also distrusted as a large and assertive power, and the Indians resident in Burma were resented because of the administrative and commercial superiority they had enjoyed under British rule.[4]

On international issues, Burma did not normally regard its neutralism as calling upon it to come up with third-road solutions for other countries' problems. Rather it tended to take positions only when, as in the Korean case, such action was inescapable. And, when it had to act, it vastly preferred to do so within the framework of the international organization. Burma also looked to the United Nations to help it with its own most serious postwar problem—the disposition of the so-called KMTs, the Chinese Nationalist troops who had fled before the advancing Chinese Communists and had then established themselves in Burmese territory.

4. Tinker, p. 353.

The presence of this growing armed force in the Shan area of northeastern Burma was a serious threat to law and order. The KMTs exacted provisions from the local population, smuggled and trafficked in arms and opium, joined forces with Karen insurgents, and encouraged the separatist inclinations of Shan princelings. However remote the area of KMT operation, resources urgently needed to pacify other more important parts of the country had to be diverted to cope with them because of the Cold War implications of their presence. Supplied from Taiwan on a regular basis, the KMT leader, General Li Mi was not merely seeking refuge in Burma; it was his avowed purpose to use it as a base for incursions into Yunnan. There was thus the prospect that China's civil war would spill over into Burma and, in addition, that the Chinese Communists might see fit to retaliate against the Burmese. In fact, China's forbearance in the years to follow caused Burma to look with more confidence upon Peking's good intentions, while, on the other hand, the KMT issue provided the occasion for terminating the U.S. aid program, resulted in tension with Thailand, and reduced Burmese faith in the UN.

The movement of Chinese refugees into Burma began to cause concern as early as 1948, and this concern was heightened in December 1949 when Peking warned neighboring countries against harboring Nationalist troops. The problem did not become serious, however, until March when Li Mi crossed the border with 1,500 men, and Burmese military action failed to dislodge him. In January 1950, a Chinese Communist force, pursuing Nationalist troops, clashed with a Burmese unit and, although this proved to be the only incident of its kind, the sense of danger was heightened. By 1951, Li Mi's "Yunnan Anti-Communist National Salvation Army" had grown considerably, established base areas and training camps, and made a number of incursions into China. Moreover, its ties with Taiwan were quite evident; in December, Li visited the island and thereafter regularly received supplies flown in to the airstrip his men had built at Mongshat. Rumors multiplied that Americans as well as Chinese were involved and that weapons were being provided from Thailand as well as Taiwan. Moreover, although the United States had agreed to raise the issue in Taipei, its efforts appeared to be having no impact.[5]

5. Oliver E. Clubb, Jr., *The Effect of Chinese Nationalist Military Activities on Burmese Foreign Policy*, pp. 2–15; Trager, Wolgemuth, and Lu, pp. 9–10.

Early in 1952, Soviet representative Andrei Vishinsky, seeking Cold War points in the General Assembly, charged that the United States was transporting Chinese Nationalist military forces into Thailand and Burma in order to mount operations against Communist China. Burma responded with alarm. Its representative, U Myint Thien, denied that any government other than that of the Republic of China was involved in maintaining the KMTs. Peking, he said, was quite aware of the situation, but had adopted a correct attitude and had not embarrassed Burma. Having made it clear to the Soviet Union that its charges were most unwelcome, he then turned to the United States and Britain and expressed the hope that their recent statements warning against Communist aggression in Southeast Asia were meant to cover all other forms of aggression as well. Concern over Cold War complications also conditioned Burma's response to a British proposal for a UN fact-finding mission. Burma, U Nu announced, would take military action against the KMTs rather than ask the UN to investigate because, if the PRC thought the inquiry "would be merely camouflage, then there would be difficulty."[6]

Military action, however, did not stem the growth of the KMT forces—estimated at about 16,000 in January 1953—or curb their activities. And when President Eisenhower announced the "unleashing" of Chiang Kai-shek in February 1953, some Burmese anticipated a general offensive against Communist China in which the KMTs would become involved. Accordingly, at the beginning of March Burma launched still another campaign against the KMTs, while also announcing that it would submit the case to the UN.[7]

Although it had never formally accused the United States of complicity, Burma nevertheless appeared to believe that its decision to seek UN condemnation of an American protégé required it to eliminate any trace of a client relationship that might be suggested by a continued American aid program. Accordingly, before submitting its draft resolution to the General Assembly, Burma asked the United States to terminate its assistance. The decision, however, was not purely one of principle. The aid program had been a source of political con-

6. Council on Foreign Relations, Richard P. Stebbins (ed.), *The United States in World Affairs* (*USWA*), 1952, p. 198; *GAOR*, First Committee, Jan. 28, 1952, p. 272; *SIA*, 1952, p. 446.
7. Clubb, pp. 16–19.

troversy, particularly after the Mutual Security Administration replaced the Economic Cooperation Administration, and charges that to accept American aid was to take sides in the Cold War had become more plausible to many. The Burmese press was especially critical of the program's procedures and accomplishments, its antagonism intensified by the aid mission's involvement in a feud between the journalists' association and the cabinet minister responsible for co-ordinating foreign aid. Moreover, while U.S. aid was adding to political contention, its economic contribution now seemed less important and necessary. With the rice market much stimulated by the Korean War, Burma's foreign-exchange earnings were very high; conversely, the obligated aid program for 1953 was half that of 1952, with the U.S. Congressional climate making apparent the likelihood of further reductions.[8]

Burma's draft resolution of March 26, 1953, noting that troops of "the Kuomintang government of Formosa" had infringed Burma's territorial integrity and violated its frontiers, called upon the General Assembly to recommend that the Security Council condemn the Republic of China and take all necessary steps "to ensure immediate cessation of the acts of aggression." Describing the charge of aggression as a monstrous one, and disclaiming any control over Li Mi, who had violated orders by entering Burma, the Chinese representative said his government had tried to persuade Li Mi to comply with Burmese wishes and would continue to do so. Nevertheless, Li Mi and his men "were regarded as heroes by all free Chinese all over the world from whom they received financial aid," and it was considered "psychologically impossible" for the Republic of China to "pronounce a moral condemnation so as to prevent the collection of funds by the representatives of those forces among the free Chinese."[9]

The ensuing debate revolved around the charge of aggression. It was agreed that Burma's situation was intolerable, that the international community was obliged to help remove the cause of the disturbance, and that neighboring countries should do everything within their power to ensure that KMT supplies and reinforcement were cut

8. Montgomery, pp. 143–144; Johnstone, pp. 64–65; Cady, pp. 619–622; Wolf, *Foreign Aid,* p. 121.

9. Trager, Wolgemuth, and Lu, pp. 10–11; *GAOR,* First Committee, April 17, 1953, pp. 658–659.

off. The Soviet Union and the Eastern European Communist countries, a number of African states, and—among Burma's neighbors—India and Indonesia, accepted the charge that the Republic of China was responsible for the presence and activities of the KMTs and was therefore guilty of aggression. Others, however, found the evidence presented by the Burmese far from conclusive. Even among the strongest supporters of measures that would bring genuine relief to Burma, there was a good deal of reluctance to proceed with the charge of aggression. Both Australia and Britain, for example, conceded that the KMTs could not have survived and expanded as they had without substantial support from Taiwan. But, using Burma's own argument in the Korean case against condemning Communist China, they and a number of other representatives pointed out that moral statements, however gratifying, were unlikely to persuade the condemned party to cooperate in solving the problem; for this, there must be arrangements involving the Republic of China for disarming and removing the KMTs.

Out of the debates came a resolution, originally tabled by Mexico, which, while making no reference to the Republic of China, deplored the presence of foreign troops in Burma and required that they be disarmed and agree to internment or departure. In the First Committee, the Republic of China and Burma both abstained; in the General Assembly, however, only the Republic of China abstained, and the resolution was passed 59 to 0. Explaining Burma's shift, its representative said, "In view of the unanimity displayed . . . and because of Burma's dedication to democratic ideals and to peace and peaceful ways, the Government of Burma felt that they would have to identify themselves with a resolution which after all fully recognized the intolerable state of affairs in Eastern Burma and sought settlement of the issue in a peaceful way."[10]

The Burmese, however, regarded the UN action—particularly since it failed to resolve the problem—as falling far short of the ideal and as illustrating the degree to which the United Nations had become the captive of Cold War considerations. "It seemed to us," said James Barrington, Permanent Secretary of Burma's Foreign Ministry, "that all the elements for the identification and condemnation of the ag-

10. Clubb, pp. 29–30; *GAOR*, First Committee, April 20, 1953, p. 670; April 21, p. 673; Trager, Wolgemuth, and Lu, pp. 11–12.

gressor were present. But the United Nations, to our disappointment did not see it that way. With great delicacy of feeling it referred to these forces as 'foreign troops.' It deplored the situation. . . . Not being an ungrateful people, we were glad to get this measure of support. . . . But we could not help but contrast the United Nations attitude in this case with the strong and swift steps taken to deal with the North Korean aggression. . . . To many of our people, it seemed that the United Nations had two yardsticks for measuring aggression, that the shorter and more handy one is used when the Communists are involved, and a longer one is used if self-proclaimed anti-communists are involved."[11]

The joint military commission, established to deal with the situation and composed of representatives of Burma, the Republic of China, Thailand, and the United States, was only intermittently successful; although by October 1954 six thousand troops had been evacuated, Burma claimed that an equal number remained. Meanwhile, friction between Burma and Thailand over controlling the KMTs continued. Early in 1953, Thailand had closed its frontier with Burma, an act causing considerable economic hardship in the eastern Shan states. In November and December, seeking out KMT concentrations, Burmese planes inadvertently bombed Thai border villages, and Thailand responded to these and other overflights by moving antiaircraft batteries to the border and giving instructions to fire on intruding aircraft. Thereafter, however, Burma apologized and offered compensation. At the end of 1954, after missions had been exchanged and the border reopened, U Nu visited Bangkok where he apologized once again, not only for the recent incident, but also for the Burmese sack of the ancient Thai capital of Ayuthia in 1767.[12]

The Theory and Practice of Neutralism: Indonesia

The basic principles of Indonesia's foreign policy were expressed well before independence. In September 1948, the Republic officially rejected the argument that Indonesia must range itself either with the pro-Russian or with the pro-American camp. Indonesia, the statement argued, must base its policy on its own interests. But it should not be a

11. Trager, Wolgemuth, and Lu, p. 13.
12. *Ibid.*, p. 12; Clubb, p. 36; Tinker, pp. 359–360.

passive policy; Indonesia should be an active agent, entitled to determine its own standpoint.[13]

Indonesia's foreign policy was succinctly described by Prime Minister Wilopo, not long after he took office in 1952. The Indonesian
government, he said, "does not forever take sides by pledging itself to
one of the two blocs, which are in controversy with each other." But
neither does Indonesia "forever pledge itself to keep aloof or to remain
neutral in every incident which may arise out of the controversy between the two blocs."[14] In the UN it would support every effort to do
away with "or at least grind off, the sharpness of the controversy
between the two trends or blocs" to help avoid conflict that could set
off World War III. By trying to stave off World War III, Mohammad
Hatta observed, Indonesia would compensate for the weakness of its
own military defenses. But to the argument that the fate of such
countries as Belgium showed the inefficacy of neutralism, Hatta replied
"Indonesia does not have common frontiers with Soviet Russia or
China. A direct threat from that direction to Indonesian independence
neither exists nor is possible." Meanwhile, as the Western powers themselves argued, the threat of domestic communism was one best met by
raising the economic level of the masses. Conversely, to take sides in
the Cold War would exacerbate domestic differences and postpone the
achievement of the internal consolidation that must be Indonesia's first
goal.[15]

Nevertheless, especially among those who led the Republic in its
first five years of independence, there remained a certain psychological
affinity with the West. Indonesia, like Burma, regarded its ability to
operate according to western democratic principles as a mark of independence and modernity. To be sure, the resentments aroused during
the independence struggle and by continued Dutch retention of West
Irian, made Indonesia quick to see vestiges of colonialism in western
actions. Thus the embargo proposed by the United States on trade with
Communist China for strategic materials—coming as it did when the
U.S. stockpile program was nearly completed and world prices for
rubber were falling—was widely seen as an effort to deny Indonesia
new markets, thereby keeping the price of rubber to its principal

13. Hatta, p. 552.
14. Stannard, pp. 54–56.
15. Hatta, pp. 551–556.

consumer, the United States, as low as possible. Moreover, Indonesian leaders regarded American and British neutrality in the West Irian dispute as, in effect, supporting the Netherlands. But for the most part, they did not see the United States and Britain as potentially threatening. "No one can say," Hatta argued, "that Britain and the United States have evil designs on Indonesia. On the contrary they are desirous of seeing Indonesia remain independent and become prosperous."[16]

Communist countries were a source of somewhat greater apprehension. Chinese Communist propaganda and diplomatic behavior did little to allay this concern. Indonesia's reactionary leaders, Peking charged in 1949, have the same outlook as Nehru, Rhee, and "other feeble-minded bourgeoisie of the East."[17] Peking's embassy seemed intent on propagandizing the Chinese community while showing contempt for Indonesia by increasing its staff and opening a consulate without prior notification. Moreover, Peking's attacks on Indonesian leaders were carried on in Djakarta itself. Early in 1951, for example, the Indonesian police confiscated 9,000 copies of a Chinese newspaper consigned to the embassy which violently attacked Sukarno and Hatta, accusing them of having provoked mass murder in Madiun in 1948. Efforts to circumscribe Chinese activities in Indonesia were reciprocated in Peking, where the Indonesian chargé was reportedly discourteously treated and restricted in his movements.[18]

Relations with Moscow were even more distant. Diplomatic relations were urged by the left but were made unattractive by the belief that Moscow had precipitated the Madiun revolt and by continuing Soviet attacks on Indonesian leaders. It was the prevailing view also that a Soviet embassy was very likely to become a center for political subversion. Nevertheless, in April 1953, the Indonesian parliament finally passed a motion calling upon the government to establish an embassy in Moscow by the end of the year. Prime Minister Wilopo took no action, and even his more leftist successor, Ali Sastroamidjojo, said that the government would carry out the motion only after it had made very careful preparations.[19]

16. *Ibid.*, p. 551; Stannard, pp. 28–36.

17. Lea Williams, "Sino-Indonesian Diplomacy," *China Quarterly,* XI (July–Sept., 1962), p. 185.

18. Feith, pp. 192–193; Holland, p. 173.

19. Fifield, pp. 144–145; Van der Kroef, *Communist Party of Indonesia,* p. 61.

In general, Indonesia's foreign policy in this period was an active one only by comparison with Burma's. There were, however, already some signs of the assertiveness that was later to become so marked a feature of Djakarta's international stance. Whereas Burma, for example, simply stayed away when it believed that by attending some international meeting it might compromise its nonalignment, Indonesia tended to take advantage of the opportunity to make its position more widely known. Thus Indonesia, unlike Burma, attended the May 1950 Baguio Conference and, once there, repeatedly declared that it would not be a party to any prowestern or anti-Communist bloc. In addition, Indonesia was a moderately active supporter of other Moslem countries. It followed Iran, Lebanon, and the Yemen, in recognizing Egypt's sovereignty over the Sudan; its leaders spoke in support of Morocco against the French; and in 1952, it took the lead in organizing UN support for Tunisian demands for home rule.[20]

Of much greater concern, however, were two issues in which domestic and foreign policy were intermingled and which interacted with each other—the proper role in the economy of foreign investment and ownership of property (for which the Dutch were still responsible for a large share), and the tactics to be followed in obtaining sovereignty over West Irian.

From the outset, the Republic had recognized its need for external economic assistance. Thus, its Political Manifesto of November 1945 declared: "We know and are fully aware that for our country and people for many years to come we shall need aid from foreign peoples for building up our country, from technicians and intellectuals, as well as foreign capital."[21] To be sure, the leaders of the revolutionary struggle saw assurances of hospitality to foreign investment as a way of persuading the Dutch and the West in general that their economic interests would be safe in an independent Indonesia. But with political independence secured, economic dependence remained; Indonesia had neither the domestic capital nor the technical capabilities to strike out on its own. The urge to nationalize and socialize—pressed by leftist and ultranationalist parties—was in clear conflict with the need to make Indonesia attractive to foreign capital. And it was the latter that remained the prime consideration with a series of development-oriented

20. Feith, p. 176; Van der Kroef, *Indonesia in the Modern World*, II, 364–366.
21. Hatta, p. 511.

cabinets whose leaders argued that the real issue was not ownership but control. Independence, they asserted, was in no jeopardy as long as the government determined the economic policies and priorities to which foreign interests must conform. But until resources devastated by war had been restored, and Indonesia had developed capital and a strong business class of its own, foreign capital would be required and was entitled to security and profit.[22]

The desire to attract foreign, particularly American, support of Indonesian economic-development aims was an important determinant of the government's approach to matters at issue with the Dutch which, from the Indonesian point of view, the Round Table Agreement had left unresolved. One of these, the federal form of government, created largely by the Dutch with little Indonesian support, could be dealt with unilaterally and was. On August 15, 1950, the Republic of the United States of Indonesia was replaced by the unitary Republic of Indonesia. Another source of friction inherited from the Round Table Agreement was the obligation it placed on the Republic to repay the debts of the Netherland's East Indies, including some of the expenses incurred by the Dutch in their efforts to reimpose their sovereignty. But, of all the controversies between the Dutch and the Indonesians, the West Irian problem was the most intractable.

The Round Table Agreement had maintained the *status quo* in West Irian pending determination of its political status through Dutch-Indonesian negotiations which were to be accomplished within a year after the transfer of sovereignty. The Indonesians read this quite literally as meaning the transfer of the territory within twelve months; in the Hatta cabinet's seven-point program of December 1949, the sixth point was "to settle the Irian issue within a year." In the same month, however, a decree organizing the future government of the territory made it obvious that the Dutch expected it to remain in their hands for some time to come. With so wide a gap between the expectations of the two sides, negotiations proceeded badly. A commission established in March 1950 in which Indonesia and the Netherlands were equally represented terminated its deliberations in August completely deadlocked. In December, at another Indonesian-Netherlands conference, the Indonesians first proposed immediate recognition of

22. John O. Sutter, *Indonesianisasi*, IV, 1182–1190; Franklin B. Weinstein, *Indonesian Foreign Policy*, pp. 310–313.

their sovereignty but with transfer to be postponed until mid-1951, after another conference had provided for protecting Dutch interests. When this was rejected, they offered, in exchange for a transfer of sovereignty, to give preferential treatment to Dutch economic interests, to employ Hollanders in the administration and allow them to immigrate freely, and to guarantee freedom of religion. The Dutch, in turn, first proposed a New Guinea Council in which an equal number of representatives of each side would determine administrative policy, sovereignty would remain vested in the Netherlands, and "in due course" the population would decide its own future in a plebiscite. Their second proposal vested sovereignty in the Netherlands-Indonesian Union, with the Netherlands retaining responsibility for *de facto* administration. Although this proposal was regarded in the Netherlands as having gone much too far and was partly responsible for the fall of the Dutch cabinet the following month, it was no more acceptable to the Indonesians than the first. On December 27, the conference broke up and, on January 3, the Indonesian government announced that "any negotiations in the future can only be held on the basis of the transfer of sovereignty over West Irian to Indonesia." Nevertheless, intermittent contacts and discussions of the issue continued until September 1952, when the newly-formed Willem Drees cabinet declared that it saw "no value in a resumption of discussions with Indonesia about the status of New Guinea."[23]

The issue was to trouble Dutch-Indonesian relations and Indonesian domestic politics for some years to come. Development-oriented governments in Djakarta hoped that conventional diplomacy and a moderate approach would be effective with the Dutch and win U.S. sympathy. They sought to avoid popular agitation, which they feared might have adverse internal consequences, especially if the Dutch proved adamant. These conciliatory policies, however, weakened the influence of their proponents in the domestic political forum and strengthened President Sukarno's ability to excite mass feelings to his own political advantage. Such feelings became easier to excite when suspicions that Indonesian dissident movements were being encouraged and supported from West Irian were fed by such incidents as the discovery of arms (believed to

23. Robert C. Bone, *The Dynamics of the Western New Guinea Problem*, pp. 68–70; Feith, pp. 155, 162–163, 197–198, 287; Holland, p. 167.

be for dissident use) in Dutch merchant vessels anchored in Djakarta.[24]

Attitudes toward other countries were also affected by the West Irian dispute. It was difficult for the Indonesians to believe in American professions of neutrality. Particularly because of American holdings in oil fields in West Irian and suspicious that the United States might one day wish to return to its wartime naval base in Hollandia, the Indonesians tended to conclude that American unwillingness to adopt their cause in fact represented a preference for the *status quo* and continued Dutch rule.[25] Relations with Australia, once Indonesia's close supporter, were also soured. Government leaders, fully supported by the Labour opposition, made it clear that, as Spender said in 1950, Australia did "not consider that Indonesia has any valid claim to Dutch New Guinea."[26] Said Spender's successor, "So far as the question of sovereignty over Dutch New Guinea is concerned, we believe the Dutch to be unquestionably in the right."[27] Australia also insisted that its own position in Papua/New Guinea entitled it to be consulted prior to any change in the territory's status. Legal issues aside, the Australians were very doubtful of Indonesia's fitness to replace the Dutch. The Indonesians, they argued, had no better claim than the Dutch on ethnic, language, or cultural grounds, and their own internal problems made it highly improbable that they could do as much as the Dutch for the territory's administration, development, and defense. Spender, moreover, saw the security of Australian New Guinea as threatened both by Indonesian pretensions and Indonesian weakness. "If the claim of Indonesia to Dutch New Guinea were conceded to any degree at all, it would be a matter of time, no matter how genuine may be assurance to the contrary, when the claim will be pushed further so as to include the trust territory of Australian New Guinea. Moreover, an Indonesian administration might not be a very effective barrier against Communist pressure. "Communism has not got any foothold yet in Australian New Guinea. Australia is determined insofar as it can to ensure that it will not."[28]

24. Feith, pp. 157–159, 197–198; Bone, p. 81; Franklin Weinstein, pp. 313, 442–444.
25. Bone, p. 110; Holland, p. 164.
26. Bone, p. 78.
27. R. G. Casey, *Friends and Neighbours,* p. 102.
28. Bone, p. 78; Watt, pp. 252–253.

The Communist Response: First Steps toward Peaceful Coexistence

During 1950, the Communists had begun to look on neutrals and neutralism with a more sympathetic eye and to differentiate among the countries of Asia somewhat more carefully in ways that affected both state-to-state relations and the behavior of national Communist parties. Although the policy of actively courting Asian neutrals was clearly in full command by 1955, it is difficult to identify the motives and stages of a shift which took place slowly and inconsistently.

It seems fairly evident that the behavior of India and other neutralists during the Korean War had a decided impact in persuading Moscow and Peking that there was indeed a third force which, properly handled, could on occasion serve their foreign-policy objectives. Before then, it was difficult to know whether Asian neutralism would really influence international affairs, or whether it would be confined to the enunciation of moral principles by countries too weak to express themselves in any other way. Moreover, from the Communist viewpoint, neutralist behavior was not inconsistent with the two-camp thesis. Although the Asian neutralists did not want to be counted among the members of the western bloc, they seemed nevertheless to retain and even strengthen their links with the West. India and Ceylon, after all, remained within the Commonwealth and, even if Burma did not, it was quite willing to receive western aid as were Indonesia and the South Asian neutrals. Thus, in January 1950, the categorical and undiscriminating militancy of the Peking meeting of the World Federation of Trade Unions was still in force; the *Cominform Journal* was commending armed revolution in Indonesia and Burma in the same terms as in Indochina, Malaya, and the Philippines, and was attacking the Japanese Communist Party for holding that the transition to socialism in Japan could be a peaceful one. But by the end of the year, there were signs of changing attitudes toward India and Burma that were to prove to be of more than passing tactical significance.[29]

India's proposal in July 1950 that the PRC assume China's seat in the Security Council as a step toward resolving the Korean conflict prompted a marked change in Peking's attitude toward Nehru and Indian neutralism. Noting that Delhi had offered only a limited "type of support" for U.S. moves in Korea and "world-wide support" for

29. Kautsky, p. 193; McLane, pp. 452–454.

Nehru's "peaceful proposals," Peking called the Indian move one of "tremendous world-wide significance."[30] The shift was more than an effort to take advantage of immediate opportunities. In December 1950, R. Palme Dutt, the British Communist Party specialist in India, in an open letter to the Communist Party of India attributed great importance to "indications of a divergence, even though still hesitant and limited of Premier Nehru . . . from the reckless aggressive war policy." Although the Indian Communists were not to support Nehru, they were to seek a broad united front and a strong peace movement and were to welcome and encourage all steps consonant with Moscow's "peace" objectives. "Supporters of peace in India," Dutt wrote, "while welcoming every step towards disentanglement of India from the Anglo-American war bloc, will press forward with unsparing vigour for the further steps which are necessary in order that India shall fulfill a firm and consistent peace policy." By January 1951, peace had become the major theme of the party weekly *Cross Roads,* and the Communists quite frequently praised Nehru for his role in promoting peace. On January 12, reporting on the Commonwealth Prime Ministers' Conference, *Cross Roads* said, "Pandit Nehru has taken a firm and forthright stand on the steps necessary to ensure world peace"; in February a CPI statement welcomed Nehru's "forthright refusal . . . to associate India with the American plan to unleash a third world on Asian soil by branding People's China as an aggressor."[31]

Changes in attitude toward Burma came more slowly and toward Indonesia more slowly still—perhaps because both countries ranked so low in international calculations. In September 1950, the new Chinese Ambassador in Rangoon noted that China and Burma had traveled parallel routes toward independence and referred to the existence of strong ties between the two countries. In 1951, Moscow praised Burma and India for not attending the San Francisco conference and treated the critical views of Indonesia and even the Philippines with respect. In December of that year, Moscow began referring to Sukarno and Hatta without disapproval for the first time since 1949. And, in the same month, the first PRC cultural mission to go abroad visited India and Burma, returning home with enthusiastic reports.[32]

30. Whiting, pp. 60–62; Shulman, p. 152.
31. Kautsky, pp. 129–134.
32. McLane, pp. 451, 454.

Approbation for neutralist positions was accompanied by an altering view of the Asia-wide efficacy of armed struggle. Disappointing party performance outside Vietnam may well have played some role in encouraging Moscow and Peking to shift toward smoother relations with the governments the Communist parties were attempting to displace. Insurrectionary activities, although certainly weakening the countries in which they took place, did not seem to be bringing the Communists any closer to power or posing serious impediments to the economic recovery of the West. The increasingly high priority being accorded to the Communist-sponsored peace movement also suggested a less automatic application of armed struggle tactics. Attempts to reconcile the broad-gauged appeal of the peace movement and militant-party-struggle doctrines were sometimes difficult. There was the added complication that the peace movement in neutralist countries was not opposing governments allied with the United States as it was in Europe; it was seeking to encourage governments that were not associated with American policies and that were frequently quite critical of those policies to continue along already-established paths.

At the Soviet conference of Orientalists in November 1951, Zhukov deplored the tendency to apply Chinese revolutionary experience automatically. "In particular," he said, "it is doubtful whether other countries of the East which take the road toward a people's democracy could expect to be able to get the most important advantage of the Chinese revolution, namely a revolutionary army."[33] It is possible, in Zhukov's statement, to see early signs of Russian concern with Chinese ambition, and this may have entered into the picture. But Zhukov's principal point seemed to be that, while Mao's four-class strategy was universally applicable in colonial and semicolonial countries, the question of whether armed struggle was the road to power had to be answered much more on the basis of the particular circumstances. The Chinese may well have been thinking along identical lines; at least one account of their role in the October 1951 change in Burmese Communist strategy suggests this. The orthodox party, the Communist Party of Burma or White Flags had been carefully treading in Chinese revolutionary footsteps, setting up its own people's democratic government in one of Burma's ancient capitals, Prome, in February 1950. Having lost its base there to government forces in May, it resolved in

33. Dallin, p. 92.

its December 1950 program, to try again. In 1951, however, a letter from Liu Shao-ch'i reportedly criticized the party for its "ultra-left" line and urged it to declare its desire for peace, form a united front, and restrict its military activities. In October, the White Flags did indeed adopt a new policy calling for a peaceful end to the fighting and for a coalition government with the AFPFL.[34]

Although the Burmese party's new line did not advance its fortunes, a similar, somewhat later, Indonesian party shift paved the way for the return of the PKI to an influential role in Indonesian politics. The party had not resumed the violent tactics that had brought it to disaster at Madiun in 1948. However, it continued to be tarred with its extremist behavior at that time. Subsequently, its bitter opposition to the first three postindependence governments (in all of which the Muslim party, the *Masjumi*, had played the leading role) had done little to improve its reputation. The shift came in April 1952, when a new cabinet was formed under the leadership of Wilopo and his Partai Nasional Indonesia (PNI). The PKI announced that it would support Wilopo as long as his government was progressive and national, an offer reported in *Pravda*, presumably as a sign of approval. Thereafter, the Communists in Indonesia increasingly stressed nationalism, wooed the PNI, and developed a new image of Sukarno, no longer a collaborator and a false Marxist but now a national rallying point for all anti-imperialists.[35]

In October 1952, a Peace Conference of the Asian and Pacific regions was held in Peking, the first to be convened in Asia, although such conferences had been fixtures on the European scene for some time. The World Federation of Trade Unions was one of the sponsors, but there were few echoes from the conference that had been held in Peking under its auspices three years earlier. Among Asian problems, Japan was accorded first place; the peace treaty and the security treaty with the United States were depicted as steps in the revival of Japanese militarism in the interest of American imperialist ambitions. There were incessantly reiterated demands for bringing the "wars of aggression" in Korea, Vietnam, and Malaya to an end, although nothing was said that suggested how this should be done in Vietnam

34. Brimmell, pp. 312–313; Kautsky, p. 152.

35. Feith, pp. 237–239; Van der Kroef, *Communist Party of Indonesia*, pp. 51–59.

and Malaya. Otherwise, national liberation movements were given little attention; those in Southeast Asia none. The report on the question of national independence, delivered by a delegate from Chile, and the resolution the conference adopted on this subject listed countries where wars of national liberation were being conducted, but mentioned only Vietnam and Malaya in Southeast Asia.[36] Most other references to Southeast Asia were made by representatives from the area who generally depicted their countries as striving for peace in the face of American efforts to control and exploit their economies, undermine their political independence, and utilize their territory for warlike purposes; none of their speeches referred to their own governments, much less attacked them.[37]

36. *People's China,* XX (Oct. 16, 1952), p. 30; *NCNA,* Oct. 13, 1952; Communist propaganda treatment of Indonesia and Burma was inconsistent for some time. In the Jan. 9, 1953, issue of the *Cominform Journal* an editorial listed Burma and Indonesia together with Malaya and the Philippines as countries in which the national liberation movement was gaining momentum. In the issue of Feb. 20, 1953, however, they were omitted from a similar listing by the General Secretary of the World Federation of Democratic Youth in an article on the "International Day of Struggle" against colonial regimes.

37. *NCNA,* Oct. 6–10, 1954.

CHAPTER 7

INTERNATIONALIZATION OF
THE WAR IN VIETNAM

In the years between the establishment of Communist rule in Peking and Stalin's death, the Viet Minh guerrilla effort against the French was transformed into a war in its own right and also into a battlefield of the Cold War. Two statements made in the wake of Chinese and Soviet diplomatic recognition of the DRV in January 1950 epitomized the political change. Communist diplomatic recognition, said Dean Acheson, "should remove any illusion as to the 'nationalist' character of Ho Chi Minh's aims and reveal Ho in his true colors as the mortal enemy of native independence in Indochina."[1] The Viet Minh military leader, Vo Nguyen Giap provided the counterpoint. "With the arrival of new China," he said, "the neodemocratic world stretches in one piece from the West to the East up to the frontiers of Indochina. Indochina has become the forward stronghold of the democratic world in Southeast Asia."[2] The military change was signaled in February when Giap announced that the guerrilla war was over and the war of movement had begun. That this was indeed the case was evident to the French not many months later. For the first time, the French admitted, the Viet Minh forces had all they needed in arms and equipment, including radios, and all their movements were well coordinated.[3]

By mid-1949, as Chinese Communist forces reached the Tonkin border, the French had been fighting the Viet Minh for three years, and no end was in sight. Fearing that Chinese support would further strengthen Viet Minh resistance, they turned increasingly to their

1. *DSB*, Feb. 13, 1950, p. 244.
2. Joseph J. Zasloff, *The Role of Sanctuary in Insurgency*, pp. 15–16.
3. Lancaster, p. 219.

Allies for help, the task facilitated by American and British desires to strengthen France in Europe and by growing Anglo-American concern that Indochina too might be lost to the Communists with seriously destabilizing effects on the rest of Southeast Asia. The United States responded by increasing its economic aid and, for the first time, by supplying military assistance as well; by mid-1952 it was pledged to support covering some 40 percent of the total French expenditures in Indochina.

The British, with more limited material resources, and heavily committed to the campaign against Communist insurgents in Malaya, joined the United States in political efforts intended to bolster French determination, deter the Chinese Communists from intervening, and secure international recognition of the three Indochinese states that had replaced the old French administrative divisions. These new Associated States had been given a degree of autonomy intended to allay nationalist pressures without abandoning French sovereignty or establishing undesirable precedents for the rest of the French empire. In Laos and Cambodia, the new dispensation seemed to be serving its purpose, at least for the moment. In Vietnam, however, the new arrangements had neither succeeded in rallying nationalist enthusiasm around Bao Dai, the head of state, nor in persuading neighboring countries that the ex-emperor was more than a puppet of the French.

Meanwhile, as the Associated States became more closely identified with the Western bloc, DRV adherence to the Eastern one became increasingly evident. And as the war became internationalized, a new American objective was added to the old: not only must the Viet Minh be defeated, but also France must be pressed to continue its efforts in the face of increasing domestic opposition to the war.

Emergence of a New State System

By 1949, a new state system was taking shape in Indochina. Before World War II, French Indochina had consisted of a number of disparately organized parts. In Vietnam, there had been the colony of Cochin China, and two protectorates, Annam and Tonkin, both under the nominal suzerainty of the Emperor of Annam. Cambodia was a protectorate. In Laos, the Kingdom of Luang Prabang was a protectorate, and the rest of the country was governed directly by the French. The new dispensation provided for three states—Vietnam,

Cambodia, and Laos—associated with each other in the Indochinese Federation, and with France and its other dependencies in the French Union. A fourth claimant to national status, the DRV, contested with France and the State of Vietnam for authority over people and territory.

After hostilities began in December 1946, there had been few contacts between the DRV and the French who became increasingly averse to negotiations with Ho. For more than a year, while attempting to pacify the country, they continued to nurture a separate state in Cochin China, where French investments were concentrated, and which, with its large rice and rubber production, was the most important economically of Vietnam's three regions. In Annam and Tonkin, Vietnamese participated in government through administrative committees established in areas restored to French control. But, by the spring of 1947, it had become increasingly apparent that, if the French were to compete with Ho and the DRV, they would have to accept Vietnam's national unity and accord it some degree of sovereignty.

Seeking a national symbol and rallying point, France turned to the former Emperor of Annam, Bao Dai, who, after cooperating briefly with the Viet Minh, had gone to Hong Kong early in 1946. It took two years to achieve the signing of the Elysée Agreements of March 8, 1949, and Bao Dai's return to Vietnam in June. The factors making for delay were many. At home, consistent French pursuit of generally accepted goals was obstructed by political instability (with four cabinets in office between December 1946 and March 1949), differences of views within and among the varying combinations of political parties attempting to maintain coalition cabinets, and differences as well between politicians and bureaucrats in Paris and colonial administrators and interests in Saigon. Also contributing to slow progress were differences among Vietnamese political groups, all of which accepted Bao Dai as the logical rallying point but agreed on little else. Meanwhile, Bao Dai himself, anxious to exact the best terms possible from the French, was a rather elusive figure.

The Elysée Agreements, while leaving much for future definition, reconfirmed Vietnam's independence and its status in the French Union and established procedures for liquidating the republic of Cochin China. France was to support Vietnam's application for membership in the United Nations. Vietnam was to have diplomatic representatives in a number of countries, but its foreign relations were to be under French control. Similarly, although Vietnam was to have its own army, the French were to retain military command until hostilities ceased. Vietnam's internal sovereignty was also limited: its currency was tied to the French; the degree of control to be exercised over its economy was left to be determined by later agreement; special rights were accorded to French nationals; and the montagnard areas were to remain autonomous under French protection.[4]

Cambodia and Laos, accorded similar status in 1949, had already advanced further toward autonomy than Vietnam. Nationalist sentiment had not been as strong there, but French interest was not as strong either and was reduced further because resources had to be concentrated on pacifying Vietnam. For their part, the Cambodian and Lao rulers were prepared to temporize, conscious of their countries' weaknesses, and wanting French assistance and protection against Vietnamese domination. Moreover, among the elite, especially in Laos, affection for the French remained quite strong.

In Cambodia, where the British took the Japanese surrender, French authority had been quickly restored. The nationalist leader, Son Ngoc Thanh, prime minister in the independent government declared by King Norodom Sihanouk, accepted autonomy within the French Union in a *modus vivendi* under which France retained control over internal security and external relations and could veto legislation and royal ordinances. Despite these restrictions, progress was made toward developing modern attributes of statehood; in September 1946, a constituent assembly was elected; in May 1947 a constitution was promulgated; and a National Assembly was elected in December 1947. In November 1949, in a treaty paralleling the Elysée Agreements, Cambodia was recognized as an Associated State within much the same framework of French controls as Vietnam.[5]

In Laos, the re-establishment of French control was made somewhat more difficult because of the anti-French policies of the Chinese, who took the Japanese surrender in the area north of Savannakhet. Never-

4. Hammer, pp. 203–244; Buttinger, II, pp. 667–734; Lancaster, pp. 179–200.
5. Michael Leifer, *Cambodia and Neutrality*, pp. 29–36; Roger M. Smith, *Cambodia's Foreign Policy*, pp. 31–39; Martin Herz, *Short History of Cambodia*, pp. 75–81.

theless, by August 1946, France was able to sign a *modus vivendi* with King Sisavang Vong of Luang Prabang whose rule was now extended over all of Laos. Meanwhile, the principal nationalist leaders—Prince Phetsarath, his brother, Prince Souvanna Phouma, and his half-brother, Prince Souphanouvong—had already fled to Bangkok where they established a Lao Issara government-in-exile.

In Laos, as in Cambodia, new political institutions were established: in January 1947 a constituent assembly was elected; in May a constitution was promulgated; and in November a National Assembly was elected. In July 1949 Laos was given the same status as Vietnam and Cambodia. Well before this, the Lao Issara had split over the question of relations with the Viet Minh, with Prince Souphanouvong leading the supporters of alliance. Its ranks divided, the hospitality of the Thai considerably diminished since Pridi's overthrow in 1946, and a greater degree of independence accorded to Laos under the July agreement, the Lao Issara government dissolved itself in October, and Souvanna Phouma and most of the other leaders returned to Vientiane.[6]

By 1949, when the State of Vietnam was established, the DRV exercised substantial political and territorial control, especially in Tonkin and northern Annam. During the brief period of cooperation with the French, the Viet Minh had seriously weakened its nationalist competitors in Tonkin. In their assaults on the VNQDD and the Dong Minh Hoi, who had bitterly opposed the March 1946 agreement, they were joined by the French; they eliminated Trotskyite and sect leaders without French assistance. After the break with the French, the DRV's political center and its main-force military formations remained in Tonkin in the Viet Bac. From this mountainous region, north of Hanoi and running to the Chinese border, the French had been unable to dislodge them, although French control had been re-established in Hanoi and the other towns of Tonkin and northern Annam by early 1947. Thenceforth, in the north, the French concentrated on maintaining their hold over the rich Red River delta. The substantial defensive force required for this purpose, however, was unable to prevent Viet Minh infiltration, harassment, and terrorism. Even in southern Annam and Cochin China, the Viet Minh had their strong points

6. Sasorith Don Katay, *Le Laos*, pp. 59–75; Sisouk Na Champassak, *Storm Over Laos*, pp. 11–20, Hugh Toye, *Laos*, pp. 69–80.

and base areas; much of the countryside was open to their activity, and there was relative security only in French garrisoned areas.[7]

The Chinese Impact

The limited autonomy the State of Vietnam had achieved by the end of 1949 reflected the strength of nationalist sentiment and the need to give the non-Communist nationalists a center around which they could rally in opposition to the Viet Minh. But the Chinese Communist approach to the borders of Tonkin played an important part as well. Grave apprehensions for the future were aroused in the United States and Britain as well as in France. The French now recognized that they would need substantial assistance from their Allies, particularly from the United States, and that, accordingly, they could not go on treating the problem as a purely internal one. But, although U.S. pressures on behalf of the nationalists began to have more impact, the French gained new leverage from U.S. apprehension over the consequences of the Chinese advance and the possibility that resistance in Indochina would collapse.

Until 1949, the United States, although concerned, had not become deeply involved. A Department of State policy paper of September 1948 recognized that continued hostilities threatened Southeast Asian stability and long-term French interests, but noted that the United States had not urged negotiations because Ho and many of his associates had Communist affiliations. The problem seemed almost insoluble. The French did not understand the situation and would probably lose. The United States had stressed that it was important to satisfy nationalist aspirations. But "our greatest difficulty in talking with the French . . . has been our inability to suggest any practicable solution of the Indochina problem, as we are all too well aware of the unpleasant fact that Communist Ho Chi Minh is the strongest and perhaps the ablest figure in Indochina and that any suggested solution which excludes him is an expedient of uncertain outcome." Added to the dilemma was the immediate and over-riding U.S. interest "in maintaining in power a friendly French government, to assist in the furtherance of our aims in Europe." The Department could conclude only that some way must be found to strike a balance between Indochinese aspirations and French interests.[8]

7. Buttinger, I, 401–409; II, 735–742.
8. *Pentagon Papers*, VIII, 144–149.

Early in 1949, it began to appear that Bao Dai might provide this solution. However, neither then nor even after the final decision to support him was there any great confidence in the outcome, while the complexities of the problems involved were reflected by divisions both within the Department of State and between the Department and the Embassy in Paris. To make Bao Dai attractive to the nationalists, further French concessions would be required. But, these could not be made except at the expense of political stability in Paris, and U.S. efforts to press the French would probably miscarry. On the other hand, if American pressures were reduced, and the French became convinced that the United States would, in any case, pour aid into Indochina to prevent a Communist takeover, their interest in anything other than a military solution would quickly evaporate. And even if Americans hoped that the French would carry out the Elysée Agreements generously and that Vietnamese nationalists would prefer Bao Dai to losing all of their autonomy to the Chinese Communists, would the Vietnamese necessarily see these as their alternatives? The nationalists might well continue to support the DRV, viewing the Elysée Agreements as promising only continued inferiority and subordination in place of the desired equality and sovereignty. A year later, American officials still held very contingent views of the future. Said the Griffin Mission, "If the majority of the Vietnamese can be convinced that the Bao Dai government will be able to achieve real independence for Vietnam and provide a competent government for the country, the fence sitters may declare for Bao Dai, and the non-Communist elements in the Viet Minh may withdraw their support for Ho Chi Minh and turn their nationalist fervor to constructive political and economic activity."[9]

The military outlook was equally bleak. In August 1950, an American military survey mission concluded that French forces were stalemated and had lost much of their offensive spirit, while failure to organize a separate Vietnamese army had intensified already deepseated dissatisfaction and distrust. Viet Minh discipline and effectiveness meanwhile had improved steadily, and they controlled major portions of the country, pinning down the French in defensive positions and making them unable to move without armed escort. The

9. Hayes, p. 61; FRUS, 1949, VII, 19–46; Pentagon Papers, VIII, 190–194, 204–210.

uncertainty arising from internal factors, the mission observed, was compounded by the serious external threat posed by the Chinese Communist presence along the northern border, where French defenses were weak and inadequate.

With the outcome so uncertain, very high stakes would have to be involved to justify major U.S. action. Civilians and military alike now saw these stakes as very high indeed. In a paper submitted to the NSC in February 1950, the State Department defined the threat to Indochina as only one phase of the Communist plan to seize all of Southeast Asia. If the Communists succeeded there, "Thailand and Burma could be expected to fall under Communist domination. . . . The balance of Southeast Asia would then be in grave hazard."[10]

Two months later, the Joint Chiefs of Staff, examining Indochina's strategic importance, agreed that if it fell, other mainland Southeast Asian countries would fall as well. The Philippines and Indonesia would then be transformed from mere supporting positions in the off-shore defensive chain into front-line bases for the defense of the Western Hemisphere. However, in both these countries and in Malaya as well, Indochina's fall would almost immediately bring about dangerous internal-security situations, and they too would probably eventually fall to the Communists. With Communist victory in Indochina assumed as inevitably meaning Communist victory in Southeast Asia, further assumptions led to the conclusion that, in due course, the ability of the United States to retain its perimeter defense would be put in jeopardy; the Chinese food problem would be alleviated; the USSR would have access to important raw materials that might shift the balance of power in its favor; and Japan, to the detriment of its relations with the United States, would be denied the Asian market and access to Asian food and raw materials.[11]

These gloomy projections did not alter the view that the Southeast Asian mainland was not sufficiently important in global strategic terms to justify U.S. participation in military operations there. But, because Indochina was now seen as quite crucial, even though outside the sphere of direct American military effort, an increasingly large investment was to be made in economic and military assistance to reduce

10. *Pentagon Papers,* VIII, 283–284, 358–359.
11. *Ibid.,* VIII, 309.

Vietnam's vulnerability and to keep the French fighting there, at least until they could be replaced by Vietnamese forces.

Britain too, as the Chinese Communists advanced, began to take a different view of a conflict previously seen as another colonial war, of concern largely because the French were handling it so very badly. British experience in 1941 had persuaded them that Indochina was the key to defending Southeast Asia against attack from the north; accordingly, a Communist victory in Indochina would further threaten Malaya, where the British, with some 40,000 troops engaged, were still deeply involved in suppressing local Communist insurgency. Thus, like the United States, although without substantial resources to commit to its success, Britain began to look with increasing favor on the Bao Dai solution.[12]

The Chinese Communist rise to power created new problems for the French without fundamentally altering their view of what the war was all about: the protection of the French Union against demands for independence, whether nationalist or Communist in origin. To be sure, French spokesmen were prepared to echo American rhetoric. Thus General Jean de Lattre, speaking to the National Press Club in Washington in September 1951, declared: "In this war . . . Indochina is not the only stake. Southeast Asia, and even the whole of Asia is at stake. Tongking is the main redoubt, the keystone of the whole structure. The loss of Southeast Asia would mean that communism would have at its disposal essential strategic raw materials, that the Japanese economy would forever be unbalanced, and that the whole of Asia would be threatened. Once Tongking is lost, there is really no barrier before Suez."[13] But French thinking remained centered in the view that General de Gaulle expressed in August 1946 when he opposed proposals for liberalizing the French Union: "United with the overseas territories which she opened to civilization, France is a great power. Without these territories she would be in danger of no longer being one."[14] What was important for France was not the impact of Communist—or nationalist—success in Indochina on Burma and Thailand; it was the impact on Tunisia, Morocco, and Algeria.

12. Saul Rose, *Britain and Southeast Asia*, pp. 165–166; Olver, *British Policy*, p. 36; Greene, p. 101.
13. *USWA*, 1952, p. 194.
14. Hammer, p. 190.

The prospects for Viet Minh success in Indochina were clearly improved by the presence on its northern border of a Communist regime. Actual military intervention could not be precluded; at the very least, it was reasonable to expect that the Viet Minh would now have substantial access to supplies, advice, and sanctuary. The French, already thinly stretched, would also need help. The point was urgently pressed in February 1950 when the American Ambassador was told "that the effort in Indochina was such a drain on France that a long-term program of assistance was necessary and it was only from the United States that it could come. Otherwise . . . it was very likely that France might be forced to reconsider her entire policy with the possible view to cutting her losses and withdrawing from Indochina. . . . Looking into the future it was obvious . . . that France could not continue indefinitely to bear this burden alone if the expected developments in regard to increased assistance to Ho Chi Minh came about."[15]

Meanwhile, military dispositions on the border and general force allocations had to be studied anew. Tactical adjustments were recommended, such as withdrawing forces from exposed positions on the border, but the more difficult problem, with military strength already dangerously drawn down in France and in French Africa, was how to meet the need for reinforcements. Allocating men and resources, moreover, became even more difficult as reactions to the invasion of South Korea faced France with further conflict between its interests as a European power and as an imperial one. The United States, its own strength engaged in Korea, was increasingly apprehensive about Asian vulnerabilities and more anxious than ever that the French stay the course in Indochina. But because Europe also seemed vulnerable, its defense too required increased resources, and a German military contribution now seemed inevitable. For France in 1950, the principle was beginning to become an acceptable one, but not to the point where the German contribution to the defense of Europe could be allowed to outweigh the French. For this dilemma there seemed to be only one solution: the organization—with American support—of a Vietnamese army that could relieve the French of some of their responsibilities.[16]

15. *Pentagon Papers*, I, A35–A36.

16. Jean LaCouture and Philippe Devillers, *End of a War*, pp. 22–24; Guy de Carmoy, pp. 137–153.

Developing Alliances

Starting at the beginning of 1949, a series of British and French exchanges of visits culminated in the arrival in Saigon in November of Malcolm MacDonald, Commissioner-General for Southeast Asia. To Bao Dai, MacDonald delivered a message from Foreign Secretary Ernest Bevin expressing the hope that he would be able to establish stable and representative government and restore peace and stability. MacDonald himself, noting the transfer of provincial and local powers to the Vietnamese, applauded the "speed, sincerity, and good will" of negotiations for the transfer of central powers envisaged in the Elysée Agreements.[17]

The United States also made encouraging statements that were intended, like those of the British, to demonstrate approval for steps already taken while making evident the need for further progress. Commenting on the Elysée Agreements, the State Department said: "The formation of the new unified state of Vietnam and the recent announcement by Bao Dai that the future constitution will be decided by the Vietnamese people are welcome developments which should serve to hasten the re-establishment of peace in that country and the attainment of Vietnam's rightful place in the family of nations."[18]

Other countries also were pressed to take cognizance of the new situation in Indochina. In October, the British successfully supported Bao Dai's application to be represented at the Singapore ECAFE conference. In January, MacDonald reported on progress in Indochina at the Colombo meeting of the Commonwealth Prime Ministers. To his argument that Vietnam would gain even greater independence as the Bao Dai regime progressed, Nehru responded skeptically, opposing recognition until it could be determined whether Bao Dai really had popular support.[19] In this instance, however, Britain showed less sensitivity than in the past to the views of India and to those of the other Asian members of the Commonwealth. In November, a conference of British officials in Singapore, agreeing that the failure of the Bao Dai experiment would mean French withdrawal from Indochina, agreed also that Britain must support him and rally the support of others. The

17. *SIA,* 1949–1950, pp. 426–427.

18. *DSB,* July 18, 1949, p. 75.

19. Olver, *British Policy,* p. 36; *SIA,* 1949–1950, pp. 430–431.

situation, they concluded, was now too urgent to allow the western nations to wait for Asian nations to act; they must recognize the new regime quickly.[20]

To make diplomatic recognition possible, however, the French government must be pressed to secure National Assembly ratification of the Elysée Agreements and the parallel agreements with Laos and Cambodia. This having taken place on February 2, 1950, the United States and Britain recognized the Associated States five days later. Neither contended that the Associated States were fully independent. The United States recognized them as "independent states within the French Union," whereas the British recognized them only as "Associated States within the French Union," with Minister of State Kenneth Younger promising in the House of Commons to press the French toward full independence.[21]

Describing recognition as consistent with "our fundamental policy of giving support to the peaceful and democratic evolution of dependent peoples," and predicting that implementation of the Elysée and related agreements would promote political stability and the growth of effective democratic institutions," the United States declared that it was considering what steps to take "to further these objectives and to assure, in collaboration with other like-minded nations, that this development shall not be hindered by internal dissension fostered from abroad."[22] Some hesitation remained. Although Acheson no longer wanted to disassociate the United States from French problems in Indochina, he feared that once aid was extended the American bargaining position would disappear entirely. Nevertheless, in May, he announced that the United States, "convinced that neither national independence nor democratic evolution exist in any area dominated by Soviet imperialism, considers the situation to be such as to warrant its according economic aid and military equipment to the Associated States of Indochina and to France in order to assist them in restoring stability and permitting these states to pursue their peaceful and democratic development."[23]

By the end of 1950 some assistance had arrived, and more was in train. In January 1951 the United States made available $23.5 million

20. *Pentagon Papers*, VIII, 223–224.
21. Lancaster, p. 204; Hansard, 5th Series, H.C., Vol. 473, Col. 1160.
22. *DSB*, Feb. 20, 1950, p. 291.
23. *Ibid.*, June 12, 1950, pp. 977–978; Gaddis Smith, *Dean Acheson*, p. 311.

in economic aid for the fiscal year ending in June 1951. In June, the first military equipment—seven Dakota aircraft—arrived. In August, regular shipments of war material began, and a military assistance group was established in Saigon. In October it was announced that the major share of the $5 billion military assistance planned for NATO for the fiscal years 1951 and 1952 would go to France and that $500 million of the military assistance funds planned for the Far East during the same years would be used for equipment for Indochina. And, in December, representatives of the United States, France, and the Associated States signed an agreement providing that all equipment and financial support supplied by the United States for establishing a Vietnamese national army would be provided to the French command; direct relations between the American military assistance group and the Associated States were expressly precluded.[24]

By the end of the year, sixteen states, in addition to the United States and Britain, had recognized the Associated States. The only Asian and Pacific states among them, however, were Australia, New Zealand, South Korea, and Thailand.[25] Even Thailand had to be strongly pressed. Phibun and other military leaders, who expected increased assistance from the United States to ensue, favored recognition; Foreign Minister Pote Sarasin, who resigned when recognition was announced, was not convinced that Bao Dai had Vietnamese support. Romulo, similarly, wrote Acheson that everyone in Asia knew that Bao Dai was a mere puppet; the reluctance of the Filipinos, who saw the lines of nationalism, Communism, and colonialism as hopelessly blurred, was never overcome. In Indonesia, rumors of American pressures led non-Communists to support an unsuccessful Communist proposal for recognition of the DRV. When Mohammad Natsir succeeded Hatta later in the year, he felt constrained to explain not why he opposed recognizing Bao Dai, but why he opposed recognizing Ho. "As regards the question about the Government's standpoint vis-a-vis the Ho Chi Minh Government; the . . . reply is . . . that recognition should be given to the whole people—should it be united by democratic procedure—rather than to a part of the people."[26] Report-

24. Lancaster, pp. 207, 220; *SIA*, 1949–1950, p. 440.

25. The others were Belgium, Brazil, Chile, Colombia, Cuba, Greece, Italy, Luxembourg, the Netherlands, South Africa, Spain, and the Vatican.

26. Dorothy Woodman, *The Republic of Indonesia,* p. 406; Holland, pp. 174, 175; Gaddis Smith, p. 312; Meyer, p. 161; Nuechterlein, p. 196.

ing in February on Asian attitudes, the American Embassy in Bangkok observed, "It is transparently clear that Asiatic neighbors of Indochina consider Bao Dai a French creation and a French puppet; despite current and anticipated actions of support by U.S. and Western powers they prepared to sell his regime short, if status Bao Dai remains un-drastically modified; even if such changes made promptly he must exert effective leadership comparable to Ho's."[27]

Just as the State of Vietnam was becoming part of the western bloc in the Cold War, so the DRV was becoming more openly and un-equivocally part of the Communist bloc. On November 26, 1949, the DRV followed the rest of the Communist bloc in recognizing Com-munist China. At the World Federation of Trade Unions meeting in Peking that month, the behavior of the DRV representatives was quite different from what it had been at Calcutta in 1948. Not only was the Chinese path accepted as the sole road to power, but also the DRV representative emphasized that, all along, the revolution in Vietnam had been following the correct Marxist-Leninist path; from 1930 on, the "leadership of the movement for national indepen-dence was assumed by the working class." In an exchange of tele-grams with Ho during the conference, Mao said, "China and Vietnam are meeting on the front line of an [anti-] imperialist struggle. With the victorious development of our struggles for liberation of the two peoples, the friendship between our two peoples will surely become closer day by day."[28] In December, the Viet Minh radio declared, "The victory of the Chinese people constitutes for us and for all the oppressed peoples who struggle in Asia a precious encouragement. For four years our people have been struggling alone against the enemy. The struggle, begun with sticks, today enters its decisive phase."[29]

Within Vietnam, the shift was signaled at the National Conference of Vietnamese Trade Unions held in December and January. Portraits of Stalin and Mao decorated the conference hall; the main report was made by Truong Chinh, secretary-general of the Marxist Study Group —the name assumed by the Indochinese Communist Party when it dissolved itself in 1945; the term "national liberation movement" re-placed "resistance war" and "independence movement" of the earlier

27. *Pentagon Papers*, VIII, 280.
28. Hinton, *Communist China in World Politics*, p. 238; Chen, p. 219.
29. Zasloff, p. 14.

period; and Vietnamese workers pledged themselves to follow the heroic example of Soviet workers. Thereafter, controls over non-Communist groups and over guerrilla activity in Annam and Cochin China were strengthened, and Communists were installed in more and more of the important civilian and military positions. DRV propaganda on international issues fell into line with that of the rest of the bloc. Internally, a campaign to learn from the Chinese was undertaken; a forced-draft effort to translate the works of Mao and other Chinese Communist scriptures occupied the attention of all available intellectuals with a knowledge of Chinese.[30]

Meanwhile, on January 14, triumphantly declaring itself "the only lawful government representing a unified Vietnamese people," the DRV announced that it was ready to establish diplomatic relations "with any government respecting equality of rights, and the territorial and national sovereignty of Vietnam."[31] Peking's response came on the same day; the Soviet Union, acting unusually both in according recognition to a regime still not victorious and in doing so in the wake of another Communist power, granted recognition on January 31.[32] The Eastern European countries and North Korea followed suit in February.

Early in 1952 the DRV's internal political structure was brought into even closer conformity with international Communist norms. At a National Congress of Unification in February, the Indochinese Communist Party reappeared as the ostensibly new Lao Dong (Workers') Party. The party's platform[33] accepted the Maoist four-class thesis: "The motive forces of the Viet-Nam revolution at present are the people comprising primarily the workers, peasants, petty bourgeoisie and national bourgeoisie, followed by the patriotic and progressive personages and landlords . . . the leading class in the Viet-Nam revolution is the working class." The platform also accepted the two-camp thesis, with the anti-imperialist democratic camp, of which the party was a member, daily coming closer to victory under Soviet leadership. In turn, the Chinese hailed the party's establishment as an indispensable step toward success: "Only under the leadership of such a revolutionary political party can an invincible people's army and an

30. *Ibid.,* pp. 43–46; Hammer, pp. 249–251; Trager, *Marxism,* p. 164.
31. Cole, pp. 95–96.
32. Ulam, p. 516.
33. Text in Cole, p. 96 ff.

invincible revolutionary united front be established, and malignant imperialism and its lackey—domestic reactionary clique—defeated."[34]

At the same meeting, the Vietnamese Communists established a more open and formal relationship with insurgents in Laos and Cambodia. France had its Indochinese Federation which, under arrangements made at the Pau Conference in 1950, served largely to perpetuate French control over such important matters as currency and trade. Now the DRV was to have its own counterpart. The Viet Minh had long been providing support to Prince Souphanouvong and his Lao followers and to dissident elements in Cambodia. Moreover, by 1950, supply routes in Laos and Cambodia had become very important to the DRV. At the February congress, attended by Souphanouvong and other Lao and Cambodian representatives, a formal alliance was urged on the basis of "mutual equality and reciprocal aid in the struggle against the common enemy." The Lao Dong platform declared, "In the common interests of the three peoples, the people of Viet-Nam are willing to enter into long-term cooperation with the peoples of Laos and Cambodia, with a view to bringing about an independent, free, strong and prosperous federation of the states of Viet-Nam, Laos, and Cambodia, if the three peoples so desire." In March still another meeting was held at which Vietnamese, Lao, and Cambodian representatives announced the creation of an alliance to struggle against the French and the Americans.[35]

Insurgency Becomes A War

In 1949, the struggle in Vietnam became politically a battleground of the Cold War. In 1950 the military situation was transformed— what had been an insurgency relying solely on small-scale guerrilla operations became a war. Without abandoning country-wide use of local forces to undermine military security and civil authority, the Viet Minh proceeded to supplement these activities with offensive actions conducted by increasingly large military formations. The contribution made to this expanding effort by PRC assistance was important but not quantifiable with any precision or certainty. With the Chinese Communists in control just over the border, Viet Minh forces in large

---

34. Chen, p. 243.
35. Cole, p. 105; Hammer, pp. 277–281; Lancaster, pp. 213–215, 248; Paul Langer and Joseph Zasloff, *North Vietnam and the Pathet Lao*, pp. 32–42, 51.

numbers could be trained in safety; as many as 18 battalions may have been trained in China in 1950 and it has been estimated that 40,000 were trained there up to the time of the cease-fire in 1954. Military equipment was provided also; the most generally accepted estimates credit the Chinese with deliveries of 10 to 20 tons of military supplies a month in 1951, 250 tons a month in 1952, and 400 to 600 in 1953.[36]

For three years after the break with the French, the DRV main force had been husbanded, trained, and expanded in the Viet Bac. In February 1950, Giap announced that the guerrilla war was over and that the war of movement had begun. In spring and fall campaigns, operating first in multibattalion and, by October, in divisional strength and making extensive and effective use of field guns and antiaircraft batteries, the Communists drove the French out of posts along the Chinese border, causing them heavy casualties and capturing substantial quantities of arms and equipment. By the end of the fall campaign a large area of northern Tonkin adjacent to China and extending from the coast to the Lao border was in the hands of the Viet Minh, who also controlled Route 4, the access road from China.[37]

A French communiqué in October recognized the change: "For the first time we have had to do with an enemy perfectly armed and equipped, who have an excellent radio network and know how to coordinate their movements."[38] Alarm stimulated action on plans for building up Vietnamese forces, hitherto organized only in token battalions. In November a school was established at Dalat to train Vietnamese officers. During 1951, four divisions were to be formed, partly by recruitment and partly by transferring Vietnamese serving with the French Expeditionary Force. The State of Vietnam was to devote 35 to 40 percent of its revenue to this enterprise, and substantial U.S. assistance was envisaged under a tripartite military agreement of December 23, 1950.[39]

The next year opened more auspiciously for France. Over-reaching themselves in their spring offensive, the Viet Minh made three efforts to drive the French from the Red River delta, and each time were

36. Zasloff, pp. 19, 27; George Tanham, *Communist Revolutionary Warfare,* pp. 63, 68–69.
37. Zasloff, p. 28; Lancaster, p. 219.
38. Lancaster, p. 219.
39. *Ibid.,* p. 220.

repulsed. Even so, the portents for the future were disturbing: into the first of its assaults the Viet Minh had thrown two divisions; into the second and third, three. General de Lattre's demand for reinforcements pointed up the French dilemma: to send conscripts to Indochina was not politically feasible; to take troops from Europe would reduce the French contribution to NATO; to take them from Africa—as it was decided to do—would weaken the French hold there. Although de Lattre managed to get reinforcements from his own government and promises of more U.S. aid more quickly delivered, the Viet Minh fall campaign put an end to any optimism generated in the spring. In this campaign, the Viet Minh concentrated on the highlands, avoiding major incursions in the delta where, nevertheless, their guerrilla activities, together with threats of further attacks, immobilized a large French force in defensive positions. But the French were also to suffer great difficulties as a result of their own initiative—the attempt to capture the Viet Minh strongpoint, Hoa Binh, on Route 6 southwest of Hanoi in hopes of interdicting movement of rice north to the Viet Bac and of military supplies south to Annam and Cochin China. By the end of February, the French, having taken Hoa Binh in November, had been forced to evacuate by a series of counteroffensives with heavy casualties to both sides.[40]

As the scale and cost of hostilities rose, so did domestic opposition in France to continuing the war. Speaking in January 1952, the Radical Socialist leader, Pierre Mendès-France, declared: "You will never succeed in organizing the national defences in Europe if you continue to send all your cadres to the East, to sacrifice every year without any result, the equivalent of the number of officers leaving St. Cyr in a year and to spend annually 500 milliard francs, representing an additional 500 milliards of monetary inflation, which will bring in its train want, rising prices, and further social unrest which will not fail to be exploited by Communist propaganda. . . . By an incredible paradox, we have accorded priority to Asia at the very time when, in opposition to MacArthur's policy, in opposition to the policy of the old isolationist Americans, the 'Europeans' from Churchill to Pleven last year, are upholding the thesis of the priority of Europe in the United States."

40. *Ibid.,* pp. 243–245; Fall, *Two Viet-Nams,* pp. 116–119; LaCouture and Devillers, pp. 28–30.

Saying much the same thing in October 1950, his had then been a lone voice; now, his position was widely discussed and widely approved.[41]

At the same time, intermittent truce talks in Korea, beginning in July 1951, were raising two questions: if peace talks eventuated in Korea, might there not also be peace talks in Vietnam? And, if Chinese forces were no longer occupied in Korea, might they not then move south in support of the Viet Minh?

In January 1952, former premier Robert Schuman, whose party, the Mouvement Républicain Populaire, for six years had vigorously opposed negotiations with Ho, declared: "If an armistice can be considered on honourable terms, France will not hesitate to make peace."[42] The following month, Jean Letourneau, Minister for the Associated States said: "If an armistice were to come about in Korea, the Government would be in favor of calling an international conference aimed at achieving a political settlement of the conflict. . . . France will not refuse to talk with the Vietminh but she will not take the first step."[43]

American officials observed these developments with some concern. In February, an NSC staff study concluded that in Indochina an armistice would be much more complicated than in Korea owing to the absence of a boundary between the two sides. Because of the weaknesses of local governments, popular attitudes, and continued Communist pressure, any settlement based on French military withdrawal "would be tantamount to handing over Indochina to communism." Accordingly, the United States should "continue to oppose any negotiated settlement with the Viet Minh."[44] In November 1952 when Acheson briefed Dwight D. Eisenhower, he noted, like the American military survey mission over two years earlier, the lack of aggressiveness of the French forces, and warned the president-elect that a strong body of French opinion, regarding the Indochina cause as lost, believed the war was bleeding France and undermining the possibility of French-German equality in European defense.[45]

The United States was also concerned over possible Chinese inter-

41. Lancaster, p. 240.
42. *Ibid.*
43. LaCouture and Devillers, p. 31.
44. *Pentagon Papers,* VIII, 474.
45. Harry S. Truman, *Memoirs,* II, 519.

vention. The February 1952 NSC Staff Study, holding that an armistice in Korea would considerably increase Chinese Communist capabilities to conduct military operations in Indochina, estimated that if Chinese Communist forces intervened directly the French would soon be driven back to a beachhead around Haiphong. Warnings against such adventures seemed clearly desirable. In January 1952, an American representative told the General Assembly that Communist aggression in Southeast Asia "would, in the view of my Government, be a matter of direct and grave concern which would require the most urgent and earnest consideration by the United Nations."[46] In the same month, British Foreign Secretary Anthony Eden, speaking at Columbia University, declared: "It should be understood that intervention by force by Chinese Communists in South-East Asia—even if they were called volunteers—would create a situation no less menacing than that which the United Nations met and faced in Korea." In April, Eden said in the House of Commons that Chinese aggression in Indochina would undoubtedly lead the French and Vietnamese governments to appeal to the UN. "We have made it clear," he said, "that in such an event Her Majesty's Government would not fail to meet its obligations under the United Nations."[47]

The solidarity of the western alliance in support of the French effort in Indochina was also increasingly stressed. In May, after American-British-French staff talks in Paris, the French premier's office announced that the United States and Britain had recognized that France represented a veritable pillar of defense in Southeast Asia and that its defeat would involve grave consequences not only for Malaya, Singapore, and India, but even for Japan. In June, an American communiqué, announcing increased aid to France, declared that the "struggle in which the forces of the French Union and the Associated States are engaged against the forces of Communist aggression in Indochina is an integral part of the world-wide resistance by the Free Nations to Communist attempts at conquest and subversion."[48] In December, French Foreign Minister Schuman successfully appealed to the NATO Council for an expression of solidarity. The Council resolution, adopted on December 17, expressed admiration for the courage

46. *USWA*, 1952, p. 178; *Pentagon Papers*, VIII, 468.
47. *SIA*, 1952, pp. 401, 421.
48. *DSB*, June 30, 1952, p. 1010; *SIA*, 1952, p. 402.

of the French forces and for the armies of the Associated States and declared that their struggle against Communist aggression, which, like that in Korea, was in harmony with the views and ideals of the Atlantic community, should receive the unfailing support of its members. Nothing was said, however, about the form that this support should take.[49]

The rhetoric of a unified response to Chinese aggression masked irreconcilable differences over how intervention, if it occurred, should be met. With 90,000 casualties inflicted on French Union forces by the fall of 1952, the French saw the problem as one of securing commitments from their Allies to reinforce them in the battle zone. To U.S. military planners, this course seemed futile, and they sought agreement—which neither France nor Britain was prepared to give—on action against China itself. In November 1952, accordingly, Acheson had to inform Eisenhower that Allied conversations had not been effective in devising agreed military solutions against the contingency of overt Chinese intervention. Meanwhile, however, the American role was growing. In June, Letourneau's visit to Washington had evoked pledges of military and financial assistance sufficient to cover 40 percent of French expenditures in Indochina.[50]

49. *SIA*, pp. 424–425; Grosser, p. 284.
50. Lancaster, p. 251.

PART III

The Geneva Settlement

CHAPTER 8

THE ROAD TO THE
CONFERENCE TABLE

The period during which France moved toward accepting a nego-tiated end to the Indochina conflict was one of exceptional division among the western Allies. Especially after Stalin's death in March 1953, Russian hints of moderation loosened the bonds created by the urge to strengthen western defenses. Russian overtures might not be accepted at face value, and compromise on vital issues might still be rejected. Nevertheless, many believed with Winston Churchill that containment had succeeded to the point where it was possible to ex-plore the feasibility of moving from confrontation toward a more harmonious international order.

Movement toward détente was widely supported in Europe. The Communist-sponsored peace movement, with its years of denigration of the United States and "ban the bomb" propaganda, had influenced the attitudes of many Europeans far outside Communist circles. Nuclear developments had heightened the fear of war and its con-sequences. The Soviet Union successfully tested a thermonuclear device in August 1953 and was known to be making great strides toward a delivery capability; American tests in the Pacific in October 1952 and March 1954 had made vivid to the world the terrifying destructive power of the new weapons.[1] Meanwhile, at the very time when Amer-

---

1. In March 1955, Winston Churchill was to say, "There is an immense gulf between the atomic and hydrogen bomb. The atomic bomb, with all its terrors, did not carry us outside the scope of human control or manageable events in thought and action, in peace or war." But with the hydrogen bomb, "the entire foundation of human affairs was revolutionized and mankind placed in a situation both measureless and laden with doom. . . . The broad effect of the latest de-velopments is to spread almost indefinitely and at least to a vast extent the area of mortal danger" (Watt, pp. 146–147).

ican nuclear superiority was clearly destined to disappear within two or three years, the "new look"—emphasizing nuclear weapons and massive retaliation and calling for reduction in U.S. forces stationed abroad—aroused fear that any hostilities in Europe would quickly take the form of a nuclear exchange.

French and British policy makers, inclined themselves toward exploring the possibilities of détente, were also pressed in this direction by popular attitudes. In France, political divisions were strong, and governments unstable. Nevertheless, there was a developing consensus around the desirability of terminating the war in Indochina and the undesirability of proceeding with the European Defense Community. In Britain, the governing Conservative Party and the Labour Party's main stream were solidly behind exploratory gestures toward Moscow and greater independence from the United States, while Labour's restless and assertive left wanted to move even further away from past policies into essentially neutralist ones.

In the United States, however, political leaders and the general public alike were in the grip of conflicting drives. The militant rhetoric of members of the executive and legislative branches—Democrats as well as Republicans—and Senator Joseph R. McCarthy's activities made it seem that the American obsession with the threat of Communism, foreign and domestic, was becoming even stronger. During the 1952 election campaign, Dulles, now Eisenhower's Secretary of State, had portrayed his party as intent upon an anti-Communist crusade. Convinced that Soviet hints of moderation were only a cover for continued aggressive designs, he argued not only that such aggression should be resisted anywhere it occurred, but also that any signs of Soviet retreat should occasion not compromise but increased pressures.[2] Conviction and political compulsions combined to evoke equally militant Democratic postures. Thus Lyndon Johnson declared in 1952: "If anywhere in the world—by any means, open or concealed—Communism trespasses upon the soil of the free world, we should unleash all the power at our command upon the vitals of the Soviet Union."[3] But, while the rhetoric of crusading anti-Communism was a potent weapon in the domestic political arena, the impact of the crusading

2. Townsend Hoopes, *The Devil and John Foster Dulles*, pp. 124–127.
3. Barnet, p. 133.

spirit on actual foreign policy was affected not only by countervailing desires for some relaxation of international tensions, but also by the growing unwillingness of the American taxpayer/voter to assume burdens in support of international crusades against Communism or anything else.

Eisenhower himself looked upon Stalin's death and Malenkov's stress on peaceful coexistence as opening up prospects for conciliation rather than increased pressures. In mid-April, marking Stalin's death as the end of an era, the President expressed hopes for concrete steps that would validate Soviet professions of peaceful intent.[4] But the two strains of thinking remained in conflict. On the one hand, a militant world view made it difficult for the United States to explore prospects for accommodation. On the other, the strong domestic pressures for cutting down overseas expenditures, reducing international responsibilities, and limiting executive freedom in foreign affairs, made it equally difficult for the United States to make commitments and concessions to its Allies that would reduce their interest in détente. In addition, these contradictory pressures, operating particularly within the majority party, gave American policy an element of unpredictability which disturbed the Allies of the United States and heightened popular demands elsewhere for some degree of disassociation from American leadership.

The differences afflicting the alliance had their greatest impact on the effort to coordinate Indochina policy. It became evident very quickly that there was no real possibility of East-West compromise on Germany, Austria, and Korea; on these problems, the alternative for each side to what had become a more or less viable *status quo* was an unacceptable capitulation to the position of the other. In Indochina, on the other hand, no *status quo* yet existed, but one might be achieved by mutual concessions at the negotiating table. Here the question was not whether action was possible—a question answered in the negative on other issues and thus easily dropped—but the more vexing one of whether possible action, since it inevitably required some concession, should be taken.

Differences in geographic perspective made it easier in Europe than in the United States to answer this question affirmatively. The Euro-

4. Hoopes, pp. 170–172.

peans were not inclined to see compromise in Indochina as in any way analogous to the compromise of Munich. With the French still unable to stem the Communist advance or to satisfy the demands of the non-Communist nationalists, Europeans tended to regard a continuing investment in Indochina as more likely to weaken the West than to strengthen it. And they found some retreat in Southeast Asia much more tolerable than in Europe or even in the Middle East.

For the United States, whose views of Communist China had already divided it from its western Allies, these answers were not persuasive. But, since the United States was not the only or even the principal actor in Indochina, it had to respond to the pressures of its Allies, and these were reinforced by the contradictory strains in basic positions and popular attitudes that bedeviled American policy makers. In American eyes the obdurate colonialism of the French was morally wrong and reduced the effectiveness of the war effort. But, if Americans did not assist the distasteful French effort to preserve some attributes of empire in Indochina, would not America's own struggle against the Communists in Indochina be lost? And could policy makers permit this struggle to be lost or abandoned when two administrations had stressed the key importance of Indochina to national security and when Eisenhower was pledged to regain the advantage his predecessor had allegedly lost to Moscow and to stem the advance of Communism in Asia? But, if the French were to prove unable or unwilling to carry on, who could then do so? The military leadership, more than ever reluctant to commit troops to the Asian mainland, viewed any additional commitments as beyond American capabilities at existing and projected force levels, especially since promised budget cuts had reduced the Army and the Marine Corps by 10 percent in 1954, and further reductions were contemplated. And there had been other promises as well. To an electorate embittered by the heavy burdens and losses of an inconclusive war in Korea, the Republican candidate for president had said in October 1952, "If there must be a war there, let it be Asians against Asians." But, there was no immediate prospect of fielding a Vietnamese force that could be effective against the Viet Minh. And not even air power's strongest advocates could argue persuasively that its use would eliminate the requirement for effective ground troops in Indochina or that Indochina would be an appropriate testing ground for doctrines of massive retaliation.

Even assuming that the administration could find a way out of this labyrinth of contradictions that would be persuasive to the military establishment, the public, and the Congress, what support could it find from its Allies in Europe? If it found little or none, was the American interest sufficiently strong to make unilateral action acceptable? All of these questions faced American policy makers before and during the Geneva Conference. Their complexity led both the President and the Secretary of State to proceed with great caution, avoiding risky commitments even though at times encouraging or permitting a degree of seeming readiness to take risks that frightened the British, confused the French, and may have induced some greater degree of caution among the Communists.

France: First Steps toward Disengagement

In December 1952 France had secured a NATO Council statement of solidarity with the French war effort in Indochina. During 1953, in concrete evidence of this solidarity, U.S. aid was to be still further increased. But it was also in 1953 that French purposes began to be drastically altered. With the growing conviction that France could neither win the war nor sustain it indefinitely, political policy began to focus on ways in which it could be ended through negotiation, while military policy focused on bringing about an advantageous base for such negotiation.

The prospect of peace talks on Korea brought by the armistice agreement of July 1953 was only one factor inclining the French toward negotiations. Long before this, concern over the many hazards and uncertainties involved in continuing the war had become more widespread. With the French Union under attack in Africa as well as in Asia, the argument that to yield anywhere was to be weakened everywhere began to be countered by the argument that France, with its limited resources, must concentrate its efforts in those of its overseas territories that were of most vital importance, and these were in Africa not in Asia. "Rabat, Dakar, Algiers," argued former premier, Edouard Daladier, "have as much importance for us as Strasbourg and Metz"; and it was there that men and material being wasted in far less important Indochina should be employed.[5] Similarly, if, as General de

5. Hammer, p. 309.

Gaulle had stressed, its overseas possessions helped make France a great power in Europe, the prolonged and inconclusive struggle in Indochina, many argued, was making it impossible for France to play its proper role in Europe where, in consequence, German military preeminence might be restored. The ever-increasing United States aid that enabled France to continue seemed to many to magnify the risks of going on. The basic American objective—the containment of Communism in Asia—was not basic to France. French interests, moreover, were threatened not only by Viet Minh successes but also by American pressures in support of nationalist demands and the prospect that, in due course, French influence would be replaced by American. To an increasing degree, therefore, the effort—which, even in the face of large-scale assistance, the French saw themselves as carrying on alone —had come to seem pointless. As General Henri Navarre was later to ask, if the French were to persist simply in order to participate in the American containment policy, renouncing their own position and privileges in the process, were they not merely pulling chestnuts out of the fire for others?[6]

In a first very quiet move toward negotiations, Prince Buu Hoi, Bao Dai's cousin, a member of Ho's delegation to the Fontainebleau conference and an eminent scientist, was sent to Rangoon late in 1952 to assure Viet Minh representatives there that France was not opposed to negotiations and would welcome contacts that could bring about clarification on both sides. Nothing came of this, and in July 1953 the new French premier, Joseph Laniel, declared that the burdens it had assumed in defending the independence of the Associated States and for the common cause of free people were too heavy for France alone. His government therefore would seek additional Allied aid, would demonstrate French good faith and encourage more active Indochinese participation in the war effort by "perfecting the independence of the Associated States," and would seek to put an end to the bloodshed by an acceptable negotiation.[7]

Laniel's promise responded to a strong political imperative; in June, Mendès-France had missed becoming premier by only thirteen votes. Nevertheless, although the domestic political balance was now quite

6. Henri Navarre, *Agonie de l'Indochine,* pp. 30, 67.

7. Hammer, p. 310; Fall, *Two Viet-Nams,* pp. 123–124; Joseph Laniel, *Le Drame Indochinois,* pp. 9–10.

heavily weighted toward peace, the government was divided. Advocates of perfecting independence and peace, led by the Premier were opposed by others, led by Georges Bidault, Laniel's Foreign Minister. Bidault, who as a candidate for the premiership in June had opposed negotiations, distrusted any move to weaken French Union authority, and still saw some prospect for military victory. All were agreed, however, that an expanded and more successful military effort would have to precede negotiations if these negotiations were to be in any sense honorable. The form the military effort was to take was established under the new commander in Indochina, General Navarre, who took up his responsibilities at the end of May.[8]

Under the Navarre Plan (largely devised by Navarre's predecessor, General Raoul Salan), the armies of the Associated States were to be expanded and trained to assume defensive responsibilities. This would free the Expeditionary Corps from garrison duties which were keeping it so occupied that, by Navarre's count, French Union forces available for offensive action were the equivalent of three divisions against a Viet Minh equivalent of nine. To provide time to prepare the Indochinese forces for their new role, the Expeditionary Corps would be temporarily reinforced, and, to permit them to concentrate on harassment and pacification in the Red River delta and in Annam and Cochin China, no major military campaigns were to be launched north of the eighteenth parallel during the 1953–1954 fighting season. Then, late in 1954, having withstood continued Viet Minh attacks and handed over the defense of now more secure areas to a transformed Vietnamese National Army, the Expeditionary Corps would launch a general offensive against the enemy main force. They would then be operating with a much more favorable force ratio than existed in the spring of 1953 and from territories less intermixed with areas of enemy control.[9]

The United States: A Different View

The Laniel and Eisenhower governments agreed that the French military effort needed reorientation and reinforcement and that rein-

8. Robert F. Randle, *Geneva, 1954*, pp. 5–13; LaCouture and Devillers, pp. 35–36; de Carmoy, p. 144; Grosser, p. 297.

9. Navarre, p. 42; Lancaster, pp. 264–266; LaCouture and Devillers, p. 37; Paul Ely, *L'Indochine dans la tourmente*, pp. 23–25.

forcement required greater infusions of U.S. aid. But the broader objectives of the Navarre Plan were viewed quite differently by the two governments. The French government wanted military success in order to improve its bargaining position in negotiations that need not come immediately but could not be too long deferred. American political and military leaders interpreted the Navarre Plan and the offer to perfect Indochinese independence as part of a new drive to win the war, a strategy more likely to be successful than earlier efforts because it seemed to satisfy requirements for rapid political evolution, greater progress in establishing a Vietnamese army, and more aggressive military tactics.

Although it does not seem that U.S. policy makers clearly perceived this difference, they did recognize that the French were approaching a turning point. In retrospect, President Eisenhower was to say, "The life of the Laniel government was important to United States policies. We were convinced that no succeeding government would take a stronger position than his on the defense of Indochina, or in support of the European Defense Community."[10] Contemporaneously, the State Department was even more vehement, urging increased aid to France because the Laniel government was almost sure to be the last "which would undertake to continue the war in Indochina. If it fails, it will almost certainly be succeeded by a government committed to seek a settlement on terms dangerous to the security of the United States and the Free World. . . . Under present conditions any negotiated settlement would mean the eventual loss to Communism not only of Indochina but of the whole of Southeast Asia."[11]

In July, Navarre arrived in Washington in an atmosphere of some optimism, since his military operations seemed to be getting off to a good start. Publicly, high officials expressed considerable confidence in French plans. The Navarre Plan, John Foster Dulles told a Senate committee, is designed to "break the organized body of Communist aggression by the end of the 1955 fighting season."[12] Privately, however, there was greater uncertainty. Lieutenant General John W. O'Daniel, reporting to the Joint Chiefs of Staff on his recent trip to Indochina, said he was convinced that the Navarre concept would

10. Dwight D. Eisenhower, *Mandate for Change,* p. 343.
11. *Pentagon Papers,* IX, 128.
12. Fall, *Two Viet-Nams,* p. 122.

achieve decisive victory by 1955. But, in passing O'Daniel's report to the Secretary of Defense the Chiefs themselves took a more contingent view: "If vigorously pursued militarily in Indochina and supported politically in France, the Navarre concept offers a promise of success sufficient to warrant appropriate additional U.S. aid." When the Joint Chiefs learned that the Secretary of Defense proposed sending their memorandum to the Secretary of State, they became even more cautious. The "promise of success" they now felt was too optimistic, especially in view of the reports they were receiving about how the plan was being carried out. They still believed that the French should receive additional support, but only if they committed themselves to implementing the Navarre Plan vigorously and were willing "to receive and act upon U.S. military advice."[13]

Uncertainty apparently persisted in some quarters; a memorandum, possibly to the Secretary of Defense, two days before the NSC meeting of September 9, remarked, "This very important and complex matter is being rushed to such an extent that there remain a number of questions which are not completely answered at this time."[14] Nevertheless, it was at this meeting that the decision was made to provide as much as $385 million in additional assistance in the calendar year 1954. The French, in exchange, were to carry out their military plans vigorously, continue to perfect the independence of the Associated States, take into account the views of the American military, and make no permanent alterations in their commitments to NATO. On September 30, a joint communiqué announced the aid decision and, in a general way, the undertakings assumed by the French.[15]

Political and Military Problems

In fact, there was ample room for concern over how French political and military programs were being carried out. The effort to perfect the independence of the Associated States, involving *inter alia*

13. *Pentagon Papers*, IX, 134, 138–141.

14. *Ibid.*, p. 144. Only an excerpt is reproduced of what seems to be a memorandum briefing one of the principals on various questions scheduled for discussion at the National Security Council meeting of Sept. 9. The summary in the Table of Contents gives the incorrect impression that the document is an account of the meeting itself.

15. *Ibid.*, pp. 153–155; *DSB*, Oct. 12, 1953, pp. 486–487.

alteration of the agreements of 1949, proceeded smoothly only in the case of Laos. There the leadership had been thoroughly alarmed in the spring of 1953 by Viet Minh incursions reaching almost to the royal capital at Luang Prabang, in the course of which Souphanouvong proclaimed a Free Lao government at Sam Neua. Wanting more than anything else to be protected from the Vietnamese, the Lao were not inclined to make serious difficulties for the French. On October 22, King Sisavang Vong signed a new treaty recognizing Laos as a fully independent and sovereign state and reaffirming its membership in the French Union. In related special agreements, various functions previously performed by the French were transferred to Lao control, while the French were empowered to station in Laos the troops necessary for its defense.[16]

In Cambodia, the French declaration of July 3 had found King Sihanouk in the midst of a campaign of his own. A year earlier, first dissolving an obstreperously nationalist Assembly and suspending the constitution, Sihanouk had promised that he himself would win independence from France within three years. In March, in Paris, he had demanded full sovereignty for Cambodia and control over its own army and police. Rebuffed by the French, Sihanouk proceeded to Canada, the United States, and Japan, holding press conferences all the way. According to his own account, he was told in Washington that, once the menace of Communism was dispelled, the United States would do everything in its power to help Cambodia gain full independence. Meanwhile, however, he was urged to join Americans and French in cooperation against the common enemy.

In May, perhaps influenced by the attention Sihanouk was attracting to his cause, France offered a number of concessions. Finding these inadequate, the King exiled himself to Bangkok, but cut short his intended stay when the Thai made it clear that they had no intention of supporting him against the French. He returned to Cambodia in mid-June, but only to Battambang, where he vowed to remain until his demands were met. After a period of some tension in Phnom Penh, the French, now committed by their July 3 declaration and anxious to concentrate their resources on their more important problems in

16. Dommen, p. 38; Australia, Department of External Affairs, *Select Documents on International Affairs, Laos,* pp. 12–13.

Vietnam, conceded on October 8 to Sihanouk's insistence upon a complete and unconditional transfer of responsibilities in all fields.[17] This included the transfer of supreme command over the Khmer armed forces, a change that was to prove of immense significance for Cambodia at the Geneva Conference.

Dealings with the Vietnamese proved by far the most difficult. The Bao Dai solution, useful as it had been internationally, had brought Vietnam no real independence. Bao Dai himself, spending much of his time on the Riviera, had failed to provide the symbol around which nationalist sentiment could solidify. For their part, the nationalists, though as disunited as ever, were also more desirous than ever of independence, as they made clear in their response to the July 3 declaration. Prompted by Laniel's promise, Bao Dai had called a National Congress to inform him of popular desires concerning future relations with France "within the framework of the French Union," and to appoint advisers to assist in the negotiations. Considerably exceeding this mandate, the National Congress on October 16 unanimously approved a motion in favor of "total independence" and, when subjected to pressures to withdraw, retreated no further than to declare that an independent Vietnam would not participate in the French Union "in its present form." In addition, the Congress demanded that any agreements resulting from negotiations between Bao Dai and the French be approved by an elected national assembly. Finally, with negotiations between France and the Communists now obviously in prospect, the Congress vigorously asserted the right of the Vietnamese people to take part in any international actions affecting their future.[18]

This very strong expression of Vietnamese views helped to crystallize French feelings that there was little point in the military effort, now once more running into difficulties, especially in Laos. Sihanouk's demands for status for Cambodia like that of Pakistan and India in the Commonwealth had already suggested that the Indochinese might come to see membership in the French Union under the terms of the constitution of the Fourth Republic as incompatible with perfected independence. Sihanouk had not pressed the point, but now the Vietnamese were doing so very sharply.

17. Roger Smith, pp. 45–49; Herz, pp. 85–92.

18. Lancaster, p. 278; Royal Institute of International Affairs, Denise Folliot (ed.), *Documents on International Affairs*, 1953, pp. 475–476.

Equally sharply, the French cabinet on October 21 called on the Vietnamese to make clear whether they intended to remain in the French Union after the war, while Laniel warned them that France itself would feel free to quit the war if they questioned "the conception of the French Union." At the end of the month, a French National Assembly resolution called for the defense and independence of the Associated States to be achieved within the French Union, and, while endorsing the expansion of the armies of the Associated States to the point where they could replace the Expeditionary Corps, urged that everything possible be done to achieve a negotiated peace.[19]

The United States also looked upon the behavior of the Vietnamese National Congress with distaste and alarm. A telegram to Saigon described the State Department's concern with "ill-considered" actions which "have jeopardized war effort upon successful outcome of which lives and property most members of Congress in effect depend. Failure of Congress to express appreciation of efforts and sacrifices of 300,000 Vietnamese fighting Viet Minh appears even more extraordinary than failure to express similar sentiments regarding essential French sacrifices and effort." Casting about for ways to foster the "mutuality of interest" that was so urgently required, the Department asked American representatives in Saigon whether the establishment of a high-level Franco-Vietnamese committee to plan for postwar reconstruction might help serve this purpose: "Prospect of fruitful cooperation in constructive work after war is won might have sobering effect on political dreamers and doctrinaires. It might divert attention from constitutional verbiage and empty demogoguery and start people thinking of and perhaps developing vested interest in the practical problems which will face the new Vietnam made possible by the current expenditure of Franco-Vietnamese blood and U.S.-French-Vietnamese treasure."[20]

The necessity for cooperation between Vietnamese and French was also stressed publicly. While visiting the Far East in the fall, Vice President Richard M. Nixon said, "It is possible and necessary for Viet Nam and France to carry on within the framework of the French Union, a common struggle in order to attain common objectives."[21]

19. *SIA,* 1953, pp. 292–297; *USWA,* 1953, pp. 277, 278.
20. *Pentagon Papers,* IX, 169–170.
21. Hammer, p. 319.

When he reported on his trip to the American people in December, he declared, "The United States supports the Associated States in their understandable aspirations for independence. But we know as they do that the day the French leave Indochina the Communists will take over."[22] In January 1954, an NSC paper called for efforts to persuade the Associated States "that it is not in their best interest to undermine the French position by making untimely demands."[23]

While French-Vietnamese negotiations continued to be bedeviled by issues relating to the prerogatives of Paris and Saigon within the French Union, the military situation remained disturbing. To be sure, a number of successful French Union operations had inflicted heavy losses on the Communists. But the important actions, which took place in northwestern Tonkin and in Laos, generally favored the Communists, especially because they dispersed French Union forces and tied them down in remote areas where resupply was particularly difficult. Moreover, the 1953 Communist campaigns in Laos had notable repercussions. The spring drive toward Luang Prabang was a major factor in the French decision to fortify and hold Dien Bien Phu. The alarm aroused by the present threat to Laos and the potential one to Thailand prompted a fateful American step: when six C-119's were provided to fly supplies into Laos for French Union forces, American civilians were recruited to fly them.

In the fall of 1953, confounding French expectations that they would again concentrate on the north, the Communists launched their principal drive westward into central Laos. In late December they captured Thakhek, just across the Mekong from Thailand, cutting Laos in two for a period of some three weeks. Then, in April 1954, a thrust into Cambodia, although of no great size, heightened the vision of an ever-widening and increasingly difficult war.

The Dialogue Begins

Meanwhile, as French desires for a way out of the impasse were reinforced by the frustrations of fighting the Viet Minh and negotiating with the nationalists, the new international atmosphere was encouraging hopes that this might be possible. Stalin's death early in

22. *DSB*, Jan. 4, 1954, p. 12.
23. *Pentagon Papers*, IX, 231.

March had seemingly provided Moscow with the occasion for more open and vigorous moves in the direction of détente, apparently in accord also with the mood in Peking. The West had not been unresponsive, although Europeans seemed more anxious to explore prospects for reducing Cold-War tensions than Americans. In a major speech in mid-April marking the end of the Stalinist era, President Eisenhower had seen a chance for peace, but he seemed to place priority on an act of contrition: the Communists, having seen the free world aroused to united action against aggression must now make clear their peaceful intentions.

It was in this spirit that the United States reacted with disfavor to Prime Minister Churchill's May 1953 proposal for a big-power attempt to negotiate East-West issues. Especially where Asia was concerned, American public opinion reinforced the policy makers' cautious approach to East-West negotiations. The Russians on behalf of the Chinese were seeking acceptance of the idea that there were now five big powers, not four. China was clearly heavily involved in Korea; that it was also heavily involved in Vietnam was a cardinal assumption of American policy. Accordingly, if Asian as well as European issues were to be discussed on a big-power basis, the PRC would almost certainly have to be present. But, if it were to be present, this would weaken the barriers the United States had erected against recognition of Communist China and its admission to the United Nations. It was necessary if unsettling, to negotiate with the Chinese on Korea, where, in any case, the West would be negotiating from strength. But, in American eyes, to negotiate on Vietnam was doubly unattractive, adding the serious disadvantage of negotiation from weakness to the general undesirability of direct dealings with the PRC. American views notwithstanding, however, through the last six months of 1953, the trend was inexorably in the direction of a negotiated settlement in Indochina.

In France especially, the approach of the Korean armistice raised both hopes that negotiations on Vietnam could somehow follow, and fears that the Chinese Communists, released from their military preoccupations in Korea, might intervene in Vietnam or at least substantially increase their aid. Earlier warnings against intervention were repeated, most notably in a joint statement by the sixteen participants in the UN combat force on July 27, the day the Korean armistice was signed. Peking, however, while apparently supplying the

Viet Minh in greater volume, made no other threatening moves. Instead, both Chinese Communist and Soviet media showed increasing interest in the possibility of a negotiated settlement.[24]

On September 2, Dulles repeated the now standard warning, its impact no doubt increased by the announcement at the month's end of substantially increased U.S. aid to the French. Taking note of the training and supplies the PRC had provided in Indochina, which he described as "part of a single Chinese Communist aggressive front," he said that if the Chinese were now to send their own army into the battle "such a second aggression could not occur without grave consequences which might not be confined to Indochina." But, he added, "we want peace in Indochina as well as in Korea." The coming political conference on Korea could bring also "if Red China wants it, an end of aggression and the restoration of peace in Indochina. The United States would welcome such a development."[25] On the same day, a *Peking Daily* editorial declared "only by applying the principle of settling international disputes through negotiations can France get out of its mess in the Vietnam war."[26]

Not long after, Georgi Malenkov, Chairman of the Council of Ministers of the Soviet Union, expressed the hope that the Korean armistice would become "the point of departure for new efforts aimed at lessening international tension in the entire world and notably in the Far East." Referring to this statement, Laniel in the National Assembly on October 27 observed that Moscow and Peking had made frequent reference to negotiations since the end of August, while France and its Allies had also accepted "the idea of negotiations, in an international framework, in order to establish peace in Indochina." Of all those concerned, he said, it is only the Viet Minh who do not seem to be willing to compromise. But, he added, "if one day Ho Chi Minh . . . should seem inclined to make proposals, the French government and other interested governments . . . would have to assess their merits and come to a joint decision on how they should be handled."[27] For the French at least, the emphasis had shifted. While the United States stressed that peace could come only if one side

24. Miriam S. Farley, *United States Relations with Southeast Asia,* p. 5; La-Couture and Devillers, p. 40; Chen, p. 256.

25. *DSB,* Sept. 14, 1953, pp. 341–342.

26. Jay Taylor, p. 11.

27. Hammer, pp. 311–312; de Carmoy, p. 143.

terminated its aggression, Laniel was now suggesting that peace could result from the willingness of both sides to make concessions.

Whether or not at this time the Vietnamese Communists were reluctant to compromise, the conspicuous silence noted by Laniel soon came to an end and, publicly at least, they joined forces with Moscow and Peking. On November 23, speaking at a World Peace Council meeting, a Vietnamese delegate declared: "To stop the Vietnam war through peaceful negotiations is completely necessary and also possible. We Vietnam people long for peace, and we stand for an end to the Vietnam war and peaceful settlement of the Vietnam question by means of peaceful negotiations."[28] Then, at the end of the month, the *Stockolm Expressen* published an interview with Ho Chi Minh in which, as though in answer to Laniel, Ho said, "If, having drawn a lesson from these years of war, the French government wishes to conclude an armistice and resolve the Vietnamese question through negotiations, the people and government of the Democratic Republic of Vietnam are ready to examine the French proposals. . . . The basis of an armistice is that the government of France should really respect the independence of Vietnam. . . . The negotiation of an armistice is essentially a matter for the government of France and that of Vietnam."[29] In December, on two occasions, the DRV reiterated its position; it was ready to negotiate with France on the basis of French respect for the independence of Vietnam.[30]

Meanwhile, events were moving toward a Big Four meeting on European matters. The United States, under pressure from its Allies, had agreed to a four-power western discussion of the German question. Although initially the Russians had reiterated their demand for a five-power discussion of world problems, they finally agreed to a four-power conference with the understanding that they would again raise the five-power issue at the conference. Late in January of 1954 in Berlin the Council of Foreign Ministers met for the first time in almost five years. In mid-February, after making no progress on European matters and with a Communist offensive under way in Laos, the Council turned its attention to Asia. It was agreed to hold an international conference on Korea; it was also agreed, with extremely

28. Chen, p. 290.
29. *Documents in International Affairs,* 1953, pp. 477–478.
30. Randle, pp. 7–8.

reluctant American concurrence, "that the problem of restoring peace in Indochina will also be discussed at the Conference, to which representatives of the United States, France, the United Kingdom, the Union of Soviet Socialist Republics, the Chinese People's Republic and other interested states will be invited."[31]

The Berlin decision accommodated American views by confining PRC participation in great-power discussions to specific Asian issues and by evading the problem of making Communist China an inviting power—a prospect American representatives found intolerable. Nevertheless, Senate majority leader William Knowland and other congressmen attacked the outcome as a step toward recognizing the Chinese Communists and as an act of appeasement, sure to lead to a Far Eastern Munich. Justifying the decision in a television address, Dulles explained that China was coming to Geneva not "to be honored by us, but rather to account before the bar of world opinion" for its role in Korea and Indochina. As to the latter, he reminded Americans, this was primarily and "quite properly a French responsibility." The United States, he said, has a very vital interest in Indochina. It is the French and the people of the Associated States, however, who are doing the actual fighting. France has a special position in Indochina, just as the United States has in Korea.[32]

Responding quite differently from their American counterparts, the members of the French National Assembly hailed the decision to discuss Indochina at Geneva. But, prompted by persistent negotiating difficulties with Premier Buu Loc and his delegation over the terms on which Vietnam's independence should be perfected, the National Assembly also reminded the Associated States of their obligations to the French Union, in which they were "indissolubly united," and advised them that, if they should repudiate their past agreements, France, for its part, would consider itself no longer bound by obligations toward them.[33]

31. *Ibid.*, pp. 26–27.
32. *DSB*, March 8, 1974, pp. 345–346; Farley, p. 9; Royal Institute of International Affairs, Coral Bell (ed.), *Survey of International Affairs (SIA)*, 1954, p. 23.
33. *Documents in International Affairs*, 1954, p. 122.

CHAPTER 9

THE PRELIMINARIES

Allied agreement to discuss Indochina at Geneva did not reflect consensus on the efficacy and outcome of the conference. The United States wanted the French to fight on, anticipating the worst from negotiating with an enemy who enjoyed the military and political advantage. It sought both to encourage the French to persist and to strengthen their negotiating position by indicating that the United States, if joined by others, would intervene militarily. In diplomatic exchanges, however, it defined its conditions for intervention carefully and with increasing rigor.

France had no intention of carrying on the war, and did not want American military intervention of a type that would oblige it to do so. In any case, the French government could not have accepted the conditions the United States put forward. But it would have welcomed help at Dien Bien Phu, because it was concerned for the fate of the defenders, feared the domestic political consequences of a conspicuous military disaster, and hoped that France could improve its bargaining position by exhibiting the strength and determination of its Allies. For this reason also, the intermittent belligerence of American spokesmen seemed helpful to the French cause.

Britain agreed with France that the war should end. But it agreed with the United States that great strategic importance should not be attached to Dien Bien Phu where any practicable form of Allied intervention was likely to be futile. And it parted company with both of its Allies on the efficacy of threatening postures. These, British policy makers feared, might escalate into wider war and, at least, were more likely than not to stiffen Communist positions. Moreover, as long as the Communists continued to emphasize their desire for peace, threatening Allied gestures were likely to antagonize neutral Asians, especially the Indians, whose cooperation Britain believed to be essential to Southeast Asian stabilization.

Developments in March and April 1954 intensified Allied disunity and revealed its extent. In these months, the issue of military intervention was dramatized by the increasingly perilous position of the French garrison at Dien Bien Phu, under siege since March 13. The question of intervention at Dien Bien Phu was settled by its fall on May 7; divisions over broader issues of war and peace remained important through May and most of June.

In the months between the Berlin Conference and the opening of the Indochina phase at Geneva on May 8, the United States was very much in the center of the stage. In February, the American military assistance group in Indochina was increased by 200 men, mostly mechanics and technicians to service the 40 medium bombers being supplied to the hard-pressed French Union forces. This move aroused Congressional alarm, but the administration denied that it had brought the United States closer to military involvement. "There could be no greater tragedy," the President said. Nevertheless, in March, administration statements stressed what Eisenhower called the "most transcendent importance" of Indochina. Simultaneously, during the Washington visit of General Paul Ely, President of the Committee of Chiefs of Staff, the administration learned that the French position in Indochina was even more discouraging than had been thought and that the prospects at Dien Bien Phu were desperate. His conversations in Washington, particularly those with his American counterpart, Admiral Arthur Radford, Chairman of the Joint Chiefs of Staff, gave Ely the distinct impression that the United States would provide air support to defend Dien Bien Phu if formally requested to do so.

Toward the end of the month, newspaper stories, obviously officially inspired, indicated that Dulles would soon announce a major policy departure. This he did on March 29 when he urged that the threat of Communism in Southeast Asia be met by "united action," even though this might involve serious risks. While Dulles' explanation to prospective adherents[1] stressed the deterrent aspects of his proposal, France, on February 4, and again on February 23, had raised the

1. France, the Associated States, Britain, Australia, New Zealand, the Philippines, and Thailand.

question of immediate military intervention by requesting U.S. air support at Dien Bien Phu. Through much of this period, speculation about imminent intervention was heightened by the dispatch of two American aircraft carriers to the South China Sea, and by a number of administration statements. These included the Secretary's statement on April 5, citing evidence provided by the French of Chinese Communist support very close to the levels that could activate earlier U.S. warnings against intervention,[2] the President's vivid use on April 7 of the domino simile in illustrating the American view of Indochina's importance, which was also heavily stressed in State Department briefings, and the Vice President's off-the-record remarks on April 16 suggesting that American troops might have to be sent to Vietnam. At mid-month, asked in a press conference whether he could envisage any satisfactory outcome in Indochina other than a complete withdrawal of the Communists, Dulles replied, "I had not thought of any."[3]

By the end of the month, however, the prospect of immediate intervention was generally seen to have evaporated. Even earlier, the British and French, publicly agreeing at mid-month to discuss collective defense in Southeast Asia, had insisted on testing the negotiating path first. On April 22, Eisenhower's press-conference remarks suggested that the United States was beginning to accept the prospect of a negotiated settlement and the desirability of what the President called a *modus vivendi* in Indochina. On the same day, British Foreign Secretary Anthony Eden solicited the help of neutralist Asian powers[4] then meeting in Colombo, a step for which Nehru had laid the groundwork in February and April when he appealed for a cease-fire. On May 7, Dulles declared publicly that there was no present basis for United States military participation. Before this could come about, he said, the French must give greater reality to their intent to grant full independence to the Associated States and place greater reliance on national armies fighting in their own homeland. Moreover, other countries must also participate in a collective effort. The situation, he

2. He was using data provided by Laniel and Bidault to Ambassador Douglas Dillon but disclaimed after Dulles used it in his April 5 appearance before the House Foreign Affairs Committee (*Pentagon Papers*), IX, 296; *SIA,* 1954, p. 29; Lyman, p. 179n.). French intelligence sources continued to cast doubt on this data (Zasloff, pp. 33–34).

3. Hoopes, p. 309.

4. Burma, Ceylon, India, Indonesia, and Pakistan.

said, may be clarified at Geneva. A settlement which does not endanger the future of the Vietnamese people would contribute to the cause of peace in Southeast Asia. On the other hand, if an armistice or cease-fire led to Communist takeover and further aggression, it would then become even more necessary to create the conditions for united action.[5]

The Issues: French and British Views

Underlying Allied differences in March and April was the question of internationalizing the war. The French had long excluded this course which, they believed, was even more likely than a negotiated settlement to result in the complete loss of the French position in Indochina, while imposing additional costs in lives and resources. Moreover, they were not confident that a wider Allied effort would deter a wider Communist effort. U.S. intervention at Dien Bien Phu, Laniel concluded, would not risk general war, because the Communists were not yet prepared for this. But both Navarre in April and Ely in June argued that an enlarged United States role over time would prompt increased Chinese Communist participation, making the war even more costly and prolonged.[6]

Unwilling to internationalize the war because they wanted to end it, the French were more anxious than otherwise to internationalize the negotiations. After years of frustration and humiliation, to deal directly with Ho was repugnant to them; Bidault carried this to the point of refusing direct contact with DRV representatives until well along in the conference. In addition, direct dealings with Ho would accentuate the difficulties with Vietnamese nationalist leaders that were likely to result even from the prospect of negotiations. The same consideration would arise with respect to the United States: however averse the United States might be to participating in international discussions on Indochina, it could be expected to be deeply offended, disturbed, and suspicious should the French embark on bilateral negotiations.[7] Seeing their problems compounded by Chinese assistance to the Viet Minh, the French assumed also that a settlement to be effective must involve the Chinese as well as the Vietnamese Com-

5. *DSB,* May 17, 1954, p. 744.

6. Victor Bator, *Vietnam, a Diplomatic Tragedy,* p. 89; Alastair Buchan (ed.), *China and the Peace of Asia,* p. 35; Laniel, p. 86; Ely, pp. 111, 167–168.

7. According to Anthony Eden (*Memoirs: Full Circle,* p. 143), the Americans were disturbed at Geneva even by contacts between French and DRV delegates,

munists. If the Viet Minh were to be joined by its Allies, France would need the presence of its friends. Should the United States prove willing to concede something to Peking's desire for legitimacy and an end to trade restrictions (or to Moscow's desire for relaxation in Europe), this might be traded off for more favorable terms for France in Indochina. Failing this, even the demonstration, through their presence at its side, that France had the support of the United States and Britain, and the appearance (even though France might reject the reality) of imminent Allied military intervention, could be used to bolster a position otherwise deficient in military and political assets.[8]

It was not always easy, however, to brandish the threat of internationalizing the war without invoking it. Thus, in April, the French found themselves in the position of having to reject the American united action proposal—arguing that it would disturb the negotiating atmosphere and provide a pretext for Chinese intervention—at the very time that they were asking for United States air-force assistance at Dien Bien Phu.[9]

Again in May, the French, once more seeking only American agreement to a single relief action, found themselves entangled in elaborate preconditions for united action. They had decided to tighten their lines—withdrawing from stretched-out positions and massing their forces in the Red River delta—and they feared that as they did so the Viet Minh forces, also regrouping and moving in the direction of the delta, would mount a massive attack supported by Chinese Mig's. It was against this contingency that the French, in bilateral discussions beginning on May 9, sought formal assurances of an immediate American air response. They apparently believed that the United States was already virtually committed to this course by its public statements about Chinese intervention and by the assurances Radford had given Ely. Perhaps to inspire greater U.S. interest, perhaps to prepare for the worst,[10] they also asked under what conditions and how the United

---

fearing they would make a deal on their own. Ironically, the French were also disturbed by contacts between Pham Van Dong and Tran Van Do (*Pentagon Papers,* IX, 647).

8. LaCouture and Devillers, pp. 102–104.

9. Randle, pp. 73–75.

10. According to LaCouture and Devillers (p. 188), the inquiry was suggested by Bonnet for the latter purpose.

States would intervene should the conference fail or be fruitlessly prolonged by Communist foot-dragging. They soon found, however, that the United States was quite willing to answer the second question with a long list of conditions, but was quite unwilling to treat the first question separately from the second.[11]

Especially to the extent that they regarded Radford's remarks to Ely as an American commitment, the French had reason to suspect the United States of advancing its numerous preconditions as a way of avoiding action. Later, an exiled and embittered Bidault said that united action "made conditions and encouraged others to get involved in Indo-China (knowing very well in advance that the others would not get involved). Only then did it suggest that the United States might consider sending aid, though not before a conference at an unspecified time was arranged by nations which had not yet made any promises. Meanwhile, the French would continue to fight for a goal dictated by the Americans."[12]

At the time, however, and to his political disadvantage, Bidault was widely seen as attempting to internationalize the war. The French public reacted to Dulles' united action speech of late March with alarm over the possibility that the war would be prolonged and enlarged by U.S. intervention. Thereafter, fed by press stories, charges multiplied that the cabinet was eagerly seeking American military intervention. The United States was attacked simultaneously from the Left and the Right: from the Left for seeking to lead France into general war; from the Right for failing to support France adequately and complicating the situation to the advantage of the Viet Minh by encouraging the importunities of the Associated States. In the National Assembly, where Mendès-France and others accused Laniel of risking general war, these charges played their part in the government's fall on June 12. Under Mendès-France, the French, moving closer to the British, abandoned the effort to use the threat of U.S. intervention to sway the Communists, but sought to replace this form of pressure by greater emphasis than Laniel had given to the possibility that France would continue the war and send conscripts to Indochina.[13]

11. *Pentagon Papers,* IX, 446–530; LaCouture and Devillers, pp. 171–189; Laniel, pp. 106–107; Ely, pp. 129–130.

12. Georges Bidault, *Resistance,* p. 198.

13. *SIA,* 1954, pp. 36, 50; Lyman, pp. 240–241; LaCouture and Devillers, p. 251; Grosser, pp. 208–209.

To the British, Allied military intervention, whether as an alternative to a negotiated peace or as a threat, was quite unacceptable: it conflicted with their estimate of the prospects for defeating Ho; with their view of their own interests in Southeast Asia; and with their analysis of Communist intentions.[14]

When he returned to office late in 1951, Eden was already quite pessimistic about French prospects, and events thereafter did nothing to alter this view. He did not believe, however, that the balance could be righted by British or other Allied military participation. British forces were heavily committed elsewhere—in Europe, Malaya, Kenya, and Suez—and, under its own new-look military policy, Britain was cutting back conventional forces while developing a modest nuclear capability. To be sure, Eisenhower, in explaining united action to Churchill, had said that it would probably not require Anglo-American ground forces. But, in the British view, reliance on air power would probably be both mistaken and dangerous. United action, Eden thought, did not really fit the facts of the case; commenting to Sir Roger Makins, British Ambassador in Washington, on Dulles' March 29 speech, he wrote: "We feel it would be unrealistic not to face the possibility that conditions for a favorable solution in Indo-China may no longer exist." More than this, if only massive Allied intervention could offer any prospect of success in Indochina, was the game worth the candle? "I did not believe," said Eden later, ". . . that anything less than intervention on a Korean scale, if that, would have any effect in Indo-China. If there were such intervention, I could not tell where its consequences would stop. We might well find ourselves involved in the wrong war against the wrong man in the wrong place."[15]

Eden was able to stand firm on this issue not only because public opinion in Britain stood behind him on Indochina, but also because there was general support for policies more independent of those of the United States and less likely, in British eyes, to imperil world peace. In late April, when it seemed that the United States was attempting to involve Britain in military action in Indochina, Churchill won cheers in Commons when he said: "The Government are not prepared to give any undertaking about United Kingdom military action in Indochina in advance of the results of Geneva. We have not entered into

14. Randle, pp. 124–127; Eden, pp. 86–119.
15. Eden, pp. 102, 104.

any new political or military commitment."[16] Eden's stance, moreover, strengthened the ability of the Labour moderates led by Clement Atlee to support the government's foreign policy and to block the efforts of Aneurin Bevan and his followers to unseat them and move Labour further to the left.

Nevertheless, Britain could not disassociate itself from the Indochina problem nor did it wish to do so. British policy in Europe required a strong and stable France, and France could be neither, as long as Indochina drained its resources and embittered its political life. The British position in South and Southeast Asia was also affected. The Communist insurgency in Malaya, now at a crucial point, had thus far been carried on without external Communist involvement. But, if the war in Indochina continued and especially if it spread to Thailand, this situation might change. Indochina seemed important also in connection with India; as the meeting-place of Chinese and Hindu cultures, Eden thought, Indochina was one area in which China and India confronted one another, "as surely as in Tibet, if less obviously."[17] Moreover, China's leaders—and Soviet leaders as well—were now courting India, and the Indians had become even more sensitive than usual on colonialist issues. Western military intervention would be suspect in Indian eyes as support for French colonialism, united action as merely a disguise for reasserting western imperialism, militant postures in advance of the conference as unprovoked rebuffs to Sino-Soviet overtures.

All of these concerns convinced Britain that a negotiated settlement was the best way out of an admittedly bad situation. This, it was hoped, would stabilize the area by accepting and legitimizing Communist gains while retaining a viable western position, strong enough to deter violation of settlement terms. Moreover, since the views and behavior of nearby states might be of some influence on the stability of the settlement, it was important to maintain close contact with the Colombo powers even though they were not to be officially represented at the conference.

Eden believed also that a negotiated settlement was consistent with the Moscow/Peking view of Communist interests. The Russians, Eden thought, did not attach the highest priority to Indochina and did not

16. Bator, pp. 71, 72.
17. Eden, pp. 85–87.

want to become involved there through some escalation of the conflict. Accordingly, they were genuinely interested in a settlement, and were prepared to put pressure on Hanoi to achieve one. The views of the Chinese he found more perplexing. More than the Russians, he thought, their interests were involved in Viet Minh success in Indochina but, especially after the distractions of Korea, he believed they wished to concentrate on economic development. Moreover, Eden believed that the Chinese perceived the threat of nuclear conflict, although probably less firmly and to a lesser extent than the Russians. However, while Eden seemed to regard what he called "the general consciousness of the peril of world conflict," as, in itself, a useful deterrent, he saw dangers in overemphasizing the threat of war; this could either cause disbelief or stiffen resistance to compromise.[18]

Differences between Britain and the United States over the question of Allied intervention posed serious problems for Australia and New Zealand, particularly for the former with its more active foreign-policy interests. Both felt more exposed than Britain to the dangers that might follow Communist victory in Indochina. Both had shown their support for the French effort in tangible ways by gifts of aircraft and other military equipment. And both had long supported the concept of collective defense in Southeast Asia and had urged the United States to provide the necessary leadership.

But at this juncture, when the United States finally seemed prepared to do so, countervailing considerations were also at work. Although Australian interest in Indochina was greater than Britain's, the area still seemed remote, much more remote than Malaya and, even there, Australia had been reluctant to involve its own forces. Then too, it was an election year, and association with moves widely seen as risking major hostilities was not likely to improve the government's prospects at the polls. And, in addition to wanting to remain whenever possible in tandem with Britain, Australia also wanted to maintain close and cordial relations with India and Indonesia.[19]

Whereas bringing about the security treaty with the United States had outweighed Commonwealth and other considerations, joining with the United States in united action in Indochina did not. Accordingly,

18. *Ibid.*, pp. 120–150.
19. Greenwood and Harper, 1950–1955, pp. 14, 17; *Keesing's Contemporary Archives,* X, 12447, 12908; Halpern, pp. 180–181.

Australian official reaction to Dulles' March 29 speech, to which the Australian public had responded with no enthusiasm, was markedly cautious. In parliament on April 7, in response to Evatt's query, Minister of External Affairs Casey, while welcoming American interest in preserving the security of Southeast Asia and the South Pacific, added, "the line of thought put forward by Mr. Dulles needs further elaboration and explanation before any new statement of Australian policy can be made on this point."[20] Further consideration led to close association with the British position and such active support as Casey, intermittently in Geneva, could lend to Eden's efforts. Casey's visit to Saigon in April, he later told parliament, had convinced him that a negotiated solution should be sought "recognizing the realities of the situation," since further military efforts appeared unlikely to be any more successful than the considerable effort already made. Allied intervention, therefore, "would be wrong. . . . It would not have the backing of the United Nations. It would put us in wrong with world opinion, particularly in Asia. It would probably embroil us with Communist China. It would wreck the Geneva Conference, and it was most unlikely to stop the fall of Dien Bien Phu."[21]

With Indian sensitivities of great concern to Australia, Casey, during his visit to New Delhi in June, detailed the Australian position to Nehru, even showing him passages from diplomatic correspondence to demonstrate that Australia was not blindly following the United States. "I said that we had been hanging onto American coattails and arguing against intervention and we believed we had some effect on their minds. We were fully seized of the need to avoid becoming embroiled in war on the Asian mainland, and particularly war with China which might easily result from intervention."[22]

The Issues: The American Dilemma

The Eisenhower administration's approach to military intervention in Indochina was closely constrained not only by the views of its Allies,

20. George Modelski (ed.), *SEATO, Six Studies*, p. 59.

21. Australia, Department of External Affairs, *Current Notes*, Vol. 8, Aug. 1954, p. 576; Albinski, *Australian Policies and Attitudes toward China*, pp. 140–141.

22. T. B. Millar (ed.), *Australian Foreign Minister, The Diaries of R. G. Casey*, p. 297.

but also and, perhaps even more, by the Congressional climate and the views of the military leadership. Reinforcing these constraints were the President's own military experience, his deep respect for Congressional prerogatives, and his orientation toward Europe and the western alliance rather than toward the Far East.

In March, with the dangers of the situation in Indochina made evident by General Ely, the pressure for American decisions intensified. Some, with Admiral Radford in the forefront, recommended urgent measures. The loss of Dien Bien Phu, Radford argued, might lead the situation in Indochina to deteriorate so rapidly that "only a prompt and forceful intervention by the United States could avert the loss of all of Southeast Asia to Communist domination."[23] There were other military leaders, however, who approached the question of intervention, whether at Dien Bien Phu or more generally, with reservations derived from long-held views about Indochina and about utilizing American military power in Asia.

No view concerning Indochina was more firmly fixed than the belief that French losses were attributable largely to their own political and military mistakes. The French were criticized for failing to take sufficient account of the force of nationalism, for not training, motivating, and adequately using abundant native manpower, and for the grave deficiencies of their strategy and tactics. Walter Bedell Smith bluntly told Bidault, "any second-rate general should be able to win in Indochina if there were a proper political atmosphere."[24] Success, said an interagency committee in February 1954, "will ultimately be dependent upon the inspiration of the local population to fight for their own freedom from Communist domination and the willingness of the French both to take measures to stimulate that inspiration and to more fully utilize the native potential."[25] Increasingly in 1954, policy makers were also concluding that the French were incapable of change, that there had been enough deference to French sensibilities, and that, in exchange for any direct intervention, the United States should insist upon much greater authority over military strategy and Indochinese training.[26]

23. *Pentagon Papers*, IX, 285.
24. Eisenhower, p. 360.
25. *Pentagon Papers*, I, Part II, p. B-8.
26. See especially memorandum from the Joint Chiefs of Staff to the Secretary of Defense, May 20, 1954 (*Pentagon Papers*, IX, 478); Randle, p. 57.

All this, however, would take time, and meanwhile what was the shape of U.S. intervention to be? In the memorandum to the Secretary of Defense in which they recommended a greater U.S. planning and training role, the Joint Chiefs also advanced a notably conservative intervention plan. They had been guided by the limited availability of U.S. forces and the undesirability of basing them in large numbers in Indochina. In any case, manpower was not the problem: French Union forces already out-numbered the enemy by five to three, and the greatest need was for training. U.S. combat involvement, the Chiefs recommended, should be limited to air-force units operating from existing bases outside Indochina and from a fast carrier force.[27]

The Joint Chiefs' caution reflected two important and long-standing strains in American military thinking: the preference for striking at the source of aggression, and the desire to avoid using ground forces in Asia. Both tenets, having been disregarded in the Korean conflict, were strengthened by the frustrations of that experience. American security interests, it was believed, were sufficiently involved in defending the Asian mainland against Communist aggression so that the United States could again become involved in hostilities there. But if this should come about, especially in Southeast Asia, United States forces should not be committed to static defense—an expensive and probably indecisive role—but to an air and sea offensive against the source of the aggression. This preferred strategic concept, however, could not easily be applied in Indochina, since the PRC's role was hardly of a scope to legitimize the kind of action against it that had seemed politically unacceptable even in response to massive Chinese intervention in Korea. And the occasion seemed hardly likely to be provided in the future. Thus, the Chiefs noted that the principal sources of Viet Minh supply lay outside Indochina and that their destruction or neutralization would reduce French problems, but they made no recommendations for action on this score. It was generally agreed that the Chinese Communists would see no need to intervene as long as the Viet Minh were doing well. Over whether they would intervene if U.S. action threatened Viet Minh defeat, there was uncertainty in the National Security Council and disagreement in the Intelligence Community which, nevertheless, was able to muster seven

27. *Pentagon Papers,* **IX,** 479.

considerations that might induce the PRC to intervene and eight that might deter it.[28]

The argument that a major American combat role in Indochina need involve only air and sea power proved impossible to sustain against the onslaughts of the Army Chief of Staff, General Matthew Ridgway, and others of his persuasion. Opponents of exclusive reliance on air and sea power attacked the notion that, even with nuclear weapons, it was possible to win in Indochina without ground forces. But the most effective argument centered on the inability of local logistic facilities to support significant air and sea action; to mount such action a very substantial American logistic force would be required and this, in turn, would have to be protected by American infantry. As General Ridgway argued, "Every little detachment, every individual, that tried to move about that country would have to be protected by riflemen. Every telephone lineman, road-repair party, every ambulance, and every rear-area aid structure would have to be under armed guard or they would be shot at around the clock."[29] If native troops could not fill the ground-force role effectively until political change and American training had transformed them, if American sea and air power could not bring victory, if Communist China's ability to sustain the Viet Minh could not be reduced, was Indochina important enough to justify the massive U.S. ground intervention that would sustain hopes for success? Ultimately, the Chiefs thought not. On May 20, they concluded that to commit a naval force to Indochina larger than the carrier task force already recommended or to base substantial air forces there would "involve maldeployment of forces and reduced readiness to meet probable Chinese Communist reaction elsewhere in the Far East. From the point of view of the United States, with reference to the Far East as a whole, Indochina is devoid of decisive military objectives and the allocation of more than token U.S. armed forces to that area would be a serious diversion of limited U.S. capabilities."[30]

28. See Special Estimate 53, Dec. 1953 (*Pentagon Papers,* IX, 206), and NSC 1074a, April 5, 1954 (*ibid.,* pp. 317–318).

29. Matthew B. Ridgeway, *Soldier,* pp. 276–277; see also Army Position (undated) in NSC 1074a, April 5, 1954 (*Pentagon Papers,* IX, 332); and memorandum from Secretary of the Army, Robert T. Stevens, to the Secretary of Defense, May 19, 1954 (*ibid.,* pp. 475–476).

30. *Pentagon Papers,* IX, 479.

Well before this, a paper prepared for the NSC had outlined a whole host of problems that the commitment of combat forces would bring in its train. It would strain the western alliance, and increase the risk of war with Communist China and even of general war. It would impose high costs in U.S. manpower and materiel, divert forces from existing missions, and have unfavorable domestic repercussions. It would associate the United States in a struggle widely regarded as colonialist and imperialist; to overcome this the Associated States and other Asian countries would have to be involved in the enterprise. But the Indochinese would support U.S. intervention only if it were on a scale adequate to defeat the Viet Minh and deter the Chinese and if the United States would assume lasting responsibility for their political independence and territorial integrity. Correspondingly, in order to involve other Asian states, the United States would have to take lasting steps to defend them. And, since the French did not really want American military intervention, if it came about they would probably try to shift the military burden to the United States by withdrawing their own forces or by failing to make good attrition.[31]

Political considerations loomed large in shaping Congressional attitudes. Influential Congressmen in both houses and both parties, however militantly anti-Communist, were opposed to a closer American association with French colonialism. Even more, they saw grave dangers in once again spilling American blood on Asian battlefields, while Allies joined neutrals, and Europeans joined Asians, in criticizing from the sidelines. Congressional misgivings were easily aroused. Learning of the French request in January 1954 for American airplane mechanics, Senator John Stennis wrote to Secretary of Defense Charles E. Wilson, "It seems to me that we should certainly stop short of sending our troops or airmen to this area, either for participation in the conflict or as instructors. As always, when we send one group, we shall have to send another to protect the first and we shall thus be fully involved in a short time. . . . I do not think we can at all afford to take chances on becoming participants in Indo-China."[32] Congressmen like Senator Mike Mansfield, who were most closely concerned with American policy in Asia, shared the view that success in Indochina was dependent upon radically changed French military and political

31. NSC 1074a, April 5, 1954 (*ibid.*, pp. 300–314).
32. *Ibid.*, p. 239.

behavior. America should help because its security was involved in denying the resources of Southeast Asia to the Communists. But "American aid . . . does not and should not involve the commitment of combat forces. Sacrifices for the defense of freedom must be equitably shared and we have borne our full burden of blood in Korea."[33] Mansfield was writing in the winter of 1953 when the prospect of defeat was clearly coming closer; Senator Edwin C. Johnson summed up majority Democratic opinion in saying he was "against sending American GI's into the mud and muck of Indochina on a bloodletting spree to perpetuate colonialism and white man's exploitation in Asia."[34] Nor was the leadership of the Republican Party of any different view. In mid-May on television Senator Knowland said he would favor U.S. intervention in Indochina only if the Chinese Communists intervened in force and that he would regard sending troops to Asia as a serious mistake.[35]

These views weighed heavily with a President who had great respect for Congressional prerogatives and was himself strongly inclined toward what emerged from the Congressional and military debate on Indochina as the majority view. He was deeply critical of the French; he believed that Indochinese troops could do the job if properly trained, motivated, and supported. Anticolonialist himself, he was sensitive to Asian anticolonialism as it applied to Indochina; he had been horrified when the French had concentrated their forces at a point so isolated, so vulnerable, and of such minor military significance as Dien Bien Phu; he did not wish to put American ground forces in Southeast Asia, while doubting the efficacy of air power used against deployed troops with good ground cover; and, although he believed the preservation of Indochina to be important to the security of the non-Communist world, he did not think that this was a task that the United States could or should undertake alone.[36]

Presidential and Congressional inclinations were reinforced by the political imperatives of an election year. The Republicans hoped to capitalize on the end of hostilities in Korea; the reaction against what was seen as dangerously unchecked freedom in foreign policy, which

33. Lyman, p. 210.
34. Dommen, p. 48.
35. LaCouture and Devillers, p. 195.
36. Eisenhower, pp. 332–375.

had produced such proposals for tight Congressional controls as the Bricker amendment of 1952 continued to be strong; and the McCarthy campaign, although approaching its end, continued to unsettle and weaken the executive branch, particularly its foreign-policy apparatus.[37] Had the President felt otherwise, his enormous personal prestige, his military standing, and the strength of American anti-Communist sentiment, might have enabled him to carry the country with him into still another military campaign in Asia. But, in fact, he did not himself regard this as the wisest course.

There remained, however, the possibility that a policy short of unilateral military intervention could be devised before the Geneva Conference that would unite America's European and Asian Allies in public support of the French war effort, thereby encouraging the French to persist, and discouraging any Communist plan to win victory at the conference by escalating the conflict. It was to serve these purposes that the doctrine of united action was put forward. Prompt acceptance by the other countries concerned—France, the Associated States, Britain, Australia, New Zealand, Thailand, and the Philippines —could eliminate, it was hoped, any immediate need for substantial combat assistance, while laying the groundwork for providing this assistance should it be required.

To be sure, the terms in which Dulles couched his proposal in his March 29 speech made it easy to conclude that he had in mind some strong and immediate action. Emphasizing as he did the strategic importance of Southeast Asia, he conveyed a sense of considerable urgency: "Under the conditions of today, the imposition on Southeast Asia of the political system of Communist Russia and its Chinese Communist ally, by whatever means, would be a grave threat to the whole free community. The United States feels that that possibility should not be passively accepted but should be met by united action. This might involve serious risks. But these risks are far less than those that will face us a few years from now if we dare not be resolute today."[38]

In the days following the speech, however, explanations to Congressional leaders and to foreign governments made it evident that what was envisaged was a stance, which, while excluding unilateral American action, would bolster the French and impress the Communists. In

37. Randle, pp. 32–33.
38. *DSB*, April 12, 1954, p. 540.

the famous meeting between Congressional leaders and Dulles and Radford on April 3, according to Dulles' own account a month later, it was agreed that the United States should not intervene unless other nations joined in, but that, even on this basis, before the United States could participate in such joint action, the French would have to move more energetically in three areas: granting independence to the Associated States, devising an effective program for training native troops, and developing an aggressive military strategy.[39] Later, the President added still another precondition—Congress would have to consent to American participation.

The exclusion of unilateral action and the requirement for Congressional authority, the Secretary said, in a message to the American Embassy in Paris on April 5, had already been conveyed to Ely in Radford's presence. In his conversation with French Ambassador Henri Bonnet on April 3, Dulles emphasized the deterrent purposes of his united action proposal. If, he said, our strength and resolution make the Chinese Communists see clearly that they cannot undertake the conquest of Southeast Asia without risk of extending the war, they may stop supporting the Viet Minh and accept a face-saving formula to cover the latter's surrender. This, however, presupposes a continued French military effort and necessitates organizing before the Geneva Conference convenes a strong coalition of nations unmistakably ready to fight if necessary.[40]

In a letter to Churchill the following day, Eisenhower repeated what Dulles had already said to Bonnet about the likelihood, in existing circumstances, that the French could end the war at Geneva only by surrender, and the consequent need "to bring greater moral and material resources to the support of the French effort." This could be

39. Dulles' own account is contained in a telegram summarizing his May 5, 1954, briefing of 25 leading congressmen (*Pentagon Papers*, IX, 426–427). Eisenhower recalls that it was agreed also that the French would have to commit themselves not to pull their forces out if U.S. forces came in (Eisenhower, p. 347). The earliest and best known account of this meeting, Chalmers M. Roberts, "The Day We Didn't Go to War," published in *The Reporter* in September 1954, describes Dulles as joining Radford in seeking congressional support for immediate air and naval intervention. Randle argues to the contrary (pp. 63–65) and, more generally, makes a detailed and impressively argued case for Dulles' great caution on the Indochina issue.

40. *Pentagon Papers*, IX, 293–294, 359, 382.

done through a coalition that "must be strong and . . . must be willing to join the fight if necessary." But "I do not envisage the need of
any appreciable ground forces on your or our part."[41] To British
Ambassador Roger Makins, Dulles also emphasized that the threat of
Allied military intervention could cause the Chinese Communists to
abandon support of the Viet Minh. The coalition, he pointed out in
conversations with Australian Ambassador Spender and New Zealand
Ambassador Leslie Munro, would be a new element in the balance
which could prevent France from seeking "a settlement at Geneva
which will amount to a sell-out," and which, while pledging its members to work together, would require them to contribute forces only "if
necessary."[42]

Even with this restricted definition, however, united action and its
implications appeared to the British and French to run counter to their
hopes of achieving acceptable terms for ending the war at Geneva,
while, on this issue, Australia and New Zealand associated themselves
with Britain. Indeed, only Thailand expressed unqualified acceptance
of the proposal, and did so within two days after its support was requested. The Philippine response was more tentative and reserved,
complicated by President Ramon Magsaysay's reluctance to commit
troops to Indochina, concern with the colonial issue, and fears of
possible adverse effects on Philippine security. On April 18, Magsaysay
declared that the Philippines would support the proposal on two
conditions. "First, that the right of Asian peoples to self-determination
is respected; and second, that the Philippines be given a clear and unequivocal guarantee of United States' help in case of attack under our
Mutual Defense Pact."[43]

Meanwhile, Britain and France had made it clear that they opposed
any early movement on united action, although in joint communiqués
with the United States in mid-April both committed themselves to
further examination of a collective defense organization for Southeast Asia. This did not dispose of the issue however; it was raised
again by French appeals for assistance at Dien Bien Phu on April 23
and on May 9 against the contingency of Chinese air intervention. On

41. Eisenhower, pp. 346–347.
42. Eden, p. 103; *Pentagon Papers*, IX, 367–368.
43. Roger M. Smith, *The Philippines and the Southeast Asia Treaty Organization*, pp. 5, 6; Meyer, p. 228.

both occasions, the United States reverted to proposals not dissimilar from its March/April united-action plan. But while there is no reason to doubt that the Secretary of State in late March believed that the plan he was proposing might be accepted, it seems highly unlikely that he could have expected anything concrete to come of the proposals he put forward in late April and again in mid-May.

Remembering their response to the original united-action proposal, the Secretary cannot have been at all optimistic that the British would reverse so quickly a decision they had reached when they already had every expectation that Dien Bien Phu would fall. To be sure, his plan, as described by Eden, would not have involved help for the French at Dien Bien Phu. Instead, British and American forces (for whose use prior Congressional authority would be sought) would make a military demonstration somewhere in the area. This military action would be accompanied by a declaration committing the Allies to the defense of Indochina. The move would not be expected to alter the military balance; it would be intended primarily to insulate the French cabinet against the political consequences of the fall of Dien Bien Phu, to help the French survive the psychological blow to the inevitable defeat there, and to encourage them to continue fighting. But to Churchill it seemed "that what we were being asked to do was to assist in misleading Congress into approving a military operation, which would in itself be ineffective, and might well bring the world to the verge of a major war."[44]

It seems even more questionable that Dulles could have expected the French to accept the preconditions posed to them on May 14, in return for an American commitment merely to request that Congress authorize a very limited air and naval contribution. These preconditions—all to be ratified by the National Assembly—included international participation (although on a somewhat narrower basis than

44. Eden, p. 117. Considering the constant failure of their minds to meet, it is possible that Eden understood Dulles to be placing greater stress on the military-demonstration feature of the proposal than the Secretary intended. Eisenhower's account of the events of April 23 is even less precise, but suggests that Dulles had in essence returned to the proposals of early April (Office of the Federal Register, *Public Papers of the Presidents of the United States,* Dwight D. Eisenhower, 1954, pp. 350–351). The one pertinent telegram from Dulles reproduced in the *Pentagon Papers* (Vol IX, p. 388) covers a conversation on April 25 after Eden had seen Churchill and casts no new light on what Dulles put to Eden on April 23.

had been outlined in the original united action proposal), guarantees of the complete independence of the Associated States ("including unqualified option to withdraw from the French Union at any time"), and French agreement to keep forces in Indochina during united action and to make arrangements with the United States concerning training native troops and the command structure.[45]

The Secretary can hardly have been surprised when Bidault responded on June 1 that to present this program of American involvement to the National Assembly, unless the Geneva Conference failed completely, would be to cause the government's downfall.[46] Dulles knew France well and his rapport with the French was much closer than it was with the British. It seems fair to assume also, if only because of the intense American interest in Indochina and the proposed European Defense Community, that the United States Embassy in Paris was reporting copiously on developments in French politics and in the National Assembly.

Presumably, therefore, Dulles must have had other considerations in mind in continuing to keep alive the prospect of united action and American intervention. If, after mid-April, he was engaging largely in atmospherics, these atmospherics were not without serious purpose. First of all, even after the President had spoken of the desirability of achieving a *modus vivendi* at Geneva, American expectations of the outcome continued to be gloomy. In order to take advantage of further military successes, the Communists might try to spin out negotiations interminably to the point where the Allies would want to break them off, or they might demand terms intolerable even to the French. Against this eventuality the concept of united action must be kept alive and pressure maintained on the French to accept the conditions that would make American participation possible. Eisenhower, for example, said of the exchanges with the French in May: "I felt that a prompt French decision to abandon their claim to exclusive direction of the fighting against Communism in the area should come soon and that they should seek instead a coalition of power to carry the burden. . . . When the French came to realize the alternatives they faced—either internationalization of the conflict or virtually abject

45. *Pentagon Papers*, IX, 451 ff.
46. *Ibid.*, I, Part III, p. A–22.

surrender—a satisfactory outcome could be expected."[47] Thus, the French were told in mid-June that although they did not have "a continuing option" to call the United States into the war under circumstances and conditions of their own choosing, a French government deciding to continue the war and supported by the National Assembly would probably find the United States prepared to respond along the lines outlined on May 14. But, the Secretary pointed out, the United States might take a different view if by this time the situation had so deteriorated that "the making of a stand in Indochina had become impracticable or so burdensome as to be out of proportion to the results obtainable."[48]

Meanwhile, Allied talk of military intervention was bound to come to Communist attention, thereby perhaps improving the Allied bargaining position and deterring rash Communist action. Dulles was not unaware of the way in which the French were manipulating this theme and, up to a point, did not disapprove. We believe, he said in a telegram to Paris in mid-May, that the principal French motive "is to use U.S. position to get better terms at Geneva. We have no objection to this provided action is consistent with the principles which we think necessary . . . to avoid thinly disguised capitulation." In this context also, it was useful to get the British position on the public record, even though it was far from according fully with American desires. Thus, the communiqué that emerged from the Anglo-American discussions at the end of June committed the two countries to press forward with plans for collective defense, whether or not a satisfactory agreement emerged from the conference. And, it was pointed out, both countries were convinced that if the French were confronted with demands preventing an acceptable agreement, the international situation would be seriously aggravated.[49]

With Allied division over military intervention well-aired in the press, the Communists might discount the prospect, but they could not disregard it. Moreover, for deterrent purposes it seemed useful to suggest that unilateral U.S. action could not be ruled out. Any overt Chinese Communist aggression in Southeast Asia, Dulles warned in a speech on June 11, would be a deliberate threat to the United States;

47. Eisenhower, pp. 358–359.
48. *Pentagon Papers*, IX, 570.
49. *Ibid.*, p. 467; *DSB*, July 12, 1954, p. 49.

while the American government would invoke the United Nations and consult with its Allies, it would have to take ultimate responsibility for decisions relating to its own right to self-preservation.[50]

Finally, as the President's Special Assistant, Robert Cutler had written in May, "the record of history should be clear as to the U.S. position."[51] To be sure, the legislative branch had made evident to the executive its opposition to any large-scale engagement of American forces in Vietnam. But this did not mean that Congress would excuse any seeming executive failure to seek to prevent the loss of Indochina by other means. In short, if another segment of Asia was to be lost to the Communists, it must be demonstrated that this was not of American doing.

50. *DSB*, June 28, 1954, pp. 572–573.
51. *Pentagon Papers*, IX, 437.

CHAPTER 10

REACHING THE SETTLEMENT

Once the United States accepted the inevitability of a compromise settlement, the concept of united action as a precursor to negotiations merged into the concept of postconference collective defense arrangements, the American role became less conspicuous, Eden displaced Dulles as the pivotal figure on the western side, and Allied differences became less intense. Nevertheless, it was not easy for the western powers to agree among themselves on the specifics of what were to be the essential elements of the final accords—military arrangements unaccompanied by political settlement, the establishment of international supervisory machinery, *de facto* partitions, and the provision for elections in 1956. On issues somewhat remote from the settlement terms, moreover, there were moments of considerable tension, with the British suspicious that the French and Americans were making plans for U.S. intervention, and Americans suspicious that the British were using the conference to pave the way for Peking's admission to the UN.

On the Communist side, if there were differences, they were not displayed. Unlike the Associated States, the DRV played an active role in the proceedings. Nevertheless, a number of the crucial Communist concessions were put forward by the Russians or the Chinese, and logic, if not evidence, suggests that the DRV may not have been entirely happy with the role played by its Allies.

Neutralist views, which had been at least in the background of British thinking before the conference, became of greater weight as the Colombo powers under Nehru's leadership addressed themselves specifically to the Indochina issue. Chou's statements both at Geneva and in the neutralist capitals to which he traveled while the conference was in recess made increasingly evident Communist interest in courting neutralist favor.

Before the Indochina phase of the Geneva Conference opened, it had been agreed that invitations to join the five principal participants would be sent to Cambodia, Laos, and the State of Vietnam by the western Allies and to the DRV by the USSR.[1] Between May 8 and May 14, at four plenary sessions both sides advanced their maximum positions. French Foreign Minister Georges Bidault stressed an internationally guaranteed and supervised cease-fire with provisions for regrouping regular forces and disarming irregulars. After the cease-fire, political questions would be settled during a transitional period which would culminate in elections. In Laos and Cambodia, where there was no civil war, all that was necessary was Viet Minh withdrawal under international supervision.

DRV Deputy Premier and Foreign Minister, Pham Van Dong, addressing the same issues, demanded that the Pathet Lao and Khmer Issarak "governments" be invited to the conference. Political agreements were to precede a cease-fire, to be supervised by joint committees representing the two sides. Thereafter, all foreign troops were to be withdrawn from Vietnam, Cambodia, and Laos; elections would be held under the supervision of representatives of both sides; and, pending the establishment of a single government in each country, each side would administer the territory under its control.

In the third plenary, on May 12, the representative of the State of Vietnam took strong exception to the proposals advanced by France and the DRV. He demanded instead recognition of the complete sovereignty, authority, and unity of the State of Vietnam under Bao Dai. The Viet Minh were to be integrated into this state with proper safeguards and with elections to be held under UN supervision. This proposal was endorsed by Under Secretary of State Walter Bedell Smith, leader of the American delegation after Dulles' departure from Geneva on May 3.

At the next plenary session on May 14, Soviet Foreign Minister Vyacheslav Molotov offered the first concession from the Communist side, modifying the DRV proposal for joint commissions by the addition of a supervisory commission composed of nations not involved in the conflict. Before this, at the third plenary, Eden had suggested that

1. That Peking had joined Moscow in issuing the invitation to the DRV emerged only later and was denounced by the United States as contrary to the agreement.

restricted sessions explore such issues as regroupment and supervision, and after May 14 there were no further plenary meetings until June 8. Restricted sessions were supplemented by private and informal meetings, with Eden exceptionally active as mediator and conciliator.

Progress was made on a number of fronts. The Allied side agreed to accept Molotov's May 21 cease-fire and regroupment proposals as a basis for negotiations. The Communists accepted the priority of a military over a political settlement and tacitly agreed to by-pass Lao and Cambodian questions temporarily. The DRV also made a regroupment proposal which seemed to accept a *de facto* partition; the French, however, were not yet prepared for partition. Finally, a start was made toward exploring arrangements on the ground (and toward direct discussions with the DRV hitherto avoided by the French) as French-DRV military staff talks got under way, first on prisoner exchanges, then on regroupment, and, beginning July 10, on partition.

During this same period a number of developments outside the conference were of some relevance to its deliberations. In mid-May, the British learned through press stories that the United States and France were exploring conditions for American intervention. An incensed Churchill described these talks in the House of Commons as "inconsistent with the spirit of the western alliance."[2] Eisenhower's remark at his May 19 press conference that appropriate Asian participation might obviate the need for British membership in a Southeast Asian collective defense arrangement added to British irritation. At the end of the month, imposing further strains on the western alliance, Thailand asked the Security Council for an observer mission to help prevent fighting in nearby Laos from spreading to Thai territory. France and Britain believed this move, supported by the United States, to be extremely untimely. Nevertheless, they voted for the proposal, which was vetoed, however, by the Soviet Union.

On June 8, the situation at Geneva took a turn for the worse. At a plenary session held at his own request, Molotov bitterly attacked Bidault, as did PRC Premier Chou En-lai the following day, both Communist representatives, in addition, advancing propositions that seemed to negate progress already made. Reverting to their original positions, they argued that political and military issues were too closely intertwined to be discussed separately and that Cambodia and Laos

2. Bator, p. 101.

must be discussed simultaneously with Vietnam and with due regard for the status of the Pathet Lao and Khmer Issarak. The new tough line was widely seen as intended, at least in part, to assist in the demise of the tottering Laniel government, which finally fell on June 12. Whether the Communists were being tough solely for this reason, and had no intention of remaining so, or whether they reverted to conciliatory tactics as quickly as they did because they feared the Allies would otherwise abandon the conference, they were given ample reason to anticipate the latter. On June 10, Eden suggested that his patience was not unlimited and that the conference might "have to admit failure." On June 15, the non-Communist states broke off the stalemated Korean talks. On the same day it was announced that Churchill and Eden would visit Washington on June 25. Discussing the visit at a press conference, Dulles said plans had long been under way, but that Eden's visit had become a practical proposition only as it began to appear that "the Geneva Conference either will be terminated or perhaps reduced to a lower level of negotiations." The next day, the President said that the British had accepted his long-standing invitation because they felt the possibilities at Geneva had now been exhausted.[3] To Communist analysts of Allied intentions it may have seemed ominous also that, within the same few days, Dulles had publicly outlined the conditions for Allied intervention and Bao Dai had asked the uncompromising Catholic nationalist and protégé of important Americans, Ngo Dinh Diem, to form a new government in Saigon.

In any case, Molotov and Chou were evidently alarmed. On the night of June 15, Molotov called on Eden but did nothing more than suggest minor changes in his position on the international supervisory commission. The next day, however, Chou offered Eden really significant concessions. The PRC, he thought, could probably persuade the Viet Minh to withdraw from Laos and Cambodia, and Peking would not find it difficult to recognize the royal governments of the two countries as long as no American bases were established there. At the restricted session on the same day, Molotov, who had previously insisted that the international supervisory committee be composed of four states—two neutral and two Communist—retreated to either a five-member commission with three neutrals or a three-member one with two neutrals. On June 17, Chou repeated his assurance respecting

3. *SIA*, 1954, p. 52; Randle, pp. 281, 290.

Cambodia and Laos to Bidault. By June 20 when, the principals having departed, the conference went into a form of semirecess, there was reason to hope that a settlement was within reach. There was also greater pressure to achieve a settlement rapidly; the new French Premier, Pierre Mendès-France, in soliciting the support of the National Assembly for his investiture had promised to achieve a cease-fire by July 20 or resign.

Between June 20 and early July when the principals returned to Geneva, the military commissions continued their work, and a number of significant meetings were held. On June 23, Mendès-France met with Chou. Breaking ground on still another issue, Chou expressed understanding of the French desire for a fairly lengthy interval between a cease-fire and elections. He also reiterated previously expressed positions respecting Laos and Cambodia, partition, and the priority of military over political issues, and agreed to ask the DRV representatives to speed the negotiations. On June 24, Jean Chauvel, the senior French professional diplomat at the conference, was authorized to meet with Pham Van Dong. Meanwhile, Communist courtship of the neutralists proceeded. Chou, visiting India and Burma, was warmly received and signed with Nehru and U Nu communiqués endorsing the five principles of peaceful coexistence which had been first enunciated a month earlier in an agreement with the PRC under which India accepted Tibet as "a region of China."

At the same time, Allied ranks were tightening. In Washington, the British and Americans, in a communiqué issued on June 28 and endorsed by ANZUS on June 30, declared they would proceed with plans for collective defense in Southeast Asia whether the conference succeeded or failed. They also agreed on seven conditions for an acceptable armistice agreement which were communicated to the French on June 29. These were not significantly different from negotiating objectives the French had already formulated. They accepted the prospect of partition for Vietnam without accepting its permanence, called for maintaining the integrity of Laos and Cambodia, and required that machinery for international supervision be included in a settlement.

The United States, nevertheless, remained reluctant to identify itself too closely with the results of the conference. Thus, when the principals returned to Geneva, Bedell Smith was not among them, and the

American delegation, led by Ambassador to Czechoslovakia U. Alexis Johnson, obviously had no more than a watching brief. This seemed to the British and French likely to do serious damage to the western bargaining position. Apparently impressed by Mendès-France, with whom he met in Paris, Dulles announced on July 14 that Bedell Smith would return to the conference.

Meanwhile, much had been accomplished by the technical working groups left behind at Geneva. However, there were still serious problems to be resolved at higher levels relating to the composition and procedures of the international supervisory commission, the demarcation line in Vietnam, the date of elections there, and the status of Cambodia and Laos. On some of these, agreement was not reached until the night of July 20. Even then, because of an unexpected Cambodian intervention into the decisions of the great powers, the deadline was met only by stopping the clock.

Problems relating to the international supervisory commissions were resolved first. Eden had originally proposed commissions made up of representatives of the Colombo powers. Molotov had retreated from his original demands for equal Communist and non-Communist membership to a five- or three-member commission with a neutral majority. The knot was cut on July 18 when Chou proposed Canada, India, and Poland. The Communists also retreated from their demand that all commission decisions be unanimous, but only slightly; decisions requiring unanimity were defined but in such a way that the most important questions fell under this heading.[4]

Early positions on the demarcation line were quite far apart—the French demanding the eighteenth parallel as the southern boundary of the DRV, and the DRV demanding the thirteenth. On July 13, the DRV proposed the sixteenth parallel but, this compromise having been rejected by Mendès-France, deadlock persisted until July 20 when Molotov proposed the seventeenth.

Agreement on elections was also reached on July 20. Initially, the French, in line with their desire to limit the settlement to military matters, had wanted to avoid even mentioning elections. Blocked in this endeavor, they sought at least to avoid fixing a date, while pri-

4. By the time this decision was reached, Bedell Smith reported that the French felt the veto would work to their advantage and that he and Eden agreed (*Pentagon Papers*, IX, 664).

vately agreeing with the British that the southern government would require at least eighteen months to establish itself and gain some prospect of an electoral victory. Pham Van Dong, however, on July 13, had proposed six months to Diem's Foreign Minister, Tran Van Do. With some fixed date seemingly inevitable, Molotov's proposal on July 20 that elections be held in July 1956 was accepted with relief by the western Allies.

Reaching agreement on Laos and Cambodia was complicated by the DRV's persistent support of its Pathet Lao and Khmer Issarak Allies; by the number of questions, technical and otherwise, requiring last-minute action owing to earlier concentration on Vietnam; and by Cambodian intransigence which gained in effectiveness because French concessions to Sihanouk on the supreme command had made it necessary that Cambodian, not French, military representatives sign the cease-fire agreements.

As Chou had promised in his conversations with British and French representatives, the DRV agreed to withdraw its "volunteers" from Cambodia and Laos. Until early July, however, it demanded political and military rights for the Khmer Issarak and the Pathet Lao which, in the case of the latter, would have brought about virtual partition. Its case for such demands in Cambodia being a very weak one, the DRV finally accepted the pledge that Khmer resistance forces would be integrated into the national community without reprisals and with the right to participate in general elections to be held in 1955. The Pathet Lao, as a more significant force, were given correspondingly better treatment. Pending a political settlement that would integrate all citizens into the national community and make possible general elections in 1955, the Pathet Lao forces were to regroup in the two northern provinces of Phong Saly and Sam Neua, the administrative status of which was left rather vague.

The Communist desire to exclude American bases from the two states and preclude their entry into the projected collective defense organization provided the occasion for the Cambodian dissent. France, it was agreed, could retain two bases in Laos and the forces necessary to garrison them, but otherwise foreign forces and bases were to be excluded from Laos and Cambodia. As to alliances, the phrase used was so permissive—none of the Associated States was to join an alliance not in conformity with the provisions of the charter—that even the United States could not object. Unexpectedly, however, and at the eleventh hour, Cambodia's representative declared that he would sign no agreement limiting his country's right to take steps of its own choice to defend its territory—including requesting the establishment of American bases. With the Cambodians obviously quite unmoved by pressures from both sides, Molotov agreed that Cambodia should be free, if its security were threatened, to request foreign military assistance and the establishment of foreign bases. Seizing this unanticipated opportunity, Mendès-France then pressed successfully for a similar grant to Laos.

On July 21, the conference met for the last time. It had before it three cease-fire agreements—two, for Vietnam and Laos, signed by the French and Viet Minh high commands, and one by the Cambodian and Viet Minh high commands. In addition, France, Laos, and Cambodia had each made unilateral declarations. France declared its respect for the independence, sovereignty, unity, and territorial integrity of Cambodia, Laos, and Vietnam and its readiness to withdraw its troops from these countries at their request. The declarations issued by Laos and Cambodia recorded their commitments with respect to integration of dissident elements, elections, alliances, and foreign bases and military assistance. The final declaration, signed by none of the participants but listing all of them, expressed satisfaction with the termination of hostilities, took note of the principal obligations accepted in the cease-fire agreements and unilateral declarations, and urged the parties to carry them out. The declaration also committed the members of the conference: to respect the sovereignty, independence, unity, and territorial integrity of Cambodia, Laos, and Vietnam; to refrain from interference in their internal affairs; and, in the last paragraph, to consult with one another on any question referred to them by the supervisory commission to determine what measures might be necessary to assure respect for the agreements.

When Eden, chairman of the final meeting, called upon the delegates to "express themselves" on the final declaration, the French, Chinese, and Russians announced their approval, the Lao made no comment, the Cambodian reserved his country's rights and interests in "Cambodian lands" in South Vietnam, and the DRV delegate, also making no comment on the final declaration, confined himself to expressing reservations concerning the Cambodian reservation. Bedell

Smith disassociated the United States from the last paragraph of the final declaration but declared that it would not use force or the threat of force to disturb the agreements and would view with grave concern their violation by any new aggression. In addition, he reiterated American support for the unification of nations "divided against their will" through free elections supervised by the United Nations. Finally, Tran Van Do, while accepting the cease-fire, protested France's arrogation to itself of the right to agree on cease-fire terms and the date of future elections, the haste with which the agreement had been concluded, and the abandonment to the Viet Minh of much territory still held by the Vietnamese Army. He then reserved for his government "complete freedom of action to guarantee the sacred right of the Vietnamese people to territorial unity, national independence, and freedom."

The Issues before the Allies

When the Indochina negotiations began, the Allies far from having coordinated their views on acceptable peace terms had not even developed national positions fully. The French at the outset seem to have envisaged nothing beyond an armistice—guaranteed by the participants in the conference—with internationally supervised machinery already in place to ensure its observance. Only after the armistice had been in effect for some substantial period would negotiations on a political settlement take place.[5]

Reflecting basic pessimism over the outcome of negotiations, the instructions given to the American delegates focused largely on what they were supposed to avoid or prevent. In a telegram drafted by Dulles, Bedell Smith was told first and foremost not to deal with the Chinese (or Vietnamese) Communists on any terms implying political recognition. The United States would not approve even by implication any cease-fire or other arrangement subverting the governments of the Associated States, permanently impairing their territorial integrity, placing French Union forces in jeopardy, or contravening the purposes for which the United States was attending the conference which were: to help the countries in Indochina "peacefully to enjoy territorial integrity and political independence under stable and free governments with the opportunity to expand their economies, to realize their legitimate national aspirations, and to develop security through individual

5. LaCouture and Devillers, pp. 100–102, 152–153.

and collective defense against aggression, from within or without. This implies that these people should not be amalgamated into the Communist bloc or imperialistic dictatorship."[6]

Eden had a different vision. He thought it unrealistic to expect that a victor's terms could be imposed upon an undefeated enemy. Accordingly, any negotiated settlement could have only one of two outcomes, "either a Communist share in the government of most of Indo-China, or complete Communist control of part of the country." He preferred the latter, primarily for strategic considerations. "My chief concern was for Malaya. I wanted to ensure an effective barrier as far to the north of that country as possible." This protective pad, as he called it, "we could prop up with western help. . . . It would be best if communism could be held at arm's length, clear of Cambodia and Laos, and halted as far north as possible in Vietnam." The Chinese and Russians might also come to see "a balance of advantage in arranging a girdle of neutral states," while, as to the Vietnamese, there was "no love lost between north and south."[7]

American policy makers likewise had early seen the alternatives as coalition or partition, but tended to reject both. In January 1954, the NSC concluded that "a nominally non-Communist coalition regime would eventually turn the country over to Ho Chi Minh." In March, the Joint Chiefs found various forms of political settlement undesirable. Coalition government would open the way to ultimate Communist seizure of control "under conditions which might preclude timely and effective external assistance." Partition "would recognize Communist territorial expansion achieved through force of arms," encourage the Communists to further adventures, and probably involve the loss of the Tonkin delta area, "the keystone of the defense of mainland Southeast Asia." Even self-determination through free elections—unlikely as it was that genuinely free elections could be held—would be undesirable, since Communist propagandists would be able to present the issue as a choice between independence and continued French rule, while Communist terrorists would intimidate the voters undeterred by any conceivable military action.[8]

By the end of April, however, it seemed that the United States was

6. *Pentagon Papers*, IX, 458.
7. Eden, pp. 97, 101, 138, 139.
8. *Pentagon Papers*, IX, 232, 267–268.

beginning to regard partition as a realistic—if far from ideal—prospect. On April 29, Eisenhower pointed out that in Indochina a course had to be steered between two extremes—the unattainable, a completely satisfactory arrangement, and the unacceptable, the disappearance of the anti-Communist defense of the area. "The most you can work out," he said, "is a practical way of getting along. . . . That is what we have been doing in Europe—the whole situation from Berlin all the way through Germany is really on a practical basis of getting along one with the other, no more. Now, I think that for the moment, if you could get that, that would be the most you could ask."[9] By the last week in May, Eden had the impression that Dulles was ready to accept partition and, in a Congressional briefing on June 23, Bedell Smith said that the administration now accepted the prospect.[10]

In the seven-point communication of June 29, Britain and the United States told the French an acceptable armistice agreement would have to preserve the southern half of Vietnam with the dividing line no further south than Dong Hoi.[11] The agreement was not to include political conditions that would risk the loss of "retained" Vietnam to Communist control or provisions that would exclude the possibility of peaceful reunification or impair the ability of "retained" Vietnam to maintain a stable non-Communist regime, to have forces adequate to preserve internal security, to import arms, and to employ foreign advisers.

The French had adopted partition as a negotiating objective only five days earlier. At that time, Mendès-France and his most senior advisers, including Ely and Chauvel, agreed that the latter, in the negotiations he was about to open with Pham Van Dong, should propose regrouping on either side of a demarcation line in the vicinity of the eighteenth parallel. Earlier, in considering how the opposing military forces should be disentangled and regrouped—part of the French armistice plan from the outset—the French had talked in terms of a leopard-spot arrangement in which French Union and Viet Minh regroupment areas would be interspersed throughout the country. This was the preference of the Vietnamese government, stemming quite logically from their demand for subordinating the Viet Minh to Bao

9. *Public Papers,* Eisenhower, 1954, p. 428.
10. Eden, p. 148; Randle, p. 295.
11. About halfway between the seventeenth and eighteenth parallels.

Dai's authority, with regroupment a step toward demobilizing the Communist forces but not toward dividing political authority—an outcome almost certain to result from partition.

The French were sensitive to these views and hesitated for some time before moving irreversibly toward partition. On May 3, the French High Commissioner in Saigon said, "The French government has no intention of seeking a settlement of the Indochina problem based upon a partition of Vietnamese territory." Writing privately to Bao Dai on May 6, Bidault (against the advice of members of his staff who wanted to preserve French freedom of action) said that "nothing could be more contrary to the intentions of the French Government than to prepare for the establishment of two states, each with an international role, at the expense of the integrity of Vietnam."[12]

Nevertheless, the French had not really excluded the possibility of partition. In mid-April, Chauvel and Navarre had already considered the modalities of partition, and Navarre had recommended the eighteenth parallel as the dividing line. Navarre had done no more than respond to Chauvel's request for his views on a contingent basis but, in mid-June, Ely strongly recommended partition as the only alternative to continuing the war. With proper safeguards, he argued, and with Viet Minh agreement to withdraw from Laos and Cambodia and terminate their activities south of the demarcation line, "France would be able to preserve the position in Indochina necessary to preserve its world position."[13] On June 18, Chauvel told U. Alexis Johnson that France had concluded that the leopard-spot solution was impracticable and unenforceable and thought it preferable to have a line behind which it would be possible to build a reasonably effective Vietnamese government and defense.[14]

Although accepting partition as unavoidable, it was difficult for the United States to accept it either as permanent—and therefore as ceding additional Asian territory to Communist control—or as temporary—and therefore as risking the loss of non-Communist Vietnam to Communist election successes, whether won by superior political strength or by manipulation and terror. To guard against Communist election abuses, the United States had insisted from the first days of

12. LaCouture and Devillers, p. 135.
13. Ely, pp. 112–113, 168–169.
14. *Pentagon Papers,* IX, 579.

the conference that they be held under United Nations supervision. Britain had supported this in a generalized way when Churchill and Eisenhower declared, in the Potomac Declaration of June 29: "In the case of nations now divided against their will, we shall continue to seek to achieve unity through free elections supervised by the United Nations to insure they are conducted fairly."[15] The British, however, apparently did not feel that joining in this statement precluded them from approving the provision in the final declaration for supervision of the elections by the tripartite commission; more consistently with its past statements, if not with the prospect of winning Communist consent as long as the PRC was excluded from the world organization, the United States reiterated its stand on UN supervision.

Whether, under some circumstances, it might be undesirable to hold elections, however supervised, was an implicit question never explicitly addressed. The French, to be sure, raised it by pointing to certain possible contradiction in the Anglo-American seven points of June 29. Was there not some conflict, the French asked the American Ambassador, Douglas Dillon, between the fourth point, which required that the armistice agreement exclude any provision risking the loss of "retained" Vietnam to Communist control, and the fifth which required that the agreement not exclude the possibility of ultimate reunification by political means? Could not the provision for elections, which would have to be included in the agreement, be the means of fulfilling the fifth requirement, but possibly only at the expense of the fourth? The French might also have noted that the third point, by excluding arrangements that could materially impair the capacity of "retained" Vietnam to maintain a stable non-Communist regime, reinforced the fourth, and therefore also conflicted potentially with the fifth.

The State Department, however, saw no real conflict. Even with an agreement that completely satisfied the seven points, Indochina might some day pass into Communist hands. To provide the best chance of avoiding this, the seven points must be observed in the spirit as well as the letter. The very possibility that elections might result in reunification under Ho made it all the more important to hold them as long after the cease-fire as possible and to avoid a fixed date and conditions that would prevent international supervision.

15. *DSB*, July 12, 1954, p. 99.

The British, who, Dulles suspected, were less serious about the seven points than the Americans, probably had less difficulty in adjusting their principled support of reunification to their practical expectation that reunification on acceptable terms was unlikely. Eden's hope to include the non-Communist segment of Vietnam in a buffer zone to be guaranteed by all parties hardly suggests that he anticipated a temporary division.[16]

Dulles' real expectations may have been little different. Nevertheless, accepting partition in principle was difficult in the American political arena where the Assistant Secretary of State for Congressional Relations felt constrained to say, "The United States will not become a party to any agreement which smacks of appeasement. Nor will we acknowledge the legitimacy of Communist control of any segment of Southeast Asia any more than we recognized the Communist control of North Korea."[17] This did not mean that the United States proposed to attempt or to encourage others to overthrow Communist control by force; indeed, it committed itself not to do so. But problems with partition combined with attitudes toward Communist China in making the administration unwilling to join in guaranteeing the settlement in the manner envisaged by Britain and France.

The French seem to have anticipated that all powers concerned in a settlement would join in guaranteeing it. But they do not appear to have thought much beyond this. Probably, although they would have liked the United States and the other signatories to join together in a guarantee—particularly since the Russians and Chinese seemed to want this—their more urgent interest lay in winning assurances of American protection for the Associated States. When Dillon suggested to Mendès-France that the State of Vietnam should be kept more fully informed and should be told about the Anglo-American seven points, at least in a general way, Mendès-France replied that he had felt it better to wait until he could assure the Vietnamese that the United States was prepared to guarantee them against further aggression and subversion. And, when he wrote to Dulles urging that the Secretary or Under Secretary return to Geneva, he emphasized that only a united West could bring about eventual military and strategic unity in Southeast Asia. "It is in this spirit," the Premier added, "that

16. *Pentagon Papers*, IX, 603, 608, 616.
17. Randle, p. 315.

the French government envisages, aside from the assurances which the conference itself could furnish, the establishment of a collective guarantee by virtue of which the signatories would declare themselves prepared to intervene, if, in Indochina, one of the three states was a victim of aggression."[18]

The British position on guarantees combined united action as a deterrent and safeguard, with a buffer area which all concerned—Communists, neutrals, and Allies—would find it to their interest to maintain. Eden elaborated on this in the House of Commons on June 23. "I hope," he said, "that we shall be able to agree to an international guarantee of any settlement that may emerge at Geneva. I also hope that it will be possible to agree on some system of South East Asian defence to guard against aggression. In other words, we could have a reciprocal arrangement in which both sides take part, such as Locarno. We could also have a defensive alliance such as NATO is in Europe. . . . These two systems, I admit, are quite different, but they need be in no way inconsistent." Later in the debate he added, "Suppose an Asian circle consisting on the one hand of China and Soviet Russia, and, on the other, of France, America, and ourselves—and perhaps India and other countries, too—could guarantee the arrangements arrived at. That would be something entirely new in our international experience. I do not say that it is likely to happen, but that I think it is possible that it might happen, and surely it is something worth trying to get."[19]

Eden's reference to the Locarno Pact of 1925 (which had guaranteed European borders as defined in the Treaty of Versailles and paved the way for Germany's admission to the League of Nations) provoked a totally unanticipated American reaction, reflecting sensitivities with respect to the PRC and to formal association with any agreement ceding territory to Communist control. In the House of Representatives on June 29, John McCormack voiced suspicions that the British had "made a deal with France and Red China at Geneva. . . . Do they expect us to enter into a Locarno agreement, so-called, which would mean at least a *de facto* recognition of Red China?"[20] On the same day the House passed a rider to the foreign-aid bill recommending that

18. *Pentagon Papers*, IX, 633, 642.
19. *Hansard*, Vol. 529, June 23, 1954, Cols. 433, 548.
20. Bator, p. 115.

no funds be "used on behalf of governments which are committed by treaty to maintain Communist rule over any definite territory of Asia." This was intended, according to the sponsor, John W. Vorys, to demonstrate "that we are buying no part of a Locarno Pact for Southeast Asia."[21] In the Senate, Majority Leader Knowland and Minority Leader Lyndon B. Johnson joined in declaring that the United States must leave the United Nations if the PRC should be admitted. Suspicions concerning the Chinese implications of the British proposal were calmed by Churchill's statement that Britain, while believing that the PRC should represent China in the UN, did not think the time had come to reconsider this matter there. Nevertheless, American opposition to the mutual-guarantee aspects of Eden's Locarno proposal remained high, and it was not mentioned in the communiqué on Indochina issued at the end of Churchill's vist to Washington.[22]

The June 28 communiqué, however, did reflect a meeting of minds on organizing collective defense, whether or not agreement was reached on Indochina. The American public, moreover, had long since been prepared by the administration for the prospect that, even if united action could not protect all of Indochina, it might still serve to insulate the rest of Southeast Asia from the consequences otherwise likely to ensue from the establishment of Communist control over some part of it. Thus, when asked at a press conference on May 11, whether the American collective security plan could succeed if one or more areas were lost to Communism, Dulles rephrased the question so as to recall the domino simile. While agreeing that it would be more difficult to keep the other dominos upright if one fell, he argued that it would not be impossible to do so if proper measures were taken in advance. "The situation in that area, as we found it," he said, "was that it was subject to the so-called 'domino theory.' You mean that if one went, another would go? We are trying to change it so that would not be the case. That is the whole theory of collective security. You generally have a whole series of countries which can be picked up one by one. That is the whole theory of the North Atlantic Treaty. As the nations come together, then the 'domino theory,' so-called, ceases to apply. And what we are trying to do is create a situation in Southeast Asia where the domino situation will not apply." I do not wish, he said, to under-

21. Farley, p. 24.
22. Randle, pp. 302–303.

estimate the importance of Vietnam, Laos, and Cambodia. "But I do not want to give the impression either that if events we could not control, and which we do not anticipate, should lead to their being lost that we would consider the whole situation hopeless and we would give up in despair."[23]

The Neutralist Voice

The neutralist role at Geneva was essentially an Indian one and derived such influence as it had from the rivalry between Britain and the Communist powers for Indian support in the broader international arena. In June 1950, Nehru had said of Vietnam, "We shall keep aloof and not recognize either regime," his stance in this regard meeting with general public approval. But, in 1953, a number of factors combined to cause a change in the Indian position. One of these related to Indochina itself: fear that the ever-increasing interest and role of outside powers could eventuate in direct and open intervention, in due course engulfing Asia in expanded hostilities. Setbacks in India's own position were also of influence because they strengthened fears of resurgent colonialism. Contrary to Indian expectations, French and Portuguese resistance to proposals that they give up colonial enclaves on the subcontinent had hardened. Moreover, increasingly close American relations with Pakistan, culminating in a military-aid agreement, aroused passionate Indian resentment. Colonialism was involved because a western power seemed to be strengthening one party to an Asian dispute at the expense of another; American justifications on containment grounds merely confirmed Indian distrust of U.S. foreign policy as unnecessarily rigid, ideological, and belligerent.[24]

As India's anticolonialist sensitivities were exacerbated, Nehru tended to express himself more often and more forcibly on Vietnam. The situation, he now concluded, was one where the right of self-determination must prevail over any fear that territory might come under Communist control. In July 1953, he said, "I have not the slightest doubt that the war is a war of independence of the South-East Asian countries. The question whether some other countries are helping them or not is another matter."[25]

23. *DSB,* May 24, 1954, p. 782.
24. Dutt and Singh, pp. 8, 15.
25. *Ibid.,* p. 8; J. C. Kundra, *Indian Foreign Policy,* p. 206.

The American concept of united action seemed to embody India's worst fears: it was further evidence that the United States opposed a negotiated settlement; it threatened wider western participation in hostilities in Asia; and it would bolster the French position in Indochina. "Whatever the motive," Nehru said, "the return of any armed forces or anything like it from any European or American country is a reversal of the history of the countries of Asia." The proposal, he charged, came close to asserting a kind of Monroe Doctrine for the countries of Southeast Asia, while V. K. Krishna Menon referred to it as "an incipient and embryonic infringement of our peace area approach."[26] Even the qualified British approval of the principle of collective defense aroused Indian ire. The *Times of India* characterized British acquiesence as "dangerously near a spineless appeasement of an importunate ally," presaging a new attempt to impose foreign domination on newly independent countries.[27]

Since Asian interests were involved, Indian leaders believed that Asians should have a greater voice in the Geneva proceedings than the western parties, particularly the United States, seemed prepared to contemplate. India's exclusion from formal participation was resentfully attributed to American pressures. Notwithstanding, India could be confident that its voice would be heard with interest on both sides of the negotiating table. Most particularly, Britain was actively seeking to demonstrate that it valued Indian advice, was tailoring its own policies to Indian approval, and hoped for Indian, and other neutralist, support and even participation in guaranteeing the final settlement. Soviet and Chinese Communist approval for India's nonalignment policies, meanwhile, was increasingly evident, and India's acceptance of the Chinese position in Tibet seemed to have removed the last obstacle to close and cordial relations.

Nehru was convinced that Indochina negotiations under greatpower auspices would run into Cold War deadlocks, and he preferred that any external conciliatory activities required be supplied by the United Nations. In his April 24 peace plan he called for an immediate cease-fire, French guarantees of the independence of the Associated States, and the initiation of negotiations in which France, the Associated States, and the DRV would be the only participants. The

26. Dutt and Singh, p. 24; *Keesing's Contemporary Archives*, X, 13548.
27. Randle, p. 84.

United States, Britain, the PRC, and the Soviet Union were to agree not to intervene, and all military aid to the belligerents was to be terminated. The final agreement would be enforced under UN auspices, and outside states would be invited to adhere to a nonintervention agreement drafted by the UN.

Not long after, India met with Burma, Ceylon, Indonesia, and Pakistan at a gathering of the Colombo powers, which had been scheduled for some time and had not originally included Indochina on the agenda. The participants, with their rather diverse views and interests, were not prepared to support all aspects of the Indian proposal. In a resolution published on April 29, they called for a prompt cease-fire and an irrevocable French commitment to independence for Indochina but, in effect, sanctioned the composition of the Geneva Conference and gave less emphasis to the UN role.[28]

While the Colombo powers were still meeting, Eden queried them regarding participation in maintaining a cease-fire in Indochina should one eventuate. Nehru's first response having been noncommittal, Eden persisted and, on May 15—the day after Molotov had proposed a neutral-nation supervisory commission—Nehru declared that India would assist in "promoting and maintaining" a settlement. Its participation, however, would be subject to its own policy of nonalignment, its limited resources, and the acceptance by all concerned of the agreements reached at Geneva, which must not favor the interests of one side over the other.[29]

Toward the end of May, Krishna Menon arrived in Geneva as Nehru's personal emissary and began to take a very active part in the informal meetings at which so much of the business of the conference was conducted. Available evidence does not reveal the extent of his influence. He himself, in an interview, laid claim to having been responsible for Mendès-France's decision to set a deadline and for other decisions as well, but he was not a man noted for modesty. He was, at the very least, omnipresent. One journalist noted "there is no antechamber where one does not find oneself face to face with Mr. Krishna Menon."[30]

28. Sar Desai, pp. 35, 40; Keesing's Contemporary Archives, X, 13548, 13576; Randle, pp. 127–129; Dutt and Singh, p. 11.

29. Sar Desai, p. 44.

30. SIA, 1954, p. 47; Michael Brecher, India and World Politics, pp. 44–49.

Whatever the extent of Krishna Menon's personal role, India's influence on British policy and the support provided to British policy by the mobilization of neutralist sentiment behind settlement were both factors of some importance. It seems quite likely also that the desire to strengthen their influence with the neutralists was one of the factors influencing Moscow and Peking toward conciliatory postures. They undoubtedly hoped that the western powers would be correspondingly influenced toward compromise by their own need to compete for neutralist sympathies. In Nehru's estimation, the conference was a resounding success, one of the "outstanding achievements in international diplomacy in the post-war era" symbolizing how peace could be attained in Asia through coexistence.[31]

The Chinese and the Russians

The Communist side conveyed the appearance of great solidarity, and its negotiating performance seemed exceptionally well-coordinated. The world press, which had little difficulty in reconstructing western difficulties on the basis of public and informed private statements, could do little more than speculate about differences among the Communists.[32] No real evidence emerged to bolster the logical suspicion that the Vietnamese Communists could not be entirely happy with compromises made at their expense.

The one insider's story, Nikita Khruschev's brief account, only obscures the picture further. At some point before the Geneva Conference, he tells us, a preparatory meeting was held in Moscow with Chou En-lai, Ho Chi Minh, and Pham Van Dong all present. The Viet Minh, Khruschev says, were on the verge of collapse and were counting on a cease-fire to bail them out. Meanwhile, they had decided to retreat to the Chinese border if necessary and, to Chou's great discomfort, had asked that China be ready to move troops into Vietnam as it had in North Korea. When Chou appealed to him to suggest a

31. Sar Desai, p. 50.

32. The passage of 20 years has altered this situation very little. On the allied side, memoirs published by many of the protagonists or accounts they have given to others, and even the documents published in the *Pentagon Papers,* have added detail and clarification without significantly changing the broad picture contemporaneously provided on the basis of thorough and discriminating use of press sources by Miriam Farley, writing in 1955, and Coral Bell, writing in 1956.

way of handling this unwelcome request, Khrushchev says he advised him to tell a white lie—let the Viet Minh believe that China will help, and they will fight harder against the French. But then, he says, the miracle of Dien Bien Phu took place and, at the first session of the conference, the French head of state, Mendès-France, proposed the seventeenth parallel, the Communists' maximum position as the demarcation line. Two years later, had elections been held, Ho would have been victorious, but this was prevented by the United States which imposed a long bloody war in Vietnam.[33]

One can see that this *ex post facto* account may have seemed useful to Khrushchev. It suggests that Peking was not prepared to help the DRV, that any concessions made by the DRV at Geneva stemmed from its own weakness not from the pressures of its Allies, and that, two years later, when the DRV had become much stronger, the United States alone cheated it of its gains. But patent inaccuracies and inner contradictions make Khrushchev's account unlikely even as a dim reflection of the truth, while leaving the motives of the Communists at Geneva and the relations among them as obscure as they have ever been.

It is hard to say how deeply concern with the risks of wider war affected Soviet and Chinese policies on Indochina. The lessons of Korea cut both ways. The United States was unpredictable; it had responded immediately and assumed heavy burdens in an area it had seemingly excluded from its strategic concern. But it was also cautious; it had taken no action against the Soviet Union, although obviously convinced that Moscow had had an important hand in the North Korean invasion, and it had not attacked China when Chinese forces entered the war. Was it not likely to be even more cautious when it had no clear provocation, when its Allies were so obviously unwilling to follow it into war, and when its atomic advantage had been so much reduced? But could the unpredictable be excluded, could threats of massive retaliation be ignored, and might not Allied hesitations be overcome if all prospects of a compromise solution were to evaporate?

In any case, the record shows that the Communists, despite periods of what seemed to be complete intransigence, pursued conciliatory tactics at Geneva to an extent unusual for that period. Obviously, therefore, they must have seen real advantages in terminating the hostilities.

33. Nikita Khrushchev, *Khrushchev Remembers*, pp. 481–483.

The advantages for Peking seem particularly evident, but Moscow stood to gain also. It is only with respect to the DRV that advantages and disadvantages were sufficiently balanced to suggest that, without the pressures of their Allies, the Vietnamese Communists would have preferred continued hostilities to the concessions they actually made.

When Moscow and Peking examined the possibility of U.S. intervention, the dangers in heightening the possibility of its own involvement must have seemed greater for Communist China than for the Soviet Union. An importunate neighbor and Ally might require actual armed support to survive against American military power. Or, even if the Chinese Communist role remained limited and concealed, American advocates of attacks on the source of aggression might be more successful than they had been in the case of Korea. Analysts of Chinese Communist actions and pronouncements during this period do not find persuasive evidence of acute concern with an imminent prospect of Sino-American hostilities, but certainly Peking would have wanted to take any steps short of abandoning major positions that could reduce this possibility.[34]

A more immediate and pressing Chinese Communist concern seems to have been with the possibility that American military power, already entrenched in Japan, South Korea, Taiwan, and the Philippines, would establish itself in strength on still another of China's borders. As Alice Hsieh has pointed out, in early 1954 the PRC was apparently giving considerable thought and attention to the American base structure in the Far East, describing it as an effort to encircle the PRC and the Soviet Union with a "global air-force ring" having a quick-strike capability.[35] At Geneva the Chinese Communists were evidently preoccupied with the possibility that U.S. bases might be established in Laos and Cambodia, and Peking was prepared to bargain away the Viet Minh-sustained local Communist position in these countries for assurances that they would not. To gain these assurances, together with recognition of Communist control of at least that part of Vietnam bordering China, must have seemed to be a valuable reinforcement of its southern defenses.

It was apparently also of high value to Peking to gain the acceptance

34. Alice L. Hsieh, *Communist China's Strategy in the Nuclear Era,* pp. 16–17; Melvin Gurtov, *The First Vietnam Crisis,* p. 118.

35. Hsieh, pp. 15–16; Millar, p. 163.

of its position as a great power that participation in the Geneva negotiations implied. Editorializing on the Berlin Conference, the *People's
Daily* attributed a special responsibility to "the major powers"—
obviously including China among them—for safeguarding peace and
security among nations through resolving disputes by negotiation. Even
more explicitly a *People's Daily* editorial of July 22 declared of the
Geneva Conference "the [PRC] joined the other major powers in negotiations on vital international problems and made a contribution of its
own that won the acclaim of wide sections of world public opinion. The
international status of the [PRC] as one of the big world powers has
gained universal recognition."[36] Even though American behavior at the
conference dashed whatever hopes Peking may have entertained for
U.S. concessions on Chinese issues in exchange for Communist concessions on Indochina, the PRC came out of the Geneva Conference
with enhanced prestige. Chou's dexterity won him considerable admiration, while China's generally moderate stance reassured Britain
and France. This was even more the case with the neutralists on whom
the impact was enhanced by Chou's visits to New Delhi and Rangoon
where he emphasized peaceful coexistence and assurances that "revolution was not for export." From the earliest days of the conference, in
fact, Chou seemed intent on cultivating neutralist good opinion. In
his first speech at Geneva, he deplored the absence of India, Indonesia,
and Burma, "which in no way can be considered as a positive aspect."
He was careful to pay tribute to the Colombo conference, and his
trip to India, dramatically announced only four days before his arrival,
was interpreted by the local press not only as intended to upstage the
Churchill-Eisenhower meeting, but also as a tribute to Indian importance and as underlining his agreement with India that Asian solutions
must be sought for Asian problems.[37]

Russian strategic interest in distant Indochina was less strong. No
more in Moscow than in Peking did there seem to be acute concern
over the possibility that continued hostilities in Indochina would lead
to armed conflict with the United States.[38] But the Russians could not
have been entirely confident of this and, in any case, would have had

36. Chae-Jin Lee, *Communist China's Policy Toward Laos,* p. 19.

37. Margaret Fisher and Joan Bondurant, *Indian Views of Sino-Indian Relations,* pp. 47, 57–58, 64.

38. Herbert Dinerstein, *War and the Soviet Union,* pp. 106–110.

to anticipate demands for assistance from their Asian comrades. In addition, any prospect of a crisis over an area of marginal importance was particularly undesirable at a time when leadership problems were unsettled, the economy was causing concern, and restiveness in the Communist bloc had only recently been manifested in East German disorders. Continued hostilities were thus, if not a major threat, not particularly desirable. Moreover, precisely because Indochina was a very low priority area in Moscow's global perspective, it was an ideal one in which to establish the authenticity of Soviet interest in détente. Peace might also advance more central Soviet concerns. Deep military involvement in Indochina was an important cause of French distrust of German rearmament proposals and, arguably, it might be useful to do nothing that would reduce or eliminate this involvement. But, although peace in Indochina might remove one French objection to rearming Germany, it might replace it by another, giving French proponents of détente additional ammunition against the proposed European Defense Community. And if France, free of the Indochina incubus, were to become somewhat stronger in Europe, might this not reduce western interest in steps that could make Germany the strongest power on the continent?[39]

It is arguable that the great debate over issues of war and peace then going on among Soviet leaders affected their thinking on Indochina. Just how is another, harder question. It is difficult to discern which side in this very fundamental debate would have seen especial advantage, or disadvantage, in a settlement, especially one costing Moscow little or nothing: Malenkov, with his confidence that Soviet deterrent strength was sufficient to permit greater efforts to improve living standards, or Khrushchev, with his emphasis on capitalist encirclement and the need for continued emphasis on heavy industry. If hostilities in Indochina could be terminated on favorable terms, this presumably would reinforce the Malenkov argument that the western alliance had become extremely fragile and that the threat of general war had receded. If they could not be so terminated, this might strengthen Khrushchev's case, but would also add to his concerns and in an area where he was to show himself quite reluctant to become involved.

39. Ulam, pp. 552–553; Dallin, pp. 153–154.

By mid-June—a crucial date in estimating Communist concern over the prospects of failure at Geneva—Malenkov's star seemed definitely on the wane. Nevertheless, even more after this time than before, Soviet tactics at Geneva seemed to mirror those prescribed in November 1953 by M. Gus, a Soviet publicist who reflected Malenkov's position. "Every agreement between the two systems should be the fruit of a reasoned, mutually advantageous, voluntary deal and not the result of the imposition of one country's dictate upon the other. . . . We always remember that our bourgeois opposite number, whether it be a trading, economic, or political bargain, will not enter upon it if he does not receive 'a just profit,' and in certain cases we are ready even to go as far as giving him an 'increased gain' but in order that we too receive a proper benefit."[40]

The Two Vietnams

The concessions made by Moscow and Peking, however, were made on behalf of the DRV and at the expense of the demands Pham Van Dong initially made at Geneva. The primacy of a political solution, early elections, recognition of the Pathet Lao and the Khmer Issarak as parties to the negotiations, all had to be abandoned. Then, when it was decided to accept partition, it was still necessary to retreat from early positions on the demarcation line.

All of this gave rise to considerable speculation at the time. The American journalist Tillman Durdin described members of the DRV delegation as saying at the conclusion of the conference that they had been forced by Soviet and Chinese pressures to accept less than they should have obtained in a settlement which constituted a form of appeasement supporting Soviet and Chinese international interests. The Sino-Soviet position on Cambodia and Laos seems to have caused the most evident disquiet to the DRV representatives; at least, for some time after the major concessions had been made, they continued to demand privileges for their Lao and Cambodian protégés that would have gone a long way toward negating the authority the Chinese and Soviets seemed ready to accord to the royal governments. Chauvel commented at the time that the Soviets and Chinese appeared to give the DRV representatives a fairly free hand to see how far they could go, intervening, however, when it appeared that DRV demands had

40. Dallin, pp. 127–128.

gone past the limit the French could be expected to accept. Writing about the conference later, Chauvel stressed Chou's role in bringing the Vietnamese to heel. On occasion, the Chinese seemed to be consciously trying to make it appear that the Vietnamese were adopting more reasonable positions because of Chinese efforts. Thus, in July, a member of their delegation told Chauvel that Chou, whose travels earlier in the month included a meeting with Ho, had had a good talk with the DRV leader, the results of which "would be helpful" to the French.[41] However, while it is reasonable to assume a degree of DRV resentment, the evidence is at best scanty, nor can the possibility of occasional tactical use of ostensible disagreement be entirely excluded.

In any event, after the conference ended, Ho described it as "a great victory for our diplomacy," and the DRV certainly had some good reasons for satisfaction.[42] For one thing, the possibility of a more active American military role posed much more immediate and serious dangers for the Viet Minh than for Moscow and Peking. The Vietnamese Communists could not be sure, under these circumstances, how much assistance either of their Allies would supply. Moreover, very large-scale aid, particularly from neighboring Communist China, could be almost as dangerous as not enough, reducing Viet Minh freedom of action and nationalist appeal. Thus, the DRV, although it had seemed to accept the prospect of negotiations somewhat belatedly, also had reason to be interested in a negotiated solution. It was after all still far from being able to drive the French out if they decided to persist, and an American intervention might postpone victory indefinitely. And, if negotiations were to be undertaken, the DRV, like France, could expect that the presence of its stronger Allies at its side might win it some advantages, even though it might have to make some concessions to their interests.

In the event, the DRV did not fare too badly. Its position in Laos, although not all that it would have liked, was nevertheless protected by the provisions concerning the two northern provinces; its position in Cambodia had not amounted to much in any case. The control that Ho's government had been theoretically accorded in 1946 was now confirmed for Tonkin and part of Annam. The rest he would have an

41. *Pentagon Papers,* IX, 623, 662; Buchan, pp. 38, 41; LaCouture and Devillers, p. 278; Zasloff, p. 69.
42. Randle, p. 360.

opportunity to win if elections were held in 1956. Aware of the insurmountable obstacles that East-West differences over modalities had placed in the way of such elections in divided Germany and Korea, Ho may have been far from confident that they would take place. But even so, he could well have anticipated that the path to the establishment of Communist political control over southern Annam and Cochin China would be much shorter and less difficult than the one he had followed from 1946 to 1954.

Whatever may have been Ho's reasons for discontent, they could not have been anything like as weighty as those of the leaders of the State of Vietnam who had been only belatedly informed by the French of crucial decisions, whose representatives at the conference had been able to do little more than make formal statements, and upon whom a wholly distasteful agreement was imposed.

Throughout the conference, moreover, the issue of Vietnamese sovereignty remained unresolved. In March, Buu Loc had demanded an unequivocal grant of independence, but once again the negotiators disagreed over the effects of membership in the French Union on the prerogatives of the Associated States. Article 62 of the French constitution[43] was read by the French government as meaning that it would direct the foreign and defense policies of an independent Vietnam. The Vietnamese refused to accept this, or the idea that they should be bound by the constitution of another member of the French Union. With the Vietnamese obdurate and the French cabinet divided, resolution of the issue was postponed. On April 28, in a joint statement, France and the State of Vietnam affirmed "their intention to settle their mutual relations" on the basis of the two treaties that had been drafted during the negotiations: one recognizing "the total independence of Viet Nam and her full and entire sovereignty," the other establishing "a Franco-Viet Nam association in the French Union founded on equality and intended to develop the cooperation between the two countries."[44]

No doubt anticipating, despite Bidault's assurances, that they would

43. "The members of the French Union pool all means at their disposal to guarantee the protection of the whole of the Union. The government of the Republic assumes the coordination of these means and the control of the policy apt to prepare and ensure this protection" (Randle, p. 133).

44. *Ibid.*, p. 135; *SIA*, 1954, p. 44.

have little if any voice in the decisions to be made at Geneva, the leaders of the State of Vietnam were careful from the outset to disassociate themselves quite specifically from agreements likely to damage their own positions. On April 28, Bao Dai declared in a communiqué that Vietnam "would never be prepared to consider the possibility of negotiations in which France, violating the basic principles of the French Union from which her authority is derived, were to negotiate with those who are in rebellion against the Vietnamese nation or with hostile powers, thereby disregarding or sacrificing her partners. Whatever may happen neither the head of the state nor the Vietnamese Government will consider themselves bound by decisions which by running counter to national independence and unity would violate the rights of peoples and reward aggression, contrary to the principles of the United Nations Charter and to democratic ideals."[45]

At the same time, Bao Dai announced that he would not send representatives to the conference if the DRV were invited. Then, after the Allies pressed him to alter his stance, he agreed in return for a Big Three guarantee that Viet Minh participation would not constitute recognition of the DRV—a position formally communicated by France to the Soviet Union on May 3.[46] Ignored and frustrated at Geneva, the State of Vietnam nevertheless succeeded in laying the groundwork for subsequent freedom of action.

45. Lancaster, p. 308.
46. *Ibid.*, p. 317; Randle, p. 159.

PART IV

The Two Directions

CHAPTER 11

SEATO:

CONFRONTATION SYMBOLIZED

The Geneva arrangements were nowhere expected to provide a permanent solution for the Vietnam problem. The elections called for in 1956 might never be held. But it was difficult to believe that Ho would rest content with control over only the North; persistent instability and division would make the South a tempting target. Nevertheless, however uncertain the future, the end of the war had removed any immediate risk of great-power confrontation in this area. Peking and Moscow, with good reason for satisfaction over the Geneva outcome and for confidence in Ho's ability to fend for himself, provided the DRV with diplomatic support and economic and military assistance. They did not appear to regard its fortunes as central to their own concerns, however, and seemed to be devoting their principal energies in Asia to winning the friendship of the nonaligned and even of western Allies. Indochina, and with it Southeast Asia, gave place to the Taiwan Straits and the Middle East as a prime threat to peace and to Africa as a center of anticolonial struggle.

The seeming decline in Indochina's importance notwithstanding, the United States saw the Geneva arrangements as a defeat for the West, with dangerous implications for the future. Motivated by this view and now committed to forwarding collective defense in Southeast Asia, the United States, departing from its earlier insistence that regional organization must stem from regional initiative, became instead the prime mover in the establishment of the Southeast Asia Treaty Organization (SEATO). This departure from past principles, however, was not one that radically extended the American commitment. With continuing low priority accorded to Southeast Asia in overall strategic doctrine, no commitments were made to ground deployments. In addition, such obligations as the United States did assume to come to the defense of Southeast Asia were limited by specific reservation to cases of Communist aggression.

The discussions between the United States and Britain, from which the essentials of the Manila Treaty emerged, reflected the same differences of outlook that had slowed agreement on ending the war in Vietnam. The United States—even though prepared to make only a very limited commitment—conceived of the treaty as still another deterrent and position of strength on the periphery of Communist power. The British too sought a device that would cushion Southeast Asia against further Communist advance. But they did not exclude some degree of neutralization and were anxious to draw as many states of the area as possible into whatever arrangements might be made.

In the event, SEATO proved to be too much of a military alliance to attract Burma and Indonesia and too weak a one to satisfy its Southeast Asian and Pacific members—Thailand, the Philippines, Australia, and New Zealand. For Thailand, however, the only one without a separate security arrangement with the United States, SEATO at least provided the previously lacking formal underpinning for an increasingly close relationship.

Until Dulles issued his call for united action, American policy makers both publicly and privately had insisted that the initiative for a regional security organization must come from within the area, not from the United States. Acheson's view in December 1949 that it might be premature even to contemplate such an organization had been rather quickly transformed thereafter into the hope that obstacles would diminish to what was regarded as a desirable, even if distant, end. But, until early in 1954, policy paper after policy paper excluded an American initiative.

In October 1953, Assistant Secretary Walter Robertson, acknowledging the pressure for American action, declared: "We continue to believe . . . that any effective Asian-Pacific organization must come about as the result of the Asians' own initiative, that it must wait upon a general appreciation among the Asians of the desirability of collective action in attacking their common problems. This is clearly not a field in which outsiders can usefully assert themselves. We do not wish to give the impression that we are trying to hustle or joggle our friends across the Pacific because we are not. Any moves to be made in the direction of regional organization are clearly up to them."[1] An NSC paper, approved in mid-January 1954, called for "measures to promote the coordinated defense of Southeast Asia," but again stressed that "the initiative in regional defense measures must come from the governments of the area."[2]

Another, even more important, restraint was the long-standing reluctance to undertake military commitments in mainland Southeast Asia. Writing in *Foreign Affairs* in January 1952, Dulles said that not the least of the many factors obstructing a regional defense organization "is the fact that the United States should not assume formal commitments which overstrain its present capabilities and give rise to military expectations we could not fulfill, particularly in terms of land forces. The security treaties now made involve only islands, where security is strongly influenced by sea and air power."[3] In proposing united action, the United States took an initiative it had previously excluded, but its continued reluctance to make fixed commitments, especially of ground forces, determined SEATO's form and the nature of the American commitment to it.

Preliminaries and Preparations

Formal planning for SEATO began only after Churchill's June 1954 visit to Washington: earlier discussions, because of their relationship to the Indochina problem, had been both acrimonious and inconclusive. On April 13, after Dulles and Eden had concluded their discussion of united action, it was announced in London that the governments of Britain and the United States were prepared "to take part, with the other countries principally concerned, in an examination of the possibility of establishing a collective defence, within the framework of the Charter of the United Nations, to assure the peace, security and freedom of South-East Asia and the Western Pacific." The next day a similar statement closed the Dulles-Bidault discussions in Paris. Apparently interpreting these statements as authorizing action, Dulles

1. *DSB,* Oct. 19, 1953, p. 522.
2. *Pentagon Papers,* IX, 228.
3. John Foster Dulles, "Security in the Pacific," *Foreign Affairs,* XXX (Jan. 1952), p. 183.

then invited the representatives in Washington of Britain, France, Australia, New Zealand, the Philippines, Thailand, and the Associated States to meet with him on April 20 and establish an informal working group to study the collective defense of Southeast Asia. When this move was reported to him by the British Ambassador, Eden was incensed over what he regarded as Dulles' unilateral effort to settle the still-debated membership question. The timing, he thought, was wrong, and India and Burma would be insulted by the failure to consult them and therefore less willing to support Allied positions at Geneva or in Southeast Asia. Dulles, although he agreed to convert the meeting into a briefing on the Korean problem, was equally irate; it seemed to him that Britain was already backtracking on its commitment of April 13.[4]

On April 30, Eden proposed that the United States and Britain begin immediately and secretly to examine the nature and purpose of a Southeast Asian collective defense organization, its membership, and the commitments to be assumed. Apparently, after their hostile encounter earlier in the month, Eden wanted to make it clear to Dulles that Britain was prepared to discuss collective security in Southeast Asia as long as this did not imply a commitment to intervene in Indochina. Perhaps also he believed that bilateral talks would satisfy the American desire for action, while avoiding the publicity he was sure would adversely affect Communist and neutral attitudes. Dulles duly reported this offer to the President but nothing came of it. Indeed, Eisenhower later described Eden's next proposal—his May 5 suggestion to Bedell Smith that the Five Power Staff Agency be convened—as Britain's first sign of willingness to do anything at all about collective defense before the Geneva Conference ended.[5]

From the available record, it is far from clear what the British had in mind. Eisenhower and Dulles apparently suspected the British of wanting to make the Staff Agency the basis for collective defense arrangements. They were prepared to have the Five Power representatives discuss ways in which their governments could contribute to a

4. Chatham House Study Group, p. 2; Eden, pp. 110–111; Randle, pp. 81, 84.
5. Eden, pp. 122, 123; *Pentagon Papers,* IX, 425; Eisenhower, p. 364. The Five Power Staff Agency was not as structured as its name suggests; essentially it was no more than the designation for meetings of the senior military officers of the United States, Britain, France, Australia, and New Zealand which had been taking place intermittently since January 1953.

cooperative defense venture in Southeast Asia, but they did not regard the Agency—a white man's club—as "a satisfactory substitute for a broad coalition which will include the Southeast Asian countries which are to be defended." By June 3, when the meeting began, American and British spokesmen were describing it as a technical-level discussion of military matters. Nevertheless, at the end of the first day, an announcement, both obscure and portentous, declared that the conversations, while not committing any of the participants, would be "of value not only to the countries represented but to other countries in the region in further conversations which may take place later on a wider basis." There were no further announcements, but discussions apparently focused on the military situation in Indochina and the steps that could be taken in response to various hypothetical contingencies there.[6]

Toward the end of June, as Allied differences over Indochina narrowed, preparations for future security arrangements began to move more rapidly. On June 28, Churchill and Eisenhower in a joint communiqué declared that without regard to whether agreement was reached at Geneva, "we would press forward with plans for collective defense." Two days later an ANZUS communiqué reiterated the pledge, describing Southeast Asia as "an area in which the three participating countries are all vitally concerned." On July 7 an Anglo-American Study Group began to discuss the treaty; thereafter, a draft was prepared in the State Department which became the basis for discussion with other interested powers.[7]

In August, with reluctant American agreement, Britain queried the Colombo powers about participating in the treaty talks scheduled to take place the following month. Only Pakistan, already the recipient of considerable American military assistance and soon to become a member of the Baghdad Pact, responded affirmatively. Ceylon's strongly anti-Communist Prime Minister Sir John Kotelewala was not so interested that he was prepared to ignore the views of India or of his own opposition party. He himself did not think that the organization would be very representative of Asian opinion, and he said that it "failed to take into account . . . that the defence of Asia must first

6. *Pentagon Papers*, IX, 435; Randle, p. 344; Chatham House Study Group, p. 3; LaCouture and Devillers, pp. 219–220.

7. *DSB*, July 12, 1954, pp. 49–50; *Pentagon Papers*, X, 747.

be an economic defence. . . . The nations of Asia, if attacked, will defend themselves to the utmost and with all the means at their command, but they do not believe that the first need is a defensive pact against aggression."[8]

Burma and Indonesia were unwilling to join SEATO, but did not seem to share India's bitter opposition. The Indians believed that participation would be inconsistent not only with nonalignment, but also with the responsibilities entrusted to them in the Geneva settlement. In addition, they regarded SEATO as subordinating Asian wishes to western decisions and as counter to their hopes, reinforced by the Indochina settlement and Peking's more conciliatory stance, for keeping the Cold War out of South and Southeast Asia.[9] SEATO was not a regional organization within the meaning of the charter said Krishna Menon, but a "modern version of a Protectorate . . . an organization of some imperial powers and some other powers who may have interest in it to join together in order to protect a territory which they say may be in danger. We are part of that territory and we say we do not want to be protected by this organization."[10] The establishment of SEATO, the Congress Party's Steering Committee declared, "had added to the insecurity of [the] region and extended the area of cold war."[11]

Formal talks opened in Manila on September 6. On September 8, the Southeast Asia Collective Defense Treaty was signed by representatives of Australia, France, New Zealand, Pakistan, the Philippines, Thailand, the United Kingdom, and the United States. At the first meeting in Bangkok on February 23, 1955, four days after the coming into force of the treaty, the SEATO Council considered working-group recommendations for implementing the treaty and for the structure of the treaty organization. At this meeting also, Bangkok was selected as the headquarters of the treaty organization and Pote Sarasin as its Director General. Further organizational decisions were made at the second meeting of the Council in Karachi in March 1956.

8. John Kotelawala, *An Asian Prime Minister's Story*, pp. 119, 129–130.
9. Royal Institute of International Affairs, Geoffrey Barraclough (ed.), *Survey of International Affairs (SIA)*, 1955–1956, p. 288; Modelski, pp. 206–207; Gupta, pp. 58–59; Sar Desai, pp. 56–58; Kundra, pp. 95–97.
10. Modelski, pp. 64–65.
11. Chatham House Study Group, p. 94.

Provisions and Structure

Two articles of the treaty defined the responsibilities of the parties with respect to collective defense. In Article IV each party agreed in the event of armed attack "to meet the common danger in accordance with its constitutional processes." For the United States, however, this commitment was to apply only to Communist armed attack or aggression; in other cases the United States would consult with its Allies.

In Article II, following a precedent set in the Rio Treaty of 1948, the parties agreed to maintain and develop through effective self-help and mutual aid "their individual and collective capacity . . . to prevent and counter subversive activities directed from without against their territorial and political stability." The provision reflected both the general view that subversion was the more imminent threat on Southeast Asia, and the difficulty of defining how it might become the occasion for invoking the treaty. The only specific requirement—"direction from without"—presumably reflected Philippine views; Romulo had earlier insisted that this qualification was necessary to exclude internal nationalist movements fighting for self-government or independence.[12] However, even though it was difficult to define the subversive threat the article envisaged, experience could be expected to provide a basis for recognizing it if it arose. No such experience was available, however, to help define the collective measures that could meet such a threat. On this subject, the treaty provided only for immediate consultation on measures for the common defense when, in the opinion of any one of the parties, a threat had arisen to territorial integrity or inviolability, sovereignty, or political independence "in any way other than by armed attack."

Article VIII defined the treaty area as "the general area of Southeast Asia including also the entire territories of the Asian Parties"[13] and "the general area of the Southwest Pacific," but only as far north as 21 degrees 30 minutes north latitude.[14] It could also be invoked to protect other states, such as Indonesia and Burma, but only with their consent and the unanimous agreement of the SEATO members. A

12. Meyer, p. 233.
13. This made it possible to include West Pakistan.
14. This made evident the exclusion of Taiwan and Hong Kong.

protocol to the treaty designated Cambodia, Laos, and "the free territory under the jurisdiction of the State of Vietnam" as eligible for SEATO protection.

Certain treaty provisions were largely reflective of the interests and concerns of the Asian members. Article III provided for economic cooperation; its attraction lay in its implication that the treaty organization might become a channel for increased aid. The "Pacific Charter," devised by the Philippines, was intended to remove any stigma of colonialism from an organization of which colonial powers were such conspicuous members. It pledged the parties to "promote self-government and independence" for all countries. However, a qualification echoing the sacred-trust doctrine—"whose peoples desire it and are able to undertake its responsibilities"—was required to secure the consent of the Commonwealth countries and France.

The structure established for the treaty organization, as compared with NATO's, was eminently simple and modest. The SEATO Council—made up of the foreign ministers or their representatives—was to meet annually. The Council representatives—the ambassadors stationed in Bangkok—were to maintain continuing consultation, perform functions assigned to them by the Council, and make recommendations to the Council. The military advisers, also to make recommendations to the Council, were to be appointed by the parties and meet periodically.

National Positions

Although the United States and Britain had differed in some respects about SEATO's role and membership, its basic structure and concept reflected the desires of these two powers and, to a degree, of France and Pakistan, much more than it did those of its Pacific and Southeast Asian members. The latter may have been conciliated by references to economic aid and independence, but their more keenly felt hopes for firm security guarantees were denied them.

Neither the United States nor Britain wanted NATO-type planning and other machinery, and neither wished to make force commitments. This was true of France and Pakistan also: France because it was primarily interested in the treaty as a means to bolster its remaining position in Indochina and to involve the United States in the defense of this position and of the Associated States; Pakistan because it valued

SEATO membership only as it might be used to reduce the weight in the power balance of India and Afghanistan, its opponents in territorial disputes. The other members, however, were disappointed that the NATO formula had not been employed; Dulles' assurances that the difference was insignificant, since, in any case, the Senate would have to consent to a declaration of war, did not wholly persuade them that the United States was providing as strong and as automatic a guarantee in the Far East as in Western Europe. The Southeast Asian and Pacific countries would also have preferred more scope for joint and advance planning than SEATO seemed likely to afford and also provisions either for stationing SEATO forces in Southeast Asia or, at least, for earmarking forces to be used there if necessary.

Although divided in their views on some subjects, the other members almost unanimously opposed American proposals for specifically directing the treaty against Communist aggression. This, it was argued, would alienate other Asians and reduce the prospect that India, Ceylon, Indonesia, or Burma might one day adhere. Pakistan did not wish to be barred from invoking the treaty against India, while Australians did not exclude the possibility of Indonesian aggression. Moreover, Japan was still feared in Australia, especially in Labour circles, even though Casey records that he encountered no appreciable dissent to his proposition that the time had come to take a more "civilized view" of the Japanese.[15] The price the others paid for the omission of the term Communist in the body of the treaty—the U.S. reservation confining its own commitment to Communist attack—was, Dulles argued, indispensable to securing Senate approval and hence, U.S. participation, without which, all agreed, the treaty would lose its reason for being.[16]

The SEATO commitment, to be sure, had moved the United States some distance away from previous doctrine governing its actions in Southeast Asia. But the American view continued to be conditioned by long-standing assumptions about the nature of the threat and about the proper use of military force, should it be required. Concern was expressed by the Joint Chiefs to the Secretary of Defense in mid-

15. Millar, p. 176.

16. Casey records (*ibid.*, p. 184) Dulles' great concern over the prospect that other countries might follow the American example and make reservations of their own.

August that SEATO commitments not strain American capabilities or tie down American forces in static defense missions. They recognized, they said, the public American commitment to a Southeast Asia collective security organization. But they had "serious misgivings concerning the military provisions of such a pact lest they imply commitments which the United States will not be able to meet." They urged making it clear that the United States was not committed either to supporting indigenous forces or to deploying American ones to the extent required to defend each signatory's national territory. As in the past, American military aid should be directed only to building indigenous forces capable of ensuring internal stability, helping support a reasonably effective response to invasion, and instilling national confidence. The treaty need do no more than provide a moral, political, and organizational framework permitting a prompt military response to overt Communist aggression, "not excluding military action against the real source of the aggression." In order to retain freedom of action, the Chiefs recommended, "the United States should not enter into combined military planning for the defense of the treaty area with the other Manila treaty powers nor should details of unilateral American plans for military action in the event of Communist aggression be disclosed to the other powers."[17]

Nothing suggests that the Chiefs' views were opposed anywhere in the policy-making hierarchy. An NSC policy paper not long after called for treaty terms: providing the President with a legal basis for ordering an attack on Communist China; ensuring that other nations would be obligated to support such action; and neither limiting U.S. freedom to use nuclear weapons nor committing U.S. forces to local defense or deployment in Southeast Asia. Less explicitly, but clearly enough, Dulles said at the Manila Conference: "For the free nations to attempt to maintain or support formidable land-based forces at every danger point throughout the world would be self-destructive." U.S. responsibilities in particular "are so vast and so far flung that we believe we serve best by developing the deterrent of mobile striking power, plus strategically placed reserves."[18]

As a Defense Department member of the U.S. delegation observed after the Manila Conference, Southeast Asia was "no better prepared

17. *Pentagon Papers*, X, 721–723, 885.
18. *DSB*, Sept. 20, 1954, p. 391; *Pentagon Papers*, X, 736.

than before to cope with Communist aggression."[19] The United States, however, was now better prepared than it had been in the spring of 1954 to cope with domestic and international obstacles to military intervention, should the occasion for it arise. Meanwhile, it was hoped, the very existence of SEATO, purposefully imprecise as were its obligations, would provide a shield behind which the Southeast Asian members, and their neighbors as well, could be strengthened against subversion, while the treaty's deterrent effect would reduce the possibility that its military provisions would need to be called into play.

The British had had rather different purposes in mind. They were equally concerned to provide what Eden had called a protective pad, behind which to strengthen Southeast Asia against the Communist threat. But they did not exclude some degree of neutralization and, accordingly, were even less inclined than the United States toward military arrangements of the NATO variety. Even after the Locarno contretemps, they seemed to envisage less a single, tightly knit, defense organization than a series of interlocking arrangements which would draw all of the regional states into guaranteeing the Geneva settlement and would also provide for economic and political as well as for defense cooperation. An American member of the Anglo-American study group described the British concept as involving a three-part organization: a general council representing the entire membership which should, if possible, include India, Burma, and Indonesia; an economic and political council which would include as many of the members as possible; and a military council in which India and other countries of similar view would not be expected to participate. Moreover, because they thought it was important to secure the membership or at least the tacit approval of as many Asian states as possible, the British wanted to proceed slowly, prepare the ground very carefully, and give the Colombo powers every opportunity to register their concerns.[20]

Countervailing interests, however, led the British to accept arrangements quite different from those Eden had originally contemplated. They still wanted in 1954 what they had not been able to obtain in 1950—an American commitment to the defense of Malaya. A similar commitment to Thailand was also important to British interests. Moreover, since the Geneva arrangements had not fulfilled British

19. *Pentagon Papers*, X, 747.
20. *Ibid.*, IX, p. 635; Eden, pp. 122, 123; John Kerry King, p. 151.

hope for reciprocal guarantees, it was desirable to underwrite the settlement in some other form. They wanted also to correct the ANZUS anomaly by joining with the Pacific members of the Commonwealth in joint defense arrangements with the United States. Finally, the British recognized that, while the prospects for Indian cooperation were remote in any case, Australia and New Zealand were very anxious to move rapidly before American interest cooled.[21]

Australia and New Zealand, also most anxious to correct the ANZUS anomaly, had been uncomfortable over the Indochina-generated friction between Britain and the United States. Including Britain in collective arrangements for Southeast Asia was not a mere matter of sentiment for them: they regarded the British presence as correcting somewhat the extreme imbalance between themselves and the United States, and they hoped that partnership would encourage Britain and the United States to remain active in Southeast Asia. In this, in extending American protection to Thailand and Malaya, and in underwriting the Geneva arrangements, SEATO satisfied the desires of the Pacific states. In many other respects it did not, since, in what was regarded as a more threatening situation than ever, no greater protection was afforded than that already enjoyed under ANZUS.[22]

The Australian government, like the American, regarded the Geneva outcome as a serious setback. In the debate on the defense budget Menzies said, "There may be some who rather wishfully think that the Indo-China 'ceasefire' permanently reduces tension and that we may now spend less on defence. So little do we agree with this view that our estimates for this financial year already disclose a substantially greater availability of funds."[23] Australia too adhered to the domino theory. "If the whole of Indo-China fell to the Communists," Casey said, "Thailand would be gravely exposed. If Thailand were to fall, the road would be open to Malaya and Singapore. From the Malay peninsula, the Communists could dominate the northern approaches to Australia and even cut our lifelines with Europe."[24]

21. Chatham House Study Group, pp. 4–5; Nicholas, p. 100; Modelski, p. 55.
22. Modelski, pp. 69–70; Norman Harper, "Australia and Southeast Asia," *Pacific Affairs*, XXVIII (Sept., 1955), p. 207.
23. Modelski, p. 65.
24. Millar, p. 196.

It might be, Casey conceded, "that the Communists will see that it suits them no less than us for the states of Indo-China to be genuinely neutral and to be an area geographically separating the Communist and non-Communist world. If so, the settlement in Indo-China may turn out to be a substantial contribution to achieving the security of the South-East Asian region." But this can be the case "only if a collective defense is built up . . . to balance the Communist military potential."[25] Australian hopes in this regard were expressed early in August when Menzies told the House of Representatives, "We are about to contract into a regional defensive arrangement which will give strength not only here but in Europe itself. The achievement of NATO will define our task. We will know specifically the nature of the forces we need, the equipment they will require, and the material support which the nation must be capable of rendering."[26]

Thereafter, at the meetings in Manila and Bangkok, and in conversations with American officials, Casey pressed hard for an organization that would permit earmarking forces and joint planning. He realized that his case was weakened by Australian unwillingness to support a defense establishment and a conscription system equivalent in terms of Australian resources to those maintained by the United States and Britain, but, in wishing to correct this imbalance, Casey was out of step with his cabinet colleagues and with public opinion generally.[27]

Disappointed in the SEATO outcome, Australia and New Zealand continued to rely on ANZUS, which both countries had wanted to retain whatever might eventuate from discussions of collective defense. In addition, in the early months of 1955, there took place a distinct shift in Australian and New Zealand defense policies. Discussing the question of force allocations with the United States, Casey had conceded that it would be wasteful and inefficient to station troops at every possible point of danger. Now, however, in pursuit of a forward defense policy, Australia and New Zealand abandoned precedent: henceforth, in any major war their troops would be used in Southeast Asia rather than the Middle East; meanwhile, in a considerable expansion of the ANZAM concept, with the nearest springboard for Communist attack having moved from South China to North Vietnam,

25. *Current Notes,* Aug. 8, 1954, p. 578.
26. Lyman, p. 268.
27. Millar, Chs. VI and VII, *passim.*

ground troops were to be provided for peacetime service in Southeast Asia. These were to be contributed to a Commonwealth Strategic Reserve in Malaya, established by Australia, New Zealand, and Britain at the London Commonwealth Conference in January-February 1955. Their presence would establish a line of defense "at the farthest point advantageous to us"; they would also join in the fight against the Malayan Communist terrorists, since they were not indigenous nationalists but insurgents acting on behalf of an outside power.[28]

Before the new policy was announced, advance American commitments had once again been sought. Washington was prepared to go no further, Menzies reported to parliament on April 20, than to agree that "in the general task of preventing further Communist aggression, the United States considered the defense of Southeast Asia, of which Malaya is an integral part, to be of very great importance. . . . I was informed that though the tactical employment of forces was a matter which would have to be worked out at the services level, the United States considered that such effective cooperation was implicit in the Manila Pact."[29] At the services level, however, Admiral Radford told Casey in August that in his view planning for the defense of Malaya assumed catastrophic disaster in the rest of Asia and that it would be quite unreal to plan against a "last-ditch contingency." It would be useful to send Australian troops to Malaya, he said, to train them in tropical warfare, but he hoped they would be available for use in emergencies in other parts of Southeast Asia.[30]

The Philippines and Thailand also advocated collective arrangements of the NATO type. The Filipinos, in addition, seemingly more sensitive than the Thai to reactions elsewhere in Asia, worked hard to disassociate SEATO from colonialism. Before and during the Manila discussions they continued to stress their two preconditions for participating in the original united-action scheme, that is, support for colonial independence and an unequivocal American commitment to Philippine defense.[31]

28. Wood, p. 25; Harper, "Australia and Southeast Asia," p. 210; Modelski, p. 78; Greenwood and Harper, p. 239; Levi, *Australia's Outlook,* p. 193.
29. Harper, "Australia and Southeast Asia," p. 210; Albinski, *Australian Policies and Attitudes toward China,* pp. 177–178.
30. Millar, p. 215.
31. Roger Smith, *Philippines and SEATO,* pp. 6–11; Meyer, pp. 231–233.

On the first point, the Pacific Charter provided partial satisfaction despite its qualifications on the right to independence. These the Filipinos rejected on the eve of the Bandung Conference when the Philippine Senate adopted a resolution stating "that the right of self-determination of subject peoples includes the right to decide exclusively by themselves their ability to assume the responsibilities inherent in independent political status."[32]

Philippine interest in unilateral U.S. guarantees was, in fact, stronger than in the adoption for SEATO of NATO-type arrangements, to which, indeed, there was some opposition on the grounds that it would be unwise to commit Philippine forces to the Asian mainland. In addition, Philippine Congressmen feared their war-making authority might be reduced if the NATO formula were adopted. Philippine efforts met with a good measure of success. The United States-Philippine Defense Council,[33] at its first meeting just before the Manila Conference, agreed to strengthen the defense of the Philippines and modernize its ground forces with U.S.-supplied equipment, while Dulles publicly pledged that an attack on the Philippines would be regarded as an attack on the United States and bring an immediate response.[34]

Since Thailand had no bilateral defense treaty with the United States, SEATO represented a new American commitment. More than any of the other parties, Thailand felt an immediate and urgent threat, one that had taken a number of forms—disturbing to the United States as well as Thailand—since the beginning of 1953.

In January 1953, the PRC had proclaimed an Autonomous Area (Hsi-shuang Pan-na Autonomous Chou) for the Thai-speaking people in the area of China adjacent to the junction of its frontiers with those of Burma and Laos and within 100 miles of Thailand's northern tip. This action was consistent with internal administrative practices of the time and might not have been intended to serve any external purpose. But the propaganda surrounding the move suggested otherwise; when Hsi-shuang Pan-na was described as providing a guide to Thai-speaking peoples who wanted autonomy and freedom from American imperialism, Thai (and Burmese as well) feared that a base was being established for Chinese-sponsored independence movements. Although

32. J. L. Vellut, *The Asian Policy of the Philippines,* p. 15.
33. Agreed to in May and formally established in June 1954.
34. Meyer, pp. 232–234; Roger Smith, *Philippines and SEATO,* p. 8.

no such use appears to have been made of this particular area, then or later, the alarm aroused was heightened by Viet Minh campaigns in Laos late in the year. In December 1953 the capture of Thakhek, just across the Mekong from Thailand, was particularly disturbing, conjuring up visions of Communist moves against the traditionally restive northeast section of Thailand where some 50,000 Vietnamese, mostly supporters of the Viet Minh, had taken refuge from the French. Even though the Geneva settlement had provided for regrouping the Pathet Lao in Phong Saly and Sam Neua provinces, well back from the Thai border, this was not very reassuring since Laos seemed more likely to be a passageway for infiltrating Communists than a barrier against them. Moreover, fears aroused by threatening Chinese propaganda were heightened when Pridi suddenly re-emerged in China. Described as the "Public Leader of Thailand," he was quoted by Peking radio as calling upon the Thai people "to wage a struggle against their rulers— American imperialism and its puppets, the government of Thailand."[35]

The sense of alarm was shared by the United States. American ambassadors and a stream of visitors seemed intent on providing frequent reminders of Thai vulnerability.[36] American aid increased correspondingly. Under the pressure of hostilities in Laos in 1953 the United States had given higher priority to military shipments to Thailand; in 1953–1954, military aid rose to $11 million from $6 million in the previous year; in the following year the amount rose to $38 million. With U.S. assistance, the defense establishment was considerably expanded. In mid-July 1954 the Pentagon announced that weapons, equipment, and training assistance would be provided to support higher targets for officers, noncommissioned officers, and technicians; by the end of the year, the army had grown to 80,000 from about 45,000 in 1952, while the police force (whose support from the United States included tanks, artillery, and aircraft) had also grown correspondingly.[37]

Closely linked to the United States through these arrangements, Thailand welcomed the more formal commitment provided by SEATO

---

35. Darling, p. 100; *SIA*, p. 292; Nuechterlien, p. 113. Edwin F. Stanton, "Spotlight on Thailand," *Foreign Affairs*, XXXIII (Oct., 1954), p. 80.

36. Prominent examples are Stanton, "Spotlight on Thailand," and William Donovan, "Our Stake in Thailand," *Fortune* (July, 1955).

37. Darling, pp. 107, 114, 115; Nuechterlein, p. 117; Wolf, *Foreign Aid*, p. 156; *SIA*, 1954, pp. 291–292.

as well as the inclusion of Laos, whose defense it regarded as essential to its own security, among the protocol states. Like the other Southeast Asian representatives, Foreign Minister Prince Wan Waithayakon pressed at Manila for arrangements that would resemble NATO's. Thailand, he said, is "anxious to have as strong a pact as possible. . . . While, in the matter of wording, there is a variety of models to choose from, it is the substance that counts; and, from this point of view, my Delegation would desire to see a commitment which in substance is as near as possible to that of NATO."[38]

Thailand, however, was somewhat equivocal about stationing SEATO forces on its own territory. Just after the Manila Conference a Thai representative said, "We will allow bases only if Thailand's security is threatened." But, at the February 1955 Council meeting, willingness to accept SEATO forces on Thai soil was at least implied. Speaking the day after Phibun had announced that 50,000 "Free Thai" troops were being massed by the PRC near Thailand's northern border, the Thai representative argued for a SEATO military command and for stationing SEATO forces in the treaty area. In July, however, Phibun, while saying that Thailand was ready to accept SEATO bases if the military advisers thought this necessary, also said he hoped this would not be the case. "I am sure," he said, "the Military Advisers . . . will not take any steps which may be construed as provocation or a challenge to the Communists." This position may have reflected Chinese efforts initiated at Bandung to reassure the Thai, although this did not mitigate Thai concern over Laos. In the same month, when resumed hostilities there seemed an imminent possibility, the Thai unsuccessfully sought a meeting of the SEATO Council to express collective concern. Notwithstanding the irritation with which the Lao government greeted this unsolicited proposal, in February 1956 Marshal Sarit Thanarat, who was to take power in Thailand the following year, declared, "If Laos is attacked, Thailand would be ready to give help right away."[39]

SEATO and the Taiwan Straits

Although the Republic of China lay well beyond the treaty area's northern boundary, the possibility that the Taiwan Straits crisis might

38. Nuechterlein, p. 115.
39. Modelski, pp. 8, 95, 98; Nuechterlein, pp. 115, 116; Darling, p. 110.

lead to war was very much to the forefront when the SEATO Council met in Bangkok early in February 1955. Taiwan's exclusion from the organization had reflected the desires of most of the members. Only the Filipinos, even though they were having problems of their own with Taipei over alleged discrimination against resident Chinese, urged Taiwan's inclusion; its omission, they argued, jeopardized their northern flank. The United States might have preferred that the alliance include Taiwan, but the problems that this would create were all too apparent; when Dulles raised the question with Eden in their early discussions of collective defense, he seems to have done so largely to discourage Eden from insisting on Indian membership. Despite Taiwan's exclusion, however, America's Allies in the Far East could not ignore the possibility early in 1955 that the contest between the PRC and the Republic of China over a number of small islands, close to the mainland and still in Nationalist hands, would erupt into hostilities between Communist China and the United States.[40]

Of the SEATO members, only the Philippines unequivocally supported the American stand. Linking Taiwan's defense to Philippine security, Magsaysay said: "Our interest extends to the measures that have been taken to defend it against aggression. . . . I welcome the decision of the United States Government clarifying its stand on the Formosa question." His statement was subsequently approved in a joint resolution passed by an overwhelming majority of the Philippine Congress.[41]

Australia and New Zealand, particularly the former, believed that Taiwan was an important link in the Pacific defense chain. Menzies, for example, declared: "The strategic position of Formosa is such that it is a portion of an island chain, the southern extremity of which is Australia, along which defeat and danger travelled only a few years ago, and which today represents a great barrier against a new Communist aggression in a great war." But, they thought the Nationalists were foolish and provocative to use the offshore islands to block trade with the mainland or to launch assaults upon it; they believed it was quite likely that Communist belligerence reflected determination to end these activities and not necessarily any intention to use the islands as a

40. Roger Smith, *Philippines and SEATO,* p. 11; Meyer, pp. 197–198; Eden, pp. 109–110.

41. Roger Smith, *Philippines and SEATO,* pp. 23–24.

stepping-stone for an assault on Taiwan; they were disturbed at what seemed to be American acquiescence in Taipei's risky actions; and, concerned lest the ANZUS tie involve them also, they did not believe the islands were "worth a great war." Regarding them as a long-run liability, Menzies nevertheless argued that Peking's truculence would merely be encouraged if the islands were simply abandoned in response to Communist threats. However, early in February, when U.S. pressure and assistance brought about the evacuation of the northernmost group, the Tachens, the move was greeted as a useful precedent for reducing and finally eliminating the Nationalist garrisons on the other islands.[42]

But the evacuation of the Tachens had done little to reduce tension when the Bangkok meeting opened on February 19. Peking had rejected a New Zealand-sponsored invitation to join in a Security Council discussion of the problem, and the United States Congress had recently passed the Formosa Resolution, authorizing the President to use armed force in any situation recognizable as part of or preliminary to an attack on Taiwan and the Pescadores. At the meeting, when Dulles talked of the close interconnection of the three Asian fronts—Southeast Asia, Japan-Korea, and Taiwan—he aroused some fear, especially on the part of France and Britain, that he considered the forces of SEATO members as potentially available in case of a conflict with the Chinese Communists over Taiwan. On his return to the United States the Secretary continued to stress possible wider involvement in any hostilities in the Taiwan area. Any "open armed aggression" by the Chinese Communists, he said, would be interpreted as a decision to "initiate general war in Asia." American forces in the area, he added, "are now equipped with new and powerful weapons of precision which can utterly destroy military targets without endangering civilian centers."[43]

Alarm in SEATO, however, reflected more than fear that Chinese belligerence on both sides of the Straits interacting with U.S. efforts to defend Taiwan and deter Communist action might lead to general war. Alarm was also aroused by the possibility that some sudden, un-

42. Albinski, *Australian Policies and Attitudes toward China*, pp. 158–167; Reese, pp. 253–255; Harper, "Australia and Southeast Asia," pp. 209–210.
43. *DSB*, March 21, 1955, pp. 459–460; *USWA*, 1955, p. 102; *SIA*, 1955–1956, p. 11; Farley, p. 49.

anticipated change in Washington-Peking relations might result from the joint ambassadorial-level talks announced in July 1955, some time after tensions in the Straits had subsided. Dulles felt called upon to state that the United States "absolutely was not prepared to abandon the South-East Asia Defense Pact," while the SEATO ambassadors in Washington were assured that the United States "contemplates no major change in policy toward Communist China at Geneva without first consulting its Far Eastern allies."[44]

44. Modelski, p. 110.

CHAPTER 12

BANDUNG: COEXISTENCE EXALTED

In the second half of 1954, increasingly in 1955, and until late in 1956, tensions seemed to be slackening world-wide. The Indochina conference had reflected the urge on both sides for some degree of détente, and its outcome encouraged hope in East-West negotiations. In fact, the treaty restoring sovereignty to a neutralized Austria was the only other agreement reached in this period on an issue directly disputed between the two blocs. Nevertheless, on the periphery of the Cold War, at least, there were encouraging signs of thaw—the lowering of voices on both sides, the return to politesse symbolized by the Geneva Summit of July 1955, the renewal of relations between the Communist bloc and an unrepentent Tito, the establishment of diplomatic relations between West Germany and the Soviet Union, and the opening of peace talks between the latter and Japan. Even in Asia, where tension between the United States and China—now focused on Taiwan—was still very high, the avoidance of seemingly imminent conflict in the Taiwan Straits in the first months of 1955 and the initiation of ambassadorial-level talks encouraged hope.

In this world of reduced tension and greater flexibility, the nonaligned, buoyed by the influence they had exerted at Geneva, and now fervently courted by Moscow and Peking, seemed likely to play a greater role in providing alternatives to the two blocs and even in moderating conflict between them. While SEATO represented the view that the need for deterrence remained, the Bandung Conference asserted that the search for peaceful coexistence led along more promising paths than the effort to establish positions of strength. The assertion seemed the more plausible since the participants included not only the nonaligned sponsors but Communist and anti-Communist states as well, joining together in what they all applauded as an important manifestation of Afro-Asian solidarity. With twenty-nine countries represented, many of them by their prime ministers, the conference brought new international prominence to the host country and to President Sukarno in particular. As the sessions proceeded, Chou displaced Nehru as the central figure on the Asian scene, and Peking's assertions of peaceful intent were reiterated to good effect.

Colombo: The Beginning

At their meeting in Colombo in April 1954, Indochina was only one of the subjects the prime ministers discussed. Others included a resolution proposed by Ceylon condemning equally colonialism and international communism, and an Indonesian proposal for convoking an Afro-Asian conference. Indonesia's Ali Sastroamidjojo had made this proposal in January when he accepted the invitation to Colombo. The invitation ironically enough had been extended only as an afterthought, Kotelewala having originally contemplated inviting only Burma and Pakistan. In joining India in opposition to Kotelewala's resolution, Ali was in the minority, as he was in his own conference proposal for which only Pakistan's Mohammed Ali expressed any enthusiasm. Discussion of Ceylon's proposal produced a revised version in which the prime ministers affirmed their faith in democracy: and "being resolved to preserve in their countries the freedoms inherent in the democratic system" they "declared their unshakable determination to resist interference in the affairs of other countries by external, Communist, anti-Communist, or other agencies." The conference issue was left to Indonesia to explore further.[1]

Ali Sastroamidjojo's stance at Colombo reflected his own ambitions for Asian leadership and the greater foreign-policy activism that was to be characteristic of his cabinet. His predecessors, whether leaders of the Muslim *Masjumi* like Hatta or of the secular, nationalist PNI like Wilopo, had given absolute priority to domestic over foreign policy. They placed far greater stress on reconstruction and on financial stability than on the long-term goal of Indonesianizing the economy, therefore working within the confines established by foreign, especially Dutch, predominance in such areas as oil, interisland and foreign

1. Gupta, p. 52; Kotelewala, p. 118; Chatham House Study Group, p. 104.

commerce, banking, and estate cultivation. Outside the government leadership, however, this policy was much criticized, and the issue of forceful police expulsion of squatters from estate land was one of the factors that brought about the fall of the Wilopo cabinet; in the 58 days it took to organize a new government, squatter resettlement and other aspects of the foreign economic role were hotly debated.

The Ali cabinet, installed in July 1953, differed markedly from its predecessors. Only four of its members had served in previous cabinets, in itself a sharp break with past practice. For the first time since independence, the *Masjumi* was completely excluded, as was Sjahrir's *Partai Sosialis Indonesia* (PSI), a small but hitherto very influential group of social-democratic-oriented, westernized intellectuals. Ali's elevation to leadership represented the triumph of the left wing of the PNI, favored by Sukarno and wooed and supported by the PKI, over Wilopo's right wing. The PKI itself, since its shift to parliamentary politics in April 1952, had advanced significantly in membership, popular support, and political impact. It was not seated in the cabinet, but two small parties very much under its influence were.

Ali, departing from the prowestern policies of previous cabinets, while continuing to welcome western investment, interpreted Indonesia's independent foreign policy as requiring more balanced relations between East and West. Accordingly, he established diplomatic relations with the Soviet Union and a number of other Communist countries and negotiated Indonesia's first trade agreement with the PRC. Domestically, as compared with its predecessors, his cabinet's nationalism was more strident, and its orientation was further to the left. Ali himself, much influenced by visions of a resurgent Asia, sought a more prominent role for Indonesia in the international politics of nonalignment and anticolonialism.[2]

Burma, in contrast, despite much internal instability, continued to be ruled by the same small group of AFPFL leaders who had brought it to independence and who had been able to reduce the Communist and other insurgent threats to manageable proportions. Their power, moreover, had been ratified in parliamentary elections held in 1951–

2. Feith, Ch. VIII, *passim;* Van der Kroef, *Communist Party of Indonesia,* pp. 57–62; Brimmell, pp. 361–362; Franklin Weinstein, *Indonesian Foreign Policy,* pp. 237–238; Sutter, IV, 1228.

1952 in which the AFPFL had won 147 of the 239 seats contested, while the Communist-oriented Burma Workers and Peasants Party had won only ten. The Communist Party itself had been unsuccessful in its efforts to play a part in coalition politics, and in October 1953 it had been formally outlawed.

In Asia, U Nu was second only to Nehru as spokesman for nonalignment. Within the ruling group, he retained the leadership he had inherited when Aung San was assassinated but shared authority with Socialist Party leaders—pre-eminently Kyaw Nein and Ba Swe—who, like Sjahrir's group were westernized social-democratic intellectuals. Unlike the PSI, however, the Burmese Socialists had a very strong power base; they constituted the principal organized group within the AFPFL coalition, dominated the leadership of its affiliated mass organizations, and held at that time nine of the twelve top cabinet positions.[3]

With this base, the Burmese Socialist Party played a leading role among the Far Eastern socialists who, their weakness in most of the countries of the area notwithstanding, were attempting to establish Asian socialist independence of the western-dominated Socialist International. The Asian Socialist Conference of January 1953 was organized by the Burmese, Indian, and Indonesia parties: the conference was held in Rangoon and was chaired by Ba Swe. Despite the pro-Soviet inclinations of some of the delegates, most notably the Indians who dominated the foreign-policy discussions, the Conference adopted a resolution which not only rejected Communism in general, but specifically condemned its "totalitarian form in the Soviet Union and its satellites."[4] In May 1954 the Anti-Colonial Bureau of the Conference, meeting at Kalaw in Burma after the Indonesian government blocked plans to meet in Bandung, heard Kyaw Nein denounce Soviet imperialism as "even more degrading and even more dangerous" than traditional western colonialism "because it is more ruthless, more

3. Richard Butwell, *U Nu of Burma,* pp. 146–157.

4. Reflecting new Soviet tenderness toward the Asian neutralists, the *Cominform Journal* (Jan. 9, 1953, p. 2) described Clement Atlee (who attended as an observer and tried unsuccessfully to persuade the Asians to remain within the Socialist International) as the principal figure at Rangoon and focused its attack on Atlee and the Yugoslav guests, not on the Asians.

systematic, and more blatantly justified in the name of world Communist revolution."[5]

Bogor: Dynamic Neutralism

When the Colombo prime ministers met again in Bogor in December 1954, attitudes toward Ali's proposed Asian-African conference had changed markedly. The prime ministers, agreeing to hold such a conference, described its purposes as: promoting good will, cooperation, and mutual interests; considering social, economic, and cultural problems; exploring problems of special Afro-Asian concern such as racialism, colonialism, and independence; and considering the contributions the Afro-Asians could make to international cooperation and world peace. It was not their intention, however, "that the participating countries should build themselves into a regional bloc."[6]

Ali had originally envisaged inviting only countries represented in the United Nations, but it was now agreed to extend the invitation to those outside as well. This made it possible to invite the PRC, whose presence Nehru had made a condition for his approval when he and Ali had discussed the project in New Delhi in September.[7]

The Bogor Conference expressed the more positive and active of the two coexisting themes of Asian neutralism: one, the view of neutralism as a way of remaining aloof from great-power conflicts over which the endangered small powers could have no control; the other, the view of neutralism as a way in which the weak, because they were not involved, could provide a bridge between the competing strong. The difference was exemplified in two statements U Nu made in 1954. In one, he described Burma's neutralism as doing "its utmost to shun any activity which is likely to create misunderstanding in any quarter." In the other, he said that the Burmese, because they were neutral between the United States and Communist China and "unclouded by prejudice," should "do something to enable both America and China to achieve their ends without resorting to bloody warfare." In Septem-

5. Trager, *Burma*, p. 257; Trager, "Burma's Foreign Policy," pp. 53–54; Alvin Rubenstein, "The State of Socialism in Asia," *Pacific Affairs*, XXVI (June, 1953), pp. 131–134; Fifield, p. 183.

6. Text in G. V. Ambekar and V. D. Divekar, *Documents on China's Relations with South and Southeast Asia*, pp. 10–12.

7. George Kahin, *The Asian-African Conference*, p. 21.

ber 1954, U Nu explicitly adopted the second theme; henceforth, he said, Burmese neutralism would emphasize positive action to ease tensions between the two blocs and promote the peaceful settlement of international disputes.[8]

The sensitivity to the views of the Colombo powers that had been shown by the two sides at the Geneva Conference encouraged the neutralists' belief that their voices would continue to be heard; in Nehru's words "the deliberations of the South East Asian Prime Ministers at Colombo had an essential and inescapable role in the Geneva deliberations."[9] This faith was reinforced by further bloc efforts to show good will to the Third World. The rapprochement with a non-aligned and unrepentant Tito was a dramatic example, but Moscow was also moving to correct the imbalance created by its failure to assist countries outside its own orbit. The first step came in the United Nations where, in the past, the Soviets had justified their failure to participate in the technical-assistance programs of the international organization by expressions of concern for sovereignty. In the summer of 1953, the Soviet Union made its first contribution to UN-sponsored technical assistance; in 1954 the Soviets began to take a more active part in the specialized agencies, joining the International Labor Organization (ILO)' and the United Nations Economic and Social Council (UNESCO), while in the Economic Council for Asia and the Far East (ECAFE), instead of concentrating their attention on the sins of the West, they stressed their willingness to expand trade and provide technical assistance and long-term credits.[10]

Although, for some time, nothing very substantial was to come of this new posture, the Burmese rice crisis of 1953–1954 afforded the opportunity for a conspicuous demonstration of Soviet interest in helping Asian countries out of their difficulties. This was a particularly attractive opportunity because of the feeling among Burmese that competition from the United States—in 1953 ranking third after Burma and Thailand as a rice exporter—was largely responsible for their

8. *SIA*, 1954, p. 297; Nu, *For World Peace and Progress*, p. 2; William Johnstone, *A Study of Factors Affecting Burma's Foreign Policy*, p. 39.

9. Fisher and Bondurant, p. 97.

10. Alvin Rubenstein, "Soviet Policy in ECAFE," *International Organization*, XII (Autumn, 1958), p. 465; John Reshetar, "The Soviet Union and the Neutralist World," *The Annals*, CCCLXII (Nov., 1965), pp. 104–105; Alvin Rubenstein, *The Soviets in International Organizations*, p. 467.

problems in disposing of a product normally bringing in some 70 percent of Burma's export earnings. With falling prices and a contracting market, as production expanded in rice-consuming countries, when the 1953 crop was being harvested early in 1954 Burma still had a large unsold surplus from the 1952 crop. The Burmese first proposed that the United States buy their surplus and distribute it under the aid program to deficit countries elsewhere in Asia. This came to nothing, however, and the Soviets and other bloc countries indicated their interest in helping. Between November 1954 and February 1956, agreements were reached with the Soviet Union, the Eastern Europeans, and Communist China, exchanging Burmese rice for bloc commodities and technical services.[11]

In Southeast Asia the new Communist line was much more actively pursued by Peking than by Moscow. Chou's trips to New Delhi and Rangoon in the midst of the Geneva Conference and his endorsement there of the Five Principles[12] had had particular impact. His exposition of Peking's policy toward the Overseas Chinese was of even wider interest to countries suspicious and fearful of their own Chinese communities. "For our part," Chou said in September 1954, "we are willing to urge the overseas Chinese to respect the laws of the governments and the social customs of all the countries in which they live. . . . The question of the nationality of the overseas Chinese is one which the reactionary governments of China in the past never tried to solve. This placed the overseas Chinese in a difficult situation and often led to discord between China and the countries concerned. To improve this situation, we are prepared to settle this question and are ready to settle it first with the South East Asian countries which have established diplomatic relations with us."[13]

Peking, in addition to identifying itself with the neutralist desire for a period of peace and concentration on nation-building, seemed also to be looking toward some more formal association of Asian states. Nehru, in particular, wanted to encourage the former but discourage the latter, since he regarded proposals for third-force organization—whatever their source—as antithetical to his own notions of a zone of

11. Trager, *Burma,* pp. 331–334; Butwell, p. 173; King, p. 237.

12. Mutual respect for each other's territorial integrity and sovereignty; non-aggression; noninterference in each other's internal affairs; equality and mutual benefit; and peaceful coexistence.

13. Chatham House Study Group, p. 66.

peace. This zone was to be created not by the organization of still another bloc but by pledges of mutual good will and noninterference and the exchange of affirmations of the Five Principles. Thus in February 1953, when Aneurin Bevan supported the Indian Socialists in advocating a third-force organization, Nehru said, "I have not been able to understand what it means. . . . If by the term is meant a power bloc, military or other, I am afraid I do not consider it desirable. . . . It would be absurd for a number of countries in Asia to come together and call themselves a third force or a third power in a military sense. It may, however, have a meaning in another sense. Instead of calling it a third force or the third bloc, it can be called a third area, an area which—let us put it negatively first—does not want war, works for peace in a positive way and believes in cooperation. I should like my country to work for that. Indeed, we have tried to do so, but the idea of a third bloc or a third force inevitably hinders our work."[14] U Nu appeared to share Nehru's view, responding in December 1954 to queries about a nonaggression pact with the PRC by saying, "Since we subscribe to the Five-Point Principle, non-aggression pacts are unnecessary." Ali, on the contrary, in May 1954, proposed that Burma, China, India, and Indonesia join together in a nonaggression pact.[15]

The evolution of Chou's views on collective peace between April and October 1954 suggested that he was amenable to Nehru's desires that the idea should not be pushed. In his opening speech at the Geneva Conference, Chou declared, "The government of the People's Republic of China believes that the nations of Asia should consult among themselves with a view to assuming mutual obligations providing for joint measures to safeguard peace and security in Asia." Two days later, Molotov declared that the Soviet Union was in full accord. Thereafter the Chinese media repeated Chou's proposal, casting no light on the type of organization he had in mind but making it fairly clear that some form of organization was contemplated. Thus *Jen Min Jih Pao* editorialized on May 12, "If the Asian countries, with more than half of the world's population, can undertake joint responsibility to safeguard peace and security in Asia, all imperialist schemes to start war in Asia will be defeated."[16]

14. Gupta, p. 49; Sar Desai, p. 66.
15. Johnstone, p. 171; Feith, p. 389.
16. *Summary of the China Mainland Press (SCMP)*, No. 797, April 29, 1954, p. 5; No. 799, May 1–3, 1954, p. 23; No. 807, May 13, 1954, p. 2.

Just before Chou arrived in New Delhi in June, the Indian Communist Party Politburo announced that Chou would discuss with Nehru "how to bring together the peoples and Governments of Asia in order to end colonialism." The party-lining *Blitz* called for mutual security pacts among China, India, and the rest of Asia. The party weekly *New Age* suggested an alliance between India and China "as the cornerstone of alliance between the Asian nations." Chou himself, in an interview with an Indian journalist, repeated his proposal that the Asian nations should seek "common measures to safeguard peace and security in Asia by assuming obligations mutually and respectively."

After conversations with Indian leaders, however, Chou's emphasis changed. In his press conference of June 27, in which he himself had selected from over sixty presubmitted questions the five he proposed to answer, he said, "in order to seek common measures for the maintenance of peace and security in Asia, it is desirable for the appropriate responsible persons of the principal Asian countries to meet occasionally to consult each other."[17] The joint communiqué, issued on June 28, stressed the efficacy of pledges of allegiance to the Five Principles in maintaining peace as did the Sino-Burmese communiqué issued on June 29.[18]

Reporting on the Geneva Conference to the Central People's Government Council on August 11, Chou repeated the proposal that he had made in Geneva in April. He added that he did not "envisage the exclusion of any country," perhaps a hint that what he had in mind was sufficiently unstructured to include countries allied with the West. Moreover, what he now described as "collective peace"—mutual pledges to adhere to the Five Principles and sincerity in carrying out these Principles thereafter—seemed very similar to Nehru's zone of peace.[19]

At the First National People's Congress in August 1954, Chou again avoided any specific advocacy of formal organization or treaty relationship. "Asian countries," he said, "should consult together and take all effective measures to promote cooperation among themselves and jointly strive to defend collective peace and security in Asia. This

17. Fisher and Bondurant, pp. 65–67, 70–72.
18. Texts in Ambekar and Divekar, pp. 7–10.
19. *People's China*, Sept. 1, 1954, Supplement, pp. 1–11.

proposal of ours by no means excludes any country outside Asia."[20]
The movement toward complete endorsement of Nehru's zone-of-
peace concept was completed with the Indian Prime Minister's visit to
Peking in October. A *Jen Min Jih Pao* editorial on that occasion
declared, "We believe that greater and more peace areas can be set up
in Asia if relations of international cooperation can be established
among the Asian countries in accordance with the five principles of
peaceful coexistence. . . . The peoples of the Asian countries should
follow this path, to strengthen their unity and strive for the establishment of collective peace in Asia."[21] Thereafter it was in these terms
that Chinese Communist media dealt with the subject of collective
peace.

It does not appear that the Soviets added anything to Molotov's
mere endorsement of Chou's proposal at Geneva. In November, however, the World Peace Council meeting in Stockholm adopted a resolution that mirrored Chou's changed approach. Prescribing six tasks to
be accomplished in Asia, however, the resolution called only for
widening and strengthening the area of peace on the basis of the Five
Principles.[22]

The Conference and After

Between Chou's visits to New Delhi and Rangoon in 1954 and the
Bandung Conference almost a year later, the PRC's relations with the
Southeast Asian neutrals had developed further, and its world stand-
ing had been further enhanced.

In the accelerating exchange of official missions, U Nu's visits to
Peking in December 1954 and February 1955 had been of particular
interest. In both he had stressed those virtues he had found in Americans who were "generous and brave" to balance the anti-American
statements of the Chinese. In the communiqué issued after the December visit, the PRC announced it would import 150,000 to 200,000 tons
of rice from Burma annually, and the two countries agreed on the
desirability of border negotiations. In February, catering to U Nu's
desire to act as a bridge between the two blocs, the Chinese entrusted
him with the message that they would be prepared to discuss issues

20. *Ibid.,* Oct. 16, 1954, p. 26.
21. *SCMP,* No. 911, Oct. 20, 1954, p. 9.
22. *Cominform Journal,* Nov. 26, 1954, p. 1.

between the two countries with an unofficial American mission. This message, which U Nu delivered to Dulles when the Secretary visited Rangoon later in the month, while bringing no results, foreshadowed Chou's use of Bandung for further conciliatory gestures.[23]

Peking's relations with Djakarta also became more active, largely in connection with negotiations concerning Indonesia's Chinese community. With PRC interest expressed even before Chou's September 1954 statement, a draft agreement was reached in April 1955 on procedures for confirming the citizenship of Indonesia's ethnic Chinese residents. The solution proposed for this complex and emotion-laden problem reflected the contradictions in which it was enmeshed: the Chinese made concessions on their traditional claim to Chinese nationality for all Overseas Chinese, while other provisions made it possible for Indonesia to obstruct Overseas Chinese acquisition of Indonesian nationality. The draft, widely unpopular in Indonesia for a variety of reasons, was of largely symbolic significance: in Indonesia it reflected the turning of the tide against local Chinese supporters of the Republic of China, and, since it was signed in the midst of the Bandung Conference, Chou was able once again to reassure China's neighbors about PRC intentions in an area of disturbing interest to most of them.[24]

When Chou came to Bandung, he came as the head of an Asian country that had been able to assert its equality both with its western great-power adversaries and its eastern Ally. In September 1954, a delegation headed by Khrushchev and Nikolai Bulganin had arrived in Peking to initiate negotiations resulting ultimately in the abandonment of those features of the February 1950 Sino-Soviet treaty—"the last of the unequal treaties"—that had been bitterly resented by the Chinese. The Soviets agreed to evacuate Port Arthur, and the joint Sino-Soviet companies for mineral exploitation and civil aviation in Sinkiang were dissolved.[25] At Bandung, Chou was to displace Nehru as the central figure of the Afro-Asian assemblage. Partly this was a dividend of the increasing irritation of other delegates with Nehru's homilies and efforts to dominate; partly it was attributable to the skill

23. *SIA,* 1954, p. 302; Kenneth Young, *Negotiating with the Chinese Communists,* pp. 43–44.

24. Feith, pp. 389–390; Chatham House Study Group, pp. 88–89.

25. Ulam, pp. 554–555; Donald Zagoria, p. 18.

and grace with which Chou was able to persuade those present that the PRC wished only peaceful and constructive relations with all other countries, even the United States.

The assemblage at Bandung—twenty-nine delegations, thirteen of them headed by Prime Ministers—included virtually all of the independent countries of the Middle East, Africa, and Asia (and two not yet independent, the Gold Coast and Sudan). There were some anomalies: the PRC was represented, the Nationalist government on Taiwan was not; the two Koreas were not invited, the two Vietnams were; in an advance over the political sophistication of the Asian Relations Conference of 1947, the Soviet Asian republics were apparently not even considered; Mongolia was also omitted from the invitation list as were Israel and South Africa; in the case of Australia and New Zealand, ethnic origin apparently outweighed location, although Nehru, sending them greetings from the conference, said that they were "almost in our region" and should come closer.

The Bandung conferees were divided among themselves in many ways, and some of their most serious divisions were bilateral ones. In international orientation they formed three groups—western Allied (or so inclined), neutralist, or Communist—with Southeast Asian countries represented in each. The Philippines, Thailand, and South Vietnam were western-oriented together with Turkey, Pakistan, Iraq, Japan, Ceylon, Iran, Jordan, Lebanon, Libya, Liberia, Gold Coast, and Sudan. Indonesia and Burma, and more tentatively Laos and Cambodia, stood with the neutralist group which included also India, Afghanistan, Nepal, Egypt, Saudi Arabia, Yemen, and Syria. North Vietnam and the PRC were the only Communist countries present.[26]

Debate was most heated on alignment versus nonalignment and on whether Communism constituted a new form of colonialism. It was the neutralists rather than the Chinese, however, who argued most actively not only for nonalignment, but also against criticism of Communist behavior. Chou tended to approach these issues tangentially and in a manner calculated to display Chinese flexibility and willingness to place unity before doctrinal purity.

The Conference communiqué,[27] in place of the Five Principles, set

26. Kahin, *Asian-African Conference*, p. 3; Watt, p. 229; Doak Barnett, *Chou En-lai at Bandung*, p. 3.
27. Text in Kahin, *Asian-African Conference*, pp. 76–85.

forth ten, many of them compromises between conflicting views. Two reflected inability to compromise: one, proposed by Pakistan, calling for "respect for the right of each nation to defend itself singly or collectively"; the other for "abstention from the use of arrangements of collective defense to serve the particular interests of any of the big powers." Romulo was an active supporter of the first of these, in accordance with his instructions to oppose any move to ask the participating states to renounce their military agreements with western powers, to endorse Peking's admission to the UN, to adopt the Five Principles, or to outlaw nuclear warfare without proper safeguards. Although criticizing the United States for its lack of "consistency and vigor" on colonial issues and its too frequent support of colonial powers, Romulo defended SEATO warmly. In response to Nehru's criticisms, he pointed out that all countries felt obliged to protect themselves—India and Pakistan, for example, were putting half their national budgets into military preparations. Large countries like India might be able to stand on their own feet; small countries had no alternative but to join in collective arrangements. Of SEATO he said: "Far from destroying the so-called climate of peace following the Indochina settlement, the Manila Pact makes it doubly certain that the signatories shall not countenance any fresh outbreaks or renewal of communist aggression in the region . . . the Communists can neither renew their aggression in any other part of Southeast Asia without risking countermeasures. One would think that this will serve to reinforce rather than weaken the climate of peace."[28]

U Nu based his case against defense pacts on their inefficacy. Burma, faced with insurgency to the point of national extinction, had found that the remedy lay in removing such causes of discontent and alienation as corruption and graft, ignorance, and economic and social injustice. "Military alliances and pacts," he said, "do not . . . provide any solution, because they do nothing to improve the lot of the common man in the country concerned. Indeed, they may often do harm since they tend to add to the existing tension." Nor do they provide real protection against aggression. For this purpose, "First, let every nation accept and strictly observe the five principles. Second, if despite acceptance of the five principles, an overt act of aggression occurs, let

28. Sar Desai, p. 273; Vellut, pp. 23–25; Kahin, *Asian-African Conference,* pp. 24–25; Doak Barnett, *Asia and Africa in Session,* pp. 24–25.

the United Nations deal with it. For this purpose, strengthen the United Nations and make it an effective instrument."[29]

Chou avoided direct attacks on SEATO while making clear PRC opposition to what he described as antagonistic military alliances. To balance even this, however, he suggested that membership in such arrangements was not necessarily a bar to good relations with the PRC, citing in this context his "mutual understanding" with the Prime Minister of Pakistan.[30]

When it came to condemning Communist imperialism, Sir John Kotelawala, who had introduced the subject, carefully distinguished between Moscow and Peking, as did Pakistan, as anxious to be on good terms with Peking as it was to get assistance from Washington. Kotelawala's examples of Communist colonialism included only the satellite states of Eastern Europe and the Cominform. Elaborating, Mohammed Ali declared, "China is by no means an imperialist nation and she has no satellites. . . . The Prime Minister of Ceylon . . . was directing his criticism against the Soviet form of imperialism by which many countries have been made satellites. . . . We have the friendliest relations with China; China is certainly not imperialist; she has not brought any other country under her heel."[31]

Some of China's neighbors showed less forbearance. None was more specific than Prince Wan who described Pridi as "organizing the training of Thai-speaking Chinese and persons of Thai race in Yunnan for purposes of infiltration and subversion in Thailand." Wan queried PRC attitudes toward Thailand's Overseas Chinese community, and recalled the threat to Thailand posed by the Viet Minh invasions of Laos in 1953 and 1954.[32] Sihanouk, who had recently embraced neutralism, saw the distrust of most non-Communist countries, even those favoring coexistence, mirrored in Cambodia's fear of China and North Vietnam. The Communist countries, he said, must reassure the rest of the world of their peaceful intentions.[33]

And it was this path that Chou followed. He thanked the delegates for their courtesy in mentioning the Soviet Union without referring to

29. Nu, *Resurgence*, pp. 9–12.
30. Ambekar and Divekar, pp. 17, 18.
31. Kahin, *Asian-African Conference*, pp. 18–20.
32. *Ibid.*, pp. 13–14.
33. Roger Smith, *Cambodia*, p. 79.

China, but explained that he could not accept this completely. "China is also a country which is governed by a Communist party. So we feel that we are also involved in it by implication." With this as a point of departure, he added simply, "We, on our part, do not want to do anything for the expansion of Communist activities outside our own country." As for the Cominform, he asked, why should it be singled out among a great number of international organizations, some of which are displeasing to China? The PRC, he pledged, would not use the Overseas Chinese to interfere in the internal affairs of others, and was ready to solve the problem of dual nationality—left behind by the old regime—in discussions with the other governments concerned. Citing Sino-Burmese relations, he asserted Chinese Communist respect for the sovereignty of other countries, even those whose border areas were being illegally used for activities hostile to the PRC. In addition, he said, where borders were not finally fixed, Peking was prepared to acknowledge this situation and would seek to alter it only by peaceful means.[34]

Speaking to Thailand, Chou said that Hsi-shuang Pan-na was being given only the same autonomy enjoyed by other national minority areas and welcomed a delegation to visit Yunnan and "see if we have any aggressive designs against others." Privately, he assured Wan that Pridi was in Peking not in Yunnan, that he was merely being given political asylum, and that to have broadcast Pridi's attack on the Thai government was a mistake that would not be repeated. He also arranged a meeting between Thai and North Vietnamese representatives at which agreement was reached on exchanging liaison groups to facilitate repatriation of the Vietnamese refugees.[35]

Romulo too was assured privately that the PRC had no aggressive designs against the Philippines, that it would be prepared to negotiate a nationality treaty, and that it would welcome Philippine visitors. Publicly Chou declared, "We . . . welcome a delegation from the Philippines to visit our coastal regions, especially Fukien and Kwang-

34. Ambekar and Divekar, pp. 15–19. According to Kotelawala, Chou responded to his private queries about the Cominform by saying the Cominform "was a Russian organization and had nothing to do with China" (Kotelawala, p. 186).

35. Ambekar and Divekar, pp. 15, 20; Barnett, *Asia and Africa in Session*, p. 12.

tung provinces, and to see for themselves whether we are carrying out any activities for purposes of directing threats against the Philippines.

To Laos and Cambodia, Chou reiterated the Geneva commitments, assuring them that the Chinese Communists had no intention of interfering in their internal affairs. In addition he arranged a meeting with the North Vietnamese at which Pham Van Dong disavowed any DRV interest in intervening between the Lao Government and the Pathet Lao. According to Sihanouk, he too received North Vietnamese assurances of respect for the sovereignty of his country.

Finally, toward the end of the conference, Chou deflected a Ceylonese attempt to push a two-Chinas' proposal and attracted worldwide attention by a press release on the Taiwan issue. The PRC, he announced, was willing to discuss with the United States "the question of relaxing tension in the Far East, especially in the Taiwan area."[36]

While Chou enjoyed the limelight at Bandung, the Soviet Union was not present, nor were North Korea and Mongolia, the two Asian Communist countries closest to it. The Russians, to be sure, unlike the Americans, had sent warm greetings to the conference, and their press had covered its proceedings enthusiastically, disregarding or playing down its anti-Soviet and anti-Communist aspects. These, nevertheless, had been a major feature of the conference, and it does not appear from the published records, or from the accounts of those on the scene, that Chou tried very hard to defend the Soviets. He did, at one meeting, say that the Eastern European countries were independent and free to choose their own governments, but that seems to have been about the extent of his effort.[37]

Specialists have asked themselves whether China's Bandung role reflected a division of labor between Moscow and Peking, or whether Chou's performance at Bandung reflected and contributed to the growing conflict between them.[38] However this may be, after Bandung Moscow certainly became more active in and laudatory of the Third World, which had again increased in tactical importance in December

36. Kahin, *Asian-African Conference,* pp. 26–27; Ambekar and Divekar, p. 20; Fifield, p. 385; Barnett, *Chou at Bandung,* p. 14.

37. Dallin, pp. 299, 312; Barnett, *Asia and Africa in Session,* p. 22.

38. See, for example, Herbert Dinerstein, *Sino-Soviet Conflict in the Underdeveloped Countries,* p. 15; O. Edmund Clubb, *China and Russia,* pp. 407–409; Harold Hinton, *China's Turbulent Quest,* p. 72.

1955 with the sharp rise in UN membership.[39] At the Soviet Twentieth Party Congress in February 1956, earlier failure to recognize Gandhi's "outstanding part in the history of the Indian people" was publicly deplored, and the policies of the Third World won warm applause. Again and again, speakers emphasized the great importance of cooperation between the Soviet-led one-third of mankind and the "peace zone"—led by India and constituting another third—against the "imperialist-controlled" remaining third. The former colonies and semicolonies were assured that the Soviet Union recognized a peaceful and even parliamentary road to socialism and that, to support their drive toward economic independence, they could obtain assistance from the "countries of socialism without having to pay for it with obligations of a political or military character."[40]

Very little of this was of any immediate practical consequence for Southeast Asia. To be sure, Bulganin and Khrushchev included Burma on their famous Asian trip toward the end of 1955, and the rice and technical-assistance agreements made then and later prompted U Nu to describe the USSR as the first country to offer technical assistance to Burma on terms suggested by its own government. Similarly, before Sukarno's visit in 1956, Moscow and Djakarta signed their first trade agreement exchanging Indonesian primary products, including sugar, rubber, and copra for Soviet iron and steel, tractors, trucks, and industrial and agricultural machinery. The total Soviet economic effort in these two countries, however, was of no great size; in its growing concern with the Third World, Moscow was much less interested in Southeast Asia than it was in South Asia—particularly India—and the Middle East—particularly Egypt.[41]

The psychological success at Bandung marked the highpoint of Chinese Communist effort; no great strides were made thereafter in tightening relations with the nonaligned, much less the aligned countries of Southeast Asia or in solving Overseas Chinese and border

39. Of the sixteen new members, seven were Middle Eastern and Asian, and the total balance was such that the United States, Western Europe, and Latin America no longer constituted a majority when voting together.

40. Reshetar, p. 195; Wolfgang Leonhard, *The Kremlin since Stalin,* p. 126; Howard Boorman et al., *Moscow-Peking Axis,* pp. 218, 224.

41. Dallin, pp. 306, 318–319; Tinker, pp. 376–377; Joseph Berliner, *Soviet Economic Aid,* p. 47; Brimmell, p. 363.

problems. Indeed, Burma and Indonesia, having moved closer to the Communist bloc, also seemed anxious to maintain the balance by moving closer to the United States. U Nu in 1955 and Sukarno in 1956 visited the United States where they addressed American audiences at length on the principles that guided their policies. In Burma, by mid-1956, the large flow of visiting Communist officials had tapered off, new agreements for American aid had been completed or were under negotiation, and the rice barter deals no longer seemed necessary. These in retrospect, had proved unsatisfactory, the goods and capital equipment received in return having done little to meet Burma's needs.[42]

In Indonesia likewise, the balance had been maintained. The *Masjumi*-led Burhanudden Harahap cabinet, which succeeded the Ali Sastroamidjojo government in August 1955, sought to re-establish closer relations with the West, partly in hopes that this would help Indonesia in renewed negotiations with the Netherlands on West Irian. Visits were exchanged with Australia and Britain, and U.S. naval vessels called at Indonesian ports and carried out an exercise in the Java Sea. U.S. technical assistance rose from $7 million in 1955 to $11 million in 1956, and on March 2, his last day in office, Burhanudden accepted a large American PL-480 surplus foodstuff agreement. Little change in foreign policy resulted from the installation of Ali's second cabinet, a more conservative body than his first, the unexpectedly strong showing of the PKI in the 1955 general elections having led to a degree of political coalescence against it. Indeed, little action was taken in any field during the twelve-month term of the Ali government, immobilized as it was not only by the same problems that had severely limited the accomplishments of its predecessors but also by its own internal divisions, by the hostility of Sukarno and military leaders, and by the growing restiveness in the Outer Islands that was soon to lead to large-scale rebellion.[43]

It was in Thailand that the Bandung Conference seems to have had the most marked repercussions. Even here, however, the effects were temporary and apparent only on the fringes of foreign policy. Moreover, Peking's new stance was only partly responsible for what proved

42. Johnstone, p. 105.
43. Feith, p. 450; Fifield, pp. 160–161.

to be no more than a temporary change in atmosphere. Other factors of importance included an internal power conflict, disappointment at the limited SEATO commitment, restiveness over the growing size and influence of the American presence, and fear that Thailand had gone too far in tying itself to the United States, especially since it now appeared to the Thai that the United States might soon achieve a rapprochement with Peking, probably without any prior consultation with its Allies.

The first sign of change came in September 1955. Phibun, who was involved in a power struggle both with General Phao Sriyanon, head of the police and widely regarded as an American favorite, and with Phao's rival, General Sarit Thanarat, commander of the military forces assigned to Bangkok, ended what had been a long period of political repression, unleashing the press and opening the doors to political party activity. A lively foreign-policy debate emerged. SEATO and the United States were criticized, the latter for undue interference in Thai affairs and for favoring neutral countries at the expense of Allies, while the advantages of neutralism and of trade with China were well-aired. A marked shift also took place in the treatment of the Chinese community and the competition within it of pro-Nationalist and pro-Communist factions. Late in 1952 the government had abandoned its even-handed treatment of the community's factions in favor of the pro-Nationalists. Now, however, police harassment and other measures began to make it evident that the pro-Nationalist element had lost its official patronage.[44]

Peking responded with propaganda shifts, abandoning references to the Thai government as aggressive and as a tool of the United States. Avoiding revolutionary themes and emphasizing nationalism and national interest, Chinese Communist transmitters warned the Thai of the ill effects of cooperating with imperialism, emphasizing the harm done by American dumping of surplus agricultural products and by the embargo on trade with China; the Chinese alleged that SEATO and the various U.S. military and civilian missions infringed on Thai sovereignty and urged the advantages of economic, diplomatic, and cultural relations with the PRC. In January 1956, a group of unoffi-

44. Nuechterlein, pp. 124–131; Brimmell, pp. 338–342; Wilcox, Rose, and Boyd, p. 189.

cial visitors, led by former cabinet minister Thep Chotunichet and including five members of parliament and three prominent journalists, was received by Mao and Chou, who stressed Peking's desire for peace and good relations with its neighbors.[45]

Meanwhile, Phibun himself was circumspect. He continued to praise the United States and SEATO, although less warmly than in the past. And it was he who initiated the first SEATO combined military exercise—Firmlink, in February 1956—which was regarded by a number of members of the alliance as unduly provocative to Communist China in proposed location and theme. But, at the same time, he made some cautious overtures. In June 1956, he announced that trade with China in rice and other nonstrategic goods would no longer be embargoed, and the PRC was permitted to appoint a Thai bank as its trading agent in Bangkok. In the same month, Prince Wan declared that Thailand recognized that Peking controlled the large majority of the Chinese people and, suggesting a new flexibility in recognition policy, said that Thailand's attitude would depend on UN decisions on representation. A month later Phibun told newspapermen that the conflict over Taiwan was a Chinese family quarrel in which Thailand did not propose to interfere. At home, meanwhile, although some members of Thep's group were arrested on their return, they were quickly released, and other visits and contacts were permitted. A number of Pridi's followers returned from China and were allowed to resume political activities in Bangkok, while the February 1957 elections were followed by the release of many previously jailed as suspected Communists.[46]

Sarit for his part attempted to win political favor by demonstrating his strong nationalism, independence of the United States, and opposition to American interference. Two newspapers supporting him in the election campaign were in the vanguard of those who attacked the United States and SEATO, and at the same time advocated neutralism and recognition of Peking. Sarit's rise to dictatorial power, however, was accompanied by a change in stance. After his first coup in September 1957, he announced that Thailand would remain in

45. David Wilson, "China, Thailand, and the Spirit of Bandung," *China Quarterly*, XXXI (July–Sept., 1967), pp. 111–120.

46. *SIA*, 1955–1956, p. 143; Nuechterlein, p. 128; Brimmell, p. 352; Modelski, p. 112.

SEATO; after his second in October 1958, firm internal political control and clear-cut external alignment were fully restored.[47]

In the Philippines as in Thailand, irritation with the United States on other grounds was usually reflected in charges that the United States favored neutrals. Such criticisms reached high levels in 1955, a year in which there was considerable debate over the economic relationship defined by the Trade Act of 1946 and the question of title to land occupied by U.S. bases. Many of the problems that had arisen under the 1946 legislation were ameliorated by the Laurel-Langley Agreement of January 1956. Residual American controls over the Philippine economy—such as those tying the peso to the dollar and prohibiting Philippine export taxes—were eliminated. At the same time, the need of the weaker partner for special protection was recognized; the transition from free trade was to be accompanied by a less rapid imposition of U.S. duties on Philippine products and a more rapid imposition of Philippine duties on American products, while most of the absolute quotas were eliminated. The base land issue, however, was less successfully handled; negotiations, opened in August 1956, broke down completely in December.[48]

Charges in moments of discontent and uncertainty that the United States did more for the neutralists than it did for its Allies reflected neither the facts of the situation nor the views of the neutralists. To the neutralists it frequently appeared that the United States failed to understand their position and, even worse, condemned it. They found grounds for this belief in Congressional debate and in some administration statements. Eisenhower, for example, lighting the national Christmas tree in December 1954, declared, "There are some who have believed it possible to hold themselves aloof from today's world-wide struggle between those who uphold human freedom and dignity, and those who consider man merely a pawn of the state. The times are so critical and the difference between these world systems so vital and vast that grave doubt is cast upon the validity of neutralistic argument."[49] In June 1956, Dulles described neutralism as a concept which "pretends that a nation can best gain safety for itself by being indifferent to the fate of others. This has increasingly become an ob-

47. Nuechterlein, pp. 127, 132.
48. Meyer, pp. 168–170; George Taylor, pp. 208–210.
49. *Public Papers,* Eisenhower, 1954, p. 116.

solete conception and, except under exceptional circumstances, it is an immoral and short-sighted conception."[50]

Generally speaking, however, administration statements on neutralism were much more moderate; the desire to preserve independence was recognized and approved even though neutralism was regarded as less efficacious against the Communist threat than the collective effort from which it was said neutralists benfited despite their refusal to assume collective responsibility. The neutralists, however, wanted greater recognition of the moral content of their position. They were not flattered by well-intended comparisons between their position and that of the infant American republic. To them the early American stance was a form of isolationism permitted by geography and the circumstances of the times, while their own stance was an effort, in the interests of global peace as well as their own safety, to find a third path from which to exert a mediatory influence between two blocs, each convinced that it had a monopoly of the truth. The neutralists did not dismiss the existence of a Communist threat, but they believed that the United States, exaggerating the danger, had adopted policies that were sometimes ill-advised or dangerous.

The United States, on its side, saw the neutralists as too easily misled by Communist blandishments and anti-American propaganda. It feared that without the confidence imparted by close ties with the strong, small countries were all too likely under Communist pressure to make concessions that would endanger themselves and others as well. Accordingly, it continued to assist neutralist countries, regarding this as a constructive contribution to their defense as well as a way in which they could be favorably influenced. Indeed, American resistance to providing major economic aid through SEATO was partly inspired by the desire to avoid any implication that henceforth economic assistance would go only to military Allies. At a Colombo Plan meeting not long after SEATO was established, Harold Stassen, head of the Foreign Operations Administration, said that the United States intended to use the money released by the end of the war in Indochina to increase aid to Asia at large. In April, presenting the aid program to Congress,

50. Michael Guhin, *John Foster Dulles*, p. 257. According to Guhin, statements of this kind were addressed to domestic opponents of aid programs and military commitments abroad. However, as he concedes, the world heard them and was not necessarily aware that the intended audience was a more limited one.

Eisenhower announced that Asian aid requirements would receive higher priority and that a special presidential fund for aid to Asia would be set up to encourage countries receiving bilateral assistance to put more of what they received into regionally based cooperative enterprises. This, it was thought, would avoid waste and duplication and, incidentally, appeal to regional-minded Congressmen.[51]

The proposal, however, was not well-received in Asia. In May a meeting of Asian members of the Colombo Plan, held at Simla at Indian invitation, expressed a distinct preference for continued bilateral assistance, and opposed elaborating on Colombo Plan mechanisms or adding to them. Only Japan showed any strong interest in regional cooperation, while some of the resistance to a new emphasis on regional economic cooperation stemmed from the fear that America's real objective was to develop new markets for Japan; considerable attention was focused on the fact that the Deputy Assistant Secretary of State for Far Eastern Affairs, looking for solutions to Asian problems, had said that "above all markets must be developed for greatly increased Japanese exports."[52]

Suspicion of the Japanese was, in any case, an almost automatic reflex, but it seems likely that the re-emergence of Japanese activity in Southeast Asia, even though on a very limited scale, had sharpened the reaction. With its economy moving out of the post-Korean War doldrums and its government strengthened after the two conservative parties merged in January 1955, Japan had embarked on a somewhat more active Asian policy. Strongly sponsored by Australia, it had already joined the Colombo Plan in December 1954; in March, ECAFE met in Tokyo. In April, a thirty-member delegation, including Diet members and important business representatives, had attended the Bandung Conference, apologizing there for wartime activities and pledging increased economic assistance. In the same month, Japan agreed to settle Thai claims for compensation for yen issued during World War II which had subsequently lost their value, while, in the Philippines, reparations negotiations, which had been resumed toward the end of 1954, produced an agreement in April 1956.[53]

51. F. Parkinson, "Bandung and the Underdeveloped Countries," *Yearbook of World Affairs*, 1956, p. 81; Farley, pp. 52–53.

52. *DSB*, Oct. 18, 1954, p. 575; Gupta, pp. 80–82.

53. Olson, pp. 21–24.

CHAPTER 13

INDOCHINA: PORTENTS
FOR THE FUTURE

The Geneva arrangements had allowed for a continued and considerable French role in Indochina. In fact, however, they proved to be the prelude to virtually complete French withdrawal and to the establishment of new patterns that thereafter were to dominate the international roles of the four states of Indochina. Cambodia and Laos, confirmed in their juridical identity and independence, moved toward neutralism. For the two Vietnams—their juridical status still unresolved and their struggle still enmeshed in the Cold War—there could be no question of nonalignment.

In Cambodia, Sihanouk held the reins. Although his policies quickly became basically neutralist, by seeming to veer erratically from one side to the other he excited both deep suspicion and ardent courtship. Cambodia's relations with its neighbors, Thailand and South Vietnam, were troubled by long-standing frictions and, in the first of periodic eruptions as in later ones, relations with the United States suffered also.

Laos, with Communist China, North Vietnam, and South Vietnam all on its borders, faced more difficult and sensitive problems in determining the course of its foreign relations; its commitment to Pathet Lao integration into national political life added further complexities. Moreover, it was even less well-equipped than Cambodia to handle the problems of national independence. It lacked the national unity of the Khmer. Its king, only recently elevated to rule over the whole country, could not claim the support of tradition for a role like Sihanouk's, nor did he have the temperament to do so. With no individual focus of leadership, the balance of power between the competing elements of the small political elite determined the degree to which the government of the day practiced neutralism and sought accommodation with the Pathet Lao.

Remaining convinced that the line against Communist advance must be held in Indochina, the United States became increasingly involved there as France withdrew, with South Vietnam the focal point of its activities. Addressing the National Assembly on July 22, 1954, Mendès-France had said, it is the end of a nightmare.[1] Dulles took a different view. Looking back some time later, he saw new opportunities for the United States to do the job right in Vietnam. "We have a clean base there now, without a taint of colonialism." Dien Bien Phu, he thought, "was a blessing in disguise."[2]

It was not only Dulles who welcomed the opportunity to put into practice the precepts the United States had long unsuccessfully urged upon the French. Across the spectrum of American political thinking, from the anti-Communist left to the anti-Communist right, there were strong hopes that a truly nationalist leader, supported by the United States and receptive to its advice, could create in South Vietnam a bulwark of political and economic democracy.[3] More and more, it appeared to Americans—some originally quite skeptical—that Ngo Dinh Diem was the man to do the job and that all available means should be employed not only to strengthen him against his Communist enemies in the North but also against his French and Vietnamese opponents in the South.

Cambodia: Assertive Neutralism

Cambodia's last-minute intervention at Geneva had shown the strength of its desire to be free to seek protection in a world where simple pledges of respect for independence and territorial integrity might not be fully efficacious. Even during the conference, according to Cambodian sources, a specific defense commitment was sought from the United States.[4] This was not forthcoming, and Cambodia had to be content with the protection afforded by the SEATO umbrella. At the beginning of October, however, when the American Ambassador presented his credentials he delivered a presidential message

1. Pierre Mendès-France, *Sept Mois et Dix-Sept Jours,* p. 35.
2. Emmet Hughes, *The Ordeal of Power,* p. 208.
3. Richard Barnet, *Intervention and Revolution,* p. 198.
4. Roger Smith, *Cambodia,* pp. 69–70.

expressing American admiration for the "Khmer struggle against Communist aggression," and offering "to consider ways in which our two countries can more effectively cooperate in the joint task of stemming the threats facing your territories and maintaining peace and prosperity in your kingdom."[5]

Armed with this expression of American sympathy, Sihanouk then sought to demonstrate that he was not aligning himself with the American camp. In November, after a visit to Burma, he declared "to safeguard themselves, the large and small nations of Southeast Asia should deploy all of their goodwill in order to create a center of pacific resistance to all pacts or alliances susceptible to provoking world conflicts. That is to say, a large group of nations should observe neutrality strictly." Shortly afterwards, Premier Penn Nouth announced that Cambodia would adopt a neutral posture; it would continue to welcome aid from the United States and France, but it would not sign any aid agreement compromising freedom of action in foreign affairs.[6]

Thereafter, Sihanouk devoted much of his attention to consolidating his internal position which, without any immediate Viet Minh threat and with independence achieved, was coming under stronger attack especially from his old adversary Son Ngoc Thanh. In February, he conducted a referendum on his policies in which he won the support of 84 percent of the voters; in March, he abdicated in favor of his father in order, he said, to be free to work more closely with his people.

Meanwhile, military assistance negotiations were underway with the United States. Perhaps anticipating Communist objections, Sihanouk assured Chou at Bandung that his arrangements with the United States would not result in an American presence in Cambodia. He then took care to publicize the outcome of his discussions with Communist leaders. "China and North Vietnam," he said, "have assured me that they will respect [the] independence, political ideology, and sovereignty of my country."[7] Sihanouk's assurances to Chou notwithstanding, however, a month after the Bandung Conference, an aid agreement with the United States provided that American military advisors would

5. *DSB,* Oct. 25, 1954, p. 615.
6. Roger Smith, *Cambodia,* pp. 73–74.
7. Fifield, p. 385.

supervise the distribution and use of U.S. supplies for the Khmer armed forces. Moreover, Cambodia committed itself under article 511(a) of the Mutual Security Act to make the full contribution permitted by its capabilities to developing and maintaining "its own defensive strength and the defensive strength of the free world." Whatever may have been their understanding of Sihanouk's explanations at Bandung, Peking and Moscow protested that the pact went beyond the legitimate Cambodian defense needs, violated the Geneva terms, and constituted "a military alliance with the United States, the leader of the SEATO Aggressive bloc."

Although the domestic political opposition echoed these criticisms, it appeared that Communist objections, having been registered, were not to be pursued further. In June, the tripartite Supervisory Commission, its Polish member concurring, concluded that the agreement did not compromise Cambodia's Geneva obligations. In reaching this conclusion, the commission accepted Cambodia's interpretation of the term "free World" as including "all freedom-loving nations, and not only the western bloc," its contention that the United States was well aware of Cambodia's nonaligned position when it negotiated the agreement, and its statement that "the Royal Government will not contribute to the defensive strength of the free world unless its own security is dangerously threatened. The commitment . . . is therefore quite illusory so far as Cambodia is concerned until a new situation arises."[8]

These explanations notwithstanding, Cambodia had gone further than other Southeast Asian neutrals in concluding a military assistance pact and in accepting aid under article 511(a). Perhaps partly because of this, Sihanouk was acutely sensitive to what he believed were efforts to make him go even further. At the beginning of February in Manila, he interpreted statements made by Filipino leaders as American-instigated attempts to push him into a more prowestern policy. He reacted by more explicitly stating his neutrality, declaring in Peking, "Cambodia is neutral . . . the SEATO has told us that we would be automatically protected. We reject such protection which can only bring us dishonor." American aid, moreover, was now to be balanced

8. Roger Smith, *Cambodia,* pp. 81–83; Modelski, p. 151; Sar Desai, pp. 122–124.

by an aid agreement with Peking, the first negotiated with a non-Communist country, under which the PRC provided some $22 million to construct a number of factories and other facilities.

Meanwhile, Cambodia had become involved in difficulties with South Vietnam and Thailand which Sihanouk, still smarting over his experience in the Philippines, believed were related to the pressures he attributed to the United States. The charges exchanged among the three Southeast Asian countries were to become familiar over the years. Thailand accused Cambodia of illegally arresting its nationals and failing to halt cross-border marauding and kidnapping expeditions; Cambodia charged Thailand with illegal occupation of disputed territory and with permitting Son Ngoc Thanh, who had taken refuge in Thailand late in 1954, to conduct raids into Cambodia. South Vietnam, although, like Thailand, closing its frontier with Cambodia, made no formal charges; it was evident, however, that Ngo Dinh Diem was irritated by a Khmer press campaign featuring accusations of South Vietnamese border violations and reviving Cambodian territorial claims in Cochin China. Cambodia accused South Vietnamese planes of overflying its territory and South Vietnamese patrol boats of seizing Khmer fishing vessels. By late April, however, the situation had calmed. The American Ambassador assured King Suramarit that the United States did not question Cambodia's neutral policy and did not hope to establish bases in Cambodia. Meeting with Foreign Minister Nong Kimny, Dulles denied that the United States had instigated Thai and Vietnamese actions or was attempting to force Cambodia to join SEATO. On April 19, the governments of South Vietnam and Thailand announced their readiness to resume formal relations.[9]

His relations with his neighbors calmed and American respect for his neutrality reaffirmed, Sihanouk then announced that he would establish relations with Communist countries "not necessarily to counterbalance western influence," he said, "but it will work that way." Paying state visits to the Soviet Union, Poland, and Czechoslovakia, he negotiated aid agreements committing Moscow to construct a hospital in Phnom Penh for which Warsaw would provide surgical facilities, while Prague promised to send a mission to Cambodia to negotiate trade and aid agreements. In November Chou and Sihanouk,

9. Roger Smith, *Cambodia*, pp. 91–104; Herz, p. 128.

meeting in Phnom Penh, paid tribute to the Five Principles, and there was soon a large Chinese economic aid mission in Cambodia.[10]

Laos: Uncertain Neutralism

In Laos, meanwhile, leadership alternated between representatives of two different strains of thinking—Souvanna Phouma and Katay Don Sasorith. Souvanna, who was in office when the Geneva conference ended, was inclined toward the West, particularly France. He wanted western interest and support, but not to a degree that would excite Chinese hostility. He suspected the Thai and the Vietnamese and regarded the Pathet Lao as strayed members of the national community who could be won back by conciliatory policies permitting them to participate in politics and government. Katay shared Souvanna's suspicions of the Vietnamese, but tended to see the Pathet Lao as irretrievably subject to the Viet Minh and as instruments of North Vietnamese expansionist urges in the Mekong valley. Like many southern Lao, he regarded the ethnic Lao living on the Thai side of the border as close kin and saw his country's interests as lying in warm relations with Thailand.[11]

By November 1954, when Katay succeeded Souvanna in office, the Pathet Lao had regrouped in the two northern provinces. There, with North Vietnamese advice and assistance, they were establishing political, administrative, and military institutions, while resisting efforts to establish royal government authority. Negotiations proceeded sporadically, the key point at issue being the government's right to take over administration in the two provinces before a general election. When elections were scheduled for December 1955 the Pathet Lao refused to participate on the grounds that their legitimate demands had not been met.[12]

Meanwhile, the Franco-American agreements of September 1954 had permitted direct American assistance to the Lao government. As they were to do even more vigorously in South Vietnam, Americans soon began to displace the French. The latter were anxious to preserve

10. Roger Smith, *Cambodia*, pp. 104–108.
11. Saul Rose (ed.), *Politics in Southern Asia*, pp. 178–179; Hugh Toye, pp. 106–107.
12. Dommen, pp. 79, 83; Langer and Zasloff, pp. 60, 62; Toye, p. 108.

their position and influence in Laos and concerned that under American pressure the government would move against the Pathet Lao to the point of precipitating renewed hostilities. The requirements of the war in Algiers, however, made them unable to maintain even the military presence authorized at Geneva or to fulfill completely their military training commitments. American influence accordingly became a new and important factor on the Lao scene. By February 1955, when Dulles visited Vientiane and assured the government of American support, a United States Operations Mission was already in place, and the United States had committed itself to budgetary support for the Lao army. By the end of the year, a Program Evaluation Office staffed by retired American officers, was overseeing the use of military assistance and beginning to take over French training responsibilities. In fiscal 1956, American aid rose from the $40.9 million of the preceding fiscal year to $75.7 million, of which about one-third was for military equipment.[13]

This increased role had not developed without controversy in the American government. In discussions beginning after the signature of the Manila Treaty in September 1954, the Joint Chiefs had argued against American support for the Lao military on the grounds that, without American advisors to supervise its training, assistance to the Lao army would be of little utility. In 1955, the Chiefs reiterated that mutual security support for the Lao army could not be recommended "from the military point of view" but conceded that the political considerations advanced by the State Department might be over-riding, as indeed they proved to be.[14]

While welcoming support from the United States, Katay also sought closer relations with Thailand. In February 1955, he visited Bangkok to discuss defense problems and the promotion of trade and communications. Thereafter, a military mission visited Thailand, several Lao army officers and a larger number of police personnel were trained there, a Thai-Lao trading company was established, and economic ties—stimulated by the transit through Thailand of most U.S. goods—were strengthened.[15]

At Bandung, responding to earlier Lao complaints about North

13. Charles Stevenson, *The End of Nowhere*, pp. 32–39; Dommen, p. 104.
14. Dommen, pp. 97–101.
15. Zacher and Milne, p. 247; Toye, p. 108.

Vietnamese interference, Chou arranged a meeting between Katay and Pham Van Dong. It was agreed that relations between Laos and the DRV were to be developed and harmonized within the framework of the Five Principles, and the DRY declared the settlement between the Lao government and the Pathet Lao to be a question of "internal order" which the two parties were "entirely free to solve in the higher interests of the country and people of Laos."[16]

Back in Laos, Katay, perhaps encouraged by PRC and DRV promises of nonintervention, moved more troops into the two northern provinces. There, however, Pathet Lao behavior seemed to reflect Pham Van Dong's words in Hanoi a month before the Bandung Conference: "For the independence of their countries, the peoples of Vietnam, Cambodia, and Laos are determined to consolidate their alliance and continue the War of Resistance with all their might."[17] Sporadic armed encounters continued despite a meeting in Rangoon between Katay and Souphanouvong late in the year.

In March 1956, Katay accepted SEATO protection. Laos, he said, "has common borders with Red China and North Vietnam and, therefore is much exposed to Communist menaces. . . . Though . . . not a signatory of the Manila Pact it lies within the protective orbit of the Treaty. It is satisfying to receive the promises of the United States [with regard to] their will to defend the principles of security and mutual aid in this part of the world."[18]

In the same month, however, Souvanna resumed office, and it began to appear that steps taken earlier by the Pathet Lao and the tripartite supervisory commission might provide the basis for an internal settlement. On January 6 at Sam Neua the Pathet Lao established what was described as a mass political party, the *Neo Lao Hak Sat* (NLHS; the Lao Patriotic Front) and issued a manifesto implying interest in a coalition government. Meanwhile, the supervisory commission, which had got off to a late start in Laos, declared that "the sovereign right of the Royal Government to establish its administration in the Lao northern provinces was undisputed." Significantly, the Polish member

16. Kahin, *Asian-African Conference*, p. 27.
17. Pham Van Dong, *Achievements of the Vietnamese People's War of Resistance*, p. 9.
18. Bernard Fall, "The International Relations of Laos," *Pacific Affairs*, XXX (March, 1957), p. 29.

merely abstained. Then in April, in a letter replete with references to peace, tranquility, and the Five Principles, Souphanouvong proposed to Souvanna that negotiations be resumed.[19]

Anxious to take advantage of the new atmosphere and at the same time to maximize pressure on the Pathet Lao, Souvanna arranged to visit Hanoi and Peking in August. According to Sisouk Na Champassak, a member of the delegation, the visit—opposed by the United States and Thailand—"had one purpose: to create a favorable climate for negotiations with the Pathet Lao." Joint declarations of non-interference, Souvanna realized, might be of little real effect but would at least leave the Pathet Lao "theoretically isolated in its dealings with the legal government." In both capitals, Souvanna was received with fanfare and warmth (as he was also in Saigon where he visited next). With negotiations under way, prospects for agreement within Laos now seemed brighter, but more than a year was to elapse before the coalition government, accepted in principle in Vientiane in August 1956, was to become a reality.[20]

Vietnam: The Division Hardens

In the years before the Geneva settlement, Americans had become convinced that the Communists were succeeding in Vietnam largely because the French did not understand the nationalist revolution. This had enabled Ho to capture a legitimate desire for independence and exploit it to his own ends. The French had failed to provide the essential ingredients of successful resistance: genuine independence, and a true nationalist leader free of colonialist ties, incorruptible, and sensitive to popular needs and aspirations. If such a leader were given well-trained troops who would fight aggressively and who would be supported by the people because their aspirations for independence, social justice, and economic betterment were being satisfied, then, Americans thought, the national revolution could be recaptured. Ho, revealed as the puppet of international communism, would no longer be able to win the nationalist competition by default.

In August 1954, the opportunity had come to apply the American doctrine. History, it seemed, had provided a clean page: the past had been French; the future would be American. There was considerable

19. Dommen, p. 84; Sar Desai, p. 178; Stevenson, pp. 31–32.
20. Sisouk, pp. 49–50; Dommen, p. 96; Rose (ed.), p. 179.

pessimism that alone, or with only French tutelage, any of the non-Communist states of Indochina could survive Communist pressures. But there was great optimism that, with American advice and support, the picture could be changed substantially.

Both strains were evident in an estimate issued by the Director of Central Intelligence in August 1954. Alone, the outlook for Indochina was bleak: "without outside support the Indochinese states cannot become strong enough to withstand Communist pressures." A continued French role would do little to improve the prospects for survival: "We do not believe there will be the dramatic transformation in French policy necessary to win the active loyalty and support of the local population for a South Vietnam government." But the outlook might be considerably altered by firm support from the United States: if the Indochinese "are given opportunity, guidance, and material help in building national states, they may be able to attain viability."[21]

The belief that it was strategically important to the United States that Vietnam should be preserved remained as strong after Geneva as it had been before. Speaking on "America's Stake in Vietnam" in 1956, Senator John F. Kennedy declared "Vietnam represents the cornerstone of the Free World in Southeast Asia, the keystone to the arch, the finger in the dike. Burma, Thailand, India, Japan, the Philippines and obviously Laos and Cambodia are among those whose security would be threatened if the red tide of Communism overflowed into Vietnam. . . . Her economy is essential to the economy of all of Southeast Asia. The fundamental tenets of this nation's foreign policy . . . depend in considerable measure upon a strong and free Vietnam."

Strength and freedom, moreover, were conceived not merely in terms of military security; social and political reform were an essential element of American doctrine. Thus Kennedy laid great stress on political and economic progress citing as "the first vital steps toward true democracy," the proclamation of a republic and the election of a national assembly, the improvement of the position of the peasants through land reform, farm cooperatives, and other measures, and the passage of legislation improving labor relations, working conditions, and wages. Much remained to be done, and American assistance re-

21. *Pentagon Papers,* X, 691–698.

mained indispensable. The United States must offer the Vietnamese "a revolution—a political, economic and social revolution far superior to anything the Communists can offer. . . . We must supply capital to replace that drained by centuries of colonial exploitation; technicians to train those handicapped by deliberate policies of illiteracy; guidance to assist a nation taking those first feeble steps toward the complexities of a republican form of government. . . . We must provide military assistance to rebuild the new Vietnamese Army, which every day faces the growing peril of Vietminh armies across the border."[22]

In August 1954, French involvement remained considerable. The nightmare might be over, but there were a few bad dreams still to come as Ngo Dinh Diem struggled to assert his primacy amidst conflicts between French and Americans over his role and their own.

The Expeditionary Corps alone amounted to 350,000 men, the Vietnamese National Army to some 250,000 more, both under French command and financial control. French ties with some of the elements of an acutely unstable local political forum were close and long-standing; the sects, for example, whose own military formations amounted to some 40,000 men, had long been subsidized by the French in return for partial cooperation against the Viet Minh. French economic interests were substantial in both North and South. Their juridical role in the South remained to be settled; the complete independence within the French Union pledged in April was not yet clearly defined, much less fully implemented. Meanwhile, as signatory to the arrangements at Geneva, France had assumed additional obligations, not only military ones under the provisions for cease-fire, regroupment of military forces, and exchange of prisoners, but also political ones having to do with civil administration, individual rights, and the projected 1956 elections.

In seeking ways to fulfill their responsibilities, reduce some of their burdens, and retain some of their privileges, the French, as usual, were divided. Three governments wrestled with these problems between 1954 and 1956, those of Mendès-France, Edgar Faure, and Guy Mollet. The French in Paris and the French in Vietnam frequently saw things differently, and the latter were divided between those whose principal thought was for preserving their own privileges and those primarily concerned with the survival of a non-Communist South

22. Wesley Fishel, *Vietnam: Anatomy of a Conflict,* pp. 142–146.

Vietnam within the French Union. French of all persuasions confronting Diem knew they confronted a man obsessed with his mission, a man who was uncompromising and bitterly anti-French. Some saw advantages to themselves or to France in promoting the fortunes of more flexible, cooperative, or venal elements, particularly those of sect and military leaders; others, like General Ely, the last French High Commissioner in Vietnam, were genuinely concerned that Diem's rigidity, his inability to work closely with those outside his narrow family circle, and his lack of contact or empathy with the general public would quickly undermine South Vietnam's prospects for political survival. Meanwhile, threats to the French position in Morocco and Algiers were becoming even stronger, making more urgent the problem of where best to employ limited French resources.

Whatever the policy inconsistencies created by these complex and conflicting strains, there remained a consistent trend toward disengagement. Mendès-France was concerned over frictions within the Atlantic alliance and was determined to avoid conflict with the United States over Vietnam in order to conserve French bargaining power in Washington for issues of greater importance to him. Under Mollet, the desire to extricate France from the Cold War and move toward active coexistence dominated foreign policy.[23]

As Dulles recognized, differing objectives were a major source of Franco-American conflict. The French, he said to Mendès-France in December 1954, "had an investment in lives and property"; the Americans had an investment in the security of Southeast Asia and were concerned with the effects there of the fate of Vietnam.[24] American policy makers, however, did not seem fully aware of the inconsistency involved in urging the French to maintain a presence—particularly a military one—to protect Vietnam in a transitional period, while at the same time pressing them to relinquish all authority there. Nor, as the United States took the first steps toward replacing the French, were American policy makers united in believing this the proper course and Diem the proper instrument.

Dulles himself, while recognizing Diem's limitations and drawbacks, believed that only under Diem was there even a prospect for preserving

23. LaCouture and Devillers, pp. 319–324; Hammer, pp. 347–350, 354–356; Buttinger, II, 872–874; *Pentagon Papers,* I, Part IV A3, pp. 1–7.
24. *Pentagon Papers,* X, p. 832.

Vietnam from Communist control—to him an urgent necessity. Military leaders were more hesitant and dubious. The Joint Chiefs were not entirely convinced of the desirability of the major effort involved in training as well as financing a Vietnamese army, and believed that American resources might be more profitably employed in strengthening the anti-Communist front elsewhere. In a memorandum to the Secretary of Defense on September 22, they conceded that Indochina was "an important part of Southeast Asia and merits limited United States support." But, they argued, existing U.S.-supported military programs in Southeast Asia "possess a capability of producing effective military forces," whereas in Vietnam "it may be several years before an effective military force will exist." Accordingly, "military support to that area, including the training and equipping of forces, should be accomplished at low priority and not at the expense of other U.S. military programs and should not be permitted to impair the development through MDA [Mutual Defense Act] programs of effective and reliable allied forces elsewhere."[25] The Chiefs' reservations, moreover, must have been buttressed by the intermittent pessimism of the President's special representative, General J. Lawton Collins, sent to Vietnam in November 1954 on what was envisaged as a short-term mission but which became in effect an ambassadorial assignment, continuing until April 1955.

The advantage lay with Dulles, however. Evading the specific questions at issue, the NSC on August 20 had nevertheless called for "every possible effort, not openly inconsistent with the U.S. position as to the armistice agreements . . . to maintain a friendly non-Communist South Vietnam and to prevent a Communist victory through all-Vietnam elections," and for "assisting . . . free Vietnam to maintain . . . military forces necessary for internal security" while "working through the French only insofar as necessary." At moments of decision this NSC-sanctioned call to action, however vague, seems to have bolstered Dulles' case; so too did Congressional sympathy for strong support of Diem. And the military leaders were willing to withdraw their objections to assuming the training responsibility, with all that this implied, if the State Department were prepared to say—as Dulles was quite eager to do—that political considerations were over-riding.[26]

25. *Ibid.*, pp. 757–758.
26. *Ibid.*, pp. 737, 789.

Once this decision was made late in October, debate tended to focus not on the American role in Vietnam but on whether Diem was its best or only instrument.

Conflicts between Americans and between Americans and French tended to arise and to be resolved in the midst of crises in Saigon. Of these, two—in September 1954 and March/April 1955—were crucial. In the first, Diem clashed with the Francophile Chief of Staff, Nguyen Van Hinh, who first won sect support and then lost it to Diem. By September 26, when Franco-American discussions opened in Washington, Diem was in control by a margin that was very thin but sufficient to enable American arguments in his support to prevail. Many of the agreements reached in Washington were to strengthen his hand. Decisions to transfer authority over the Vietnamese armed forces to the Vietnamese government and to provide American aid directly to the Vietnamese government gave him access to the levers of control. In addition, the French, who had already transferred responsibility for the administration of justice, public safety, and civil aviation, agreed to cancel the Pau Agreements, through which much of their economic authority was exercised, and to permit the Vietnamese to issue their own currency. France also agreed to retain elements of the Expeditionary Corps in Vietnam, while the United States agreed to consider providing the French forces and those of the Associated States with financial support. Finally, the two governments agreed to support Diem in establishing and maintaining a strong anti-Communist and nationalist government and to urge all anti-Communist forces to cooperate with him.[27]

Before January 1, when the transfers of authority envisaged in the Washington agreements were to take place, American support for Diem was strongly and publicly recorded. In mid-October, Senator Mansfield, returning from a two-month study tour in Asia, endorsed Diem's intense nationalism and incorruptibility and recommended that, if he lost control, the United States should consider suspending its aid to Vietnam and to the French Union Forces. On October 23, President Eisenhower, in a letter to Diem, reaffirmed promises of aid, indicating at the same time that he expected in return adherence to performance standards and necessary reforms. He expressed American hopes for a

27. *Ibid.*, p. 765; LaCouture and Devillers, pp. 340–343; Buttinger, II, 862; *DSB*, Oct. 11, 1954, p. 534.

government "so responsive to the nationalist aspirations of the people, so enlightened in purpose and effective in performance, that it will be respected both at home and abroad and discourage any who might wish to impose a foreign ideology on your free people."[28]

Arriving in Saigon in November, General Collins declared that the United States was "not interested in training or otherwise aiding a Vietnamese Army which does not give complete and implicit obedience to the Premier." He had not been there long, however, before he developed grave doubts, strengthened by his discussions with General Ely, over Diem's prospects for success. In January he reported to the NSC that Diem's position seemed somewhat stronger and that there was now "at least an even chance that Vietnam can be saved from Communism if the present programs of its Government are fully implemented." Already many members of the U.S. mission were deeply involved in this effort. Colonel Edward Lansdale, who had earlier played a key role in Magsaysay's successful counterinsurgency campaign in the Philippines, had long been providing Diem with advice and assistance in his efforts to bring the sects under control. Collins had discussed with Diem the reorganization of the armed forces; other American officials were helping with plans to resettle refugees, create a National Assembly, regulate foreign exchange, and establish import controls, while Michigan State University was about to sign a contract to provide training in public administration and police methods. But, as Collins observed, efforts to persuade Diem to broaden the base of his government had been of no avail.[29]

In February, when arrangements for the American training role were just getting under way, tensions revived, as sect leaders, no longer subsidized by the French, sought to force Diem into new arrangements. In a crisis that waxed and waned throughout March and April and into May, Diem faced the strongest challenge he was to meet until 1963. Collins joined the French in urging that the Diem regime must be replaced by a more broadly based government, meeting with some Defense Department sympathy, where it was argued that the "concept of making U.S. support dependent exclusively on Diem's continuance in power is not valid." Dulles, although prepared to face the prospect

28. *Public Papers,* Eisenhower, 1954, p. 949; Lancaster, p. 351.

29. Lancaster, p. 352; Edward Lansdale, *In the Midst of Wars, passim; Pentagon Papers,* IX, 866–876.

that Diem might have to go—at least to the point where State Department officers drafted telegrams setting out elaborate procedures for replacing him—nevertheless remained reluctant to endorse this course. He doubted that there was a better candidate. And, at least as a debating point, he advanced the argument that U.S. credibility might be at stake. "It is widely known," he cabled to Collins, "that Diem has so far existed by reason of U.S. support despite French reluctance. If, however, when the showdown comes, the French will prevail then that will gravely weaken our influence for the future both in Vietnam and elsewhere. Removal of Diem under the circumstances may well be interpreted in Vietnam and Asia as example of U.S. paying lip service to nationalist cause and then foresaking true nationalist leader when 'colonial interests' put enough pressure on us."[30]

Once again Congressional views tended to reinforce Dulles. A State Department memorandum prepared on April 30 recorded that Mansfield had issued a long statement supporting Diem the day before and that Knowland and Hubert Humphrey also backed Diem as did many others in the Senate and House. Moreover, as time passed and Diem was able to divide and defeat his enemies with the tools American support had given him—notably control of the purse strings and command of the army—American doubts again subsided. This was made unquestionably clear by the new American Ambassador, G. Frederick Reinhardt, who said on May 27, "I came here under instructions to carry out United States policy in support of the legal government of Vietnam under Premier Ngo Dinh Diem."[31]

Thereafter, Diem seemed to move from strength to strength. In October 1955 in a referendum, which it is generally agreed he would have won even without the pressures he chose to employ, 98 percent of those voting favored the dethronement of Bao Dai and the establishment of a republic with Diem as its president. By February 1956 a campaign against the sects initiated in 1955 had brought them under complete control. Constant pressure on France, no longer inclined in any case toward vigorous resistance and still heavily dependent on American assistance as it sought to retain its empire in Africa, brought a rapid end to the French presence. In April the Expeditionary Corps, now very small, was withdrawn at Vietnamese request, and the French

30. *Pentagon Papers,* IX, 908, 930, 945.
31. Buttinger, II, p. 886.

High Command was dissolved. In August, South Vietnam established a mission for liaison with the trilateral supervisory commission to replace the mission withdrawn by the French, at the same time disclaiming any responsibility for implementing the Geneva agreements.[32]

Meanwhile, the DRV was also going through a period of internal consolidation. It was evident from what Pham Van Dong had to say to the DRV's National Assembly in 1955 that this, rather than any immediate action in the South, was the first task. "To consolidate the North means to consolidate the essential bases which will be the decisive factor in the struggle for national liberation, in the basic and immediate struggle to consolidate peace and realize unity." To be sure, while carrying out the essential tasks in the North—economic development, national defense, and land reform—it was necessary to pay attention to the compatriots in the South. But theirs, it seemed, was to be largely a holding operation. "We must make our actions thoroughly understood to our compatriots in the South so that they are more enthusiastic, confident, and actively take part in the nationwide struggle."[33]

With a strong and cohesive leadership, a disciplined cadre structure, and a battle-proved army, the DRV did not face the political problems that were so destabilizing in the South. It had the will and ability to destroy any domestic opposition, and its problems in this regard were diminished with the flight of 65 percent of its Roman Catholic community to the South.[34] Nevertheless, its administrative and economic problems were formidable. Viet Minh experience in administration had been largely in the rural and less-populated areas. Now in taking over the North—a process completed when the French left Hanoi in October 1954—it was assuming responsibility for urban areas and for the most modern and industrialized segment of Indochina's economy. The latter, moreover, had felt most sharply the impact of wartime destruction; there were difficult tasks ahead of restoration and reconstruction.

These tasks and the burdens they imposed on the general population were not lightened by the regime's rigidly ideological approach.

32. Randle, p. 473.

33. Pham Van Dong, *Our Struggle in the Past and at Present*, pp. 54, 55.

34. Estimates of the number of Catholics among the approximately 900,000 refugees run from 600,000 to 800,000 (Buttinger, II, 900).

Transportation and the industrial sector were to be restored and military forces were to be enlarged and re-equipped. And achieving both of these tasks at a forced-draft pace was to be given much higher priority than the welfare of the general population, which was subject, in addition, to a radical and ruthlessly enforced land redistribution program begun and dropped in 1953 but resumed late in 1955.[35]

There had been some hope in France when the war ended that a continued role in the South could be combined with a relationship with the North, preserving French interests and influence there and limiting Hanoi's dependence on Moscow and Peking. Mendès-France apparently shared this hope, although he was not willing to pursue it to the point of causing serious difficulties with French opponents like General Ely or with the United States. A principal proponent was Jean Sainteny, who had negotiated the March 1948 agreement with the DRV and regarded himself, with some justice, as personally acceptable to Ho and other Viet Minh leaders.

In August 1954, Mendès-France announced that Sainteny had been appointed Delegate General of the French Republic in Hanoi. Arriving in October, Sainteny was cordially received by Ho but was unable to further his principal mission: the establishment of a cooperative economic relationship based on the extensive French commercial and industrial interests in the North. Despite Sainteny's own hopes, neither side approached this prospect with any real enthusiasm. On the French side, business interests as well as the government were influenced by American opposition. In addition, having already experienced Communist expropriation measures in South China, businessmen were unable to take very seriously the prospects of a profitable relationship with the Vietnamese Communists. The DRV itself seemed quite disinclined toward such a relationship. Its own concept of how the economy should be organized barred any real or lasting cooperation with French capitalists. It regarded the French as accomplices with the United States—in SEATO, in maintaining Diem in power, and in planning to ignore the Geneva requirement for elections in 1956. Its hostility had been accentuated, moreover, by the extensive removals of industrial equipment that had accompanied the French evacuation. Before the end of 1955 the DRV had made its policies

35. *Ibid.*, II, 819–916; Fall, *Two Viet-Nams,* pp. 152–168.

clear; the French-owned enterprises—some 150 in number—had been nationalized with no compensation except for the Hon Gay coal mines and the Hanoi public transportation system.[36]

To the extent that the DRV looked abroad for economic assistance, it turned to its fellow Communist countries. In 1954 and 1955 two agreements were negotiated with Communist China, one with the Soviet Union. The first agreement with Peking provided manpower, equipment, and technical assistance for restoring the railway the French had built from Hanoi to Kunming, and for building another line to the Chinese border, as well as for restoring highways, dikes, and canals. In addition, the DRV was assisted in restoring the civil aviation, postal, and telecommunications links between the two countries. In the aid agreement of 1955, assistance to the amount of $200 million was provided, Chinese technicians were assigned to North Vietnamese factories, and Vietnamese workers were sent to Chinese factories for training. In the same year an agreement with the Soviet Union brought $100 million in aid. As under the agreement with Communist China, Soviet technicians were sent to North Vietnam and Vietnamese workers to Russia. Rice, obtained in the Soviet barter arrangements with Burma, was provided to relieve desperate shortages. Barter and aid agreements were also signed with Czechoslovakia, Hungary, Poland, and Rumania.

The DRV joined other members of the Communist bloc in promoting peaceful coexistence. Nehru was an early and honored visitor to Hanoi. In the joint statement issued during his visit in October 1954, the DRV expressed its adherence to the Five Principles and its desire to apply them in relations with Laos, Cambodia, and other countries as well. At Bandung, Pham Van Dong, following Chou's wake, reiterated the DRV's peaceful intentions toward Laos and Cambodia and toward Thailand.[37]

Whatever its real expectations of the Geneva provision for elections in 1956, the DRV kept the issue well to the fore, starting early in 1955. In April of that year in a joint communiqué issued during Pham Van Dong's visit to New Delhi, India and North Vietnam supported free elections in Vietnam and reunification under the Geneva

36. LaCouture and Devillers, pp. 352–360; Buttinger, II, 901–903; Hammer, pp. 341–344.
37. Lancaster, pp. 368–375; Hammer, pp. 344–345.

terms. On June 6, the DRV declared its willingness to enter into the consultations concerning the 1956 elections which the final declaration of the Geneva Conference had scheduled to begin on July 20, 1955. Not long afterward this initiative was endorsed by Bulganin and Nehru while, on July 5, Peking joined with Hanoi in reiterating the demand for elections. On July 19, Pham Van Dong wrote directly to Ngo Dinh Diem formally proposing that representatives of the North and South begin consultations.

Diem's response, emerging piecemeal and slowly, was clearly negative. His government, he said in a broadcast on July 16, did not consider itself bound by the Geneva agreements which had been signed against the will of the Vietnamese people. He supported reunification and did not exclude free elections as a means of bringing it about, but such elections must indeed be free and "faced with a regime of oppression as practiced by the Communists we remain skeptical concerning the possibility of fulfilling the conditions of free elections in the North." In August a government statement reiterated this position, adding that "nothing constructive could be achieved in the way of reunifying the country through elections as long as the Communist regime in North Vietnam does not allow each Vietnamese citizen to enjoy the democratic freedoms and fundamental rights of man." In September, Diem announced that there could be "no question of a conference, even less of negotiations."[38]

To all of this, and to the obvious prospect as the date approached that the scheduled elections would not take place, the international response was quite bland, even more so in 1956 than in 1955. The United States generally endorsed Diem's contention that it was fruitless to expect genuinely free elections in the North and that, since South Vietnam had neither signed the cease-fire agreement nor accepted the final declaration, it was not bound by the Geneva election provisions. France and Britain preferred to maintain the *status quo*, particularly as it began to appear that Diem had succeeded in stabilizing the political situation. Had Moscow pressed strongly, their position might have shifted, but this, it became apparent, Moscow had no intention of doing. At the Geneva Summit, Molotov raised the question with Eden; when the western powers agreed to join the Soviet Union in urging

38. B. S. N. Murti, *Vietnam Divided*, pp. 183, 184; Franklin Weinstein, *Vietnam's Unheld Elections*, pp. 24–39.

Diem to comply with the Geneva provisions he did not press for further action. Again in 1956 formal moves were undertaken, at least for the record. In April and May, at British initiative, the cochairmen met in London for talks which, according to the British note, were to be directed primarily toward preserving peace and only "secondly towards the eventual achievement of a political solution in Vietnam." As a result of these deliberations, the governments of North and South Vietnam were invited to submit their views concerning the timing of consultations and elections, and were urged, in view of the dissolution of the French High Command on April 28, to cooperate with the tripartite supervisory commission. Neither government in responding made any specific recommendations about consultations or elections; both affirmed their commitment to a peaceful solution and their willingness to cooperate with the supervisory commission.[39]

Thereafter, although the DRV continued to condemn the failure to hold elections, it received little more than propaganda support from Peking and Moscow. The Soviet position reflected a more general shift to the principle that the reunification of divided countries was a matter to be decided between the governments of both countries. To others, it now appeared—whatever might be the ultimate aspirations of Saigon or Hanoi—that, as in divided Germany and divided Korea, a *status quo* had been accepted which might persist for some time to come. The problems of Vietnam had not retired into the obscurity from which they emerged in 1949. But in the world of 1956, soon to be faced with Hungary and Suez, and with little ability to foresee crises to come, Indochina's problems no longer loomed very large.

39. *SIA*, 1955–1956, pp. 272–274; Brian Crozier, "The International Situation in Indochina," *Pacific Affairs*, XXIX (Dec., 1956), pp. 310–314.

BIBLIOGRAPHY

BOOKS, MONOGRAPHS, AND ARTICLES

Acheson, Dean. *Present at the Creation.* New York: W. W. Norton, 1969.

Albinski, Henry S. *Australian Policies and Attitudes toward China.* Princeton, N.J.: Princeton University Press, 1966.

———. *Australia's Search for Regional Security in Southeast Asia.* Unpublished dissertation. University of Minnesota, 1959.

Ambekar, G. V., and V. D. Divekar. *Documents on China's Relations with South and Southeast Asia, 1949–1962.* Bombay: Allied Publishers Ltd., 1964.

Anderson, Benedict R. O'G. *Some Aspects of Indonesian Politics under the Japanese Occupation.* Ithaca, N.Y.: Cornell Modern Indonesia Project, 1961.

Asian Relations, being the report of the proceedings and documentation of the First Asian Relations Conference. New Delhi: Asian Relations Organization, 1948.

Barnet, Richard J. *Intervention and Revolution.* Cleveland, Ohio: New American Library Inc., 1968.

———. *Roots of War.* New York: Atheneum, 1972.

Barnett, A. Doak. *Asia and Africa in Session: Random Notes on the Asian-African Conference.* New York: American Universities Field Staff, May 18, 1955.

———. *Chou En-lai at Bandung: Chinese Communist Diplomacy at the Asian-African Conference.* New York: American Universities Field Staff, May 4, 1955.

Bator, Victor. *Vietnam, a Diplomatic Tragedy: The Origins of United States Involvement.* Dobbs Ferry, N.Y.: Oceana, 1965.

Beloff, Max. *Soviet Policy in the Far East, 1944–1951.* London: Oxford University Press, 1953.

Benda, Harry J. *The Crescent and the Rising Sun.* The Hague and Bandung: Van Hoeve, 1958.

Berliner, Joseph S. *Soviet Economic Aid.* New York: Praeger, 1958.

Bidault, Georges. *Resistance.* New York: Praeger, 1967.

Blackton, Charles S. "The Colombo Plan," *Far Eastern Survey,* XX (Feb. 7, 1951).

Bone, Robert C. *The Dynamics of the Western New Guinea Problem*. Ithaca, N.Y.: Cornell Modern Indonesia Project, 1958.

Boorman, Howard L., et al. *Moscow-Peking Axis*. New York: Harper & Bros., 1957.

Brackman, Arnold. *Indonesian Communism: A History*. New York: Praeger, 1963.

Brecher, Michael. *India and World Politics*. New York: Praeger, 1968.

Brimmell, J. H. *Communism in Southeast Asia: A Political Analysis*. London: Oxford University Press, 1959.

Buchan, Alastair (ed.). *China and the Peace of Asia*. New York: Praeger, 1965.

Buttinger, Joseph. *Vietnam: A Dragon Embattled*. 2 vols. New York: Praeger, 1967.

Butwell, Richard. *U Nu of Burma*. Stanford, Cal.: Stanford University Press, 1963.

Byrnes, James F. *Speaking Frankly*. New York: Harper & Bros., 1947.

Cady, John F. *A History of Modern Burma*. Ithaca, N.Y.: Cornell University Press, 1958.

——. *The History of Post-War Southeast Asia*. Athens, Ohio: Ohio University Press, 1974.

Callis, Helmut G. *Foreign Capital in Southeast Asia*. New York: Institute of Pacific Relations, 1942.

Casey, R. G. *Friends and Neighbours*. Melbourne: F. W. Cheshire, 1954.

——. *Personal Experience, 1939–1946*. London: Constable, 1962.

Chatham House Study Group. *Collective Defence in Southeast Asia*. London: Royal Institute of International Affairs, 1956.

Chen, King C. *Vietnam and China, 1938–1954*. Princeton, N.J.: Princeton University Press, 1969.

Clubb, O. Edmund. *China and Russia: The Great Game*. New York: Columbia University Press, 1971.

Clubb, Oliver E., Jr. *The Effect of Chinese Nationalist Military Activities on Burmese Foreign Policy*. Santa Monica, Cal.: The RAND Corp., 1959.

Coedès, G. *The Making of South East Asia*. Tr. by H. M. Wright. London: Routledge & Kegan Paul, 1966.

Cole, Allan B. *Conflict in Indo-China and International Repercussions: A Documentary History, 1945–1955*. Ithaca, N.Y.: Cornell University Press, 1956.

Collins, J. Foster. "The United Nations and Indonesia." *International Conciliation*, No. 459 (March, 1950).

Council on Foreign Relations. *The United States in World Affairs* (USWA). New York: Harper & Bros. (John C. Campbell, ed.), 1945–1947, 1947–1948, 1948–1949; (Richard P. Stebbins, ed.), 1952, 1953, 1955.

Crocker, Isabelle. *Burma's Foreign Policy and the Korean War: A Case Study*. Santa Monica, Cal.: The RAND Corp., 1958.

Crozier, Brian. "The International Situation in Indochina." *Pacific Affairs*, XXIX (Dec., 1956).

Dallin, David J. *Soviet Foreign Policy after Stalin.* Philadelphia: Lippincott, 1961.

Darling, Frank. *Thailand and the United States.* Washington, D.C.: Public Affairs Press, 1965.

de Carmoy, Guy. *The Foreign Policies of France, 1944–1968.* Chicago, Ill., University of Chicago Press, 1970.

de Gaulle, Charles. *The War Memoirs.* Vol. III. *Salvation.* New York: Simon and Schuster, 1960.

Devillers, Philippe. *Histoire du Viet-nam de 1940 à 1952.* Paris: Editions du Seuil, 1952.

Dinerstein, Herbert S. *Sino-Soviet Conflict in the Underdeveloped Countries.* Santa Monica, Cal.: The RAND Corporation, 1964.

———. *War and the Soviet Union.* New York: Praeger, 1962.

Dommen, Arthur J. *Conflict in Laos: The Politics of Neutralization.* Rev. ed. New York: Praeger, 1971.

Donovan, William. "Our Stake in Thailand," *Fortune,* LII (July, 1955).

Drachman, Edward R. *United States Policy Toward Vietnam, 1940–1945.* Rutherford, N.J.: Fairleigh Dickinson University, 1970.

Dulles, John Foster. "Security in the Pacific," *Foreign Affairs,* XXX (January, 1952).

———. *War or Peace.* New York: Macmillan, 1950.

Dunn, Frederick S. *Peace-making and the Settlement with Japan.* Princeton, N.J.: Princeton University Press, 1963.

Dutt, Vidya Prakash, and Vishal Singh. *Indian Policies and Attitudes Towards Indo-China and S.E.A.T.O.* Twelfth Conference of the Institute of Pacific Relations. Kyoto, 1954.

Eden, Anthony. *Memoirs: Full Circle.* Boston: Houghton Mifflin, 1960.

Eggleston, F. W. *Reflections on Australia's Foreign Policy.* Melbourne: F. W. Cheshire, 1957.

Eisenhower, Dwight D. *Mandate for Change.* New York: Garden City, 1963.

Ely, Paul. *L'Indochine dans la tourmente.* Paris: Librairie Plon, 1964.

Emerson, Rupert. *From Empire to Nation: The Rise to Self-Assertion of Asian and African Peoples.* Cambridge, Mass.: Harvard University Press, 1960.

Fall, Bernard B. "The International Relations of Laos," *Pacific Affairs,* XXX (March, 1957).

———. "Tribulations of a Party Line," *Foreign Affairs,* XXXIII (April, 1955).

———. *The Two Viet-Nams.* 2nd ed., rev. New York: Praeger, 1967.

Farley, Miriam S. *United States Relations with Southeast Asia.* New York: Institute of Pacific Relations, 1955.

Feis, Herbert. *Churchill, Roosevelt, and Stalin.* Princeton, N.J.: Princeton University Press, 1957.

Feith, Herbert. *The Decline of Constitutional Democracy in Indonesia.* Ithaca, N.Y.: Cornell University Press, 1962.

Fifield, Russell H. *The Diplomacy of Southeast Asia, 1945–1958.* New York: Harper, 1958.

Finkelstein, Lawrence S. "U.S. at Impasse in Southeast Asia," *Far Eastern Survey,* XIX (Sept. 27, 1950).

Fishel, Wesley R. *Vietnam: Anatomy of a Conflict.* Itasca, Ill.: F. E. Peacock Publishers Inc., 1968.

Fisher, Charles A. *South-east Asia.* London: Methuen, 1966.

Fisher, Margaret W., and Joan W. Bondurant. *Indian Views of Sino-Indian Relations.* Berkeley, Cal.: University of California Press, 1956.

Fitzgerald, C. P. *China and Southeast Asia since 1945.* London: Longman, 1973.

Fosdick, Raymond. "Asia's Challenge to Us: Ideas Not Guns," *New York Times Magazine* (Feb. 12, 1950).

Furnivall, J. S. "Twilight in Burma: Reconquest and Crisis," *Pacific Affairs,* XXII (March, 1949).

———. "Twilight in Burma: Independence and After," *Pacific Affairs,* XXII (June, 1949).

Gilchrist, Huntington. "Colonial Questions at the San Francisco Conference," *American Political Science Review,* XXXIX (October, 1945).

Golay, Frank (ed.). *The United States and the Philippines.* Englewood Cliffs, N.J.: Prentice Hall, 1966.

Grattan, C. Hartley. *The United States and the Southwest Pacific.* Cambridge, Mass.: Harvard University Press, 1961.

Gravel, Mike (ed.). *The Senator Gravel Edition: The Pentagon Papers.* Vol. V. Boston: Beacon, 1971.

Greene, Fred. *U.S. Policy and the Security of Asia.* New York: McGraw-Hill, 1968.

Greenwood, Gordon. "Australian Attitudes toward Pacific Problems," *Pacific Affairs,* XXIII (June, 1950).

———, and Norman Harper. *Australia in World Affairs, 1950–1955.* Melbourne: F. W. Cheshire, 1957.

Grosser, Alfred. *La IV*e *République et sa politique extérieure.* Paris: Librairie Armand Colin, 1961.

Guhin, Michael A. *John Foster Dulles: A Statesman and His Times.* New York: Columbia University Press, 1972.

Gupta, Sisir. *India and Regional Integration in Asia.* New York: Asia Publishing House, 1964.

Gurney, Natalie. *History of the Territorial Dispute between Siam and French Indochina.* Baltimore, Md.: Johns Hopkins University Press, 1950.

Gurtov, Melvin. *The First Vietnam Crisis: Chinese Communist Strategy and United States Involvement, 1953–1954.* New York: Columbia University Press, 1967.

Haas, Ernest B. "The Attempt to Terminate Colonialism: Acceptance of the U.N. Trusteeship System," *International Organization,* VII (Feb., 1953).

Hall, D. G. E. *A History of South-East Asia.* 3rd ed. New York: St. Martin's Press, 1968.

Halpern, A. M. (ed.). *Policies Toward China: Views from Six Continents.* New York: McGraw Hill, 1965.

Hammer, Ellen J. *The Struggle for Indochina, 1940–1955.* Stanford, Cal.: Stanford University Press, 1966.

Harper, Norman. "Australia and Southeast Asia," *Pacific Affairs,* XXVIII (Sept., 1955).

——. "Security in the South West Pacific," *Pacific Affairs,* XXIV (June, 1951).

——, and David Sissons. *Australia and the United Nations.* New York: Carnegie Endowment for International Peace, 1959.

Hatta, Mohammad. *Portrait of a Patriot.* The Hague: Mouton Publishers, 1972.

Hayes, Samuel P. *The Beginning of American Aid to Southeast Asia.* Lexington, Mass.: Heath, 1971.

Henderson, William. *Pacific Settlement of Disputes: The Indonesian Question, 1946–1949.* New York: Woodrow Wilson Foundation, 1954.

Herz, Martin. *Short History of Cambodia.* New York: Praeger, 1958.

Hinton, Harold C. *China's Relations with Burma and Vietnam.* New York: Institute of Pacific Relations, 1958.

——. *China's Turbulent Quest: An Analysis of China's Foreign Relations Since 1949.* Rev. ed. Bloomington, Indiana: Indiana University Press, 1972.

——. *Communist China in World Politics.* New York: Houghton Mifflin, 1966.

Holland, William L. (ed.). *Asian Nationalism and the West.* New York: Macmillan, 1953.

Hoopes, Townsend. *The Devil and John Foster Dulles.* Boston: Little Brown, 1973.

Hsieh, Alice L. *Communist China's Strategy in the Nuclear Era.* Englewood Cliffs, N.J.: Prentice Hall, 1962.

Hudson, G. F. "Will Britain and America Split in Asia?" *Foreign Affairs,* XXXI (July, 1953).

Hudson, W. J. *Australia and the Colonial Question at the United Nations.* Honolulu: East-West Center Press, 1970.

Hughes, Emmet J. *The Ordeal of Power.* New York: Atheneum, 1963.

Hull, Cordell. *Memoirs.* Vol. II. New York: Macmillan, 1948.

Iriye, Akira. *The Cold War in Asia.* Englewood Cliffs, N.J.: Prentice Hall, 1974.

Isaacs, Harold R. *No Peace for Asia.* Cambridge, Mass.: MIT Press, 1967.

Jenkins, Shirley. *American Economic Policy toward the Philippines.* Stanford, Cal.: Stanford University Press, 1954.

——. "Philippine White Paper," *Far Eastern Survey,* XX (Jan. 10, 1951).

Johnstone, William C. *Burma's Foreign Policy.* Cambridge, Mass.: Harvard University Press, 1963.

——. *A Study of Factors Affecting Burma's Foreign Policy.* Washington, D.C.: Johns Hopkins University School of Advanced International Studies, Burma Research Project, No. 15, 1958.

Jones, F. C. *Japan's New Order in East Asia: Its Rise and Fall, 1937–1945.* London: Oxford University Press, 1954.

Kahin, George McT. *The Asian-African Conference: Bandung, Indonesia, April, 1955.* Ithaca, N.Y.: Cornell University Press, 1956.

——. *Nationalism and Revolution in Indonesia*. Ithaca, N.Y.: Cornell University Press, 1952.

Karunakaran, K. P. *India in World Affairs, 1947–1950*. London: Oxford University Press, 1952.

——. *India in World Affairs, 1950–1953*. London: Oxford University Press, 1958.

Katay, Sasorith Don. *Le Laos*. Paris: Berger-Levrault, 1953.

Kattenburg, Paul M. *The Indonesian Question in World Politics, August 1945–January 1958*. Unpublished dissertation. Yale University, 1949.

Kautsky, John H. *Moscow and the Communist Party of India*. Cambridge, Mass.: MIT Press, 1956.

Kennedy, R., and P. M. Kattenburg. "Indonesia in Crisis," *Foreign Policy Reports*, XXIV (Dec. 15, 1948).

Khrushchev, Nikita. *Khrushchev Remembers*. Boston: Little Brown, 1970.

Killen, E. D. L. "The ANZUS Pact and Pacific Security," *Far Eastern Survey*, XXI (Oct. 8, 1952).

King, John Kerry. *Southeast Asia in Perspective*. New York: Macmillan, 1956.

Kotelawala, John. *An Asian Prime Minister's Story*. London: George G. Harrap & Co., 1956.

Kundra, J. C. *Indian Foreign Policy, 1947–1954*. Groningen: Wolters, 1955.

LaCouture, Jean, and Philippe Devillers. *End of a War: Indochina, 1954*. New York: Praeger, 1969.

Lancaster, Donald. *The Emancipation of French Indochina*. London: Oxford University Press, 1961.

Langer, Paul F., and Joseph Zasloff. *North Vietnam and the Pathet Lao*. Cambridge, Mass.: Harvard University Press, 1970.

Laniel, Joseph. *Le Drame Indochinois*. Paris: Plon, 1957.

Lansdale, Edward Geary. *In the Midst of Wars*. New York: Harper and Row, 1972.

Leahy, William D. *I Was There*. New York: Whittlesey House, 1950.

Lee, Chae-Jin. *Communist China's Policy Toward Laos, 1954–1967*. Lawrence, Kansas: University of Kansas Press, 1970.

Leifer, Michael. *Cambodia and Neutrality*. Canberra: Australia National University Press, 1962.

Leonhard, Wolfgang. *The Kremlin since Stalin*. New York: Praeger, 1962.

Levi, Werner. *Australia's Outlook on Asia*. East Lansing, Mich.: Michigan State University Press, 1958.

——. *Free India in Asia*. Minneapolis, Minn.: University of Minnesota Press, 1952.

London, Kurt (ed.). *New Nations in a Divided World*. New York: Praeger, 1963.

Lyman, Princeton N. *Alliances and the Defense of Southeast Asia*. Unpublished dissertation. Harvard University, 1961.

McHenry, Dean E., and Richard N. Rosecrance. "The 'Exclusion' of the U.K. from the ANZUS Pact," *International Organization*, XII (Summer, 1958).

McLane, Charles B. *Soviet Strategies in Southeast Asia.* Princeton, N.J.: Princeton University Press, 1966.

McVey, Ruth T. *The Calcutta Conference and the Southeast Asian Uprisings.* Ithaca, N.Y.: Cornell Modern Indonesia Project, 1958.

——. *The Development of the Indonesian Communist Party and Its Relations with the Soviet Union and the Chinese People's Republic.* Cambridge, Mass.: MIT/CENIS, 1954.

——. *The Soviet View of the Indonesian Revolution.* Ithaca, N.Y.: Cornell Modern Indonesia Project, 1957.

Mansergh, Nicholas. *The Commonwealth and the Nations.* London: Oxford University Press, 1948.

——. *Survey of British Commonwealth Affairs, 1939–1952.* London: Oxford University Press, 1958.

Mendès-France, Pierre. *Sept Mois et Dix-Sept Jours, Juin, 1954–Fevrier, 1955.* Paris: René Julliard, 1955.

Meyer, Milton W. *A Diplomatic History of the Philippine Republic.* Honolulu: University of Hawaii Press, 1965.

Millar, T. B. (ed.). *Australian Foreign Minister, The Diaries of R. G. Casey.* London: Collins, 1972.

Millis, Walter (ed.). *The Forrestal Diaries.* New York: Viking, 1951.

Modelski, George (ed.). *SEATO, Six Studies.* Melbourne: F. W. Cheshire, 1962.

Monk, W. F. "New Zealand Faces North," *Pacific Affairs,* XXVI (Sept., 1953).

Montgomery, John D. *The Politics of Foreign Aid: American Experience in Southeast Asia.* New York: Praeger, 1962.

Mosely, Philip E. "Soviet Policy in the Two-World Conflict," *Journal of International Affairs,* VIII (1954).

Murti, B. S. N. *Vietnam Divided: The Unfinished Struggle.* New York: Asia Publishing House, 1964.

Navarre, Henri. *Agonie de l'Indochine.* Paris: Plon, 1956.

Nicholas, Herbert. *Britain and the U.S.A.* Baltimore, Md.: The Johns Hopkins University Press, 1963.

Northedge, F. S. *British Foreign Policy: The Process of Readjustment, 1945–1961.* New York: Praeger, 1962.

Nuechterlein, Donald. *Thailand and the Struggle for Southeast Asia.* Ithaca, N.Y.: Cornell University Press, 1965.

Olson, Laurence. *Japan in Postwar Asia.* New York: Praeger, 1970.

Olver, A. S. B. *Outline of British Policy in East and Southeastern Asia, 1945–1950.* London: Royal Institute of International Affairs, 1950.

——. "The Special Commission in South-East Asia," *Pacific Affairs,* XXI (Sept., 1948).

Palmier, Leslie H. *Indonesia and the Dutch.* London: Oxford University Press, 1962.

Panikkar, K. M. *In Two Chinas.* London: George Allen & Unwin, 1955.

Parkinson, F. "Bandung and the Underdeveloped Countries," *Yearbook of World Affairs* (1956).

Perkins, Whitney T. "Sanctions for Political Change—The Indonesia Case," *International Organization*, XII (Winter, 1958).

Peterson, Alec. "Britain and Siam: The Latest Phase," *Pacific Affairs*, XIX (Dec., 1946).

Randle, Robert F. *Geneva, 1954: The Settlement of the Indochinese War.* Princeton, N.J.: Princeton University Press, 1969.

Reese, Trevor R. *Australia, New Zealand, and the United States: A Survey of International Relations, 1941–1968.* London: Oxford University Press, 1969.

Reshetar, John S., Jr. "The Soviet Union and the Neutralist World," *The Annals*, CCCLXII (Nov., 1965).

Ridgeway, Matthew B. *Soldier.* New York: Harper & Bros., 1956.

Roberts, Chalmers M. "The Day We Didn't Go to War," *The Reporter* (Sept. 4, 1954).

Roberts, H. L., and P. A. Wilson. *Britain and the United States.* London: Royal Institute of International Affairs, 1953.

Rose, Saul. *Britain and Southeast Asia.* London: Chatto and Windus, 1962.

———. (ed.). *Politics in Southern Asia.* London: Macmillan, 1963.

Rosecrance, R. N. *Australian Diplomacy and Japan, 1945–1951.* Parkville, Australia: University of Melbourne Press, 1962.

Rosinger, Lawrence K. *India and the United States.* New York: Macmillan, 1950.

———, and Associates. *The State of Asia.* New York: Alfred Knopf, 1951.

Royal Institute of International Affairs. *Documents on International Affairs.* London: Oxford University Press (Diane Folliot, ed.) 1953, 1954.

———. *Survey of International Affairs* (SIA). London. Oxford University Press (Arnold J. Toynbee, ed.) 1939–1946; (Peter Calvocoressi, ed.) 1947–1948, 1949–1950, 1952, 1953; (Coral Bell, ed.), 1954; (Geoffrey and Rachel F. Wall, eds.) 1955–1956.

Rubenstein, Alvin Z. *The Soviets in International Organization: Changing Policy toward Developing Countries, 1953–1963.* Princeton, N.J.: Princeton University Press, 1964.

———. "Soviet Policy in ECAFE," *International Organization*, XII (Autumn, 1958).

———. "The State of Socialism in Asia—The Rangoon Conference," *Pacific Affairs*, XXVI (June, 1953).

Russell, Ruth B. *A History of the United Nations Charter.* Washington, D.C.: Brookings Institution, 1958.

Sar Desai, D. R. *Indian Foreign Policy in Cambodia, Laos, and Vietnam, 1947–1964.* Berkeley, Cal.: University of California Press, 1968.

Schlesinger, Arthur M., Jr. *The Bitter Heritage: Vietnam and American Democracy.* Boston: Houghton Mifflin, 1967.

Selden, Mark (ed.). *Remaking of Asia.* New York: Pantheon Books, 1974.

Shaplen, Robert. *The Lost Revolution.* New York: Harper and Row, 1965.

Sherwood, Robert. *Roosevelt and Hopkins.* New York: Harper & Bros., 1948.

Shulman, Marshall D. *Stalin's Foreign Policy Reappraised.* Cambridge, Mass.: Harvard University Press, 1963.

Silverstein, Joseph (ed.). *Southeast Asia in World War II.* New Haven, Conn.: Yale University Southeast Asia Studies, 1966.

Singh, L. P. *The Politics of Economic Cooperation in Asia: A Study of Asian International Organizations.* Columbia, Mo.: University of Missouri Press, 1966.

Sisouk Na Champassak. *Storm Over Laos.* New York: Praeger, 1961.

Smith, Gaddis. *Dean Acheson.* New York: Cooper Square Publishers, 1972.

Smith, Roger M. *Cambodia's Foreign Policy.* Ithaca, N.Y.: Cornell University Press, 1965.

——. *The Philippines and the Southeast Asia Treaty Organization.* Ithaca, N.Y.: Cornell University Southeast Asia Program, 1960.

Spender, Percy. *Exercises in Diplomacy.* New York: New York University Press, 1969.

Stannard, Raymond E., Jr. *The Role of American Aid in Indonesian-American Relations.* Unpublished thesis. Cornell University, 1957.

Stanton, Edwin F. *Brief Authority.* New York: Harper & Bros., 1956.

——. "Spotlight on Thailand," *Foreign Affairs,* XXXIII (Oct., 1954).

Statuts et Résolutions de l'Internationale Communiste. 2nd Congress. Leningrad, 1920.

Stevenson, Charles A. *The End of Nowhere: American Policy Toward Laos Since 1954.* Boston: Beacon Press, 1972.

Strausz-Hupé, Robert, Alvin J. Cottrell, and James E. Dougherty. *American Asian Tensions.* New York: Praeger, 1956.

Sutter, John O. *Indonesianisasi: Politics in a Changing Economy, 1940–1955.* 4 vols. Ithaca, N.Y.: Cornell University Southeast Asia Program, 1959.

Tanham, George K. *Communist Revolutionary Warfare: The Vietminh in Indochina.* New York: Praeger, 1961.

Taylor, Alastair M. *Indonesian Independence and the United Nations.* Ithaca, N.Y.: Cornell University Press, 1960.

Taylor, George E. *The Philippines and the United States: Problems of Partnership.* New York: Praeger, 1964.

Taylor, Jay. *China and Southeast Asia: Peking's Relations with Revolutionary Movements.* New York: Praeger, 1974.

Thien, Ton That. *India and Southeast Asia, 1947–1960.* Geneva: Librairie Droz, 1963.

Thompson, Virginia, and Richard Adloff. *The Left Wing in Southeast Asia.* New York: William Sloane Associates, 1950.

Tinker, Hugh. *The Union of Burma: A Study of the First Years of Independence.* London: Oxford University Press, 1957.

Toye, Hugh. *Laos: Buffer State or Battleground.* London: Oxford University Press, 1968.

Trager, Frank N. "Burma's Foreign Policy, 1948–1956," *Journal of Asian Studies,* XVI (Nov., 1956).

———. *Burma—From Kingdom to Republic: A Historical and Political Analysis.* New York: Praeger, 1966.

——— (ed.). *Marxism in Southeast Asia: A Study of Four Countries.* Stanford, Cal.: Stanford University Press, 1959.

———, Patricia Wolgemuth, and Lu-yu Kiang. *Burma's Role in the U.N., 1948–1955.* New York: Institute of Pacific Relations, 1956.

Truman, Harry S. *Memoirs.* Vol. II. *Years of Trial and Hope.* New York: Doubleday, 1956.

Ulam, Adam B. *Expansion and Coexistence: The History of Soviet Foreign Policy, 1917–1967.* New York: Praeger, 1968.

Vandenbosch, Amry. *Dutch Foreign Policy since 1815.* The Hague: M. Nijhoff, 1959.

———, Amry and Mary Belle. *Australia Faces Southeast Asia.* Lexington, Ky.: University of Kentucky Press, 1967.

Van der Kroef, Justus M. *The Communist Party of Indonesia: Its History, Program, and Tactics.* Vancouver, B.C.: University of British Columbia Press, 1965.

———. "Indonesia and the West," *Far Eastern Survey,* XX (Feb. 21, 1951).

———. *Indonesia in the Modern World.* 2 vols. Bandung: Masa Baru, 1954 and 1956.

Van Mook, Huburtus J. *The Stakes of Democracy in Southeast Asia.* New York: Norton, 1950.

Vellut, J. L. *The Asian Policy of the Philippines, 1954–1961.* Canberra: Australian National University Press, 1965.

Watt, Alan. *The Evolution of Australian Foreign Policy, 1938–1965.* Cambridge: Cambridge University Press, 1967.

Weinstein, Franklin B. *Indonesian Foreign Policy and the Dilemma of Dependence.* Ithaca, N.Y.: Cornell University Press, 1976.

———. *Vietnam's Unheld Elections.* Ithaca, N.Y.: Cornell University Southeast Asia Program, 1966.

Weinstein, Martin. *Japan's Postwar Defense Policy.* New York: Columbia University Press, 1971.

Whiting, Allen S. *China Crosses the Yalu.* New York: Macmillan, 1960.

Wilcox, Wayne, Leo E. Rose, and Gavin Boyd. *Asia and the International System.* Cambridge, Mass.: Winthrop Publishers, 1972.

Williams, Lea. "Sino-Indonesian Diplomacy: A Study of Revolutionary International Politics," *China Quarterly,* XI (July–Sept., 1962).

Wilson, David A. "China, Thailand, and the Spirit of Bandung," *China Quarterly,* XXX (April–June, 1967), and XXXI (July–Sept., 1967).

Wolf, Charles, Jr. *Foreign Aid: Theory and Practice in Southern Asia.* Princeton, N.J.: Princeton University Press, 1960.

———. *The Indonesian Story.* New York: John Day, 1968.

Wolfers, Arnold (ed.). *Alliance Policy in the Cold War.* Baltimore, Md.: Johns Hopkins Press, 1959.

Woodman, Dorothy. *The Republic of Indonesia.* London: Cresset Press, 1955.

Young, Kenneth T. *Negotiating with the Chinese Communists*. New York: Mc-Graw-Hill, 1968.

Zacher, Mark W., and R. Stephen Milne (eds.). *Conflict and Stability in Southeast Asia*. Garden City, N.Y.: Anchor Books/Doubleday, 1974.

Zagoria, Donald S. *The Sino-Soviet Conflict, 1956–1961*. New York: Atheneum, 1964.

Zasloff, Joseph J. *The Role of Sanctuary in Insurgency: Communist China's Support of the Viet Minh, 1946–54*. Santa Monica, Cal.: The RAND Corp., 1967.

OFFICIAL PUBLICATIONS

Australia

Department of External Affairs. *Select Documents on International Affairs*. No. 16. *Laos*. Canberra, 1970.

Burma

Nu, U. *An Asian Speaks*. Washington, D.C.: Embassy of Burma, 1956.

——. *For World Peace and Progress*. Rangoon, 1954.

——. *From Peace to Stability*. Rangoon: Ministry of Information, 1951.

——. *Resurgence: Premier U Nu at Bandung*. Rangoon: Director of Information, 1955.

Democratic Republic of Vietnam

Dong, Pham Van. *Achievements of the Vietnamese People's War of Revolution*. Hanoi: Foreign Language Publishing House, 1955.

——. *Our Struggle in the Past and at Present*. Hanoi: Foreign Language Publishing House, 1955.

India

Ministry of Information and Broadcasting. *The Conference on Indonesia: Jan. 20–23, 1949*. New Delhi: United Press, 1949.

New Zealand

Wood, F. L. *The New Zealand People at War: Political and External Affairs*. Wellington: Department of Internal Affairs, 1958.

United Kingdom

Documents Relating to British Involvement in the Indo-China Conflict. CMD. 2834. London: HMSO, 1965.

Donnison, F. S. V. *British Military Administration in the Far East, 1943–1946*. London: HMSO, 1956.

Woodward, E. Llewellyn. *British Foreign Policy in the Second World War*. London: HMSO, 1962.

United Nations

Documents of the United Nations Conference on International Organization, San Francisco, 1945. (UNCIO) Vols. III and X. New York: 1945.

United States

Department of State, *American Foreign Policy, Basic Documents, 1950–1955.* 2 Vols. Washington, D.C.: GPO, 1957.

Department of State, *Foreign Relations of the United States* (FRUS). Washington, D.C.: GPO.
    1942, Vol. II, Europe.
    1943, Vol III, The British Commonwealth, Eastern Europe, The Far East.
    1943, China.
    1943, The Conferences of Washington, 1941–1942, and Casablanca, 1943.
    1943, Conferences at Cairo and Teheran, 1943.
    1943, Conferences at Washington and Quebec, 1943.
    1944, Vol. III, The British Commonwealth and Europe.
    1944, Vol. V, The Near East, South Asia, Africa, The Far East.
    1945, Vol. I, General: The United Nations.
    1945, Vol. VI, The British Commonwealth, The Far East.
    1945, Vol. VII, The Far East, China.
    1945, Conferences at Malta and Yalta.
    1945, Conference of Berlin (Potsdam). Vol. I.
    1946, Vol. VIII, The Far East.
    1947, Vol. VI, The Far East.
    1948, Vol. VI, The Far East and Australasia.
    1949, Vol. VII, The Far East.

House Committee on Armed Services, Department of Defense, *United States-Vietnam Relations, 1945–1947 (Pentagon Papers)*, Vols. I, VIII, IX, X. Washington, D.C.: GPO, 1971.

Notter, Harley. *Postwar Foreign Policy Preparation, 1939–1945.* Washington, D.C.: GPO, 1949.

Office of the Federal Register, *Public Papers of the Presidents of the United States.* Dwight D. Eisenhower, 1954. Washington, D.C.: GPO, 1960.

INDEX

Library of Congress Cataloging in Publication Data
(For library cataloging purposes only)

Colbert, Evelyn Speyer, 1918–
    Southeast Asia in international politics, 1941–1956.

    Bibliography: p.
    Includes index.
    1. Asia, Southeastern—Foreign relations. 2. World politics—20th
century. I. Title.
DS518.1.C587   327'.0959   76-28008
ISBN 0-8014-0971-3

Southeast Asia in
International Politics
1941–1956

Designed by R. E. Rosenbaum.
Composed by York Composition Company, Inc.,
in 11 point Intertype Baskerville, 2 points leaded,
with display lines in Baskerville and Deepdene.
Printed letterpress from type by York Composition Company
on Warren's Number 66 text, 50 pound basis.
Bound by John H. Dekker & Sons, Inc.
in Joanna book cloth
and stamped in All Purpose foil.